You will also be interested in:

GOD IS MY ADVENTURE
BY *ROM LANDAU*

THE PERSONALITIES AND TEACHINGS OF THE FOUNDERS OF MODERN RELIGIONS AND THE SPIRITUAL MOVEMENTS WHICH THEY INITIATED — KRISHNAMURTI, BUCHMAN, OUSPENSKY, GURDJIEFF, STEINER, KEYSERLING.

ALFRED A. KNOPF, *PUBLISHER*

MEN WHO HAVE WALKED WITH GOD

MEN WHO HAVE WALKED WITH GOD

BEING THE STORY OF
MYSTICISM THROUGH THE AGES
TOLD IN THE BIOGRAPHIES OF
REPRESENTATIVE SEERS AND SAINTS
WITH EXCERPTS FROM
THEIR WRITINGS AND SAYINGS

BY

Sheldon Cheney

New York : *Alfred A. Knopf* : 1945

Copyright 1945 by Sheldon Cheney. All rights reserved. No part of this book may be reproduced in any form without permission in writing from the publisher, except by a reviewer who may quote brief passages or reproduce not more than three illustrations in a review to be printed in a magazine or newspaper.

Manufactured in the United States of America

Published simultaneously in Canada by The Ryerson Press

FIRST EDITION

Contents

Preface		viii
I	The Golden Age and the Mystic Poet LAO-TSE	1
II	The BUDDHA, the Great Light, and the Bliss of NIRVANA	38
III	The Age of Reason in Greece: PYTHAGORAS and PLATO	86
IV	The Tardy Flowering of Greek Mysticism: PLOTINUS	118
V	Christian Mysticism, from the Founders to SAINT BERNARD	143
VI	The Mediæval Flowering: ECKHART and the Friends of GOD	176
VII	FRA ANGELICO, the Saintly Painter and Tool of GOD	212
VIII	JACOB BOEHME, the Shoemaker-Illuminate of the Reformation	238
IX	BROTHER LAWRENCE, the Lay Monk Who Attained Unclouded Vision	285
X	A Mystic in the Age of Enlightened Scepticism: WILLIAM BLAKE	309
Afterword		378
A Descriptive Reading List, with Acknowledgments		385
Index	*follows page*	395

List of Illustrations

	FOLLOWING PAGE
Lao-Tse on a Water Buffalo. Chinese, Sung	10
Sage in Contemplation. In the style of Ma Yuan	20
Sage in Contemplation under a Pine Tree. By Ma Yuan	34
An Arahat Entering into Nirvana. By Lin Ting-Kuei	80
Socrates	102
Christ Appearing to the Apostles. By William Blake	146
Saint Paul. By El Greco	154
Augustine Recording His Vision of the City of God	160
Saint Bernard. By El Greco	170
Saint Francis Receiving the Stigmata. School of Giotto	178
Meeting of Saint Francis and Saint Dominic. By Fra Angelico	182
The Garden of Paradise. School of Cologne, about 1400	204
The Annunciation. By Fra Angelico *Portrait of Fra Angelico.* By Carlo Dolci	216
The Naming of Saint John. By Fra Angelico *The Visitation.* By Fra Angelico	222
The Annunciation. By Fra Angelico *The Annunciation.* By Fra Angelico	226
Coronation of the Virgin. By Fra Angelico *The Nativity.* By Fra Angelico	232
The Flight into Egypt. By Fra Angelico	236

LIST OF ILLUSTRATIONS

FOLLOWING PAGE

Glad Day. By William Blake — 250

When the Morning Stars Sang Together. By William Blake — 318

Then a Spirit Passed before My Face. By William Blake
Saint Paul Preaching at Athens. By William Blake — 326

Satan Rousing the Rebel Angels. By William Blake
The Great Red Dragon and the Woman Clothed with the Sun. By William Blake — 338

Satan Smiting Job with Boils. By William Blake
Then Went Satan Forth from the Presence of the Lord. By William Blake — 356

The Ancient of Days Laying out the Circle of the Earth. By William Blake
Blake Dethroning Urizen. By William Blake — 362

The Angel of the Revelation. By William Blake — 374

THE author and the publisher wish to record their thanks to the Department of Education and Museum Extension of the Metropolitan Museum of Art, and to the Photograph Library, School of the Fine Arts, Yale University, for providing certain of the illustrations of Fra Angelico's paintings; and to Miss Elizabeth Mongan of the Print Department of the National Gallery, Washington, for exceptional aid in assembling the photographs of William Blake's drawings and prints. Our indebtedness to museum directors and to photographers is more directly recorded in the captions under individual illustrations.

Preface

In the final analysis there is only one subject of permanent interest, the soul. It is a truth easily forgotten in the press of practical undertakings. The busy modern man, sped on his way by machines, ambitious, social, political, is likely to discount the importance of the spiritual life, if he does not overlook its existence. Especially in a world feverishly at war, he easily excuses himself for mislaying the wisdom of the spiritual prophets, for slipping into a life of practical expediency and neglect of the soul.

There are nevertheless a great many men who believe that the apprehension of spiritual values in mortal things is the real substance of living. Many of them go on to belief that there is an experience open to the soul, in the nature of divine communion or mystical union with God, which is the highest boon that can be bestowed upon a mortal being. To-day even the sceptics and the scientists among us, baffled at the end of every inquiry into the source of life or the nature of spiritual awareness, concede that there may be completion of happiness only in the activities of the soul. They grant even a reality to the mystical experience.

This is a book about certain artists and poets and spiritual prophets who have been close to God in the special mystic way. They have known the experience of union with God. The writers and artists among them have believed, in some cases, that their writings and pictures were composed as if by divine dictation; or they have thought of art as a special mode of revelation of the rhythm or vital order of the universe. The recognized spiritual prophets among them are men who have spoken intuitively, out of divine awareness, expressing in each case truths of such power and intensity that they swayed vast numbers of less intuitive men. Beside the founders of the great religions I have placed some obscure monks and recluses who, despite their humble positions, managed to bring illumination into their own lives, and to set examples, usually bolstered by writings, that deeply affected other men.

When I started to write the book its plan was this: as background a concise running account of historical mysticism as it has developed East and West, with at least allusion to every widely known mystic leader; and, in the foreground, full-length treatments of a dozen outstanding figures. In other words, within a lightly sketched historical framework I intended to insert rather long biographical studies of certain prophets and saints who seemed especially to illustrate the varieties of the mystic way of living.

My thought was that by concentrating upon the stories of the chosen figures, and especially upon the human side of their lives, I might afford common readers access to a subject often treated abstractly, even esoterically. Illustrating through each one the personal working, and the triumph, of the mystic spirit, I might — if I were successful — offer living and persuasive proof that mysticism is not a subject for initiates only: that it offers an essentially human and normal way to completion of otherwise incomplete living. By developing, in the background history, several half-length figures, and by sketching in a half-hundred lesser biographies, in miniature size, I still might afford a sense of the universality and the continuity of mankind's hunger, and search, for participation in divine union.

In the end I am aware that I have compromised my plan, devoting the greater proportion of my pages to eight or nine figures, and somewhat abridging the historical review. The study of the Buddha Gautama and his mystic religion, running to nearly fifty pages, and the even lengthier chapters devoted to the Reformation mystic Jacob Boehme and to the dissident saint William Blake, are — as paper and type and wordage are measured in war time — small books in themselves. But I believe that these studies, with those of Lao-Tse, Plotinus, Eckhart, Fra Angelico, and Brother Lawrence, will leave the reader with a fuller sense of the joy attained by men through the mystic experience than would twice the number of shorter sketches.

The book, if too unbalanced to be called a history in the schoolmen's exact sense, yet affords an outline survey of its subject. Its real unity, however, is in the likeness of the vision and the messages of these many explorers of the realm of the spirit: in the like result, in each separate life, of a human soul rendered content and invulnerable, in the finding and the praise of a "way" leading to Heaven and to the joy of divine union.

Of all words "mysticism" is the one the most often employed ignorantly or wrongly, and therefore some readers may expect to find the author's definition on page one. It has seemed to me preferable to let the definition grow as the story unfolds; for assuredly there are aspects of the mystic experience not to be compassed in words. It is, moreover, part of my plan to stress the likeness of the experience among peoples who speak of God and among those who make an abstraction of the Eternal and the Divine; to emphasize that a mystic philosophy is at the core of religions, or ways of life, as different as Christianity, Buddhism, Neo-Platonism, and Taoism.

The commonly inscribed basic definitions — which are, let us say, "union with God," "intuition of the Divine," "realization of the Eternal," and "mergence of the soul in the Absolute" — are one in meaning, though each might seem limiting or incomplete when tested by one or another manifestation of "illumination and inundation" East or West. There is, after all, no ideal or all-embracing definition of the rapturous reality that is the mystic experience.

Throughout the writing I have tried to keep in mind "the common reader" spoken of above. There are specialized and scholarly books enough for the initiate, about theoretic mysticism and about each of the mystics to whom I have devoted chapters. But the common reader, when he has asked for introductory books about the men who have walked with God, has been but poorly served. Vaughan's *Hours with the Mystics,* at once excellent in parts, informative, and strangely unsympathetic, published in 1856, is almost the only readable general history of the subject now on the shelves.

In planning to present a bird's-eye view, through a generalizing lens, I gave over all desire to reveal new knowledge or new subtleties of knowledge in the manner of the research scholar. I recognize that I am not equipped to compete with, say, specialists in Plotinian or Boehmian philosophy, nor do I desire to do so. The book pretends no more than to afford an all-over introductory view.

To certain scholars, no doubt, it will seem superficial. Nevertheless, to the reader who has heard that Boehme or Blake or Lao-Tse offers a feast of spiritual riches if one can get at it, my chapter-study of that seer may be just the needed bridge from ignorance to the difficult ground of the specialists where the feast is more fully spread. That is my hope. I have tried to build my bridges plainly, compactly, in common idioms.

I am indebted to innumerable scholar-specialists for my materials. I have mined from the books of Legge and Waley and Carus and Giles, of Stephen Mackenna and Rufus Jones and

PREFACE

Evelyn Underhill. I have built upon their researches, and I have borrowed (with permission) from their writings and their translations, and from many others.* But, having disavowed so much as scholar and writer, I must add that I have worked with a certain conviction, even a sort of vision, and I hope that the reader will detect this in the pages that follow. My scholarship, so far as it goes, has been, I believe, honest and painstaking.

As I have set up no definition as a reference point, so I have tried not to let my personal beliefs too strongly colour my interpretations. I may even have laid myself open to the charge that I am credulous and inconsistent. It has simply seemed to me best to approach Lao-Tse or the Buddha, or the Catholic Eckhart or the Protestant Boehme, with all the understanding possible, from as near the point of view of a believer as I might. If to believe in their visions, their miracles, their closeness to God, is credulous, I am guilty of credulity. The mystic life is an epitome of the visionary and miraculous things that do happen to the individual human being. In believing in imagination or poetry or mysticism one commits oneself to a faith suspect among "realists."

A writer who deals favourably with the mystics is open to one further misinterpretation. He will be charged, not only by intellectual sceptics but by many not irreligious folk who live primarily by the processes of reasoning, with wanting to do away with all that mankind has accomplished through using reason as a tool. He will be charged even with condemning what has been accepted as the "normal" life in the age of rationalism.

There is justice in the complaint; but it arises, I believe, from overstatements by the mystics, not out of the nature of their beliefs. Almost without exception the seers and saints here treated have attacked rationalism and Reason (spelled with a capital R to indicate that it has been deified); but if I have read their works aright, it is the common over-reliance upon reason — upon thought, logic, disputation — that they oppose. They have witnessed eras of war, of moral degradation and spiritual unenlightenment, follow hard upon the ages of Reason; and they plead for use of the other half of man's equipment, call it intuition or imagination or divination.

* My debt to each and my thanks are recorded in a special appendix in which I have combined the purposes of the usual "Acknowledgments" and those of a reading list. In every case the writers and their publishers have been co-operative, even generous.

They seek no more than to place reason under control of the powers that are nearer to the divine source of everything mortal. From the Buddha's cry, "Learning availeth not," to the repeated pleas of William Blake that reason be put under control of Imagination (which he called also Poetic Genius, and Vision, and Perception of the Infinite) there is a series of assaults upon reason or rationalization as enthroned in civilized society. Sometimes the epithets of condemnation have been hurled in a passion of protest (as in Blake's case). But, in general, mystics are the gentlest and most understanding of men, and the most of them have recognized and praised the works that proceed from reason — laws, government, material invention, system — *in their subordinate place*. There is, they say, a better sort of knowledge, a higher source of knowledge. Reason, whatever its importance, is ultimately less sure as a basis for action than is Vision, Intuition, Clairvoyance (in its original sense).

As to the suggestion that the mystic way of life departs from the "normal," need I note more than that it has been urged upon men by Jesus and the Buddha Gautama, by Lao-Tse and Plato, by every one of the prophets and seers quoted in the following pages? One needs to be very sure that one is not arguing from the ground of materialism and atheism before venturing the thought that the mystic is "abnormal."

If poetry is abnormal as an expression of human vision in these times, then mysticism too may be said to depart from the normal. I believe, however, that even in the world's latest and most destructive lapse into realism and scepticism, most men recognize that it is common living that has departed from the verities, that poetry and mysticism and spiritual idealism are on the high, the vital side — and are "normal."

As among poets, so among mystics there have been men and women, some of them very great in spirit and gifted in expression, who have totally forsaken the affairs and the rewards of the world, and others whose mystic insight and spiritual raptness have been associated with signs commonly attributed to mental instability or aberrance: spells and hysteria and indulgence in self-torment. But we do not discount the importance of poetry or knowingly persecute our poets because genius — that is, awareness of eternal values and divine rhythms — sometimes carries its possessors close to the realm of dreamy irresponsibility, of hysteria, even of madness. No more need we suspect mysticism, in its profounder aspects, because Santa Teresa (as she confessed) could hardly separate her visions of God from a frenzied torment, a hysterical ecstasy, or because Saint John of the Cross succeeded in arriving at the "spiritual betrothal" of his soul to God only after the suffering and the torments which he described as "the Dark Night."

If poetry is the language of imagination, mysticism is Imagination itself, the unlimited, eternal thing at which poetry or music or painting hints. It is pure spiritual experience, the actuality of vision, the foretaste of the soul's perfect rest.

All of us speak of the mystic life at times as a refuge. But that is because we have rendered the ordinary world so nearly untenable for the soul. From the prison of mortality we sometimes look upon the mystic quest as an escape. But the truer image is that of the mystic wanderer returning from a joyous voyage, to illuminate everyday living with the light of divine understanding. Aside from the isolated plungings of the adept into union with the Absolute, I conceive the mystic life to be less a forsaking of reality than a search to discover that which gives the lustre of reality to all; and, after the mental discovery, a constant detection of eternal values in every object and facet of mortal life.

Mystic living as we know it on earth is thus not an absolute thing, demanding detachment from all else. We are all to a certain degree mystics; that is, partakers of the one Divine Life. What I remind my reader of is that the choice of degree belongs to the individual.

Some men, among them the greatest spiritual prophets, have forsaken all else to seek entry into God's presence. Some have gone into the deserts and mountain fastnesses to escape worldliness, while others have withdrawn by the way of mortification and abstinence. But far greater is the number of those who have remained within the community life, not permitting their inclination to God to disturb unduly their obligations to family or fellow men, or it may be to their students or their churches. These mystics who abide in society are the ones all men can term normal. Certainly ninety-nine out of every one hundred of my readers will aspire to no greater degree of mystic consciousness than one that will leave them free to discharge their mortal duty, as they conceive it, to society, and family, and their own hearts.

My point is that participation in the mystic life *is* a matter of degree — certainly not a plunge out of the richness of life, and certainly not retreat into a cult; and that to attain to the first degree of vision and belief is to gain rewards beyond calculation. At this first stage there is an immediate and constant pressure upon the mind to live life only in a way consonant with the soul's nobility, and a consequent lessening of self-interest, growing attention to the natural dictates of compassion and love, and, in every sense, purification.

While the everyday life is thus re-formed, without withdrawal, there is revealed, beyond, the prospect of the soul's life as it will be, perhaps at higher stages of the quest in this existence, the rapturous experience of union; as it certainly will be in that final inundation when mortality has been outworn. From the first the soul has found a philosophy that renders it invulnerable, the world around is enriched — for Divinity has come clear in all things — and the pilgrim feels the presence of, though he does not yet know utterly the joy of walking with, God. He apprehends a future of delight that will be his, of which the signs are revealed to him daily, hourly, in a world become miraculous.

Perhaps my book, which, in relation to the transcendent subject and the exalted souls about which it is written, is so halting, so imperfect — perhaps my book is worthy only to light the way of a few readers to this first stage of mystic vision and awareness. To do so much will, I believe, have its usefulness, not only for the gains of those who thereby arrive at what seems to me the essential — that is, the spiritual — reality of life, but because the next forward movement of men in the mass waits upon individual vision and regeneration. To help even a few to get back to the ground of the soul, to help them to recognize the Divine actuality of life and to apprehend the joys of mystic union, may be a social as well as an individual service.

S. C.

Westport, Connecticut
February, 1945

MEN WHO HAVE WALKED WITH GOD

I. The Golden Age and the Mystic Poet Lao-Tse

The Chinese have a simple way with history. They admit to the record a likely legend or a bit of folk-lore as readily as a truth proved by dated document or sculptured monument. They avoid the fuss raised by Western historians over a discovered inscription or a bit of primitive human bone. They place their trust in the account that is spiritually true to the people, the time, and the place. Their writing of history results in a warmth and perhaps an intrinsic authenticity not achieved in the scientific West.

Under the Oriental method historical record is carried into an antiquity not to be written of in terms of document and relic. But certainly we shall understand the Chinese peoples better for having toured, so to speak, back into their Golden Age; for having met the elusive Yellow Ancestor; for having heard of the first man, P'an-Ku, who laboured heroically for eighteen thousand years to shape a habitable world out of chaos, and of the lovely Hsi-Ho who bathed the Sun in the Pools of Sweetness. History so written illumines the intangibles of man's existence, his religious inclination, and his strange divine-material duality.

Soon after the world became habitable, the Chinese say, there appeared five guides for mankind, five Lords. They were celestial rather than human beings, possibly half dragon, but their business was to arrange matters on earth, and in Heaven in so far as that might be, for the advancement and the happiness of mankind. One of them, the Lord of Man, had ample opportunity to bring in the elements of civilization, for he ruled through forty-five thousand years. He introduced clothing, shelter, and agriculture, and he fostered the religious spirit. It was an era when there was hardly any difference between divine and human beings.

Toward the end of his time the Lord of Man appointed kings or emperors as his assistants. These were the first earthly rulers. At the beginning they took pains to extend the gains for humanity. They invented hunting snares and fish-nets, undertook flood control, instituted marriage, and established the custom of giving gifts. While they thus carried on the work of human improvement, the union of divine and human life was continued.

But the Hsia Dynasty, founded by one of the earthly kings late in the third millennium before Christ, degenerated in the course of four hundred years. It came to a bad end in the figure of one Chieh, a dissolute and cruel tyrant. He was killed — for wholly human ways of improvement had now been instituted — by a rival king.

The arts by this time were flourishing, especially music and sculpture, and there were the beginnings of a written language. But religion, or spontaneous divinity, no longer controlled men's minds. Animistic beliefs and rituals addressed to Heaven, Earth, and Ancestors had unduly developed. Neither in that fundamental of religion, the closeness of the individual soul to God or the Source, nor in that important by-product of religion, morality, had the conditions of the Golden Age survived.

The following Shang Dynasty ended too, after five hundred years, with an avaricious and tyrannical monarch, who was overthrown in 1122 B.C. The empire was now greatly expanded; but the power of the state was lost to a set of feudal lords and princes, and wars among the lords brought misery to the people.

Just before the princely quarrels and the bloodshed reached their climax (in a period known as the Era of the Fighting States), when the blessings of the Golden Age seemed to have slipped out of men's grasp for ever, there met together in the capital city of the State of Chou two of the world's greatest philosophers, Lao-Tse the mystic seer, and Confucius the ethical sage. This was late in the sixth century B.C., the very time of the Buddha Gautama's enlightenment and teaching in India, a hundred years before Socrates and the flowering of Greek philosophy, and more than five hundred years before the ministry of Jesus in Palestine.

Confucius and Lao-Tse met as strangers, though their reputations had been carried far and wide in the feudal states. Both were humane, tolerant, and considerate, and both, in a turbulent and degenerate time, visioned salvation for man in a return to the conditions of the Golden Age. There the resemblance ended. Confucius saw the Golden Age as a time of good manners and noble actions among men, and of a science of etiquette and a just code of law. Lao-Tse visioned instead a time when man lived in communion with the Spirit, in natural innocence; when he was in tune with the harmony of the universe, and thus required no instruction to make him act nobly. Confucius looked back only to a period when rulers were benevolent and virtuous and subjects law-abiding and loyal, Lao-Tse to an age before rulers were necessary. In short, the one sage was a practical reformer, busying himself with laws, regulations, proprieties, and conventions; the other possessed the Golden Age in his heart. When they met, Lao-Tse was an old man, in his eighties. Confucius was thirty-four.

Lao-Tse was librarian and keeper of the secret archives of the State of Chou. Confucius had argued to himself that a man who was both archivist and sage would have learned a great deal about the laws and the ceremonies of the old times. In constructing his outlines for the reform of society, such knowledge would be invaluable. As a teaching philosopher he took along, on his visit to the older man, a retinue of disciples and pupils.

But his questions brought disagreement and even chiding from Lao-Tse. Confucius having asked how it might be possible to bring back the glories and the happiness known to the sages of the Golden Age, the other replied: "The sages of whom you inquire died, and their bones long since crumbled. Their words alone remain. If a sage in his own time is understood, he mounts to honour, but if the age does not understand him, his gifts are blown away by the vagrant winds. Surely a good merchant, when he has concealed rich treasures, makes no show of them. So the true sage, though he be illumined, puts on no appearance beyond the average. Come, Sir, leave off your proud airs, conquer your desires, get free of all this show and fuss. Such things add nothing to your worth."

How much of his philosophy Lao-Tse outlined to Confucius we do not know. Perhaps he spoke of his favourite doctrine of the *Tao,* or Way of Heaven; of the Spiritual Oneness of all that is; of the natural as against the artificial man, and his necessity to conform with the rhythm of life; of action without assertion, and of non-interference; of the need to have quietude in the soul; and of the natural honesty and compassion of people not educated to shrewdness and righteousness and morality.

Confucius went away discomfited, knowing that a vista had been opened upon a majesty and a mystery he could not fathom. He went away to become the world's greatest ethical teacher — "The Perfect Sage," he was called during the ages of Reason. He went away to write his books of instruction and admonition, to teach uncounted millions of men how to be virtuous, respectful, thrifty. Undoubtedly he helped more than any other one — excepting possibly Lao-Tse — to shape the Chinese people into one of the most law-abiding, virtuous, and philosophical of the nations of the earth.

He had, nevertheless, caught glimpses of a realm of living that eluded his maxims and his analects. He had been afforded a glimpse into a Golden Age beyond his dreaming. Calling together his retinue of students after he had gone from Lao-Tse's presence, he said to them: "I understand the ways of birds, and how they can fly, and no less the ways of fish that swim, and of the animals that run. The running animal can be trapped, the swimming fish can be snared in nets, and the flying bird can be brought down with an arrow. But there remains the question of the Dragon. I do not understand how the Dragon mounts among the winds and clouds, and enters Heaven. To-day I have been with Lao-Tan.* Shall I call him the Dragon? . . ." He added that the mystic doctrine of the *Tao* seemed to demand suppression of the worldly self and a deliberate retreat into obscurity: aims not easily cherished by the practical reformer.

Long afterward an imaginative historian, the Taoist Chuang-Tse, reported another meeting of the sages, one probably apocryphal, but, as an invention, illuminating. Confucius started to read to Lao-Tse an abstract of the Twelve Classics.

"Too involved," said Lao-Tse; "let me have the substance of them in brief."

"They advocate Charity and Righteousness," Confucius said.

And the philosopher of non-interference answered: "Do Charity and Righteousness constitute the being of man? . . . Take note of the heavens and the earth, how they move in effortless order, of the sun and moon that unfailingly return with their brightness, and of the stars that preserve their courses without exertion. There are, too, the birds and the beasts, which need not be told to flock with their kind; and the trees grow naturally upward. Conform to this natural rhythm, follow this Way, and you will attain to wisdom. No need then of straining and struggling after Charity and Righteousness. Stop going about as if you were beating a drum. . . ."

Lao-Tse went on to caution Confucius about introducing confusion and disorder by his moral meddling. In effect he said (as

---

* Lao-Tan was the contemporary name of the one who, since his canonization in the seventh century of the Christian era, has been known as Lao-Tse — "Tse" meaning "saint" or "Sage." Similarly the reader will find on a later page that Chuang-Tse in speaking of himself employs the name by which he was known in his own time, Chuang-Chou.

indeed he shaped the thought for another): "Take care, my young reformer, not to interfere with the natural goodness of the heart of man. It is possible to depress the heart or to excite it unduly. . . . In repose it is profoundly still; it is capable, nevertheless, of every freedom, of every orderly movement, of heavenly flight. . . . Do not wake men out of their natural purity, avoid excess of arguing, trust to quiet conformance with Order."

When Confucius returned from the interview he did not speak for three days. Then one of his pupils broke the silence to say: "Master, you have seen Lao-Tan. In what way did you admonish him?"

The great sage answered: "Yes, I have seen the Dragon. It is true that the Dragon is coiled in a body, but going out from the body is the Dragon soul. It rides the clouds of Heaven and takes its nourishment from the Soul of the Universe. My mouth fell open and I could not shut it. How should I admonish Lao-Tan?"

And so the Dragon, Lao-Tan or Lao-Tse, went uncorrected. Dragon he was, the one human who epitomized the spiritual genius of the Chinese; the guardian that was the symbol of the race; the dragon whose element was water (which Lao-Tse so praised as being lowly, seeking the valleys unobtrusively, but permeating everywhere, conquering all); the dragon that breathed fire, yet equally breathed out the winds that quicken life at the beginning of spring.

A very few years after his meeting with Confucius, Lao-Tse gave up his post as archivist and left the Kingdom of Chou. He went away to the Westward and was never heard of again. Somewhere in the West, it was believed, there was a realm where sages lived under conditions surviving from the Golden Age, where rules and rulers were unknown, where life was not interrupted by the change called death. There one took one's place among the Men of Perfect Wisdom.

The Spirit of man longs to return to God or to the Source — a way of returning home. Therefore the conception of a Golden Age or an eternal Paradise is common to the great religions. It is a product of the soul's inevitable nostalgia. The more imaginative seers, the poets and philosophers and mystics, have depicted the land of the Golden Age as intangible, spiritual. It is, above all, a realm where the distinction between gods and men is unknown. For the poets who visualize the Great Source as God, it is a Kingdom wherein men walk with God at will. For those who distrust imaging, who rise above sense-picturing, it is the ocean of Spirit in which the soul is immersed when it returns home. It is the Eternity, the Infinitude, the Absolute, transcending creation, mortality, and reason. There the released soul is assimilated in the Divine. There it experiences the bliss of perfect rest, of mergence in immortal Being.

There evil is unknown. There is no death. All are brothers in the communion of the Divine. Wisdom and Understanding take the place of knowledge. Holiness — which means merely living wholly or being Whole — is there the natural state.

The peoples of the Far Eastern countries, China, India, and Japan, philosophically more mature than those of the Western nations, have looked to Paradise without the necessity to endow it with fruits and flowers, silver and rubies, silks and perfumes. They have been content to vision the rapture there as of a different order from that commonly vouchsafed to mortals in terms of sense. They have been able to read into abstract terms — supreme wisdom and divine communion and universal love — a meaning, an experience, transcending any known to the bodily faculties. Their dream ends rather in absorption into abstract bliss.

In the West, Paradise is frequently painted as a higher sort of pleasure ground, in terms of material things commonly considered good. A garden is a thing near to God, and it is the best of our Western imagining that our Eden or Paradise is a celestial garden. It is well, too, that we endow our Golden Realm with the natural elements at their most tranquil and placid level — with sense-lulling warmth, and serene music, and sweet-scented breezes. But beyond that, as the Eastern seers and our own poet-mystics have so often observed, we Christians of the West, and the Jews, and the Mohammedans even more notably, have dressed Heaven and the Golden Age, in our sacred books, in the trappings common to our worldly dreams. We have let our egos and our cravings intrude. We have painted the vision of Paradise as if it were an answer to our earthly desires. We have been slow to relinquish the idea that Heaven in the hereafter must minister to our appetites, our lust for gold and rare jewels, our hunger for magnificence.

The major Christian prophets, to be sure, and most of all Jesus, have maintained the Oriental abstract view. The Kingdom is within; Paradise and Hell are not exterior and physical, but of our own mental making; the reward in Heaven is of a sort eye hath not seen nor ear heard. The end is that we shall stand in the presence of God.

The differences between the conceptions of Heaven in East and in West, among different nations, do not profoundly matter. What greatly signifies is that men of every race have devised the concept of a Paradise, as if universally the human mind recollected something of the glory of its Source. Sometimes the emphasis is on the Divine ruler or God; at other times it is merely the Soul of the universe that is glorified; or again it is the simple primeval state known to the first children of men, a vague time and place of innocency and peace, as pictured by Lao-Tse.

The Chinese speak freely of a Heaven, and their seers invented or recollected many variations of the Age of Gold and of its Paradise. But God as an imageable concept is absent from both the Taoist and the Buddhist books of wisdom, which are their chief treasuries of religious lore (and absent, of course, from the ethical and social treatises of Confucius). Paradise is rather a shadowy abode of "the Ancients" — meaning the Ancestors. There is mention of a Divine Gardener, or Divine Farmer, but this represents a mortal promoted to Heaven for his services to man and to agriculture, rather than a father deity.

The idea of mystery and of mystic communion, nevertheless, is in no way absent because of the lack of a concept of God. An abstract conception (difficult for Western minds to "feel into") of the One, or the Source, or the Rhythm of Life permits ample play to dreams of detachment, deliverance, peace, and divine communion.

Ancestor worship, so crudely interpreted by the West, bears within it a complex of conceptions and activities permeated with mystic feeling and symbolic significance. It is the idea of creation that is exalted, of a considered, reverent continuity of life. Each ancestor in turn has become immortal in carrying on the chain of generation. He is the link backward to the procreative beginnings of the Universe, to a revered all-comprehending One, and to all the creators in his own line; he is honoured as the link forward toward whatever glory shall crown man's continuance.

Filial piety is man's bond with the Eternal. Family, clan, and race afford a channel of "worship" and "devotion" paralleled by the functions of the church in the West. Nor is there reason to believe that any church doctrine or ritual more effectively engenders the sense of consecration, of a universe conceived out of love, of a personal bond with the body of divine wisdom and human knowledge. If we prefer to term the abstract Source or One "God," we may say that the approach to God and to the mystery of one's own being is facilitated rather than hindered by the interposition of the spirits of one's ancestors along the devotional path.

For mystics, and indeed for all those whose minds are set upon God or Ultimate Spirit as the one goal, it matters not very much what is the helping figure the mind fixes upon *en route*. The "way" may prove easier because the pilgrim reverently asks guidance of the Virgin Mary or of a collective Ancestor, or of Sophia, Wisdom, visualized as a guardian other self. Lao-Tse kept his eyes steadily upon the ultimate goal or Soul or Attainment; but he nowhere registers disapproval of his countrymen's reverence for the ancestral chain linking the individual to the Source.

"The mystic East" is a phrase common in literature. In the Orient the characteristic search for means to the individual's union with the Absolute has been more at the heart of religion than in the West. It is no accident, then, that the two seers who are the purest advocates of the mystic life, who most unconditionally put the interests of the spirit above the body, are of the Far East — Lao-Tse and the Buddha Gautama. Both hold to Spirit as the ultimate reality; both preach the cleansing, the sacrifice, of the self; the illusiveness of desire and "busyness" and riches; the travelling of the way from personality to impersonal mergence in the sea of the divine. Both posit inward peace, quietude of mind, and tranquillity of soul as the highest earthly good.

Lao-Tse, because he is the less austere figure, because he is the less exacting and the more human — and each pilgrim begins his pilgrimage on human ground — may prove the more appealing guide into the treasury of Oriental mysticism. His emphasis is so clearly on the ways to find abundant life, not on repression and escape, and his thesis is so definitely the naturalness of the spiritual way of life, that he is doubly persuasive. "The man who is wise," said Lao-Tse's apostle, Chuang-Tse, "takes his stand upon the beautiful orderliness of the world." The Buddha the more sternly condemns, or at least discounts, the constituted world.

It is Lao-Tse's insistence upon the sweetness of life (when illumined from Heaven) that makes him perfectly the prophet of the restored Golden Age. He is himself un-self-conscious, effortlessly harmonious, serenely joyful. He is innocent — even when pointing out the artificiality and pretentiousness of rulers and reformers, or explaining the inevitableness of savagery once war is condoned — innocent of bias or resentment or guile. He simply speaks out of intuition, out of an understanding of the world as it was before evil arose.

He passionately holds to humility, peace, and the liberty of the soul. He also profoundly enjoys contemplation of the harmonious processes, the rhythmic movements, of nature. He urges the duty of creativeness, but on the quiet, spiritual, effortless side, out of "the Valley of Spirit, from which came Heaven and Earth: a fountain inexhaustible, ceaselessly flowing, to be used."

Of all the seers of the East, Lao-Tse is the one who has the morning light most upon him, who is radiant, golden, crystalline.

The sage known as Lao-Tse was a member of the Li (Plum) family, and his personal name was Er (Ear). He came to be called Lao-Tan, Lao meaning Old, and Tan meaning Long-lobed. Hundreds of years later, when he was, as they say, canonized, the name Lao-Tan was changed to Lao-Tse, signifying the Old Sage or Old Philosopher.

Because Tse means child as well as sage, Lao-Tse has been known at times as the Old Boy. This circumstance opened the way to the legend that he lay in the womb for eighty-one years and was born with snow-white hair. There is a legend, too, that he was the Yellow Lord reborn, an incarnation of one of the all-wise guides of mankind, of that age when there was no distinction between divine and human leaders.

Lao-Tan was born about the year 604 B.C. in the village known as Good Man's Bend, in the Thistle District of Bramble Province.* He rose to be an official of the State of Chou — literally the State

---

* Here I have followed the account by Sze-Ma-Ch'ien, a Chinese historian of the second century B.C., as interpreted by Paul Carus. I am indebted also, for historical data, to Lin Yutang, Tsui Chi, Arthur Waley, Dwight Goddard, and other writers. A detailed acknowledgment, with the names of the books drawn upon, will be found in an appendix. I have made my own version of the *Book of Tao*, based on the reputedly literal translation by James Legge, with frequent reference to the texts of Ch'u, Lin, Carus, Waley, Goddard, and seven others. Of the more than two hundred and fifty lines quoted in this chapter, none duplicates any other translation.

of Everywhere, the King of Chou then being emperor of all China; that is, of all the known world. If the place names, like those applied to the sage himself, have a legendary aspect, as if to symbolize the seer's overcoming of handicaps and his rise to world eminence, nevertheless the places are real ones, to be identified on the maps.

For a great many years Lao-Tan served the King of Chou as librarian and archivist. He probably acted also as state historian, a fact that might be taken to explain his fluency with the brush and his poetic style. He lived virtuously and modestly. Of his many years at the capital of Chou, comprising almost a lifetime, the only attested incident is the visit of Confucius, about 517 B.C.

At that time Lao-Tan had already developed the ideas of self-effacement, non-interference, and pacifism, which would conform but oddly with the duties of a retainer at the court of an emperor and war-lord. His dream of a Golden Age of quietude and contemplation could in no way be reconciled with the martial activity, the ostentation, and the material splendour of his surroundings — this, too, against a background of poverty, serfdom, and plundering. He saw with candid eyes the evidences of decay of civilization. Finally he forecast the collapse of the proud Chou State and thus the disintegration of the empire (a prophecy fulfilled within a generation). He could stay at court no longer.

He made his way to the western frontier. If he did not actually believe that beyond lay "the Western Paradise" or "the Abode of Peace" as a survival of the Golden Age, he at least visualized, in retirement and obscurity, a life free of hypocrisy and restless striving; looked forward to an existence permitting serenity, natural conformance with nature, and spiritual illumination.

At the frontier the guardian of the pass, Yin-Hi (whom later Taoists immortalized for his service to mankind), recognized the sage. He said: "Since you have decided, Master, to retire from the world, I ask you to put down in a book the ideas by which we may remember you." Lao-Tse tarried long enough to compose a poetic treatise consisting of hardly more than five thousand ideographs or words. Giving the manuscript to Yin-Hi, he went through the pass into the mountains beyond, and disappeared.

The *Book of Tao,* or the *Bible of Tao,* as Lao-Tse's composition is known in simplest words, at first bore in Chinese the title *Tao Teh*.

LAO-TSE ON A WATER BUFFALO. BRONZE STATUETTE. CHINESE, SUNG DYNASTY. WORCESTER ART MUSEUM.

The word *Ching* of the commonly used title *Tao Teh Ching* means "canon" and was added when the book was recognized as canonical — that is, as the work of a saint or prophet — twelve hundred years after the writing.

Because the words *Tao* and *Teh* cannot be exactly or completely translated, there have been almost as many forms of the title in English as there have been translators. Important versions have appeared under titles as dissimilar as *The Way and Its Power* (Arthur Waley's translation), *The Canon of Reason and Virtue* (Paul Carus), and *The Providential Grace Classic* (Edward Harper Parker). A Christian student, having in mind the pregnant words of Jesus to Philip, might consider *The Canon of the Way and the Life* the most suggestive transcription. For essentially the *Tao Teh Ching* treats first of a Way of Heaven, in the double sense of the "manner" of the running of the universe, and the road to Eternity; and second, of a rhythm of life, a conformance to natural rhythmic processes, by which the Wayfarer attains to *Tao* — or, it may be, to a harmonious flow of life given him out of the infinitude of *Tao*.

Lao-Tse wrote his book without indications for dividing the poems or sections from one another. Later, scholars cast the material into the form in which it appears to-day, in two parts containing eighty-one named poems or stanzas of unequal length, each self-sufficient in structure and meaning.

Interpolations and corruptions have crept into the text. There is, nevertheless, an extraordinary unity of sense and feeling in the composition. There is little continuity from poem to poem; and those commentators may be right who call the work a compilation of Lao-Tse's aphorisms and sayings. But the originality, vigour, and cogency of the verses argue for a single author, and for the existence of a poet profoundly intuitive and imaginatively inspired. The combination of grandeur and conciseness, the clear-speaking along with inexhaustible connotative meanings, the illumination out of occult penetration — all this seems unthinkable as a product of collective authorship.

The spirit of Lao-Tan the man and of Lao-Tse the inspired philosophic poet abides in the text of the *Book of Tao*. If obscured and confused in parts (and utterly incomprehensible to the mind that takes its stand upon rationalism and pragmatism), the book yet sets out one of the great coherent systems of transcendental and practical philosophy. To the mystics of both East and West it has appealed as the revelation of a Seer's way of finding Heaven.

There is in the nature of Chinese writing — that is, of ideographs descended from picture-symbols, each ideograph covering a wide range of "meaning extensions" — ample reason for the extraordinary differences of thought in the Western translations of the *Book of Tao*. This language is incomparably rich in overtones, incomparably inexact. The picture element makes for vividness and abundant allusion. But nouns are not distinguished as singular or plural, and verbs have not past, present, or future tense. There is no "I," "you," "he," or "they." Beyond knowledge the translator (something of a falsifier at best) needs the spiritual equipment of intuition and divination. It may be added that never has the profound meaning of a book eluded mere scholars so substantially. The most literal philological transcriptions are the least useful.

Lao-Tse's rhythmic structure can to an extent be echoed — the parallelisms and the occasional changes of movement; but the subtler poetic values, the secondary rhythms, and especially the use of symbols with (to the Chinese) double meanings, may as well be marked off by the translator as impossible of reproduction. And in his imagery Lao-Tse veils or hints at infinitely more than is stated.

If ever a book cried out for expression of the spirit rather than the letter, of the vision and the insight and the mystery of feeling, it is the *Tao Teh Ching*. The very words and symbols have a different meaning and purpose than would have been the case if one encountered them (as one does) in the texts of the intellectual Confucius. The latter, indeed, employs the word *Tao* frequently; but it is not the primitive, Heavenly *Tao* of Lao-Tse.

Lao-Tse did not invent the word *Tao*. It quite simply signifies "way" in the several meanings, concrete and abstract, that Western dictionaries give to the word: as, path; direction; manner of doing. But when a religion of Taoism arose, it was Lao-Tse's philosophy, personal and mystic, that lay at the heart of it. The word *Tao* signifying a path of life — a religion, in short — had existed as early as the seventh century B.C. But the sixth century seer clothed the conception with magnificent new import.

What is the *Tao*? It is the Absolute, the Infinite, the One. It is at once all that is and the cause or mystery behind the all. It is limitless; therefore Lao-Tse says, in the opening lines of the Book of Tao: "When *Tao* can be spoken of, it is not the all-embracing *Tao*; for a name cannot name the eternal. Nameless, it is the source of Heaven and Earth; with names one comes to creation, and things."

The *Tao* was, before creation. It is, before existence. It is all that mortals have vaguely tried to convey in the words "God" and "logos" and "Providence." It is the Spirit, the soul, the nature of the universe, beyond cosmos and life and truth. It is the harmony of all processes and all things. It is the indivisible unity existing before the dualism of the *yang* and the *yin*, the male and the female, the hard and the soft, the aggressive and the yielding, the luminous and the dark of mortal life.

The ineffable and the nameable, the unmanifested of the source and the manifested in life, are, says Lao-Tse, "in essence the same." And he continues:

> *The sameness holds deep upon deep of mystery.*
> *Over deep and deep extends the mystic way;*
> *It opens gates to the wonder of living.*

The mystery is touched upon in these lines concerning the "invisible, inaudible, intangible" *Tao*:

> *Endless, ceaseless, continuous,*
> *The One if we try to name it,*
> *Disappears in nothingness —*
> *Which yet is filled:*
> *For this is the form of the formless,*
> *The shape of the shapeless,*
> *The look of the invisible. . . .*
> *In the unfolding of* Tao
> *The unseeable is imaged.*

And of *Tao* as source, and as model, of all that is, Lao-Tse wrote these lines:

> *Before the being of Heaven and Earth*
> *There existed the nebulous One,*

> *Unnamed, silent, formless,*
> *Changeless, eternal, unfailing,*
> *The fathomless womb of all things.*
> *Baffled, I speak of it as* Tao,
> Tao, *the Supreme.* . . .

In another sense *Tao* is the Heavenly *Way*. It is the path to be trod, the perfection to be emulated, the "admirable operation" with which one must come into accord. (Western students, and especially missionaries, visualizing religion as primarily moralism, have dryly translated the phrase as "the correct road" or "the path of virtue.")

Tao is, again — for the stubborn human brain will explore every explainable aspect of the unexplainable — the harmonious interaction of man, Earth, and Heaven. It is the flow of the vital essence, the moving of absolute love, the progressive order of being, growth, and fruition. Man may busy himself with the affairs of the outer life, with the manifested, without regard to Heaven's flow. He may act wholly on the plane of appearances and desires and events. But the wise man, counsels Lao-Tse, will recognize the relationship of manifested to unmanifested, of Earth to Heaven, will divest himself of earthly desires, and thus will enable his soul to rise into the flow of harmony — and so embrace *Tao*.

To merge silently, freed, into the stream of infinitude is the greatest good of life. The two aims of the world's mysticism are here set forth: first, to find the eternal in given life, to feel the emanation of Spirit in every manifested thing; second, to take on the sense of the flow of Spirit, to bathe in consciousness of the stream of divinity, in union with the Soul and all souls.

One finds *Tao* everywhere; one is filled with *Tao*. In discovering the vital flow in all, one is relative to all that is. In giving oneself up, in being permeated by Tao's light, one becomes the sanctuary in which a perpetual holiness is celebrated. Lao-Tse wrote of the dual aspect of the Way, and of man's necessary regard to both the world and the Source, thus:

> Tao *existed before the creation,*
> *Yet* Tao *mothered all the sons of the world.*
> *Know the Mother,*

> Enter into the brotherhood of the sons;
> Know brotherhood,
> You are at one with the Mother:
> Then can you meet no harm. . . .
> To understand the small, yet exalt the great,
> To be strong in guarding tenderness;
> To employ the earth-light,
> Yet share in Heaven's illumination:
> This is to escape earthly cares,
> This is to merge in the ageless.

Sometimes directly, sometimes indirectly, Lao-Tse utilized the metaphor of flowing waters, unassertive but pervasive, signifying *Tao:*

> A man's excellence is like that of water;
> It benefits all things without striving;
> It takes to the low places shunned by men.
> Water is akin to Tao. . . .

And:

> In all the earth nothing weaker than water,
> Yet in attacking the hard, nothing superior,
> Nothing so certain in wearing down strength:
> There is no way to resist it.
> Note then: The weak conquer the strong,
> The yielding outlast the aggressors.

The thought is implicit in many passages, without direct statement, as:

> Tao *is like the emptiness, the capacity of a vessel:*
> Its uses cannot be counted.
> It is deep and inexhaustible,
> The fountain-source of all things.
> It blunts all sharpness,
> Unties all tangles,
> Tempers all glare,
> Quiets commotion:
> A spring continuously pure and still.
> What is it? Where from?
> A vision in the boundless mind of the Ancestor?

If the grandeur and the all-inclusiveness of the conception of *Tao* put it, humanly, on the remote side, there is a way of approach in understanding *Teh*, the word forming the other half of the title *The Canon of Tao Teh*. For *Teh* (though as difficult to define in a phrase) has to do with mortal life, with experience, with living harmoniously in this world. It is *Tao* in action.

Teh links the *individual* with the purpose of Heaven. It is the rhythm of the spirit brought down to life, the unfolding of *Tao* in the being of the individual. It is the spontaneous flow of the "power" attained from *Tao*. It is conformance to, and movement in, the natural rhythm or orderliness that Lao-Tse so extols as harmoniously animating nature.

Embracing *Tao*, the wise man takes on *Teh*. (In this sense, the translation of *Teh* as "virtue" is understandable and right.) Conversely, *Teh* is the quality in the man that brings him to the realization of *Tao*. There is here the connotation of a position in life similar to that achieved by Christian "grace" — a resting in divine favour and an understanding conformance with unseen directives.

A man's grasp of *Teh* begins in a sense of the harmonious flow of a single Spirit through Heaven, Earth, and Man. It ends in attainment of peace and in the power to rise to the experience of Unity or communion. It is the power compelling the Wayfarer to the Way.

In the art of living, "the art of being in the world," to be possessed by a spiritual rhythm or movement of the spirit is to be endowed with *Teh*. In a narrower sense *Teh* is the equipment and the method by which the mystic attains, first, awareness of the divine or cosmic in each object in life, and, secondly, conscious union with the One or God or *Tao*.

There are those who speak of Lao-Tse as a writer for initiates, for ones already enlightened. And indeed he seldom puts his thought as directly and simply as did the Buddha Gautama in his sermons, or Jesus in his addresses. But cryptic as his style is, and condensed his thought, the purport of each poem emerges when taken in relation to the whole book.

> Tao *produces all things of earth;*
> *The outflowing* Teh *sustains them.* . . .
> *Therefore let a man exalt* Tao
> *And honour* Teh, *its expression.*
> Tao *animates living things;*

> Teh *nurtures them,*
> *Gives them increase,*
> *Completes them, protects them,*
> *Provides shelter and food.*
> *Yet* Teh *claims no possessions,*
> *Supplies without owning,*
> *Guides without ruling:*
> *In this the clue to life's mystic operation.*

How is one to conduct oneself in human affairs in order to possess the harmonious power of *Teh* and attain *Tao*? Primarily, writes Lao-Tse, by practising *Wu-Wei*, a phrase commonly translated "non-action," but meaning more exactly "non-resistance" or "action without assertion." The word contains a caution against striving, shrewdness, unnatural activity, and interference. But it does not imply a wisdom of utter passivity, an existence of inaction.

The ideal, says Lao-Tse, is to move in accordance with the effortless movement of nature, to be at one with the flow of the Spirit of *Tao* through all life. There is a beautiful orderliness of the universe. Take your stand upon this, upon its non-striving, its effortlessness, its inevitability. Create no complications, no argument, no strife. Fall in with the life-rhythm of the Spirit. All else will be cared for.

Wu-Wei is the means of preparing oneself for the consciousness of *Tao*, as *Teh* is the expression of *Tao*. It is the dedication to a mortal life of unresisting co-operation, of spontaneous, unstudied action. It is the choosing of a path avoiding extremes, leading away from compulsion and strain. As water and earth and sun and bird are obedient to the *Tao's* "way," so man must be passive as material, without self-will.

Action without striving implies the killing out of arrogance and conceit, the stilling of the restless scheming mind. It means surrender of the self to the keeping of the Spirit. It means entry into a life of simplicity, peace, and compassion. Paradoxically, it means accomplishment of the greatest deeds.

To accomplish without trying: that is the central practical lesson. Lao-Tse, as he looked about him at the disorder, the suffering, the running about, among humans, perceived that the way to peace lay through a return to the ideal of simple action, of controlled desires, of non-resistance.

> Though he does not step outside the door,
> Man may comprehend the universe.
> Though he does not look beyond the window,
> He may know the Way of Heaven.
> When far he goes from the Source,
> Pale becomes the light.
> Therefore the sage runs not about:
> Though he looks not, all is illumined.
> Though he strives not, all is accomplished.

The power of non-resistant and non-insistent action is summarized thus:

> The softest of things
> By persistent dripping
> Wears away the hardest.
> The gentle flow of Spirit,
> Movement without substance,
> Enters the creviceless solid.
> In this I see the power
> And weight of non-interference.
> To convey the lesson without speaking,
> To reach the goal without striving:
> That is the Sage's rare attainment.

And:

> He who aspires to shape the world
> Will not succeed.
> The world is a spiritual vessel,
> Beyond man's shaping.
> He who tampers spoils it,
> He who holds, loses.
> Thus the wise man avoids excess of doing:
> He wins by not contending.

Reserve of action is to be practised even in speaking — a warning as regards glib talkers:

> The one who knows the Secret does not speak:
> The one who speaks does not know the Secret.

Spontaneous, unthinking action is frequently praised, as in a line thus elaborated by Chuang-Tse:

> *Perfect kindness acts without thinking of kindness.*

Lao-Tse is celebrated for his paradoxes and parallelisms. Nowhere else do so many appear as in the poems dealing with *Wu-Wei*. In verses that might be entitled "On Catching Difficulties While They Are Easy," he writes:

> *You will never have an important difficulty*
> *If you regard every difficulty as important.*

The Taoist who follows the philosophy of non-striving, avoiding extremes, tends to level great and small. Therefore Lao-Tse says (in the same poem):

> *Careless of greatness,*
> *The Sage becomes great.*

It is this poem that includes the line in which the Chinese seer anticipates an utterance of Jesus destined to become immortal in the Western world:

> *Repay injury with kindness.*

The lesson of *Wu-Wei* is, in the end, not inaction but action restrained, action deferred until one feels the effortless, unerring wisdom of *Tao* inspiring, guiding one. Then it will be action so natural that there will be no need of insistence, or contriving, or straining. Having seen the way, one is poised, relaxed, released, and then one's action is spontaneous, free, intuitive. The *Book of Tao* sums up the results of practising *Wu-Wei* thus:

> *The Way of Tao is this:*
> *It strives not, but conquers;*
> *It speaks not, but all is made clear;*
> *It summons not, but its house is crowded;*
> *It contrives not, but the design is perfect.*

The avoidance of over-striving is a step in the preparation for mystic understanding as recommended by the sages of all lands. Lao-Tse is even more directly the mystic counsellor when he goes on to distinguish between learning, or secondary knowledge, and intuition, or "good" knowledge; and especially when he speaks of quietude of mind as basic for progress in the Way.

The man who has no conception of *Tao*, who lives by desires and sense-satisfaction and by material possession, "gets along" by exercise of knowledge and reason. But if he have not intuitive intelligence, a natural apprehension of an inner flow of Spirit through life, education can lead to no permanent happiness.

Knowledge can be useful, reason will solve many minor problems; but neither can bring man into the kingdom of the Spirit. Indeed, progress may have to begin, says Lao-Tse, with unlearning a great deal that civilization has sanctioned as valuable knowledge. Otherwise the mind cannot act as the pure mirror of *Tao*.

The technique of contemplation — Lao-Tse implies rather than states that a discipline not unlike that of yoga is necessary — involves dismissal of knowledge, a deliberate stilling of the brain; but the unlearning process of which the Chinese seer oftener speaks is of a more general sort. It is escape from the system of knowledge that has led man out of his original estate of natural simplicity and intuitive goodness. It is liberation from the false activity, the material enterprise, and the law-regulated morality that "knowledge" and pragmatic education have brought into human life.

> *Throw away learning,*
> *Cast off excess knowledge:*
> *Reap thus a hundredfold gain.*
> *Banish cumbrous benevolence*
> *And interfering righteousness:*
> *Then will the people return*
> *To filial love, to brotherhood.*
> *Void the ideals of scheming and getting:*
> *Robbers and thieves will disappear.*
> > *Education has failed,*
> > *Hold fast to intuitive good:*
> > *Be simple; be natural;*
> > *Check ambition; curb desire.*

Such verses, with their end-summary of rules for simple living, are as concrete and terse as any schoolmaster could ask. Equally plain and logical are the lines linking the idea of simplified living

SAGE IN CONTEMPLATION. PAINTING IN THE STYLE OF MA YUAN. CHINESE, SUNG DYNASTY. MUSEUM OF FINE ARTS, BOSTON.

(through *Wu-Wei*) with that of the blessed quietude so prized by the mystic:

> *Through return to simple living*
> *Comes control of desires.*
> *In control of desires*
> *Stillness is attained.*
> *In stillness the world is restored.*

China in the latter years of Lao-Tse's life as a government official was a disordered and afflicted land. When he arrived at the western border, self-exiled from the realm, he had already prophesied the collapse of the Chou State and the lapse of the peoples of China into aggravated conditions of misery, bloodshed, and exploitation. In the *Book of Tao* he condemns the rulers' struggle for power, the resort to war, and the enslavement of the masses. But he places the greater emphasis on the causes of those evils. He blames the wide-spread aspiration for power, for extravagant display, for so-called honour. He stresses the emptiness of the enjoyment of earthly fame, of caste distinctions.

Beyond that, he had observed the frivolity, the callousness, and the actual degeneracy among rulers and courtiers, who feasted, dallied, and intrigued at grievous cost to the people. He saw the vast structure of governmental regulation, law, and armed enforcement as designed to perpetuate social evils. And the saddest part of it was, he pointed out, that no one was really made happy. For the rulers and courtiers gained only the illusory enjoyments of the flesh, and they were periodically harassed, harried, and overcome by rival rulers.

What was the answer, then? Go back and recognize the fundamental mistake. Give up egoism, aggression, and personal scheming. Forego regulation (which the Taoist defines as interference). Avoid argument, bustle, and acquisitiveness. Instead of building up one's ambition, wealth, and position, one must discover the joy of flowing along with nature's harmonious current.

Lao-Tse's references to the rulers and the ruling class are often apt and revealing, and his advice to rulers about war is wise and sound. The ultimate ground upon which every pacifist stands is illuminated in a single line:

> *When the great armies go to war, Sorrow is the sole winner.*

And there is a paradoxical bit about victory:

> *Victory proves a bitter blessing:*
> *He who wins is lowered,*
> *A slaughterer of men. . . .*
> *Let the victors listen —*
> *Those are funeral bells!*

There is a poem, sometimes translated under the title "The Art of Government," which explains that the wisest ruler is he who trusts to *Tao* and adopts a policy of "let alone"; then:

> *How do I know this?*
> *The thicker the rules and restraints,*
> *The more poverty-stricken the people;*
> *The sharper the weapons of enforcement,*
> *The deeper the common misery;*
> *The more police and soldiers,*
> *The less rewarded the labourer;*
> *The more numerous the laws,*
> *The more thieves and robbers.*
> *Consider then the Sage's words:*
> *I withhold action:*
> *The people return to honesty.*
> *I cultivate repose:*
> *The people become tranquil.*
> *I avoid busyness:*
> *The people prosper.*
> *I rest my mind upon* Tao:
> *The people are simple and docile.*

Because rulers have not followed the way of the sage, the art of government has steadily deteriorated:

> *In the Golden Age,*
> *Rulers were unknown.*
> *In the following age*
> *Rulers were loved and praised.*
> *Next came the age*
> *When rulers were feared.*
> *Finally the age*
> *When rulers are hated.*

There may be conditions, Lao-Tse admits, under which guidance and correction are necessary to government, but the central principle is to leave the people, as much as possible, to follow natural ways of doing things; then they will labour honestly, respect one another, be content with simple pleasures, and create no disturbance. The seer's advice to the rulers, as to the common man, thus contains much of the sense tied up in our folk sayings "Easy does it!" and "Go with the current." It is all summed up in a single admonition:

> *You should rule a great country*
> *As you fry a small fish —*
> *With the least turning.*

When the world is at crisis, caught in chaotic violence and threatened with catastrophic ruin, as it was in Lao-Tse's time twenty-four hundred years ago, as it is in the mid-twentieth century, spiritual leaders return to the truth that salvation cannot come from without, and certainly not from governments. They know that peace and ordered life depend upon change in the life-ideals of the individuals making up a social community. Nothing can save the world except wide-spread personal regeneration. Lao-Tse may pause to address advice to the world's ruling class; but his deepest concern is with the individual, with the individual's soul.

In his own country, and in the wider world, he has been accused of advocating a humility, a passiveness, and a spirit of acceptance that are less than manly, that lead to a show of masterfulness on the one side and cringing on the other. The accusation falls when one plumbs the full depth of meaning of the poems. For it is a glad acceptance of natural ways of life that he counsels, a joyful falling in with the rhythmic course of nature. He counsels quietude because the bliss of communion can be attained only with stillness, never with assertion. He does not once suggest a rigid asceticism or mortification as a step on the road to salvation.

Frugality, moderation, and gentleness may lead to withdrawal from the overactivity of the world. But this frugality enriches one, this gentleness leans on strength. Withdrawal from excesses intimates no retreat into nothingness, no assumption of puritan austerity.

The Sage may seem to have withdrawn, because he is indifferent to so much that a fevered civilization counts important. He may seem to be a jelly of indecision and non-resistance. That, says Lao-Tse, is because he not only meets goodness with good but returns good to all; not only meets faith with faithfulness, but is faithful to the faithless — in the deeper sense of adjusting his purpose to the fundamental need of every individual. Having lost everything, living in peace, rendering himself a vessel through which flows the harmony of Heaven, he knows that in the end his not-doing, his not-striving, will bring the regard of men to him.

Withdraw from materialistic living, he counsels, in order to enter fully into life. Withdraw from the cross-purposes of an artificial and violent civilization in order to move harmoniously in the one purpose of the natural universe. Abandon self-will; in so doing, one merely opens the way to the most vital activities of the true — that is, the spiritual — self. Exert no influence; only thus can one ultimately influence all.

Perhaps because he had been taxed with the apparent frivolity of advocating nothingness, the seer wrote one of his most provocative poems on the utility of emptiness. Superficially, it is a spun-out paradox. Within the lines, nevertheless, is hidden one of Lao-Tse's profoundest thoughts, that in renouncing excessive busyness we are but making room or capacity for the spiritual tides of life. Let us, he says, see the positive structure of our existence as something that can be transformed to make space for the soul's expansion.

> *The wheel's hub holds thirty spokes:*
> *Utility depends on the hole through the hub.*
> *The Potter's clay forms a vessel:*
> *It is the space within that serves.*
> *A house is built with solid walls:*
> *The nothingness of window and door*
> *Alone renders it usable.*
> *That which exists may be transformed.*
> *What is non-existent has boundless uses.*

Lao-Tse opposed the rule-makers, Confucius among others, and deplored their interfering and their conceit. One hesitates, then, to quote any poem of his as offering "rules for individual living."

THE POET LAO-TSE

Yet these practical lines on the ordering of mortal life seem common-sensical and memorable:

> *I know three precious gifts. Hold them fast!*
> *The first is love,*
> *The second, being frugal,*
> *The third, renunciation.*
> *When one is filled with love,*
> *There is no room for fear.*
> *When one is frugal*
> *One has everything to give.*
> *When one renounces high position,*
> *One opens the door to service.*
> *To-day men rule by fear, not love,*
> *They would be liberal without saving,*
> *Would advance without serving —*
> *That way lies decay.*
> *Love alone resists all, conquers all:*
> *With love in one's heart*
> *One is armed with the power of Heaven.*

The "way" of renunciation as known to many mystics, the path of sense-abnegation and of quietude, is recommended in lines that might have been written by a Buddhist Bodhisattva deploring the prison of the senses:

> *He who closes his mouth,*
> *Who shuts the sense channels,*
> *Is blessed in life.*
> *He who opens the sense gates*
> *And busies about*
> *Cannot be saved.*

Humility and lowliness and gentleness have been celebrated consistently by the great spiritual prophets down the ages, especially by Lao-Tse, the Buddha, and Jesus. By humility each one meant, not weakness and subservience to other men, but that profound surrender to God or natural harmony or *Tao* which is the most joyful experience of the mystic. One becomes quiet, unassertive, inconspicuous, empty, that one may be filled with God.

The pliancy, the passiveness, and the temperateness necessary to mergence in "the natural course of life" are brought out by Lao-Tse in one of the world's most cogent sermons on the rewards of humility:

> Be humble and take on completion;
> Yield to bending, and become straight;
> Be as an empty vessel, and be filled;
> Spend yourself, and be renewed.
>
> Take little, and gain all:
> Contend for much, reap frustration.
>
> The wise man immerses himself in Tao,
> He reflects the lustre of the Way.
> Free of self-assertion,
> He finds himself exalted.
> Free of self-display,
> He is seen by all.
> Cleansed of pride,
> He is honoured.
> Rival of none,
> He meets no rivalry.
> The Ancients said,
> "To be lowly is to reach the Highest."
> Yielding is of the wisdom of Tao.

And what of sin? The individual sinner nowhere claims Lao-Tse's attention. Later, Western religions centred upon the eradication of sin and sinfulness. The sacred books are filled with commandments and rules. But Taoism offers the thought that if each individual gains the light of *Tao*, resumes simple honesty, and lives by the ideals of equality, co-operation, and non-resistance, society will automatically be rid of sin and crime.

The main thing is that, extricating himself from false activity, the man "take on" the harmonious action of *Tao*, the natural rhythmic flow of "all that is." Not only does the wise man follow the promptings of the flow in his own heart; he also finds a supreme delight in experiencing the rhythmic pulsing of the universal order within his own being, and in observing the process of growth, life, and decay endlessly occurring in the world around.

This order, this rhythm, this ceaseless transformation is the subject of certain of Chuang-Tse's imaginative stories about Lao-Tse.

In one of them Confucius is pictured as interrogating Lao-Tan, and the latter is speaking of the beginning of things. He speaks of the antecedent duality of *yang* and *yin*, and of the fusing of these "principles" so that "a harmony ensued and orderly production began."

A power induced and controlled all this, but it is formless and unknowable. Growth and relapse, empty and full, alternating light and dark, the orderly march of the sun, the changes of the moon: these continue, but the force behind is unseen. . . . Behold the spring, how the water wells up effortlessly and overflows. It does not act; that is its nature. Thus it is with the man who conforms to *Tao*. He does not plan or will any action. Yet the right action flows out of him, influencing all. Then he is like Heaven, which is naturally high, like Earth, which is naturally solid, like the sun and the moon, which of themselves give light. What need of willing and striving?

And:

Without talking about it, Heaven and Earth carry on their functions with beautiful efficiency. Without discussion, the four seasons continue in their appointed cycle. The ten thousand created things move through life according to kind, and no one issues a proclamation.

The man who is wise takes his stand upon this beautiful orderliness of the world. He moves in accordance with the one constitution of all things. Therefore the saying that the man of wisdom carries out no action of his own; even a Master among sages originates nothing, beyond sharing in the Rhythm of the universe.

The end of Lao-Tse's advice to the individual is, then, that he shall take on mystic awareness. The heart of Taoism is in the celebration of a natural flow of the Spirit, of the rhythmic essence of life, through all manifest things.

Be aware of the Eternal in the transient. Feel life as the expression of Infinitude. A cycle of growth, fulfilment, and decay is implicit in every birth. Immortality stands guard over every death.

The transient reveals unending movement, ceaselessly unfolding order. Behind all the pulsating, alternating dualisms, and behind the interaction of the *Tao* of Heaven, the *Tao* of Earth, and the *Tao* of Man, is the boundlessness of the all-embracing *Tao*, the home of the soul. Find the gateway in yourself, counsels Lao-Tse. Rest in *Tao*. Savour its ebb and flow. Merge in its infinitude.

One day in the spring of the year 478 B.C. Confucius died, honoured by his friends but wearied and disappointed after decades of rebuffs at the courts of the provincial princes. Long since, Lao-Tse had disappeared over the mountains to the Westward. China's two greatest sages had gone from the earth.

Though the disciples of Confucius mourned for three years, the country was too confused and miserable, in the midst of warfare and public destitution, to take heed of the death of a philosopher. Yet such was the power of his writings and sayings, and the zeal of his students and disciples so great, that hardly had peace, or comparative peace, returned to the land when Confucianism became the guide to conduct for millions of Chinese.

The acceptance of Taoism was longer deferred. It was not until A.D. 666, nearly twelve centuries after Lao-Tse's death, that he was canonized, by an emperor of the Tang Dynasty. Then he was hailed "The Supreme One, the Mystic Author, Most High."

At that time Confucianism and Taoism had developed through many centuries side by side. In one reign the system of Confucius would be set up as the official Chinese "religion"; in another Confucianism would be proscribed and Taoism proclaimed the national faith.

Ultimately a religion of Taoism crystallized, with divinities, temples, icons, rites, a hierarchy headed by a "pope," and an extensive minor priesthood. But the Taoist church became so entangled in a complex of witchcraft, divination, and pious fraud that the original doctrine was all but obscured. It is best, indeed, in studying the pure thought of Lao-Tse, to close one's eyes to the institutions and the priesthood operating to-day in the name of Taoism—as the founder, if he were on earth, would be constrained to do. Nevertheless he and the *Tao* he celebrated have profoundly affected the lives of millions of people, affording them spiritual sustenance, lifting them from the leaden life of materialism so overwhelmingly prevalent in both East and West.

In the first place the idea of *Tao*, without being lifted to the eminence of a religious faith, entered profoundly into the Chinese character. In the second place, minor Taoist groups *have* preserved the pure core of the master's message, have lived by the philosophy, have developed upon the foundation laid in the *Tao Teh Ching* one of the great bodies of spiritual literature. Because, moreover, *Tao* escapes those claims of exclusiveness and divine sovereignty implicit in some religions, it fused easily with a version of Buddhism when that faith was introduced into China; and from the fusion came the Ch'an or Zen Buddhism which represents to-day (as it has represented for fourteen hundred years) one of the fairest flowers of Oriental spiritual activity.

It was the adaptability of the doctrine of *Tao*, and a certain tolerance and unconstraint bred in its adherents, that permitted the deeper philosophy of Taoism and the outward, ethical precepts of Confucianism to act together upon the collective soul and character of the Chinese people in the three centuries following the passing of the founders. Confucius was, as he said of himself, an adapter, a gatherer of other men's ideas about the good life — and a marvellously wise and witty composer of epigrams. When he had, so to speak, fastened good manners and the outward virtues of loyalty and kindliness and thrift upon the Chinese, there still was room for the cultivation of their spiritual faculties.

Confucianism is not, in the full sense, a religion. Its founder was, if not a sceptic, an indifferent advocate of the spiritual life. He had no notion of what it is that a mystic faith or mystic philosophy does for the human being. For the mass of people a wholly non-spiritual life, though lived peacefully and ethically, fails to satisfy. China found Confucianism insufficient.

Taoism was at hand to supply the spirituality, the sense of a rhythmic order pulsing in Heaven and Earth and in man's veins, a conception of a divine essence that might be called Nature or God or the Great Ancestor. Taoism supplied, moreover, a supporting moral impetus, gave depth and reason to the sometimes commonplace moral instructions of Confucius. And certainly in Lao-Tse and his doctrine of non-assertion and reserved action is the root of the passivity, the patience, and the pliancy of the Chinese character, which have served to carry the nation intact through the crises of more than two thousand years. The people are submissive and peace-loving, and out of submissiveness they have built a vast reserve power. The victory is to the non-doing, said Lao-Tse.

Nor was the influence greater upon the people than upon the Chinese rulers. No major country has enjoyed less of governing. The fact may seem to signal disability at any given moment; but over the years the uncomplicated government, and the resultant reliance upon non-government, have enabled China to survive — the only one of the great ancient nations to remain great and independent. It is likely, too, that in China the ore of life has assayed higher in spiritual contentment than in Western lands where the mining has been done under highly organized coercive law. The riches of contentment are most easily gained where ruling begins in self-government by the individual.

Taoism as a philosophy, then, helped develop passiveness and self-reliance in the Chinese people, and it is perhaps Lao-Tse's greatest service to mankind up to this time. But Taoism as a faith, as a mystic religion, has persisted in purity through an unending succession of disciples and interpreters; and the purely spiritual benefit from Lao-Tse's having lived and written may yet prove the greater.

Seldom has a Master been blessed with two such brilliant disciples and apostles as followed Lao-Tse in the two hundred and fifty years after his death. In the fourth century B.C. there was that "rider upon the winds," Lieh-Tse, and a little later, living through the first quarter of the third century, the imaginative and witty Chuang-Tse.

Lieh-Tse may have written his own books, though many scholars have preferred to consider them stories and sayings brought together later by his disciples. He was especially the apostle of natural living. He thought that men should avoid complication, interference, and artifice; that they should follow the harmonious course of *Tao* and be simple, responsive, compassionate — natural.

Lieh-Tse's lessons are presented usually in the unfolding of an anecdote, a parable, or an allegory. His reverence for the rhythm or harmony that runs through all things is illustrated in many of the stories. There is a fable of a sailor who made a practice of swimming in the sea, to whom the sea-gulls came, playing about him as friends. But one day the sailor was asked by his father to catch and bring home one or two of the gulls. Next day when he went to swim as usual, not a bird came down to him. Though he did not do a thing in any new way, they had become aware that he was a man and different from themselves. The harmony that had once prevailed among men and birds had been disturbed.

On this point Lieh-Tse elsewhere says: "There were men of deep wisdom in the olden times who knew by intuition the feelings and the ways of all living things. They perfectly understood the languages of the different kinds of animal. When they called, the animals gathered together and listened to their teachings, just as if they had been human beings. . . . These sages felt that there was no considerable difference, and they neglected no species that came asking for instruction."

A little fable that might be entitled "How We Fool Ourselves" is this: "A man missed a sum of money. It occurred to him that it might have been stolen by a son of his neighbour. Sure enough, the youth had the furtive manner of a thief, and his expression was sly. Indeed, all his actions and ways marked him as a thief. A little afterward the money was found where it had been washed into a drain. The owner took another good look at his neighbour's son. The youth had neither the manner nor the look of a thief."

Chuang-Tse (who died in the year 275 B.C. or thereabouts) was one of the outstanding writers of his time and, next to Lao-Tse, the greatest mystic seer of early Chinese history. His work as the Saint Paul of Taoism was brilliantly accomplished. As Lao-Tse had left but the one brief, cryptic book, it fell to Chuang-Tse to elaborate and expound the ideas of his master. His comparatively voluminous writings are filled with expositions of the harmonious nature and boundlessness of *Tao*, of the expediency of practising *Wu-Wei*, and of the ways of contemplation and attainment of illumination.

The expositions are embedded in stories and anecdotes: for Chuang-Tse is that rare seer, a romantic philosopher, an entertaining apostle. He rode always with a loose rein upon his imagination. The disciples of Confucius have felt that Chuang-Tse misrepresented and slandered their humane master in fictional treatments of his meetings with the sage of Taoism. Nevertheless the author's inventions are a means of illuminating the truths of a creative philosophy and a profound religion. The basic doctrines of non-interference and of flowing with *Tao's* stream are thus expressed:

> He who knows what is God's part and what is Man's part has reached Understanding. He is then inclined toward God. . . . In the Golden Age true men had no ambition to over-

ride others, to force their way as heroes. They avoided scheming. Thus, whatever the outcome, it brought neither repentance nor pride. They were enabled to climb to great heights without fear, and to walk unharmed through fire and water: this was part of their knowledge of *Tao*. They slept dreamlessly and woke without anxiety. They took little thought for eating. Their breathing was deep and rhythmic. . . . The true men put no emphasis on love of this life; they harboured no fear of death. Birth into life brought rejoicing, departure from it no resistance. They came and went composedly, remembering whence they had sprung, content to know whither they would return. Acceptance of birth, a fair and unconfused passage, then restoration: that is Man's part. It is the way when one does not resist the orderliness of *Tao*, when the human does not interfere with the Divine. It is the way of true Understanding.

From such unadorned dialectic it is a far jump to Chuang-Tse's lighter, even romantic imaginings. One of his favourite questions is: How do we know that this sense-life is not illusion? On the subject of illusion he wrote a little fable:

> I remember a time when I, Chuang-Chou, dreamt that I was a butterfly. I spent my life flying about and I tasted all the joys of being a butterfly. I had no consciousness of being a man. Suddenly I awoke and there I was — I seemed to be again the veritable Chuang-Chou. How do I know whether I was then a man dreaming I was a butterfly, or now a butterfly dreaming myself a man? Surely there must be some distinction between a man and a butterfly? . . .

In a great many of his passages about *Tao* and the doctrine of action without striving, Chuang-Tse paraphrases sections of Lao-Tse's *Canon;* and a great deal of the rest is illuminated with one or another of the Master's sayings. It is this that removes the follower from a position near the top of the list of the world's greatest mystic philosophers. His writings form one of the most revealing (and readable) treasuries of spiritual wisdom known to East or West, but the originality belongs substantially to Lao-Tse. It is possible to note at once the likeness to Lao-Tse's terse, aphoristic style and a certain brilliance and wit that are Chuang-Tse's own. Of aphorisms:

No use to praise the ocean to a frog who lives in a well. No use to speak of the grandeur of winter to a fly that lives and dies in a summer day. Is it worth while then to speak of *Tao* to a pedant who has shut himself in a prison of intellectual knowledge?

The nostalgic longing for the perfections of ancient times is implicit in this bit:

From the beginning, men had certain natural endowments. They wove and clothed themselves. They cultivated the ground and fed themselves. All acted alike, in ways learned from Heaven. In the Golden Age when they thus acted from instinct and there were no class distinctions, they moved serenely; and they looked out at the world with heads held high. . . . How could there be any distinctions of good and bad? Unspoiled by knowledge, what need to invent virtue? Without evil desires, men were naturally, simply honest. It was an existence near the perfection of Heaven.

Then appeared the people of too much learning, exercising what they called charity and showing righteousness — and doubt was born among men. There was also all that fuss and gush about elaborate music and intricate ceremonies: thenceforward the empire was divided.

When it seemed that Chuang-Tse was not far from death his disciples gathered about him and broached the matter of a worthy funeral.

"Well," said Chuang-Tse, "for my coffin and tomb I shall have Earth and Heaven. For my funeral regalia there are the sun and the moon, and the countless constellations of stars. And will not all creation escort me on my way? Do we need invent something else?"

Chuang-Tse pictures more fully than does Lao-Tse the Taoist pilgrim's way that ends in the mystic experience — almost in Nirvana:

The follower of the Way is profited when benefits are spread among all men. He finds repose when his gifts are shared with all men. When travellers have lost their way, he is their comfort, like a mother to grieving children. He has abundance and knows not whence it comes. He has food and drink, but no care for its source. . . . When such a one attains highest spirituality he rides up into the glory of heaven. His body is no more. This is called mergence into the Light. It is the realization of all one's powers, divine as well as earthly. From the corporeal world of man he has risen joyously to God. Mortal things have melted away. All is as It is, infinite, in the primal estate. This is called losing oneself in the Immortal.

Of the influences serving to shape Chinese art, religion has been paramount. Among the influencing religions, Taoism has been pre-eminent. Painting especially has taken on a spiritual inwardness, a pregnant repose, and an evanescent radiance from the mystic attitude toward nature discovered in Lao-Tse's philosophy. The picture is a distillation of the artist's feeling toward the universe. It is a crystallization of his vision, formed after months or years of contemplation, of absorption in the atmosphere surrounding his subject, of harmonious living with it.

In China, where reportorial activities are not considered creative, it is pretty well understood that the work of art will be as the artist's character is, pure or corrupt, spiritually deep or superficial, inspired or empty. The artist is a medium, a bridge between the soul of the world and the consciousness of other men. He deals with essences, with emanations, with the Spirit. His mystic understanding of the universe, as a revelation of *Tao*, is a source of his powers of expression. He paints out of intuition and vision — and his own crystalline clarity. It is, indeed, himself that the artist paints, far more than in the West: his art is a revelation of his way of living, his dreaming, his honest habits of thought or his scepticism and dishonesty. He is a vessel filled according to his capacity, out of Heaven's inexhaustible stuff. Ideally he is a mirror reflecting the harmonies and rhythms of the *Tao*. He must, therefore, be pure, clairvoyant, spiritual-minded.

The aim of the Chinese painter is to express the intangible. His business, in Lao-Tse's phrase, is to image the imageless, to communicate the incommunicable. To accomplish this he must go farther back and know the unknowable: that is, pierce to the mystery in which all things have their beginning. He must surrender his self-will, lose himself in *Tao*, become one with all that exists, understand the essence, the Spirit, animating existence.

The artist therefore is a mystic. He practises the discipline of

SAGE IN CONTEMPLATION UNDER A PINE TREE.
PAINTING BY MA YUAN. CHINESE, SUNG DYNASTY.
METROPOLITAN MUSEUM OF ART.

a mystic. He prizes stillness, is reserved in speech, is without desire for personal success. By contemplation, by surrendering himself to the rhythmic flow, the inner nature, of his subject, he is enabled to vision its inward essence. He discards as a husk the outward look of it. He arrives at understanding rather than knowledge of it. This all may be accomplished when one has gained the Way of *Tao*, when one has fallen in with the ordered flow of Spirit, with nature's rhythmic movement. There will be no artifice, no straining, no clever adorning or gesturing; only expression as effortless, as profound, as still, as the movement of the sea, as the growing of a tree.

Operating in the light of that "æsthetic," the Chinese painters have created a body of art surpassing that to be found in any other land in those qualities that most delight the spirit. The typical Chinese picture is simple, reposeful, harmonious, powerful, radiant. Its power is coiled, restrained, its strength expressed but held in check. The artists are masters of movement; but the movement is resolved rhythmically, ends in repose.

These pictures touch upon, share, and hold immanent something of the Eternal, the Absolute, the Holy. How else explain them except by realizing that the artists have — in Lao-Tse's way — entered into *Tao*, understood Heaven's design, and made themselves the transmitters of spiritual rather than material truth? Indeed, no artists elsewhere have so generally discarded the earthy materials of art.

The Chinese painters are supreme draughtsmen, conveying marvels in the subtle turning of a line. No one else has made space so living, so pregnant with suggestion. They are past masters of the form-organization or plastic orchestration which is the invisible element, the animating power, of the picture, sought by the leading schools of Western modernism.

Fourteen centuries ago the Chinese æstheticians were concerned with the nature, and even the labelling, of the mysterious thing that to-day is called the "form element" in the painting. They spoke of it as the "rhythmic vitality" of the picture, or the "spiritual rhythm of life" animating it, or the "life movement of the spirit." The words (from a treatise by Hsieh Ho of the sixth century) say nothing unless one sees behind them the Taoist philosophy of the fathomless, all-pervading, vital force that pulses in every created thing.

Our Western artists would seem to need beyond all else, for the enrichment of their comparatively factual and materialistic art, this insight and awareness and illumination. They are not likely to attain to so much without cultivating those other gifts of the individual mystic, humility, non-assertive living, tranquillity of mind, and a sense of absolute rest in the soul.

The manipulative arts are only extensions of the supreme art, the art of living. The Taoist faith provides a blueprint for "the art of being in the world." In it, as in the Chinese painting, "the life movement of the Spirit" is everything. The necessity to take a stand upon "the beautiful orderliness" of the universe is stressed. It is one of the most beautiful faiths devised by the seers among men.

Lao-Tse, in the one poem that is marked by the commentators as autobiographical, spoke of the contrast between the rewards offered by the worldly life and those of the mystic who has put the world in its place and found God. Early translators, knowing nothing of the bliss of divine illumination, missing the significance of the contrast suggested in the final lines, have spoken of the poem as one in which the seer voiced his bitterness and his hurt from the world's neglect. Instead — assuredly — the mystic will understand it as a hymn of thanks in the spirit of one who says in gratitude: "They have everything. I have nothing — but I have the Spirit."

> *The men of the world are merry-making,*
> *As if life were an endless feast,*
> *The world a terrace in springtime.*
> *I alone am still. I wait.*
> *Like a new-born babe, unsmiling,*
> *I appear homeless, forlorn.*
>
> *The men of the world have riches;*
> *I alone go empty-handed.*
> *I seem to others witless,*
> *Unheeding, vague — a fool.*
>
> *The men of the world are knowing;*
> *I seem unenlightened.*
> *They are clever, sharp, alert;*
> *I am reserved and silent,*
> *Motionless as the sea.*

> *The men of the world are useful;*
> *I am a tool outworn.*
> *But — alone and different —*
> *I am nourished at the Holy Breast*
> *By the divine one, the Mother-Spirit.*

Lao-Tse leaves in the mind no doubt of his faith that the best in life is in that spiritual sustenance. Because that is so, the most fitting conclusion of an essay about him is to be found in a fragment of one of his poems, which might well be entitled "The Mystic Way":

> *Void the mind,*
> *Open the being to God,*
> *Abide in stillness.*
> *Life arises, and passes,*
> *Birth, growth, and return,*
> *A rhythmic arc from Source to Source.*
> *In the life rhythm is quietude,*
> *A tranquil submission;*
> *In the soul's submission is peace,*
> *Absorption in Eternity.*
> *And so, the Great Light!*

II. The Buddha, the Great Light, and the Bliss of Nirvana

In one of the later Buddhist tales there is the story of a disciple who comes before the Master, confessing his doubts. Is it necessary for salvation, he asks, to give up not only the sense-pleasures of this life but the promise of a sensuously beautiful Heaven? He is uneasy, as a mortal clinging to worldly ideas is bound to be in the presence of one who sees life singly, who is clairvoyant and holy and purified.

"Master, must we relinquish the promise of a Paradise? Is there no Heaven?"

The Tathagata — for that is the name by which the Buddha is known between his enlightenment and his passing into final Nirvana — the Tathagata in turn asks a question: "What is this promise of a Heaven?"

"It is said," answers the disciple, "that there is a Western Paradise, which is called also the Land of Purity. It abounds in all that is precious, silver and gold and flashing jewels. There are lakes and streams, decked with lotus flowers, and bordered with golden sands and promenades. There is sweet music, and thrice daily there are showers of petals. The birds sing a haunting song, which evokes a spiritual yearning. There one becomes aware of the Buddha and the truth.

"It is said that the Wanderer who devoutly and faithfully repeats the praises of the Immortal Buddha will be transported to the Pure Land. At the change called death he will come into the presence of the Blessed One and his sainted followers. There he will know perfect peace."

The Buddha-to-be said: "There is indeed a Paradise such as you describe; but the place is a spiritual one, and it is open only to those who have given ascendency to the Spirit. You have said that it is in the West. The meaning is that Paradise should be sought where he has passed who has enlightened the world. When the sun goes down, one seems to be left in darkness. The night of death descends and the body is claimed by Mara, the Earthly One. But the sunset need not mean extinction. What may seem extinction is, indeed, entry into infinite light and everlasting life.

"If in your devotion to the Immortal One you have cleansed your heart and have desired only to serve the Truth, then you have in yourself the lamp that will guide you to the Western Paradise."

Then, seeing that the disciple was still troubled — for dreams of jewels and gardens and heavenly music are not easily given up — the Tathagata continued: "The description you have given of Paradise is, as men say, beautiful. But there are no terms to describe the glory of the Pure Land. The worldly think and speak of it in worldly images. But to the enlightened, the spiritual Paradise is beyond the beauty possible for the mortal mind to imagine. Even while he is in the body, the Tathagata lives in the Pure Land, and knows its bliss. The Tathagata preaches the doctrine of enlightenment, to you and to the world, in order that you and your brother-men may present yourselves undefiled, and attain that Pure Land, which is, in truth, the bliss of supreme wisdom, utter peace, and infinite light."

The story is a late one — and indeed no saying or report of the Buddha Gautama was committed to writing until several centuries after his lifetime on earth.* It indicates, nevertheless, the two ways of his service to mankind: his teaching of a spiritual philosophy which is as high and pure and holy as any revealed by the prophets among men; and his legacy of a doctrine destined slowly to be transformed into a faith not quite so high and austere as the original "way," a little more worldly, and describable in terms of the sense-understanding, yet sufficiently spiritual and mystic to lead millions of followers into paths of regeneration and sanctity.

The Nirvana which is the Buddha Gautama's Paradise is at once extinction and blissful absorption into the light of Infinity. The "region" of it is wholly spiritual, as he insisted in answering the disciple. To-day, twenty-five centuries after he formulated the doctrine, there are millions in the Orient who follow his ideal of

* The story of the Pure Land is from the Chinese treasury of Buddhist tales. It was incorporated by Paul Carus into his useful and readable compendium of Buddhist stories, entitled *The Gospel of Buddha, Compiled from Ancient Records*. I am deeply indebted to this, the best of all brief accounts of the life and preaching of the Buddha Gautama. I have drawn also on many of the sources to which Carus went, on the books of Samuel Beal and Rhys Davids and Henry Clarke Warren; and on other books written or compiled since Carus wrote, especially those of Dwight Goddard (notably *A Buddhist Bible*) and Ananda Coomaraswamy. My acknowledgments and thanks to these authors, and to their publishers, are recorded in the appendix entitled "A Descriptive Reading List, with Acknowledgments."

renunciation of the world and his regimen of saintly living and spiritual search, in anticipation of entry into Nirvana. These are the truest, the primitive, the most selfless followers of the seer.

But the greater number of those who bear the name "Buddhist" are of the persuasion represented by the disciple. They belong to sects less austere than the primitive brotherhood. It is they who have, often enough, accepted the picture of Paradise as painted in terms of the sense-pleasures. Absorption into Nirvana is imaged less as extinction and entry into light than as eternal living in idyllic gardens, among heavenly sights and sounds, in an unceasing bounty of birds and flowers, of perfumed breezes and delectable foods. There are other compromises, too, that have made it possible for masses of men, without giving up their accustomed places in society, to follow the Buddhist path of enlightenment, controlling rather than extinguishing mortal desires, ever mindful of the law of Karma and of the eightfold rules of noble conduct, finding signs of the oneness and infinity of life in natural objects, rather than relegating attainment to a time after death.

If these millions do not know quite the pure bliss foretasted by the Tathagata, before his passing into final Nirvana, they nevertheless, each in accordance with the stage of purification and spirituality reached, attain some measure of mystic penetration and spiritual joy. As Buddhism of all the major religions puts the fullest stress upon emancipation from worldliness and upon absorption in the ultimate light or wisdom, its adherents form the largest brotherhood of mystic seekers in the world. Numbers hardly matter except as testimony to the effectiveness of a founder's appeal. But the Buddha Gautama issued a call which, either in its original purity or as adapted and compromised by Indian, Chinese, and other interpreters, has, through the ages, been heeded by more religious seekers than any other.*

"I reveal," Gautama said, "suffering and the extinction of suffering." In words as simple he added: "Suffering exists, there is a

* There are possibly four hundred to five hundred millions of Buddhists in the Orient today, compared with half as many Hindus. The Hindus, incidentally, profess beliefs profoundly influenced by the Buddha. There are perhaps as many Mohammedans as Hindus. The great religion of the Occident, Christianity, ranks next to Buddhism in numbers. Attempts have been made to place Christianity first; but candid examination of the figures would seem to indicate that estimates above three or four hundred millions include a vast reservoir of sceptics and atheistic intellectuals because they live in predominantly Christian communities.

cause of suffering, the cause of suffering can be removed." Gautama thus began by speaking a language understood by all men. From the generalized promise that "the cause of suffering can be removed" he went on to the more specific promise that a religion, realization of a truth, would bring cessation of suffering. By following the "path" the pilgrim would reach extinction of sorrow with extinction of desire, lust, and egoism.

The doctrine (thus far) was not greatly different from that of the Vedantism professed by the Brahman caste of the Hindus, and concurred in, presumably, by the fighter and the lower castes of Indian society in the Buddha's time. The new religion was, indeed, so similar that, so far as India proper was concerned, it was destined to be absorbed back into Hinduism, the Buddha finding place in the pantheon of the Hindu gods.

The Buddhist philosophy, nevertheless, was more elementary. It discouraged both the mortifications of the body and the abstruse exercises of the mind that made Vedantism (in its purer form) so "special" a religion. The Buddhist doctrine was simple, appealing, uninvolved. Yet it promised in the end mergence in the divine, or in the Light, or whatever one prefers to call the ocean of bliss beyond the created universe.

The mysticism of Gautama is of a special sort. He dreams and speaks of the bliss of a life eternal, of mergence in the uncreate, of the inexpressibly blissful illumination of Nirvana. Oftenest his word for mystic realization is "enlightenment" (though again "enlightenment" is preparation, on the way to supreme attainment). It would be incorrect, in strictest interpretation, to speak of Gautama as one of the men who have walked with God. His mind rejected the idea of personified deity, and he discouraged his disciples from speculating upon the nature of that which is above all, which is the cause of all — upon the nature of Oneness.

No other man among men, it has been said, was so godless while so godlike. Nevertheless his glorification of the Law (standing above man-made authority and laws), his conception of the Boundless Light of immortality and of a Supreme Wisdom, and his teaching of an inevitable movement or process beginning in a Cause: all these ideas tremble upon the verge of a conception of deity or God. In the spiritual region to which the mystic rises, it would seem to matter little whether the yearning has been toward a somewhat visualized or personalized God, or toward an Absolute or a Light or Liberation. In the sublimest spiritual consciousness the imaging and reasoning powers have long since been swallowed up in the surge of purified feeling. One initiate may speak of the consummation as the going into a Presence, another as absorption in the Absolute; the two experiences are hardly to be differentiated.

The specialness of Gautama's mysticism is rather that of the preliminary stages, the ways of conduct and of meditation along the preparatory path. No other major prophet has so singly urged the extinction of sense-desire and of egoism; no other has so insistently counselled a fixing of the consciousness upon the final blissful mergence into the ocean of the uncreate; no other has been so certain that speculation is unnecessary, even harmful, outside the chain of one cause, one effect, one cure — sense-craving, suffering, extinction of suffering, spiritual enlightenment.

Gautama was a man of infinite compassion, and he laid before the world a design of self-conduct that forms one of the most admirable of humanitarian programs, as animated with love as the systems set forth by Lao-Tse and by Jesus. But as the path is straighter, simpler, with him, there is an austerity about his teaching, and an effect of other-worldly disregard of mortal interests. In short, no other seer ever put so bluntly the thought that common life in the mortal world is not worth living unless one sees and accepts the way of liberation from suffering, sickness, and illusion; unless one puts first the following of the path into eternal illumination.

For the peoples of the West, committed to the ideals of materialistic competition, conquest, and self-expression, peoples educated pragmatically, peoples almost perpetually in the fever of war, no better tonic could be prescribed than study of the mystic doctrines of Gautama Buddha and of Lao-Tse. The peace that lies at the heart of these two religions; the stressing of self-conquest before conquest of others; the truth that moral conduct grows naturally out of personal holiness; and the natural welling-up of respect, compassion, and nobility among men who have known mergence in the divine — call it God, or Enlightenment, or the *Tao:* all this is profoundly and tragically needed in the crisis of the spiritual paralysis of the West. We should find, incidentally, a startling correspondence with the basic teachings of Jesus.

India at the time of the coming of the Buddha, the India of the sixth century before Christ, was a land advanced both culturally and spiritually. Europe was then a continent of which only isolated fringes — especially that fringe toward Asia — had received the elementary light of civilization.

India, or at least the northern territories lying along the foothills and the plains at the foot of the Himalayas, harboured a mixed or divided people. The majority were descendants of the dark-skinned "original" races of the South. The outnumbered ruling castes were of the Aryan-speaking tribes that had migrated down into the Indus valleys through the Khyber and other passes, from some Iranian or "steppe country" reservoir of blue-eyed northern people: contingents of those adventurous Aryans who spread so far East and West that they are oftenest known by the blanket name "Indo-Europeans." They were the forefathers of the Brahman and warrior castes of the Hindus, of the Persians and the Greeks, and of confusing Northern European language-groupings that to-day are the most easily identified in the Teutonic and Anglo-Saxon countries. The Buddha spoke a language akin to the English of these lines.

The classics of Hinduism and of the tangent Buddhism may, indeed, be accounted the first great spiritual expression of a mother culture from which we, as Anglo-Americans, derive. The truest evidence is in the language we speak. (It is for this reason that some scientists have insisted that the word "Aryan" should be used as a label for the language-groupings alone; though its usefulness as tracing migrations, racial strains, and rudimentary physical characteristics is hardly to be denied.) *

Not only is the language-structure substantially that of Sanskrit, itself a later crystallization of the *Pali* which Gautama spoke, but many of our everyday words are but variations of common ancestral words. *Is* was once *est* in Latin, *esti* in Greek, and *asti* in Sanskrit. *Mother*, the German *Mutter*, is the Greek *meter* and the Sanskrit *matar*; and so through *father, brother, sister*, and *son*. So too the Sanskrit *manas*, which gives us *mind* or *mentality*; the Hindu fire-god Agni, from which our *ignite*; and even our words *deity* and *divine*, as compared with Sanskrit *deva*, meaning god, or the shining one, giver of light. These are among the many Aryan words entering into our common speech.

---

* Recent rank misuse of the word by the German Nazis has weakened its effectiveness. By a curious ironic twist the German word for honour, *Ehre*, is derived from "Aryan." Originally "Aryans" meant "the noble people," or "the honourable people."

So close then is the language used by the Buddha Gautama when he spoke to his disciples and to crowds of pilgrims in upper India twenty-five centuries ago. The heritage of thought and word, and of many other elements of civilization — benevolent government, agriculture, industrial arts, science, music — was then old. It is likely that the mother Aryan tongue had been in use several thousands of years.

Northern India was then divided into small kingdoms or principalities, each ruled by a family of the noble or Aryan caste. Though caste lines were not so rigid as they were to become in later times, the immigrant race held to the privileges and position of an aristocracy. They considered themselves the guardians of thought, and they put up social barriers against contamination from what they considered lower sources.

The dominant class constituted, roughly, two groups in society: the soldier-rulers, and the Brahmins or philosopher-teachers. As in China, so in India it was the custom for kings or princes to seek advice of sages in matters bearing upon the welfare of the country. Within the Aryan caste, women enjoyed an equality hardly known elsewhere in the Eastern world.

The civilization of India in the sixth century B.C. was pastoral and pleasant. There were dangers, of course: from wild beasts and occasionally from envious rival communities. But in general the people's existence was peaceful. It was a land of comparative plenty, hardly less than idyllic in parts. Above it towered the Himalayan Mountains, which have immemorially held a fascination for the spiritually-minded.

Perhaps the natural features of valley and mountain, of running water and receiving ocean, had some subtle effect upon the human mind and hopes. Already the cultivated man turned especially to philosophy and spiritual aspiration. Whereas the Aryan-speaking peoples who turned westward were to develop over the centuries a genius for political conquest and worldly adventure, for commerce and invention, and were to fail to develop a lasting religious faith (for Christianity was not originally Western), their brothers of the East considered philosophy or religion the one subject most worth pondering.

Their wise men had by the sixth century established speculation upon the unseen, upon the nature of creation, existence, and immortality, and study of the ways of putting oneself into communion with the Absolute, as the first aim of learning, if not of life. Yet in India there was no priestly dominance over men's minds. The soul was known to be the most important thing in the world, but the way of salvation was not prescribed.

Vedantism was already a fully constituted religion. If its priests were philosophers and teachers, without desire to police men's lives, they yet occupied an honoured place in the community. And the thousands of ascetic "wanderers" who gave up all else to go out in search of God were supported as a matter of course by the tradesmen and the workers.

Vedantism had its gods, Indra and Agni and ultimately many more; but somehow they all merged in a monotheistic conception of a One, an Absolute, above division or limitation. Those humans who could not conceive of a god fully depersonalized or abstract doubtless worshipped and propitiated "Him," and thought of "Him" as in a substantial heaven. But seldom in history has a popular faith risen so spontaneously into the realm of the absolute, conceiving an infinitude of spirit to which each individual soul is joined: a web of immortality from which a thread of consciousness reaches out into the life of each man. The Brahmins and the Wanderers knew that it was possible, by holiness in living and by a spiritual discipline, to project the consciousness along the thread, even before death, and to enjoy, as it were, periodic reunion with the infinite, the divine.

Indeed, India before Buddha owned a religion overwhelmingly mystic. If one begins a study of Indian seers with Gautama, it is because the names and the teachings of a hundred earlier prophets are lost to us — as must be the case where the saintlier the man, the deeper went his desire to remain inconspicuous and anonymous. The Hindu mystic philosophers before 500 B.C. must have been legion. The earliest Vedas, the holy texts or books of divine knowledge, are usually given a date at least as early as 1400 B.C. But no towering name emerges from that period's history. The Buddha Gautama is, indeed, the first world-renowned figure in the records of India.

It is fitting that the nation should be known first through the fame of a holy man. Spiritual activity was the most characteristic trait of the Hindus, then as so often in history. The outstanding fact about the Emperor Asoka, the first celebrated political figure, is that he was converted to Buddhism and tried to remake his forcibly won empire into a Buddhist paradise. In later Indian history there are many world-famous seers, from Sankara to Ramakrishna and the saintly leader Gandhi.

The Brahmins who were (indirectly if not directly) the teachers of Gautama would regard education as a fitting of the individual, not in relation to a community or a work to be done, but in relation to the universe, especially the spiritual universe. They would stress a way of conduct which the West would consider ethical and benevolent, but not for the West's reasons; they would see the utility of it in the soul's better preparedness for re-entry into the divine. They would teach the sanctity of the common custom (sometimes called anti-social) of abandoning ordinary living in order to follow the spiritual path toward the Absolute, whether as Wanderers or as forest hermits.

They would preach the superior reality of the inner life and the illusiveness of worldly things. They would teach that spiritual perceptions and the seeming miracle of rising above mortal limitations are possible to all men, and that the Absolute, or Brahma, has its part, or *Atman*, in every individual. The doctrine is that the *Atman* or soul is the eternal portion of each self; it is the *Atman* that is to be freed to rise back to God in the mystic experience. The progress of the soul toward the day of final release is dependent upon a man's balance of good and bad works; that is, of his Karma. So long as the final swinging of the balance to the side of good is not accomplished, the soul is subject to transmigration, or rebirth in further individual bodies.

Such roughly is the teaching the youthful Gautama would have received — until his father became alarmed lest the youth be unfitted for ruling, and so surrounded him with the means to experience worldly rather than spiritual joys. Certainly the young noble could not have escaped, in the last quarter of the sixth century, the consciousness of multitudes of men about him aspiring to union with the divine, whether as souls craving return to their true home, the Brahman Absolute, the ocean of Spirit, or as sages grown so wise and pure that they were enabled to lift themselves periodically into realization of the Absolute.

A youth inclined to gentleness and speculation could hardly escape the wisdom of these teacher-mystics. It was only natural that, in becoming the greatest seer and prophet among them, he should have adopted and adapted much of their Vedic doctrine.

THE BUDDHA

The child destined to become the Buddha was born about the year 560 B.C. His father was the ruler — King or Prince — of the little state of the Sakya clan and had his capital at a city named Kapilavastu, so-called in honour of a Rishi or spiritual teacher, Kapila, of a century earlier. Kapilavastu was near the western border of what is now upper Bihar, in north-eastern India.

The King — he is called "King" in the Buddhist books, though his state was probably only semi-independent, in suzerainty to the ruler of Kosala, whose larger state lay to the south or west — the King was known as Suddhodana. He had married two sisters, princesses, by name Maha Maya, or Lady Maya, and Maha Japiti, daughters of a neighbouring king. Thus the child came into the world a member of the warrior caste and a royal prince. His mother was the Queen Maya, but she died seven days after his birth, and her sister Maha Japiti became his foster-mother.

About the child's birth there grew up innumerable legends, mostly of a miraculous nature. The Buddhist accounts begin at a point many generations before the birth, detailing adventures of Gautama's soul in earlier incarnations; and the Blessed One incorporated into his parables recollections of experiences from his other lives. The stories of prophetic signs and miracles accompanying his birth are of the sort usually told of a spiritual leader who attains deification. Nor is it possible wholly to disentangle what the Western historian somewhat arrogantly terms actual fact from the surrounding web of legend, unverified surmise, and fact acceptable to the miracle-admitting Oriental mind.

Though Suddhodana had been married to the sister queens for many years, no child had been born, a matter of deepest sorrow to all three. But the Buddha-to-be was ready to enter upon his last incarnation, and it was divinely decreed that Maya should be the mother. She dreamed one night that she was transported by the Four Guardians of the World to a lake in the Himalayas. There a white elephant came to her and touched her right side, and from that moment the child was in the womb. When she told the dream to King Suddhodana upon waking, he called in the Brahman sages. They prophesied the birth of a remarkable child who would become either an incomparable world ruler or, if he should choose the path of religion, a universal saviour.

When the date was nearing for the delivery of the child, the Queen Maya set out with her retinue to visit her parents. Her time came upon her when she was half-way from Kapilavastu to the capital of her father's kingdom. In a park, among gardens and orchards, under a sandalwood tree, the babe was born. At the moment of birth a sage named Asita, a hermit of the Himalayas, divined the cause of the pleasure of the gods and transported himself through the air to Kapilavastu. Resuming the ways of a mortal sage, he gained entry to the palace. When he had seen the child and had prostrated himself at the Blessed One's feet, he repeated to King Suddhodana the prophecy of the court Brahmins.

When a third time the prophecy was repeated that the child, named Siddhartha,* would have the choice of becoming the mightiest of world rulers or the supreme Buddha, King Suddhodana inquired what measures might be taken to link the baby prince's destiny to the kingship that would be his by right of succession. If, the wise men said, it should be possible to keep Siddhartha ignorant of the existence in the world of sickness, the decay of old age, and death, he might then avoid a life of religion. But almost immediately occurred the miracle of the babe's holding motionless the shadow of a tree under which he sat. The King was all but convinced that this was the Buddha-to-be.

He contrived, nevertheless, that Siddhartha's youth should be spent where no signs of the world's evil would come before his eyes. In those days, the Master told his disciples many years later, he wore silks and went into the streets only with servants who bore a white parasol to shield him from the sun. He was, however, an accomplished athlete and hunter; and possibly it was the fate of hunted animals that first uncovered the spring of compassion within him.

As he neared manhood he was given, as was customary with princes, three houses or palaces, one for each season, and palatial gardens. He was surrounded by dancing-girls and story-tellers

---

* Siddhartha was the given name of the Prince, Gautama the family name. After his enlightenment he was to be known sometimes as Sakyamuni; that is, the Sage of the Sakya people. "The Buddha" is a bestowed title, meaning the Enlightened One, or the one who has attained Supreme Wisdom. Since complete detachment from the world is implied, the title is seldom used in telling the story up to the time of his passing into Final Nirvana. Between the day of the Enlightenment and the day of his final passing the title "the Tathagata" is used, meaning "the one who has come," or "the one who has attained." Other titles commonly used are "the Blessed One," "the Master," and "the Lord Buddha." Since other men may attain Supreme Wisdom — that is, the state of Buddhahood — it is customary to qualify the name where confusion might arise; whence the common form, "the Buddha Gautama."

and gaming companions, and tempted with all the allurements of worldly pleasure. For his father dreaded the appearance of any signs of ascetic preference or religious interest.

When the time came for the Prince to be married, certain neighbouring rulers whose daughters were eligible demurred, saying that Siddhartha, apparently pampered and meditative, lacked the character and strength to be expected in one of the warrior caste. A tournament was arranged, and Siddhartha met rival nobles in tests of mind and body. He confounded with his brilliance even the sages who conducted the mental examinations; and he surpassed every rival in wrestling, bowmanship, and other physical accomplishments. Then he chose his own wife, the gentle and beautiful Yasodhara, a princess and his cousin.

King Suddhodana was delighted, because he felt that this tie would hold Siddhartha to the court life and the world. When Yasodhara gave birth to a son, Siddhartha bestowed on the child the name Rahula, which means "tie" or "fetter," for he too felt that he was being fettered to earthly things. Already he had sickened of the worldly pleasures set before him by the King's aides, and his tendency to meditation and philosophical speculation increased.

When the Prince Siddhartha had desired to go into the city, or to ride out to the neighbouring hamlets among the rice fields, the route had always been predetermined and the way cleared of every person or thing that might suggest the existence of sickness or old age or death. Now the Prince said that he would again ride forth, and the King's agents had the streets gayly adorned and made sure that all diseased and decrepit ones were kept indoors.

But the time for completion of Siddhartha's education had come. The gods, the books say, sent their own emissaries to open the Prince's eyes to the truth about suffering. He and his charioteer Channa drove through the city streets in a gilded chariot drawn by four white horses amid admiring crowds. When they reached the country roads, Siddhartha bade Channa draw up, for he had seen what had never met his eyes before: a bent old man with wizened face, hardly able to walk.

"What sort of man is this?" he asked. And the terrified Channa replied, not knowing how to evade the truth: "This is a man in old age. Once he was a babe, then a youth, and a man in full strength and beauty. But now his strength and beauty are gone. He is withered and wasted. It is the way of life."

"How is it possible," Siddhartha asked, "to take pleasure in life that inevitably ends thus in decay?"

The pensiveness and moodiness of the Prince increased, but King Suddhodana tried harder than ever to beguile his interest with pleasures and diversions. When Siddhartha and Channa drove again to the country, however, there appeared on the roadside a sick man, prostrate and groaning and horribly emaciated. When Siddhartha asked: "What sort of man is this?" Channa could only explain that every man is subject to sickness. Upon a third excursion, they came on a funeral procession, following a corpse on a bier. The attendants were crying and beating their breasts. Again Channa explained: "It is death. He has been taken from those he loved, and from his home. His life is ended."

The Prince asked: "Are there other dead men?"

"All men must die. There is no way of escape."

Siddhartha returned to the palace. Thenceforth he could only ponder the riddle of men living sensually, carelessly, heedlessly, in a world teeming with sickness, decay, and the evidences of death. When Yasodhara tried to comfort him he answered: "I am downcast and miserable because everywhere I see signs of change and decay. Men grow old, sicken, and die. I can only seek to free mankind from this cycle of suffering."

At the time of ploughing he once more rode forth. He bade Channa stop the chariot where he could see the serfs toiling, and he was distressed in mind because they laboured pitifully, and again because the oxen strained and struggled under the lash and the goad. Thus his education of misery was complete.

As he and Channa moved away he encountered another sort of man, a mendicant, a hermit monk. He wore the simple robe of a religious order and carried a begging-bowl. His eyes were clear and untroubled, his face serene and restful. "Who, then," the Prince asked Channa, "is this man of so great dignity, who is at peace?" And Channa answered: "This is a religious brother, an ascetic, who has renounced the world. He has no desires, for he gains his food by begging. He knows nothing of wealth or ambition or fetters. He gives his life to solitude and to seeking enlightenment."

It is said in some of the books that this Wanderer had been sent invisibly by the gods to intercept Siddhartha (for the King was still having the roads guarded), and that the monk entered into converse with the young man, telling him that there is a way out of the evils of the world, a way of peace, a path to Nirvana.

When the Prince spoke of the grief his father and his wife would feel if he renounced worldly life, urging that the time might be inopportune for such a drastic step, the venerable man answered: "No time can be inopportune for cleansing life and turning to the joy of the spirit." When Siddhartha returned to the palace he knew that he too must become one of the homeless seekers for enlightenment.

That night Yasodhara dreamed that great storms arose and desolated the land and tore from her the jewels she loved and her very clothing. Next day Siddhartha perceived in the dream confirmation of his beliefs, a further sign that ignorance and desire and all they represent can be stripped away, even that mortality can be overcome. He told Yasodhara that all would be well if she kept faith in him — for he perceived in her both honesty and devotion — and that he now saw the way of wisdom.

He explained to the King his wish to go forth, free of all fetters, to seek enlightenment upon man's imprisonment to sense. The King could not restrain his tears. "What is it," he asked, "that you desire? I would willingly retire and give you my kingdom — all." The Prince answered: "I desire but four boons: to hold my youthfulness, to be free of sickness, to escape death, never to know decay. There is a way out of these limitations, these sufferings. I ask your permission to go forth seeking that way." The King granted permission. But secretly he doubled the guard about the palace and on the roads, hoping thus to delay his son's going.

Siddhartha was a man of great beauty, princely in bearing, graceful and majestic. On the day before his departure he went out into the city streets. As he passed the palace of a warrior family, a beautiful girl came out upon the roof. Seeing the Prince, she made up a song: "Blessed is the mother of a being so glorious; blessed is the father of a being so glorious; blessed is the bride of a being so glorious."

When he had heard this song the Prince passed on. But he meditated upon the girl's pleasure, and he thought: "She has said simply that a father or a mother or a bride may be gladdened by looking upon another who is manly and noble. She has found blessedness in this. She felt nothing of desire, or envy, or infatuation." And in her pure delight he found a clue. He who had known that he must go forth homeless to seek enlightenment perceived suddenly what it was that lay at the end of seeking — Nirvana, extinction of craving. Saying that the virgin had carried him a step further in wisdom, he unloosed a necklace of pearls from his throat and sent it as a fee to the girl. Then he returned to his own palace for the last time.

Not many days later there came the call he had awaited, voices that said: "Rise and go. Seek the Light. Finding it, share it with all men."

Though he knew that the palace gates were bolted and the roads guarded, he felt no fear that his escape would be prevented. The King made a last attempt to divert his mind; he had the palace filled with the most beautiful girls of the kingdom and bade them beguile the Prince's affections. By every loveliness and every wile known to the temptress they tried to attract his interest. Never before had so lavish a show of the charms, tendernesses, and allurements of woman been spread before an inattentive man. But Siddhartha's mind was the more firmly fixed on his coming pilgrimage and search. After a while, the books explain prosaically, the temptresses, tired out by their fruitless revelry, went to sleep; and the Prince was reminded of their mortality and of the transience of sensuous and sensual allurements.

In the darkness before the dawn he rose and called his charioteer Channa. While Channa was busy with the horses Siddhartha went to the room where his wife Yasodhara and his son Rahula were asleep. His love for them was great and he longed at least to clasp them to him and say farewell. But he recollected his determination to renounce all that stood in the way of enlightenment. "If she awakens," he said, "I must delay going. Some day, when I have found the Light, I shall return, and she and my son will be here."

He stooped and pressed his lips lightly to Yasodhara's foot. Then he left the room, and it is said that his sorrow was more for the suffering she would feel from the parting than for his own anguish at breaking the tie.

He went away on his horse Kanthaka, with Channa following behind. Miraculously the gates all were opened silently, while the guards of both the palace and the roads slept as if they had been drugged. Mara, the Evil One, alone endeavoured to stay Siddhartha. He offered him dominion over all the earth, if he would but postpone his going seven days. But the Prince Siddhartha had chosen. He and Channa rode on. He turned once to look back at the city, saying: "I will not look upon Kapilavastu again until I have found a way of dominion over suffering, old age, and death."

They rode until they came to the edge of a forest. There Siddhartha dismounted. "Channa," he said, "I am going now to become a wanderer. Do you take these jewels and return to Kapilavastu. Tell my father the King that I have gone on my pilgrimage, homeless and comfortless, but uplifted in spirit." Because he had an affectionate understanding of animals, he thanked Kanthaka for his faithful service and for his part in the flight, and bade the horse farewell. As a last act in renunciation he took Channa's sword and cut off the long locks of his hair and with them the symbol of his royal rank.

Channa's love for his master prompted one more appeal to spare the royal family and the Sakya people the sorrow of this parting. When he saw that he was again refused, Channa asked that he too might lose himself in the life of a wanderer. Siddhartha said: "If you love me so much, go first without grieving, and bear my message to the palace." Before the faithful charioteer turned back, a hermit appeared, clothed in the coarse robe of a religious seeker. The Prince took off his rich garments and gave them to the hermit, and put on the simple russet robe. He disappeared into the forest. Siddhartha at the time was twenty-nine years old.

Siddhartha had cast aside his jewels and his regal clothing, but he could not disguise the beauty of his own being or a certain grave and princely bearing. He took up his duties as a student of wisdom at a retreat in the hills outside the city of Rajagaha, capital of the state of Magadha. There, in caves and rude shelters, many recluses meditated and studied. Each day, clad in his russet robe, he took his begging-bowl, descended to the streets of the city, and begged from door to door. The people, noting his holiness and his courtly bearing, bowed to him instinctively and gave freely. Soon there was talk on every side about the mendicant who had the grace and majestic bearing of a noble of the Aryan caste. Some said this was Brahma himself come to earth.

King Bimbisara of Magadha heard of the strange pilgrim, had him followed, and one day went to his retreat in the hills. When he found that Siddhartha seemed indeed a prince, with the graces and accomplishments of a noble, and at the same time was of a saintly and compassionate nature, King Bimbisara asked him to accept one-half of his kingdom. He promised all that the worldly heart desires, palaces, power, beautiful women, riches. Siddhartha refused, explaining that he had renounced worldly dominion, that he had no other desire than to attain spiritual enlightenment. He commended the King, however, for his benevolent way of ruling, and he promised that, when he found the light he sought, he would return and preach the doctrine first in Rajagaha.

Among the hermits was a celebrated sage named Alara Kalama who taught the doctrine of the Brahmins. Siddhartha listened respectfully to his teachings, and upon some matters he gained new light. But he was unconvinced when Alara insisted that the self or ego of the individual persists when the soul ultimately gains freedom from the body. This was opposed to his own vision of the self extinguished when the soul passes into bliss. Nor could he yet be sure that the path of deprivation, of extreme asceticism, which led these hermits to deny themselves every comfort and to live only on uncooked foods and water, was not a road of additional suffering.

When he quitted the group that Alara had assembled about him, Siddhartha sat at the feet of the sage Udraka. He learned more thoroughly the doctrine of Karma — and to this he was to adhere in later years — but again he shrank from the teachings that the *Atman* or soul persists as an extension of the self. It seemed to him that in this Brahman belief there lurked a new danger, a threatened persistence of the ego; if, indeed, the whole idea were not a subtler form of desire, of selfish future desire. He debated these matters with Udraka, and then parted from him.

Leaving the company of the hermits, Siddhartha joined for a time the ranks of those who sacrifice in the temples, and he studied the ceremonies of the priests. Having the sympathy with animals and the understanding of their ways that are part of the nature of the truly compassionate one, he was grieved by the cruelties he saw practised.

"These priests," he said, "are shedding blood. They claim that thus they are honouring the gods. Would they not do the gods more honour by an example of holy living than by destroying life? They believe that the one who brings an animal for sacrifice thereby purifies himself. But the man who has purity in his heart has no need to kill." Ever afterward he preached against the Brahmins who counted sacrifice, ritual, and incantations a part of religion. Sometimes he stayed the hands of priests about to kill animals, and always his superior humaneness won over those who had thought to win advantage for themselves.

He went back now to the hermits. In the forest of Uruvela he encountered five ascetics who had been disciples of Udraka, and it seemed to him that these anchorites had travelled a considerable way along the road of purification. Their desires and passions were controlled by rigorous self-discipline, and they had arrived at a stage of compassionate understanding unknown to the priests of the temples. Perhaps, he reflected, he had been wrong in repudiating asceticism. The way to the light might be through the rigours of self-denial and the discipline of uninterrupted meditation.

So he set out to destroy the body and its needs in so far as that might be without completely extinguishing the fire of life. He suppressed every want except that for food, and gradually lessened his ration until his body was nourished by no more than a grain of rice a day. He practised the disciplines by which the adept leaves behind all attachment and distractions, by which the senses are stilled, the attention concentrated, and the consciousness projected into realization of infinite being.

For six years he persisted in a course of mortification and meditation. His beautiful body was wasted away until outwardly he was no more than bones and parched skin. In his eyes shone still a native holiness. The birds and beasts went to him as if he were one of themselves. The five hermits, by reason of Siddhartha's steadfast self-torturing, agreed that he was the holiest ascetic among them. Gradually word went forth of his incredible self-denial, and pilgrims came to stand in awe at sight of his wasted frame and to seek his blessing. They believed that as he had diminished mortal life he had drawn close to the estate of a god.

At the end of six years Siddhartha realized that all his mortification, penance, and fasting had not brought illumination. His weakness and suffering had become such that he was losing the power to concentrate upon the quest for Nirvana, or to push farther in search of wisdom. At last he understood that mortification could not lead to spiritual understanding. "I will eat and drink again," he said, "for one without strength cannot follow the path."

Painfully he dragged himself to the river's edge, believing that he might be sufficiently refreshed by bathing to go in search of food. He struggled into the water and lay there exhausted. When he wanted to return to the bank he could not rise. The five bhikshus came to look at him and said: "The holy Siddhartha has come to the end."

After a time, however, he was able to grasp the drooping branch of a tree. Painfully he dragged himself to the shore and crawled toward his home in the forest. Half-way he fell helpless.

In the near-by village, where the hermits had been accustomed to beg their food, there was a certain girl, the daughter of a wealthy farmer, who had prayed that some day her offering of food might be proffered to the Buddha-to-be, and that in this small way she might help him to persist on the way to enlightenment. Now she divined that the day of fulfilment of her prayer had come. Skilled in preparing the purest of foods, she boiled milk taken from consecrated cows and cooked rice. And knowing that this was no ordinary occasion — for the world was bright with signs that the hour of the Buddha's Great Enlightenment was at hand — she put the milk-rice into a golden bowl and covered it with a snow-white cloth. She went to Siddhartha, where he was sitting under a tree, and put the golden bowl into his hands, saying: "This is my offering. May it bring you as much good as it has brought me."

Siddhartha ate of the food, and he felt his strength return as a warmth of the body. At the same time his mind cleared; and he too knew that he was about to receive illumination. The five hermits, however, seeing him eat freely, cried out that he had broken his vows and had forfeited his sanctity; and they deserted him.

Siddhartha went once more to the river for purification; then he sought for the tree he had visioned as his shelter during the Enlightenment. Passing a meadow where a man was mowing grasses for his cattle, he begged an armful of the green grass. He carried it until he came to the tree, and spread it underneath like a carpet. He sat in the fashion of the meditating sage. At the hour of dawn he experienced Enlightenment.

During that night the world was filled with signs of the great event. The heavens were lighted, the earth shook, happiness descended upon all the peoples, the sick were healed. Mara, the Evil One, alone attempted interference. He loosed terrifying storms over the tree under which the Prince sat calm and unmoved. When the winds were changed to perfumed breezes, and the rains had become showers of lotus blossoms, Mara tried the way of beguilement. Beautiful nymphs came before the holy one and tempted him.

"A great rock remains undisturbed in a storm," say the Buddhists. No more did Siddhartha note the seductive graces and inviting charms of the nymphs. Instead his mind was filled with light and understanding, and with thankfulness that he had at last been enabled to comprehend the way of emancipation from mortal suffering.

During the hours of illumination the Blessed One experienced all the stages of mystic consciousness and communion. He gained perfect comprehension of the finite and the infinite, of the cycle of man's soul through birth, mortal life, and death, and through its rebirths and its sinking into the ocean of Oneness. He attained understanding of the riddle of man's suffering, perceived clearly the chain of causation from desire to evil to sorrow. He saw before him the vision of mankind freed from the prison of the senses, craving annihilated, the soul delivered from the bonds of delusion. His consciousness was extinguished in the bliss of Nirvana, the peace of the Absolute.

In that moment, that eternity, Gautama became the Buddha. He had completed the journey from darkness into light. The rapture and the peace of immortality were his. He might have elected to remain in the blissful splendour of that experience, to be extinguished (so far as the world is concerned) in Nirvana for ever. And indeed Mara, who now conceded that he had no power to seduce the Blessed One with worldly temptations, came before him saying sanctimoniously that Heaven after all was the place for so great a saint, and that the enlightened one, having entered into the highest bliss, would not wisely return to the confusion of the mortal world.

But the Buddha knew that the Tempter wished to hold the realm of mortality for his own. Moved by his love of men and his great compassion for every living thing, he drew back from entry into Final Nirvana. He decided to spend upon earth the remaining years of a natural lifetime, preaching to as many men as might be prepared for enlightenment the doctrine of emancipation by extinction of desire. He held, as it were, to the privilege of periodic entry into Nirvana, but he postponed final annihilation of being until a chain of wisdom should be established that would reach down through all the ages of man's existence on earth. To Mara he said:

"Evil One, there shall be a brotherhood to instruct men, self-consecrated brothers who will teach and preach and afford example of holy living, and lay disciples who will follow the eightfold path of virtue. This shall be my work on earth, to proclaim the religion of Buddhahood, of a final heaven of bliss for all men, and to draw into that religion an order of wanderers and teachers. I will not enter into Final Nirvana until I have thus helped mankind to escape from the ocean of ignorance and delusion."

When he had experienced the Great Enlightenment, the Tathagata — for now he was "The One Who Has Come," though not yet finally the Buddha — sat in silence under the Tree of Wisdom for forty-nine days. For so long did he meditate upon the way and the doctrine, savouring the blissful peace of emancipation, reviewing the search for the truth and the wonder of final enlightenment, and visioning the life ahead, of preaching, of spreading the doctrine of the eightfold path, of binding untold numbers of men by their own vows to a brotherhood.

At the end of the seven weeks two travellers came by, merchants from Burma. Attracted by the peace and nobility of the Tathagata's countenance, and by a radiance that ever after lighted the place where he was, Bhallika and Tapussa approached him and gave him food, the first he had tasted since the farmer's daughter had prepared the golden bowl of milk-rice. These two listened to the Blessed One's exposition of the doctrine, and they became the first of his disciples. They were, however, lay disciples and not members of the brotherhood of bhikshus or monks.

The Tathagata decided to make his way to Benares, a celebrated centre of religious interest, and to find there the five ascetics who had so recently repudiated him. On the way he met an aristocratic Brahmin. Noting the peace and beauty that surrounded the holy one like an aura, the Brahmin asked what faith and what master had brought him so great calm and contentment. The answer came: "I have no master, and my faith is of the simplest. Those who harbour no ill will, who have restrained the senses and freed themselves of desire, those who have escaped selfishness, they open the way to immortality."

The Blessed One went to the Deer Park at Benares, where the five ascetic monks were staying. When he approached, they agreed that because he had broken the vows of self-denial they would not honour him, nor even rise when he came among them. But the majesty and serenity of his presence and the love he felt for them were so compelling that they rose without thinking. Involuntarily they tended him as if he were their master, one taking his robe and bowl, another bringing water to bathe his feet.

It was to the five ascetic monks that he delivered his first sermon. Because they had been accustomed to practise mortification as a way to holiness, he prefaced his discourse with an exposition of the doctrine of the "middle way." The holy man, he said, would, like all spiritual seekers, avoid the road of self-indulgence, passion, and ambition; but he would equally avoid the road of mortification of the body, penances, and painful austerities, for, he said, these practices accomplish neither the cleansing of a man nor the opening of a way to emancipation. Between the road of self-indulgence and the road of self-immolation lies the middle path, the path of self-control, the path of selfless devotion, from which the growths of desire, lust, envy, and uncleanness have been cut away; the path that leads to understanding, wisdom, and the peace of Nirvana. In this counsel to avoid the extremes of austerity the Tathagata established one of the greatest differences separating his faith from that of the Hindus, who to this day are celebrated for the great number of ascetics who mortify the flesh.

He went on to preach the "first sermon." It is known as "the first turning of the wheel of truth," by reason of his use of the simile of the wheel of conduct. "The spokes of the wheel are the man's eightfold right conduct . . . and his constant mindfulness is the hub upon which the axle of truth is borne." He spoke for the first time of the Four Noble Truths, noting that sense-craving is the origin of suffering, and that only control or riddance of the desire for gratification can emancipate the individual from suffering. There is, he continued, a way of conduct by which one rises above the sense-imprisonment of self.

He then laid down the doctrine of the Eightfold Path of Virtue, which was to remain at the heart of Buddhist moral teaching ever afterward. In brief, the path of the eight ways is this:

right seeing	right work
right aspiration	right enterprise
right speaking	right meditation
right behaviour	right spiritual rapture

The five monks offered themselves as disciples, for they recognized the authority and the wisdom and the exaltation of a great spiritual prophet. Kondanna, the first among them to attain full enlightenment, thus became the first Buddhist leader after the Master, a Bodhisattva.

Five days after the first discourse the Tathagata delivered another historic sermon. In it he expounded the second great difference by which the Buddhist faith was to be separated from Vedantism. He spoke of the *Atman*, or soul, and said that so long as the soul is conceived of as something representing self, having its own sensations (as one speaks of a "sixth sense") and persisting after death, there can be no idea of an ultimate sinking into the blissful peace of Nirvana.

Now the order or brotherhood began to grow spontaneously. Disciples appeared from all sides. A rich youth of Benares, named Yasa, overcome by brooding upon the sorrows of the world, came to ask the Blessed One if there were indeed a way to extinguish suffering. He was won by an exposition of the doctrine of emancipation from desire. Desiring to join the brotherhood, he looked with dismay at his own richly adorned garments. The Tathagata said that just as a hermit in rags in the jungle would be worldly if his thoughts were worldly, so a man richly dressed might be holy if his thoughts were holy. "We shall make no distinction," he said, "between the lay member and the hermit member, if both have conquered self." Yasa, however, took the vows of a monk and assumed the plain habit of a religious.

Yasa's father, come in search of the youth, heard the Blessed One speak and was convinced. He took the oath as a lay member; and it is said that he was the first to repeat the standard declaration for lay membership: "I take refuge in the Buddha, our Master. I take refuge in the doctrine revealed by him. I take refuge in the brotherhood he has founded." In later years this concise declaration was elaborated into a service of ordination for monks. But the simple placing of trust in the Buddha, the Law, and the brotherhood is still a sufficient way of profession for lay adherents.

When the Tathagata, bearing his begging-bowl, went to the house of Yasa's father, both the mother and the wife of the youth took the lay vow of refuge in the Buddha. They were the first women to become members of the order. Certain of the young friends of Yasa went to the Deer Park in search of him, hoping to recall him to a life of worldly pleasure. But they too were converted when they heard the words of the Master.

When the brotherhood of monks numbered sixty members, the Master sent them out to teach. "Go forth," he said, "and preach the doctrine. With compassion for all men, go forth and preach the extinction of desire. Proclaim the eightfold path that leads to wisdom, peace, and Nirvana."

The Blessed One went himself to Uruvela, where three renowned ascetics, brothers, had brought together a thousand disciples. Uruvela Kassapa, the most celebrated of the brothers, and all the disciples were fire-worshippers. It was then that he delivered the third or "Fire" sermon.

He said that craving is a flame. So, too, the torments of sickness and old age, of birth and death, are no more than the fires of misery, kindled by sense-desires. He showed his hearers how the flames might be extinguished by right living, and the self at last extinguished in Nirvana. And Kassapa and his two brothers and all their disciples were converted by the Fire sermon, and took vows.

The Tathagata remembered now his promise to King Bimbisara, and he went to Rajagaha with Kassapa and many of the new disciples. The people of the city were puzzled, for they had considered Kassapa the greatest of religious sages; but the King knew unerringly that a greater prophet had appeared. He took refuge in the order, and many of his subjects followed his example. King Bimbisara then presented to the brotherhood a beautiful park known as the Bamboo Grove, that those who believed in the coming of the Buddha might have a meeting-place and a monastery. This was the first centre of the Buddhist faith, a faith to which, twenty-five centuries after, so many monasteries and shrines and temples are dedicated, in so many lands, that no one has been able to count them.

The Blessed One went to the Bamboo Grove, and thereafter he made that park his centre while he was in Magadha. Thither came many pilgrims, and from among them the order gained innumerable disciples. They were from all classes, for the Tathagata discouraged caste distinctions. There were two accessions of sages so wise and holy that the Tathagata said as they approached the park: "These two are destined to be my chief disciples"; and in time Sariputta and Mogallana became leaders in the brotherhood and formulators of the doctrine.

There was also a great merchant, a man of wealth and a philanthropist, named Anathapindika, who was visiting in Rajagaha. He heard of the coming of the Buddha and went to the Bamboo Park. After listening to the Tathagata he wished to enter the brotherhood. Asking whether he should renounce his riches and leave the world, and whether a man might retain his wealth and fulfil the obligations of a lay member by doing good works, he received the answer that one could indeed live a life of selflessness and love if one's mindfulness were always for the truth and for the service of others.

Anathapindika returned to his home at Savatthi, the capital city of Kosala. He sought to buy the pleasure garden belonging to the Prince of Kosala, that he might present it to the Buddhist brotherhood. The Prince, learning what was to be done with the park, insisted upon becoming a co-giver with the rich merchant. They built a great hall for meetings of the brotherhood and to accommodate the pilgrims who appeared wherever the Tathagata went.

When the Blessed One came to dedicate the park, which was called Jetavana, the King of Kosala sought him out and asked about the principles of truth in relation to ruling. He answered: "Even a King's good and evil deeds follow him like a shadow. The key to good ruling is a loving heart. Regard your people as a man regards his only son. Remember the transiency of life and the illusiveness of earthly possessions. Search your mind, control your body, walk in the path of faith. Then will your conduct be kingly and virtuous, and your happiness real."

At the Jetavana Park the Blessed One preached a sermon on Nirvana which is celebrated among his followers. For he expounded the law of the uncreate, the eternal, which is beyond all that is created, different from all that changes, beyond the thoughts of being or origination, beyond birth or ending, beyond space or form — the only refuge from suffering.

It was now seven years since the Prince Siddhartha had ridden away from the palace at Kapilavastu to become a homeless seeker of enlightenment. While he was at Rajagaha the word was taken to his father, King Suddhodana, that he had become a great religious prophet. The King sent emissaries repeatedly to Rajagaha to ask that Siddhartha return home and receive honours among his own people. Each time the messengers and the men of their retinues were converted to the brotherhood and did not return. Finally the King exacted a vow from his Minister that he would go to Rajagaha and that even if he entered the brotherhood as a disciple he would urge the Tathagata to return to Kapilavastu.

When the one-time Prince Siddhartha was known to be on the way home, a park was made ready for him and his twenty thousand followers. When, however, the Blessed One took his alms bowl and begged his food in the streets of Kapilavastu, the King was torn between his love for his son and pride and anger and shame. His son, royally born, had become a beggar!

Being reproached for disgracing his family and dishonouring his noble heritage, he answered: "The way of my true inheritance, the way of the succession of Buddhas, is this." When he added the appeal to set aside all else and enter the path of pure living, in order to attain bliss, his father the King was foremost among those who took vows; and the King attained the first stage of enlightenment.

There was yet one meeting more difficult, one sterner test of the Blessed One's steadfastness, for Yasodhara had stayed away from the meetings at which Siddhartha had been welcomed by his family and friends. She had said to herself: "If I have any value in his eyes, as mother of his son, he will come to me. Then I shall pay homage in my own way."

As they went to her simple chamber he said to his two attendants: "If this woman embraces me, or even touches me, we must in the name of compassion suspend our rule. Do not prevent her." When they were in the room, Yasodhara was momentarily torn by a conflict between her old love for Siddhartha and her new pride in and awe of the radiant saint before her. Then she threw herself before him, clasping his ankles and bowing her head against his feet. The Blessed One was silent.

After a few moments she regained her composure, rose, gazing steadily at her husband, and with dignity stood apart. And this was in keeping with her dress, for now the Master noted that she wore the plain russet robe of an ascetic; and her hair was cut short.

It was King Suddhodana who told him the story of Yasodhara's renunciation. When she had heard that Siddhartha had exchanged clothes with the hermit the night of his going, she too had assumed the russet robe. When she heard that he slept no longer in a bed, she placed a mat upon her bedroom floor and slept upon it. When it was reported that he accepted food but once each day, she ate but once, and then from an earthen bowl. Thus during the seven years the gentle-born Princess had matched the wandering Prince's austerities with her own. King Suddhodana concluded: "Such, despite her grief, has been her goodness and her purity. She is worthy."

The Blessed One was moved, but he was not surprised, remembering the gentleness, the understanding, and the devotion of Yasodhara in the old days. To her he said: "The path I have opened is for you too." When he preached again, this time to his own people, she found a place among his listeners, and she asked that she might be taken into the order, not as a lay member but as one who had given up the world. Many others of the family and of the court circle offered themselves for dedication to the work of teaching and preaching, for nowhere had the nobility and spirituality of the Tathagata been more clearly perceived.

Among the converts were two cousins — both had been among the nobles Siddhartha had defeated in the tournament preceding his betrothal to Yasodhara — one of them, Ananda, destined to become the best beloved of the disciples and his personal attendant, the other, Devadatta, to be a troublesome plotter and heretic. But although many became monks, Yasodhara was refused because the Blessed One doubted that women should be admitted to the preaching order.

A week after the return of the Blessed One to Kapilavastu, Yasodhara called her son Rahula to her and said: "The holy saint who has come among us, who is godlike in appearance and bearing, is, indeed, your father. He owns great treasures. Go to him therefore and say that you wish to claim your inheritance." The boy went to his father and straightway asked that he be given what treasure his father possessed. The Tathagata answered:

"I have neither gold nor precious jewels, nor power, to bequeath. But I see the design in your coming. I shall bestow on you the truths that lead to noble living." And with the concurrence of the disciples he bestowed on the child membership in the brotherhood. Thus he made glad the heart of Yasodhara. And in later years Rahula was counted one of the wisest apostles of the Buddhist way.

King Suddhodana, however, was distressed because again a Prince in the line of succession had been taken into the religious order, and the throne left without an heir. (Devadatta, as the nephew of the King, had been designated as Siddhartha's successor, until he too had taken the vow.) The Tathagata, seeing justice in the complaint, decreed that thereafter no minor should be accepted into the order without his parents' consent.

The Master, because his mission was to lead people into the path of enlightenment, did not remain in one place, and he left Kapilavastu as he had left the monasteries established in Rajagaha and Savatthi. But he returned when he heard that his father was near death. The Blessed One went to him and taught him the way of complete enlightenment, and King Suddhodana died and attained Nirvana.

When the King was gone the Queen, she who had been fostermother to Siddhartha, decided that she would like to join the preaching order. She and Yasodhara, who had already been refused, and a great many noble ladies, widows whose husbands had been killed in the wars, went to the monastery where the Tathagata was staying and petitioned for admission. But the Master was firm in his refusal. The women returned home, but somewhat later they again assembled, donned ascetics' robes, and cut their hair. With their begging-bowls they set out to walk the distance to the monastery, although many of them had been accustomed all their lives to travel only in carriages or on elephants. Even their bleeding feet did not avail to change the Master until Ananda interceded for them.

"Are women, then, not competent to attain to sainthood?" he asked; and, "Is the Buddha born into the world only for the benefit of men?" The Tathagata gave in, for he could not deny the logic of Ananda's arguments or the sincerity and holiness of the applicants. He prophesied that the structure of the brotherhood would be weakened, but he laid down rigid regulations for the discipline of the nuns. The Queen was the first among the women of the order to attain Arahatta; that is, the rapture of Nirvana.

For forty years thereafter the Blessed One carried on the work of preaching to pilgrims, teaching the disciples, and organizing the brotherhood for continuing service in spreading the doctrine. The way of his life was this:

He owned nothing except his robe and underclothing, his alms bowl, his water-strainer, his tooth-stick, his razor, and a needle. During the long season of fair weather he was a wanderer, without home, sleeping at night in any proffered shelter or under a tree. Often he walked twenty miles a day, usually accompanied or followed by groups of bhikshus. He begged his meals. But his holy aspect was such that he would be invited frequently to enter the house of the charitable one. Then, when all had partaken of food, he spoke to the host and members of the household on spiritual and philosophic matters. In this way he gained many converts. His modesty and simplicity were winning, and he stressed always that he wished no one to come to him except as he might help with counsel, by throwing light upon the path. For, he said, every man must liberate himself; there is no saviour who can take upon himself another's burden of slavery to sense, of impurity, a burden that can be cast off only by self-conquest.

During the three months of the rainy season he would stay at one or another of the monasteries, perhaps in the Bamboo Grove at Rajagaha, or at Jetavana, or at shelters erected by pious kings and nobles in their gardens. There, after early rising and the usual purification, he would retire into solitude for meditation. During the morning he would go to a near-by settlement, carrying his alms bowl, and beg his food. The rest of the day and evening he would spend, with intervals of meditation and rest, speaking in the great hall of the monastery to pilgrims and discoursing to the disciples, answering their questions, clarifying the doctrine, and sometimes resolving doubts and strengthening the always loose structure of the brotherhood.

During the years of ministry there were occasional enmities and jealousies, even quarrels and schisms. The unhappy Devadatta, who wished to be designated as the Tathagata's successor in leadership of the order, attempted a division of the brotherhood. He claimed that the rules of the order were too lenient, and he founded a rival sect given to mortification. Failing to draw away the Blessed One's followers, he intrigued and finally conspired to have the Master murdered. But the drunken elephant let loose by the evil-doers in the path of the Blessed One became gentle in his presence and kneeled before him. The would-be murderers were overcome by the love and saintliness of the one they had planned to kill, confessed, and were forgiven. Devadatta on his death-bed repented and asked to be taken to the Master to seek forgiveness, but he died on the way. Some of the books say that as he approached the monastery, borne on a palanquin, the earth opened and he was sucked into a pit of flames.

Religious teachers from whom the Master attracted disciples became jealous of his success. At one time they plotted a subtler way than Devadatta's to rid themselves of his rivalry. They sought to dishonour him by proving that while preaching emancipation from desire he was secretly indulging in carnal pleasure. They bribed a young woman to visit the monastery often and then to claim publicly that she had been intimate with the Blessed One. She made up her clothes as if she were pregnant, but the ruse was discovered, and she, too, it is said, disappeared when the earth opened under her, dropping her into a lake of fire.

The Tathagata's response, when the disciples urged him to take action against the envious ones who tried to hurt him, was this — and it might be a quotation from Lao-Tse: "Hatred can be overcome only by non-hatred." At another time he said regarding injuries: "If a man shall do me wrong, I will offer in return my full love. The greater the injury he attempts, the greater must be the good I offer in return." And again he said: "A truly virtuous man cannot be injured. One who attempts an attack upon him is like a man who flings dust at another while the wind is contrary."

In his administration as leader of the brotherhood — of the Sangha, as it is called in the Sanskrit — the Enlightened One was successful as only the saint, utterly devoid of selfishness, envy, and ambition, can be successful. His transparent purity, his serenity, and his majestic bearing created an atmosphere in which pettiness and minor differences melted away. Nevertheless he put into effect many improvements in the regulations for the conduct of the brothers, and something like a code of laws was established.

The disciples and their leader at first considered it a virtue to wear the most frayed and faded of robes, often no more than rags reclaimed from rubbish heaps. The Master perceived that in this matter they were holding to a remnant of extreme asceticism, and, though he permitted a choice to those who preferred the old way, he made standard the plain but durable and clean yellow robe. When he was opposing the demands of Devadatta for a return to the practices of mortification, he declared for a healthful attention to the body, in these words: "The true ascetic does not gratify his body; but he cares well for the body that he may advance in the spiritual life. Cared for, it is the better vessel for truth."

When it was seen that the Blessed One was aging — although it was remarked that he was even more beautiful of body and presence, endowed with a more commanding calm, in the later years

— questions arose as to the future conduct of the Sangha and of the preaching work. The Enlightened One preached a number of sermons, constituting a charge to his disciples.

He forbade that any one of them should work miracles; for, he said, the ignorant are diverted and misled by miracles, and ask themselves whether the doer is man or god, and the heart of Buddhism is in the knowledge that each man may do for himself all that is necessary for salvation. The attainment of enlightenment, the bathing of the soul in the waters of immortality, gives the Arahat seemingly miraculous powers, and there are times when it is wise to exert these; but claims of supernatural power lead easily into rites and incantations and the rise of a dishonest priestcraft.

"But," the Master added, "there is no more wonderful thing, and seemingly miraculous to the sceptic mind, than a man who has been mired in the transient pleasures of the world turning to holiness and finding bliss."

The rules of membership were lenient. A bhikshu who found himself unsuited to the life of a monk could withdraw without ceremony. As long as he remained a member he must wear the simple yellow robe and beg his food. He must not eat other than the one prescribed meal daily. The order had no officers; instead, a natural deference was paid to the founder and the older disciples. The Blessed One asked the bhikshus to meet in frequent assembly and to act in concord, but to learn the uses of solitude and be faithful to meditation.

"The brotherhood," he said, "may be expected to prosper and not to decline so long as the brothers remain emancipated from craving and follow the dictates of holy living, so that men of purity will want to come and live among them; . . . so long as they shall not be stopped by attainment of some lesser thing, short of entry into Nirvana; so long as they exercise themselves in the seven ways, of mental speculation, philosophic search, joyfulness, serenity, initiative, contemplation, and poise. . . ."

The Tathagata suggested also a code of moral injunctions. This is sometimes put down as a panel of ten commandments, very like the thou-shalt-nots of the Western faiths. They begin with "Kill not, but husband life," and go through familiar prohibitions to "Hate not, even your enemies" and "Escape from ignorance into truth." The central code, as given affirmatively in the exposition of the Eightfold Path, appears in innumerable variations in the reports of the sermons of the later years, all illustrating "the way that ends in the annihilation of suffering."

The Blessed One established the rule for observance of a Sabbath; and he suggested that at the seventh-day meeting any monk whose conscience troubled him should confess his offence before the assembly of brothers. "A fault when confessed will rest on him but lightly," he said. Many other rules came into being after the monks, experiencing temptation, sought counsel at the gatherings.

When women were permitted to join the order, the Blessed One was asked what should be the bhikshu's conduct toward a woman. Beyond the advice to see her not as a woman, and to regard her as one regards a mother or a sister, he could only suggest a general tightening up of defences against betrayal by the heart or by desires. "Arm yourselves with the weapons of uprightness, wisdom, and single-mindedness, and fight the five cravings. Woman's beauty is a beclouding thing. . . . Steel your heart, for her ways are as so many snares. . . ." Once when the beloved Ananda asked for further advice about women, the Master could only say, not without humorous implications: "Avoid them altogether. If you can't do that, then stay wide awake, Ananda." Women gave some of the most desirable of the meeting-places and monasteries presented to the brotherhood by grateful converts, and the Tathagata dealt with them in these and other matters. But from the moment of assuming a wanderer's robe he was in personal life the perfect saint.

During the later years of the Buddha's ministry he preached many more sermons that are celebrated among the faithful. Not only was his wisdom outstanding, but he had a genius for storytelling. He spoke in parable and allegory, and he had a gift for imagery and aphorism. He was skilful too in fitting his discourse to the time and place and to the nature of his audience, whether a group of sages or an assembly of uninstructed pilgrims or a householder's family. On this matter he said to Ananda:

"I was accustomed, whenever I was to go before an assembly, before I took my seat, to take on the colour of the audience. My voice became their voice. I spoke in their language, and with spiritual discourse I attracted, gladdened, and instructed them. My doctrine has the qualities of the ocean. Both become gradually deeper. . . . Like the ocean that has but one taste, my doctrine has but one taste, of emancipation. . . . Likewise it cleanses all without distinction. There is room in it to receive all, men and women alike, the strong and the weak, those in high places and in low. . . . Having attracted, gladdened, and instructed them, I would then vanish."

The wisdom that is so often summed up in a phrase, and the stories that are so humanly absorbing, can be hardly more than referred to here. The discourses upon surrender of self and upon non-action — so suggestive of Lao-Tse's insight — should be read in their entirety. A line spoken to a general in one of them has become a classic saying in the East: "Great is a general who defeats many armies; but he who conquers himself achieves a greater victory."

And there is a saying that should be in every statesman's mind when he ponders civilization's unending cycle of wars: "Victory begets hatred, for the vanquished is left galled. Let a man rise above the ideas of victory and defeat. Only then can there be happiness."

The Buddha's sayings about the intellect, reason, and learning are in perfect accord with those of mystic leaders from Lao-Tse to William Blake: "Learning is a good thing, but in the end it availeth not. Experience, not learning, leads to wisdom and the bliss of Immortality."

In his later sermons the Blessed One spoke often of the mystic attainment that lies at the heart of Buddhist aspiration. Avoiding the terms in which men's conceptions of Paradise are usually clothed, he yet conveyed an impression of the richness and the surpassing peace of immersion in the Absolute. "The gods themselves might envy the rapture of him who has annihilated passion and reached the ocean of Nirvana. He is cleansed of impurities and freed of illusion. He may live in the world and yet be unsoiled . . . for craving is extinguished and the way attained. This is deliverance, salvation, and the bliss of Heaven and the life everlasting."

The Master also preached sermons dealing, though somewhat vaguely, with the ways of preparation and meditation and concentration. Through all flows the feeling, so common in mystic writings, of the surpassing value of serenity, of the wisdom of guarding one's times of silence, of the high uses of solitude and seclusion.

The Blessed One in a debate with a great Brahman sage said: "I came to preach not death but life"; and he pointed out that those who fear death and have anxiety about the after life are really anxious lest they lose the pleasures of the self in Heaven. When one conquers the self, one removes the cause of the fear of death, and one thereby gladdens life.

The Master himself, in his last years, looked forward to death of the body as a natural consequence of the mortal processes of change and decay; but as he had lifted his spirit into the realm of changelessness, he could not grieve or fear. Rather he felt the joyous apprehension of final attainment. He could not but be uplifted in spirit, for the end would be immersion in the eternal peace of Nirvana.

It was when he was nearing eighty years of age that the Blessed One and a great number of his followers went, upon invitation of the beautiful and rich courtesan Amra, to take their meal at her mansion. She was a woman of deep wisdom, serene-minded and pious, and hearing the Master speak, she perceived that this was indeed the Buddha, the enlightener of the world. She prepared the food herself and served the holy ones. Then she took her place on a low stool before the Blessed One and said: "Lord, I give this mansion and property to the brotherhood of which you are the chief." He accepted the gift, and she was gladdened by the acceptance and by his discourse on the spiritual life. Thus in his eightieth year he was still serving the purpose, established at the time of his enlightenment, of extending the work of the brotherhood.

When the rainy season came that year he was severely ill. He resolutely subdued the sickness, because his work was not quite done. He called together the bhikshus and preached to them his farewell sermon. He perceived that the brothers could not escape grief at his going, and that they were puzzled as to the leadership. "Be ye lamps unto yourselves," he said. "Be your own reliance. Hold to the truth within yourselves as the only lamp."

A little later he spoke to Ananda about his approaching death. "All things that are constituted must grow old and pass away. . . . At the end of three months the Tathagata will die." And he repeated the prophecy to the brothers in assembly. The Blessed One was himself very happy at this time.

Attended by the beloved Ananda, and with a large company of bhikshus, he made his way to Pava, where they stopped to rest in the grove of a smith named Chunda. The smith felt great joy at this honour, and he begged that he might provide the next day's meal for the holy ones. Though the food was carefully prepared, the Blessed One suffered a sudden illness after partaking of it. As soon as the pain abated a little he and Ananda set out for Kusinara, for there, it had been foretold, the Master was to die.

He lay down under a tree, and there came to him a pilgrim, a young seeker of wisdom named Pukkusa. The Blessed One expounded the doctrine, and Pukkusa was converted and joined the brotherhood. He presented two golden robes to the Master; but when they were put about him it was noted that their brightness faded. The seeming change, however, was due to the clear brightness of the body of the Tathagata. "It is thus," he said, "on two occasions: when the Buddha-to-be first attains Enlightenment, and at the time when he finally puts off mortality."

He asked that he might have solitude for meditation. After a time he rose and went with Ananda to the river and bathed. Then he spoke to Ananda about Chunda the smith. "Some may grieve Chunda," he said, "by recalling that I died after his offering of a meal. But let him not feel remorse." He recalled the offering that the farmer's daughter had brought to him the day before his Enlightenment. "This offering too, the last before final attainment, is holy. You will see Chunda and tell him, Ananda, that he is blessed in having provided the last meal. He has thereby laid up great rewards."

When they came to Kusinara, with a great number of the bhikshus following them, the Master lay down between two sala trees, with his head toward the Himalayas. He was serene in mind and spoke clearly. But Ananda knew that he was dying and drew apart until he should master his grief. When the Blessed One called for him he went and sat by his side, and the Blessed One comforted him, saying that it is natural for the body to pass, that the doctrine would endure, and that as there had been Buddhas before him, there would be Buddhas again.

He spoke also to the people of the near-by town, who came weeping bitterly and grieving; and he spoke to the assembled brothers, saying that he knew that each one of them, having found the way of emancipation, would know cessation of suffering and attainment of peace.

Then for a time he was silent, and it was as if a great calm settled over the land. Only once again he spoke, saying to the disciples: "I ask you to remember, transiency is in the nature of all created things. Seek diligently for emancipation." He then sank deeper and deeper into meditation; consciousness and feeling ceased, and he passed into the eternal bliss of Nirvana.

Men and gods paused, and they expressed their grief in their various accustomed ways. But among the disciples there were some who had completely conquered passion and gained enlightenment, and they were glad and comforted their brothers.

In assembly the bhikshus made simple arrangements and rules for the carrying on of the work of the order. There was no division of opinion among them, and no one strove to become leader of the brotherhood. The truth, they said, is the spirit of the Sangha, and the truth is the Buddha. In order that the truth might go on perpetually, undefiled and uncorrupted, they appointed certain ones to codify the rules and the guiding principles — such as those of the Four Noble Truths and the Eightfold Path — and others to memorize the sermons and sayings of the Enlightened One. For some centuries the words of the Buddha and the stories about him were thus handed down orally by trained Buddhist sages, before they were written down.

The people of Kusinara insisted upon paying honour to the dead seer. While the body lay in the sala grove they brought wreaths and garlands and flowers, and perfumes and spices. They gave themselves up to lamentation and dancing and hymns. Finally they placed the body on a regal funeral pyre. But when the torch was applied the pyre did not take fire. Finally it was seen that a flame sprang from the heart of the Blessed One, and the pyre and the body were consumed.

The charred bones alone were left. Many peoples and communities asked for these relics. The bones were divided into eight parts and were enshrined reverently in stupas or dagobas in various of the countries in which the Buddha had taught the doctrine. One portion was thus honoured by the Sakya peoples at Kapilavastu.

But the truest memorial to the Blessed One, as an elder disciple said to the multitude at the funeral pyre, was the truth he taught, which cleanses men and leads them to bliss.

In India the Buddhist faith grew and spread, but it failed to develop the strength to stand against the Hinduism which had been the original religion from which the Buddha sprang. The Brahmins never ceased claiming the seer Siddhartha as one of their own. After a dozen centuries they were able to re-absorb Buddhist doctrines into their own creed, and to install the Buddha (who had spoken against deification) into their elastic gallery of gods as an incarnation of Vishnu.

Thus one of the purest and profoundest of philosophies, one which through a millennium attracted the devotion of nobles and kings and serfs, wealthy and poor, sage and illiterate, ran a brilliant course and then was extinguished in the land of its origin. Certain of the Buddha's doctrines profoundly influenced the Brahman faith. Nevertheless the hold of the Brahman priests upon the people, the popular love of ceremonial and belief in sacrifice, and the shrewd manipulation of the caste system determined that Buddhism should be stamped out, except as parts of its philosophy might be merged with Vedantic wisdom.

The period of Buddhist ascendancy in India was the five or six centuries after Asoka's reign. It was just before the middle of the third century B.C. that the youthful Emperor Asoka was converted. True to the pacifism proclaimed by the Buddha, he renounced war and tried to repair the injuries done to countless people in earlier campaigns. (His armies had just slaughtered 100,000 persons.) In one of the most remarkable of state edicts he proclaimed righteousness, love, toleration, and non-interference as the corner-posts of his kingdom.

He called on his subjects to refrain from violence, passion, evil thought, and envy; and he made clear that he had vowed to live and to rule in righteousness. He forbade luxury and waste in his own palace (though it is doubtful how far beyond his own apartments the prohibitions operated). He forbade sacrifices and urged his subjects to have compassion toward every living thing. He asked his people to foster the personal virtues of self-restraint, cheerfulness, gentleness, and upright living.

But above all he emphasized his own abjuring of war — war being the greatest curse of civilization, producing more of man's suffering and unhappiness than all other causes together. He admonished — in a rock-cut edict — his sons and their sons to abstain from war, saying that moral or religious conquest is the only defensible sort. He urged upon his descendent rulers, too, forgiveness, forbearance, and leniency in punishment. Already, he said, "the sounding of the war-drums serves as a summons not to battle but to righteousness."

Although the edicts inform us of Asoka's own intention to follow the path even to the attainment of Arahatta, his injunctions are almost solely upon the ethical side. He promises that compliance will bring his subjects happiness in this world and in Paradise; but that is the only mention of the future state. Nevertheless he did more than any other to spread the faith into other lands in its purest mystical form. He sent emissaries in all directions, wisely charging them to dispense not only the Buddhist doctrine but such blessings as medical science. His own son went as a missionary to Ceylon, where Buddhism remains to-day overwhelmingly the religion of the people. Other lands that accepted the faith and still harbour great numbers of adherents are Tibet, Burma, China, and Japan.

Asoka ruled for nearly forty years, and Buddhism seemed destined to become the light of India. But his sons and grandsons failed to remember the admonitions against war and luxury and conquest; and the Brahmins began their gradual centuries-long drive to recapture the loyalty of the people. Eventually the Buddhist shrines and monasteries in India were taken over or neglected. Asoka's dream of a pacifist state, supported by subjects treading the eightfold path of virtue with their eyes upon the bliss of Nirvana, faded from the world. India was not ready for so stern, so austere, a faith.

What noble service Buddhism rendered to Indian art is known to every student of sculpture and painting. The Buddhist holy books are among the world's foremost treasuries of spiritual literature. Embedded in the sermons, stories, and verse are some of the most telling arguments for the mystic enrichment of life in the whole range of religious literature. In the pages of the books produced in the two divisions of Buddhist development there are innumerable noble passages dealing with the nature of Nirvana, the ways of attainment, and the relationship of life, Karma, rebirth, and the ultimate ocean of bliss.

The two chief historical schools of Buddhism are known as the Hinayana, the primitive or Southern school, which grew directly out of the doctrine as interpreted by the disciples immediately after the death of the Buddha, and the Mahayana, the Northern school, of somewhat later development and much wider-spread. Hinayana and Mahayana mean "The Lesser Vessel" and "The Greater Vessel," or, as some translate the word, the lesser and greater "vehicles" — referring to the vessel or vehicle of salvation.

The Hinayana texts are in the Pali language or dialect; the Mahayana in Sanskrit.

Beyond these treasuries are those of the Chinese, Tibetan, Japanese, and other "foreign" Buddhist bodies. In the nature of the faith, there is no one to say that such and such scriptures are canonical and others apocryphal. The latest convert may add an acceptable text if his vision of the truth is sufficiently clear and pure, and his spiritual and literary inspiration adequate. Asvaghosa, the most eloquent poet of Buddhism, lived probably in the first century of the Christian era, five centuries after the Buddha passed into Nirvana.

Although the Buddhist faith is essentially one of joy, presuming a way of life purified of sorrow and illumined by the light of eternity, the logic of the teaching begins in the realization of human suffering. There is a story about the universality of suffering, the Story of the Mustard Seed, which perfectly prefaces any summary of the Buddha's teachings.

There was a girl named Kisa Gotami, who had been born very poor but through her virtue had married the son of a man of property. She had an only child, but he died while hardly more than a babe. Distracted by grief and love, the mother went from house to house, clasping the body in her arms, asking people to give her medicine for her baby. The neighbours felt pity for her, but among themselves they said: "The girl has lost her senses. The child is dead." But then Kisa Gotami came to one who answered: "I cannot give you medicine that will cure your child. But there is one who can help you." And he directed her to the Sage of the Sakyas, who was the Tathagata. Kisa Gotami went to the place where the Master was staying, and made reverence to him and said: "Lord, give me the medicine that will cure my child." He answered: "I can help you. But I shall need a handful of mustard seed." The girl cried out joyfully, for any householder would give her a handful of seed. The Buddha added: "There is one condition. The seed must come from a house where no one has lost by death a son or a parent or a husband or wife."

Kisa Gotami went forth, still clasping the child's body to her, and she stopped at each house as before. When she asked for a handful of mustard seed each householder was quick to respond; but when she asked whether death had entered the house she received like replies from all: "I too have lost my son," or "I have lost my beloved parents," or "My husband has died." One said: "It is the living who are few. The dead are many. Do not remind us of our sorrow." Kisa Gotami wore herself out in the search. Finally she sat down by a roadside overlooking the houses of the town. She reflected: "It is true. There is here no house, no family, from which death has not taken a loved one. Sorrow is known to all. Life flames up and is extinguished, and mortal suffering is all about. I have been selfish in grieving for my child."

She went with friends to a forest, and they buried the body. Then she returned to the Buddha. He asked her: "Have you brought the mustard seed?" She answered: "Lord, the lesson of the mustard seed is learned. There is no house to which the parting called death has not brought misery. They have told me that the living are few, the dead many." The Master spoke to her of the transiency of all living things and of the one way in which there is emancipation from sorrow. Kisa Gotami then, as the Buddhists say, entered into the stream that flows to the ocean of Nirvana.

Life is transitory and impermanent. Desire and personal love and the pleasures of the self are transient and illusory. This is the beginning point of the cycle of thought at the heart of Buddhist philosophy. Change, decay, exists; mortal life is a flow, of which the very nature is change; sorrow results from attachment to the things that decay. Recognize, therefore, the cause of suffering: attachment through desire, passion, selfish ambition, the craving to possess. Seeing clearly, then, the existence and the causation, one may go on to remove or extinguish the cause. The extinction is at once a sort of bliss and a deliverance into eternal rapture.

The filling in of this stark outline belongs to books of philosophy (which, in the West, have too often overlooked the Buddha, Lao-Tse, and the other Oriental sages), and not to a book on the mystics. It is necessary only to recall briefly the characteristics of the faith as they determine the individual's life on the way to emancipation and illumination, and to ask what is the mystic nature of Nirvana.

Unlike Hinduism or Brahmanism, this, in its purest form, is a religion without gods, priests, or rites. No supreme deity is recognized, nor any supernatural or miraculous power except of the sort that every man may attain by exercise of his spiritual nature. The brothers of the Buddhist order have no priestly authority or function. They preach and counsel, but they administer no sacraments. Lay members are their own guides; a light has been kindled within. "Be a lamp unto yourself," said the Blessed One. There is no saviour, no lifting of the burden of sorrow and mortality by an outward agency. The Buddha does not bring deliverance; he has shown the path. The pilgrim's own effort leads to emancipation.

Since there is neither god nor saviour (nor the intercessors of the Christian Church), there is no worship. Especially forbidden is sacrifice. Penances and all forms of self-mortification are discouraged as morbid and a peril to the health of the mind as of the body.

Departing from the Brahman faith, again, is the disbelief in a persisting self. The soul, at the end of a series of rebirths, at the end of a succession of lives, is extinguished in the boundless light of Nirvana. It is here that both Brahman thought and Western thought pause, hesitating to follow into a realm where the individual soul loses personal identity. The Buddha expressed it (roughly speaking) this way: The self has no more abiding reality than the other appurtenances of mortality. As long as you are thinking of it as "your self" you are holding to a thing that cannot survive. There is, nevertheless, something representing immortality in you — nameless, unnameable, indescribable, inexpressible — and this returns to the ocean of immortality.

Or again, if one renounces worldly life for a holy life only in the hope of a personal self's surviving to enjoy rewards in eternity, one is substituting one form of mortal craving for another. Full extinction of self, and a conception of the soul as so intangible and impersonal that at death it disappears in the Absolute as candlelight disappears in the effulgence of sunlight: this, the Buddhists say, is necessary to the passing from worldliness into immortality.

The average man, impelled by "the lord that is self," lives a life in slavery to senses. But the self, the ego, like the senses and their craving, is a part of the mortal existence, subject to change, illusory, to be denied. In debate with a Brahman who defended worship and sacrifice the Master said: "The sacrifice of self is more effective than the offering of bullocks. He who offers up his evil desires need spill no blood at the altar. . . . The cleaving to self is a continuous dying; existence in truth is a partaking of life unchanging, of Nirvana."

The Buddhist denial or discipline of self, in so far as it means escape from bondage to the senses, is, of course, common to the method of all the great mystic religions; it is a standard part of the groundwork for illumination. Equally the Buddha discounted reason as other than a mortal, instrumental thing, as do the mystics in all ages. "Reason passes, but wisdom endures," he said. One must reason from a premise, but truth has neither beginning nor end.

For the rest, Buddhism agrees substantially with Hinduism. The Brahman and the Buddhist teachings about Karma and transmigration are alike, and there is the same emphasis upon the overwhelming importance of spiritual enlightenment as the first aim of human life.

The doctrine of Karma, or the law of cause and effect as applied to human conduct, of recompense for good and evil action, is of the very texture of both faiths. A man's Karma is his balance of righteousness and unrighteousness, of merit and demerit according to universal law. It is the resultant of his moral doing, the sum of his thoughts and deeds and their consequences. Man in being evil or good affects the whole balance of the universe. He builds up an account with all creation and with what lies beyond; he develops a character continuing (and gradually being perfected) through all incarnations. His "treasury of virtuous acts" is all he takes with him at death.

The doctrine implies a wider application of the familiar truth, "You shall reap what you sow." The Buddha put it this way: "Not in the heavens above, nor in the farthest reaches of the sea, nor by transporting yourself to the remotest valleys of the mountains, will you be able to hide from the consequences of your own evil actions. Likewise, certain are the blessings growing out of your good actions."

The doctrine of transmigration of the soul was adopted by the Buddha from Brahmanism. There is the difference that he rejected the conception of a surviving self-entity. Rather there is a transmission of a character or Karma-clot. Sometimes, however, he seemed both to reject and to admit an individualized soul: "When men die after complete emancipation from the bonds of lust, covetousness, and selfish cleaving to existence, they need not fear. . . . Nothing then remains but their Karma of good thoughts and good deeds, ending in the bliss that recompenses righteousness. Just as rivers must flow at last into the unbounded ocean, so their souls will be reborn in a higher place, pressing on to the eternal ocean of truth, the peace of Nirvana."

The doctrines of Karma and transmigration or rebirth lead to an ethical code among the most admirable devised by man. More detailed and regulatory than the Taoist, yet suggesting Lao-Tse in its emphasis upon non-interference, it is less particularized than the Christian. More stress is laid on getting one's *intention* right. More responsibility is put upon self-discipline. Buddhist morality is perhaps the most humane and compassionate of all the widely practised systems. The Blessed One gave point to his teachings when, coming with a group of monks upon a bhikshu who, they said, was too loathsomely ill to be nursed or touched, he bathed and tended the dying man himself.

"Those who have failed to work toward the truth," said the Buddha, "have missed the purpose of living." Truth to him is eternity, immortality, the essence, the uncreate. For the individual it is final liberation, emancipation. To attain emancipation is to attain Nirvana, at once extinction and entry into illumination. Nirvana is the ocean of peace, unlimited bliss.

The true purpose of living, then, is a mystic one: deliverance and absorption, annihilation, immersion. How does this attainment differ from the divine communion or illumination or absorption described by other spiritual seers? What is the special nature of the mysticism of the Buddha?

It is, first of all, if not an austere, remote, dehumanized conception of a soul-experience, at least the farthest removed from any experience to be described in sensuous or emotional terms. Only by forgetting the senses that are portals of the self, by repression of sense-images, by escape from the nets of personal attachment, can one imagine the nature of Nirvana. The bliss it postulates is the purest, least tainted by ideas bred of mortality. It is existence in a Heaven abstract and starless.

It should be added, nevertheless, that the austerity of the teaching as set forth in the word of the Buddha was, even by his own sayings, sometimes softened and eased. Accepted literally, the admonition to turn the mind from all that changes, to fix the attention solely upon the unchangeable, would seem to exclude love of nature. Yet the Blessed One is pictured as looking upon a familiar vista of river and village and trees with love in his heart. And is not the compassionate regard for "every living thing" a

ARAHAT ENTERING INTO NIRVANA. PAINTING BY LIN TING-KUEI. CHINESE, SUNG DYNASTY. MUSEUM OF FINE ARTS, BOSTON.

tacit recognition of a unity underlying all that is — a sort of extension of the thread of the immortal into each object of creation, rendering it lovable?

Other major bodies of mystics link the universal element in nature with the Absolute or the Divine. On the one hand they aspire to mergence in the Absolute; on the other they identify themselves with the sign or signature of immortality, the essence, in every encountered phenomenon. They detect the eternal and the holy quality in every thing, and their hearts stir toward it.

The Buddhist may, and often does, rise into the meditation or abstract reverie that spells forgetfulness of surroundings and happenings; but when he is free of that sort of intense concentration he finds a source of joy in nature and feels a communion with men and animals. He does not

> . . . See a World in a grain of sand
> And a Heaven in a wild flower . . .

nor does he trace God in a cloud. He stops far short of the Taoist obsession with the beauty of "unspoiled" nature. But the sense of the immanence of the Spirit in nature is strong in him. It softens a little the seeming rigidity of his injunction to abandon the world of changing phenomena. Even his warning against "attachment" to what is transient, which may seem inhuman because it rules out personal love, is somewhat negated by the obvious affection felt by the Blessed One for his favourite disciple and attendant, Ananda. Nor is there a clear line to be drawn between compassion as individually applied and love for the individual. Certainly the disciples confessed a warming affection for their Master.

The Buddha specifically exempted lay members of the order from several of the rules laid down to govern the conduct of the preaching brothers, those who had given up the world. He commended freely the lay members who decided against taking the monastic vow, approving kings who ruled wisely in the light of knowledge of the Path, and rich men who used their riches humanely, with loving-kindness, while renouncing luxury and lust and envy. He clearly promises that these actively compassionate lay members are on the way to entry into Nirvana. Apparently he believes also that, like the bhikshus, they may while still mortal know that liberation, that tasting of immortality, which is the mystic experience.

Of himself, in the period after attainment of Enlightenment and return to the world to complete his mission, he said: "Even while he is in the body, the Tathagata lives in the Pure Land, and knows its bliss." He approved those preparatory exercises, in the nature of retirement into seclusion, meditation, and concentration, that lead to loss of self in mystic consciousness of the Absolute. It is said that he neither approved nor forbade the set yoga practice as it was brought by converts from Brahmanism, the concentration by which the yogi attains detachment from worldly consciousness and entry into an ecstatic spiritual trance. It will be remembered that "right rapture" is the final stage in the Eightfold Path of Noble Conduct, and that it follows the seventh stage, "right meditation."

"I have during this life entered into Nirvana," he said, "and the life of Gautama is extinguished. The self has disappeared. The Truth has taken up its abode in me. The body is Gautama's; in due time it will be dissolved. . . . That dissolution will constitute the final extinction after which nothing survives to form another self. None can then say, the Blessed One is here, or there. It is just as with a flame in a sea of blazing fire. It has been, but it is gone. The flame has vanished, and one cannot say, it is here, or it is there."

It is the anticipation of the experience of Nirvana that sustains the Buddha during the return to life in the world, between the Supreme Enlightenment (at the age of thirty-five) and the entry into Final Nirvana forty-five years later. All the misery of the world, all the annoyances of administration of monasteries, all the obstacles and calumnies introduced by heretics and dissenters, fail to dim a radiant light and a flaming faith that the end is in bliss, eternal peace.

The spoken emphasis is, nevertheless, on cessation, deliverance, extinction. "There is, O Bhikshus," he once said to the disciples, "an escape from the cycle of the born, the originated, the created, the constituted; for there is the state of the unborn, the uncreated, the unconstituted. . . . It is a state where there is not earth or air or fire or water, neither space nor awareness, neither perception nor non-perception, nor nothingness. It is the uncreate. . . . It is the changeless, the eternal that is not originated and does not end. There is the extinction of suffering."

The Buddha Gautama left, indeed, little room for description of the blissful state. In erasing the self the doctrine seems to extinguish the experiencing power. Perhaps it would be fairer to say that the Buddhist places the emphasis upon the Absolute, not on the "I" participating in the Absolute. The Absolute, immortality, is Buddhahood, is finality. The average mystic of other faiths, though taken out of himself at every experience of union with the divine, looks forward — as a self — to further blissful experiences of that union in this life; all pointing, however, to final absorption and illumination not very different from the Buddhist Nirvana.

The word Nirvana, or *Nibbana* as it is in the Pali tongue of the time, meant, before the Buddha gave it a special religious or mystical significance, an extinction or a dying-out as witnessed in a dying fire. It was used in the sermons to denote the extinction of the flames of lust, craving, anger, and the like in the life of the Arahat. But shortly it came to mean the whole process of final liberation and emergence into illumination. Deliverance, emancipation, salvation, enlightenment (in the final sense): all this is implied in the term.

The Blessed One made a distinction between Nirvana and Final Nirvana. It was Final Nirvana, which is coincident with death or the final passing from mortality, that Mara, the Evil One, urged the Buddha to accept in the last of the temptation scenes; for he had already reached Nirvana, or, as it were, tasted Nirvana, in the moment of the Great Enlightenment. He then knew its radiancy, its bliss, was granted insight into the oneness of all that is, perceived the relationship of cause and effect, saw the Way and the Truth. But he then drew back from finality of absorption.

The "discipline by meditation," which prescribes five steps of preparation, appears in a late Buddhist document that may or may not be based on authentic utterances. It has, none the less, a suggestive interest. It begins: "First is the meditation upon love, in which your heart is enlarged until it longs for the well-being and the happiness of every living being, including the well-being and happiness of your enemies." The second meditation is upon compassion; the third upon joy; the fourth upon purification. The fifth details that other prerequisite so important to mystics of every time and clime, a serene mind: "Fifth is the meditation upon serenity; in this you rise above questions of riches or want, of conquest or slavery, of love or hate; you face your destiny, indifferent to self, calm, tranquil, in peace." Thus the initiate is prepared to enter into "the limitless light of truth."

Again there is a listing of the four stages of contemplation or states of vision on the way to final ecstasy or perfection, the four *Dhyanas*. The first is the state of seclusion, in which one puts aside the last traces of sensuality and desire. The second is the state of utter tranquillity. The third is passionless immersion in spiritual gladness. The fourth is the state of unconditioned perfection, of blissful release.

Because the Buddha wished, as he told the doubting monk, to keep the conception of a Paradise or Heaven on a spiritual plane above descriptions in sense terms, his sermons are bare of those opulent figurative passages in which mystical literature elsewhere so abounds. In *The Questions of King Milinda,* an early Pali book not generally considered canonical, there is, however, one such picture of the Buddhist after-world, suggestive of the Christian City of God, but instructively different, too, by reason of the abstract descriptive words: "A glorious city, stainless and undefiled, pure and white, ageless and deathless, secure, calm, and happy." Perhaps the writer of those lines had in mind a statement of the Blessed One recorded in an early canonical book, the *Mahavagga*: "I attained to the highest birth, and I found enlightenment. To you I have shown the noble path leading to *the city of peace.*" The lines are part of the sermon on "The Goal," quoted earlier, that ends: "This is deliverance, salvation, and the bliss of Heaven and life everlasting."

The mind harks forward twenty-four centuries to the words of an English poet: "If the doors of perception were cleansed, every thing would appear to man as it is, infinite." To the Tathagata, the Buddha-to-be, the cleansing had to be by fire. The doors of mortal perception — that is, the senses — must be cleansed, and their cravings and lusts annihilated in flame.

The thought is not far different from that of the quoted English poet — William Blake — for in the same verse he wrote: "The whole creation will be consumed and appear infinite and holy." He had in mind, one may believe, the cry of the Apostle Paul: "Our God is a consuming fire."

With these three religious mystics, two Christian, the other the founder of Buddhism, there is infinitely more of identity than of difference. When Blake, the Christian, cries, "Annihilate the selfhood in me!" he completes the line, addressing God, with the supplication, "Be Thou all my life." Annihilate my self so that I may disappear in Thee! The way of expressing the prayer is Christian; but substitute the word Nirvana for *Thee* (or *God*), and the sentence appears a paraphrase of a dozen statements from the sermons of the Buddha.

The burning away is identical. Cleanse, purify, sear the senses. Let the world of sense-cravings, of desire, of lust, be consumed. Cauterize the soul, to rid it of the infection of self. Burn away the passion for possessions, the carnal craving, the brutal reach for power, the greed for fame. Purify man of covetousness, cupidity, envy, anger, egoistic pride. When the flames die down there will be that other extinguishment, the mergence of the individual: in God in the one case, in Nirvana in the other.

Does it matter that Paul and the poet Blake called the place of attainment the City of God, while the Buddha named it the City of Peace? that the Christians termed it the Heavenly Jerusalem, while the Buddha spoke of it as the Universe of Delight?

The Blessed Buddha was one in an unending line of seers who have cried down the sense-ridden, self-infected mortal existence; who have celebrated as the highest and holiest aim of life the attainment of divine consciousness or Enlightenment or spiritual rapture. The "way" is by the fires of purgation, and the end is immersion or absorption — in Nirvana, or in God.

III. The Age of Reason in Greece: Pythagoras and Plato

Greece played the most glorious and at the same time the most tragic rôle in the drama unfolded by the nations of the ancient Western world. For a brief period of perfect integration and eventful climax the Greeks accomplished heroic deeds in the realms of the mind. No other triumph has been quite so bright and shining. But thereafter the descent to self-destruction was swift and unequivocal. The dénouement, as is right in serious tragedy, ensued from a defect of character, a basic shortcoming if not corruption in the life of the protagonists: the Greeks had no religion, or, more accurately, no common spiritual faith.

The ancient Greek tongue had no word for religion. To-day's books of the sacred writings of the world include no chapters from the Greek. Or if an editor ventures to insert, for the sake of coverage, a selection of myths and stories, they prove, in comparison with the profound spiritual literature of the Chinese, the Hindus, and the Hebrews, superficial, romantic, and unworthy. The Greeks conceived their gods as they did their art, in the image of man. The measure was not big enough. They believed in gods, but they had no God. They celebrated divinities symbolizing natural powers, but they knew no Divinity. The gods of Olympus were human beings magnified and embellished. They were human beings without mystery. They acted from common noble and ignoble motives, not seldom from envy or jealousy or lust — or from caprice, which least of all should be attributable to deity.

The Periclean century saw the perfecting of one of the two or three major ways of art. Then the Western clear-seeing, rationalizing mind brought to culmination the idealistic glorification of physical man. In the buildings on the Acropolis Greek architecture flowered with a simple beauty that was to be copied by builders down to the twentieth century. In poetry and drama Æschylus, Sophocles, and Euripides touched heights of literary and theatric expression never after surpassed. Western philosophy then found its form and texture: clear, rational, utilitarian. There was splendour in all this.

The gods of Olympus were not without their typically Greek

attributes of splendour, idealism, and robust healthiness. There is radiant beauty in the conceptions of Apollo, Aphrodite, and others. Nevertheless the whole constellation is basically literary and theatrical. It is Homer and Hesiod who give to the divinities their ranking and their attributes, their lineage and their functions. They are set up artificially. They are chosen and combined and crystallized out of a confusion of hundreds of native animistic "spirits" and imported gods, demi-gods, demons, and heroes. Their divinity is haphazard, unfocused.

Worship, if Greek homage to the Olympians can be called that, was official and hardly more than perfunctory. In the city-states the chief magistrate — politically elected or a buyer of the office, or chosen by lot — was high priest. In the end it was the politicians who fanned life into the state religion. With the spread of intellectual enlightenment, men of brains had fallen away into scepticism. The man of deep religious intuition was absent.

There were two circumstances that somewhat redeemed the shallowness of the Greek polytheistic religion. Philosophy, upthrust as a human expression in the place of a spiritual faith, gradually acquired some of the elements of religious belief. An immanent God appeared vaguely in the speculations of a line of reasoners pointing to Socrates and Plato. And for a chosen few in every community the mystery cults afforded a way into communion with God. If it were not for the comparatively small number of initiates, the mystery sects might be set forth as representing the real spiritual life of the Hellenes. And indeed the splendour of the Greek theatre was partly a result of the spirit of the mystery initiates who became playwrights and actors.

In general the Greek creative philosophers ignored the Olympian gods and legends or, like Plato, acknowledged them only sufficiently to stave off official persecution. (Socrates was, of course, put to death as an apostate and a teacher of heresies. Protagoras was condemned for impiety and died in exile.)

The ideas of God and of the immortality of the soul incorporated into Greek philosophy from the sixth century on were derived by one thinker after another from Egypt and Asia. There was also a link between philosophers and the mystery fraternities, which were, again, an imported institution, generally considered alien to the Greek genius. One finds Pythagoras, in the sixth century, modifying the teachings of his academic masters and accepting the ideas of a divine derivation of man, of immortality, and of divine experience through purification, atonement, and regeneration; one sees him, even, founding a brotherhood mystically inclined. Thus a search for mystic wisdom, even any generalized search for a sense of the divine among the Greeks, uncovers before Plato's time only two germane developments: the mystery religions and the Pythagorean brotherhoods. Unfortunately the Eleusinian and Orphic Mysteries, secret by nature, have left only the scantiest literature; and Pythagoras wrote no books. Plato, who inherited richly from Pythagoreanism, is the first major figure — with Socrates a preparatory and tentative prophet of Platonism.

Of Plato Emerson said that he compassed the excellences of Europe and Asia. He added that Plato "substructs the religion of Asia" under the metaphysics and natural philosophy that express the genius of Europe. The American sage saw that the greatest of Western philosophers had brought into his own mind illumination from the East. He had incorporated conceptions of the unbounded Infinite into the Western science-bound philosophy. Unfortunately his inclination toward Oriental transcendentalism affected the Greek nation and the drift of Greek history not at all. The Greeks continued in a course marked by religious dispersion, growing scepticism, and moral degeneration until their national heritage was hopelessly destroyed.

Plato escaped the Greek distrust of all that cannot be comprehended by reason. He posited a cosmic Good. Within it he placed man; man has, it appears somewhat hazily, a soul in the image of One God — a soul that returns to immortality. (To the Greeks generally, immortality is a blessing reserved for the gods.) But if these concepts imply a personal monotheistic religion and a personal moral uprightness, even an open door to mystical experience of the divine, Plato failed to impress them upon his followers.

Platonism never thereafter dies. But the schools of philosophy that immediately grow out of the master's teachings neglect the mystical aspect. They are scientific, utilitarian, and Godless. The first great figure in the mystical Platonic line after the founder is the Hellene Jew Philo, a contemporary of Jesus. Nor does the transcendentalism implied in Plato's words come fully ripe for still another two hundred years. Only then, in the third century after Christ, when the Greek nation has been five hundred years under foreign rule, does Greek mysticism arrive at flower. It is Plotinus, of Roman-Egyptian stock, trained in the Greek schools of Alexandria, writing in Greek, who mutes the scientific and political strains in Platonic doctrine and brings to full beauty the Orientalism of it. Plotinus is the first "possessed" mystic in the Greek line, the founder of Neo-Platonism, and a forerunner of the great mystics of the Christian Church.

After Plotinus, the stream of Neo-Platonism flows back to Athens, where it sweeps into Plato's own Academy; lends force to the effort to renovate Classicism as a rival of Christianity; then flows strongly into the Christian Church — through Augustine, who has been schooled in the Plotinian *Enneads* before his conversion, through Boethius in the sixth century, through Erigena, or John the Scot, in the ninth century. If only because his works inspired Plotinus and gave name to successive groups of mystic seekers, even to the Cambridge Platonists of the seventeenth century, Plato must be considered the key figure in substructing under the philosophy of Europe a base of Oriental transcendentalism; that is, of mysticism.

At the time of Plato's coming, Reason had become the keystone of the structure of Greek philosophy, and the life of Greece was built around those ideas that can be squared with reason: self-expression, competition, acquisition, physical health, a realistic art, a realistic polity, conquest by arms. The Greek centuries constitute the first Age of Reason.

Plato introduced doctrines repugnant to the apostles of Reason; and as he was forced to pay lip service to the gods of the official pantheon, he was forced likewise to compromise his faith, to keep silent, except for intimations and rare allegories, about his belief in the unity of all that is, the omnipotence of God, and the good that the soul may experience when it enters into "divine company." Nevertheless the foremost of Greek philosophers is a figure historically great in the succession of the world's spiritual prophets.

During the centuries of the triumph of reason it was the mystery religions that kept alive in Greece the ideal of divine dedication and the expectation of immortality. Obscured as the thread is at times, confused as are the lines of development, the mysteries persisted as an expression of the intuitive spiritual powers of man.

Their beginnings are lost in the haze that shrouds the waves of northern peoples coming into Greece. The end, more than a millennium later, is in a confusion of genuine mystery sects with a plethora of Oriental and pagan orgiastic cults, not seldom dedicated to the least spiritual forms of self-indulgence — the cults that, in the Roman world, lend such a lurid background light to the spectacle of Christians shaping a new and holy church. The Hellenic mysteries are of interest to us, not only intrinsically, but because they formed a channel leading into the supreme Western religion of resurrection and divine communion. The heart of the Greek celebrations, whether Eleusinian, Orphic, or Dionysian, was in a drama of death and resurrection.

For the individual, the climax of the mystery was initiation into divine wisdom. While the discipline became entangled at times in such sensational rites as the Bacchanalian orgies, it was essentially, for the novice, a discipline; and it led to a life of soberest, most courageous rectitude. Only a holy way of life on earth, according to the teaching, could lead to a blessed immortality after death.

The Hellenes, despite their devotion to Reason and the anthropomorphic measure, had divine capacity, and with not a few there was the nostalgia of the soul that compels flight to God. At times, the historians state, "the mystery religions swept Greece."

The denial of immortality in the Olympian religion, the lack of any conception of the divine in the human soul, the visualizing of man as material, egoistic, and self-sufficient — all this was insupportable for the intuitively religious person. Conformance, or worship of the conventional sort, though it might satisfy the masses and a certain number of intellectually mature but spiritually blind leaders, did not suffice for minds that had obtained glimpses or intimations of a life as "child of both Earth and glorious Heaven."

The mysteries of Eleusis were the most famous in Greece, and Athens, when Eleusis ceased to be a free city, took over the Eleusinian celebrations. A good deal is still to be learned about the rites (for the nature of the initiation and the drama formed a secret not to be divulged under penalty of death); but it seems established that at Eleusis the initiate was promised immortality in the future world and a happy life in this one, without the feature of divine communion or "possession by the god."

It was rather the Orphic and Dionysian mysteries that brought in richly the mystic element. To the rites of purification and the imparting of secret, sacred wisdom, was added the ceremony of union with the divine. Once a savage rite in which the celebrant partook of raw flesh (symbolizing the god), the sacramental act later took other forms, all symbolic of the re-entry of man into divine estate. In one a marriage of the soul to the god or goddess was consummated. In another there was shown the birth of the god, symbolizing personal attainment of godhood.

At Eleusis the drama of suffering, death, and resurrection centred upon Demeter, goddess of the fertile Earth, and Persephone, her daughter. The Orphic mysteries retold the story of Orpheus, who, it will be remembered, descended into Hades, charmed Persephone there with his music, led out his beloved Eurydice only to lose her again, and was torn to pieces by the Thracian women during a Dionysian orgy. It is likely that Orpheus was a real man (although traditionally he was the son of Apollo and of the Muse Calliope), a surpassing musician, and a prophet or priest of a Dionysian sect. Probably when he had established Dionysian rites he was martyred by his followers, torn to pieces as the Dionysus of the myths had been. In any case the Orphic and Dionysian mysteries became inextricably intermingled. And in the end the resurrection drama has elements of the stories of Demeter, Orpheus, and Dionysus.

Plato wrote — and the passage touches upon an essential doctrine of the Orphists — that "the founders of the mystery rites said in a figure that the man who passes without purification and uninitiated into Hades will remain in the dark of hopelessness; but he who comes there after initiation and sanctification will dwell with the gods." He adds the "figure": "Many are they that bear the wand, but few are the Bacchoi" — or, as Jowett translates it, "few are the mystics." That is, the Orphic teaching is that man living by ordinary standards, unenlightened spiritually, taking no steps to draw up out of the average materialistic life, bears no chance for immortality, can never dwell with the gods. Only a few, the mystics, by purification and dedication and regeneration, are prepared to lead the holy life in the wisdom that forecasts the soul's immortality, its return to the gods. These initiates, it is clear, in a subtle way *become* the god. They are possessed by him, they enter into him, they are identical with him.

Thus, though no name stands out as prophet or seer from among the *mystae* or initiates, the members of the Greek mystery fraternities are to be recognized as of the universal order of mystics. Their aim is union with the divine, resurgence of the god within themselves. They bring to Hellas (even before the philosophers) a conception of the human soul as divine by nature. They introduce self-discipline and holy living as means to immortality. They infuse ceremony with the highest spiritual feeling. They teach that spiritual consciousness can transform common life, much as Christian mystics were to preach illumination of everyday living by practice of the presence of God.

In the lesser or preparatory stages, too, the mystery religions parallel the more ancient religions of the East. The practices of purification and meditation, the study of the doctrine of suffering, symbolic death, and rebirth in divinity, and the withdrawal as far as possible from the sense-cravings and the contaminations of heedless worldly living, are familiar in every period of mystical awakening.

Much is made, moreover, of the uses of silence. The final words of the hierophant to the initiate, at the end of the mystery rites, were "Go in peace!" For the mind mystically aware they are words bearing overtones almost of rapture. "Go in peace!" When we exist in peace the mind is still, the soul is serene, the heart is tranquil; we move in harmony with the rhythm of the spheres; we partake of the sense of oneness of all that is. We are aware of the divinity of being.

Iamblichus of Syria early in the fourth century after Christ undertook the writing of a biography of the Greek philosopher Pythagoras. He approached his subject as a perfect biographer should: "under divine guidance, and with a quiet mind." He wrote: "I wish to set forth the fundamentals of religion as determined by Pythagoras and his followers. The test of all that they did or abstained from doing was consonance with divinity. Their first aim was converse with God. They shaped their lives in order to accord with his will. That is the foundation of their philosophy, because, they say, to search for good from any but the divine source is foolish."

Pythagoras, who was born on the Island of Samos about 580 B.C., departed the farthest of all Greek philosophers from the norm of Reason. It has been said, reproachfully, that he tried to shape philosophy to the outlines of the mystery religions. Again and again in the reading of the biography by Iamblichus, one is reminded of the typical Oriental seer, who so closely links religion and philosophy that one despairs of classifying him as a prophet in the one sphere or the other. Pythagoras is at once the most spiritual of Greek philosophers and the most philosophical of Greek religious leaders.

He took freely from the mystery faiths, and like the founders of the mysteries he organized a brotherhood of spiritual seekers. But if he inherited from Orphic doctrine, he added richly from other sources. As a young man he studied with the aged Thales of Miletus, counted first in the line of Hellenic philosophers, and with Anaximander, whose theory of the boundless or the infinite doubtless widened his mental horizon. When Pythagoras had completed his studies with the Ionian teachers, Thales insisted that he go to Egypt to learn from the priests, who "were the source of Thales' own reputation for wisdom." He is said to have spent twenty-two years with the Egyptian seers.

Where else Pythagoras travelled in the search for knowledge and inspiration is not fully known. He may have gone as far as Babylon and India. When he returned to Samos he achieved fame as philosopher, scientist, and teacher, and also was renowned for his "beauty, wisdom, and divine graciousness." About the year 529 B.C. he emigrated to Crotona, one of the fairest of the Greek cities in lower Italy. There he established his school and brotherhood. From this centre Pythagoreanism spread over all the colonies as well as the states of Greece proper.

The Pythagorean brotherhoods were celebrated for the holiness of their members. They were unlike the mystery fraternities in that the initiates lived together in communistic groups; and the "celebrations" were continual rather than occasional. On the other hand, Pythagoras as a philosopher established more than the sort of school or academy identified with the ancient philosophic teachers. Conduct, not faith or learning, was the test of membership. The cenobites first participated by reason of belief, but they remained only by reason of strict observance of rules of abstinence and conduct worthy of the basic aim, "consonance with God." The school at Crotona was a residential university, perhaps the earliest in Europe.

Eventually politicians and mobs came to resent the influence of the bands of Pythagoreans. They were attacked, their homes sacked, their assembly halls burned, and the members sometimes killed. It was about a hundred years after the founding of the brotherhood at Crotona that the worst wave of intolerance swept over both Greece and Italy. Sometimes the charges of heresy sufficed to stir the mobs, at other times charges of subversive political aims. Though the members were scattered, they did not change their way of life; and bands of Pythagoreans are heard of through the following five centuries. In some isolated cases they ruled their towns through generations.

Pythagoras was an eminent scholar in the field of mathematics and astronomy, one of the greatest of ancient times. His interest in numbers was both scientific and mystical, and his geometry was not unrelated to his theories of the cosmic order or "harmony"; though he is best known, in the science-led world, as a founder of the mathematical sciences. He was the first to discover the mathematical bases of music, and music entered generously into the spiritual training of his disciples.

It is said also that Pythagoras coined the word *philosophia*. It is easy to believe that "friends of Wisdom" came naturally to his mind as an appellation for his band of spiritual seekers. The word *sophia* alone had before sufficed among the teachers we now call philosophers. For a considerable time to be known as a philosopher was to be known as a Pythagorean.

In spiritual philosophy Pythagoras may have gone little ahead of the hierophants of the mystery cults. They too had inherited from Egypt and the East. Nevertheless he is the first known seer to have taught, in Greece, the divine origin of the human soul, the expectation of immortality, a pervading harmony of the spheres (hardly to be detached from the conception of a benevolent God), and the kinship of men and beasts. He taught also the doctrine of the transmigration of the soul.

His theory of a divine or immortal soul in a perishable body posed a certain opposition of spiritual and physical living. Without descending to mortification and rules of extreme abstinence, Pythagoras urged on his disciples a becoming asceticism.

He lived his own life with a saintly purity of purpose. He was temperate, putting strict limits upon the use of wine. Believing in transmigration, he was a vegetarian at table. He urged no celibacy upon his followers, and indeed he had a wife and children; but he trained the young people of the community to abhor incontinence and to combat with almost Buddhistic discipline the cravings of the senses. Pythagoras was the first teacher in Greece to admit women to higher education.

The teachings of Pythagoras about the conventional Greek gods were tolerant and expedient, except in the matter of blood sacrifices, which he forbade. Accept the popular gods, he advised, in so far as you must, to avoid offending believers; but if you feel the need to worship or to erect temples, do so in honour of the Muses, who stand for harmony, rhythm, and concord; or to gods who may be considered symbolic representations of the one unknowable Divinity.

If an understanding tolerance distinguished the attitude of Pythagoras toward the popular religion, it was little different from his stand regarding government and rulers. He foreshadowed a state or republic in which philosophers — in the Pythagorean true sense, as lovers of Wisdom — would be supreme; and it must have been difficult not to meddle in politics. But he cautioned his followers (and he had as many as six hundred at one time in the community at Crotona alone) to remember the wisdom of non-interference. His advice to them was: "Do not poke the fire with a sword."

Despite his caution he could not keep his community disentangled from local politics. His philosopher-saints may have done no more than become a noticeable aristocracy of intelligence; or they may have advocated purification and reform in the government. Some believe that their case was hopelessly complicated when a notorious politician and tyrant was denied membership in the brotherhood. The mobs at Crotona, stirred to violence, whether by charges of heresy or at thought of a flouting of democracy, stormed a building in which the members were meeting, killed those who resisted, and drove the rest from the city. Pythagoras may have been murdered then; or, as other accounts have it, he may have escaped to Metapontum, to die of starvation some time after.

Pythagoras wrote no books, and when one attempts analysis of his mysticism there are only stray sayings of his, or the second-hand or third-hand summaries by biographers who did not know the man. Occasionally a quoted aphorism illuminates his vision or his way of teaching. He said that "To begin is half the accomplishment." He spoke many precepts regarding silence, including this: "Of all forms of continence, the bridling of the tongue is the most difficult." The familiar testimony to the need for aloneness is in the admonition: "Leave the public roads, and walk in unfrequented paths."

By precept the Pythagoreans avoided conversation in the morning until they had prepared the mind and attained inner serenity. To this end they took long walks in solitude, to temples or groves or other sacred places. They also listened to music especially composed to foster a quiet clear-mindedness. Such recreational activities led, however, into strict routines of study and labour. Pythagoras said: "Do not offer the gods wine from an unpruned vine." He cautioned his disciples not to exhaust their energies by useless worry or the nursing of grievances. "Consume not your heart," he said. And to blusterers: "Threaten not the stars."

Of the doctrine of the oneness of all that is, and of the resulting kinship of men and beasts, Sextus Empiricus says: "The followers of Pythagoras, as of Empedocles and the other Italians, state that there is a bond of union which links a man not only to other men and to the gods, but also to the unreasoning animals. For there exists throughout the universe a pervading spirit, a sort of world soul, that binds us to the animals. . . . These philosophers appealed to men to spare creatures having a living soul; they said that it is an evil act when men 'stain the altars of the Divine with warm blood.'" Many stories have been told of Pythagoras's kinship with animals, not unlike those concerning the Taoist and Hindu sages, and similar to the legends of Saint Francis of Assisi.

The belief in a world soul is hardly to be distinguished from the Pythagorean belief in the rhythmic cosmic movement or order. The One exists not statically or substantially, but as a flow of life. The origin of all, the being of all, the kinship of all, is in the harmonious flow. To be perfectly in the rhythm is to be divinely attuned. Health is perfect bodily rhythm. Education is the opening of the being to the rhythm.

It is the attainment of the rhythmic movement — not merely numerical beat, symmetry, measure, harmonious proportion, but the strange, creative, unaccountable, asymmetrical rhythmic movement — that endows a work of art with life of its own, yet links it to the one Unity. Great art is the expression of the totality of life, its flow and its pausing, its regularity and its breaking of the measure.

Pythagoras, who was the first to measure musical vibrations and intervals, invented the curative use of harmony and melody of sound. In composing he combined his scientific knowledge with inspiration out of his awareness of the universal rhythm. Iamblichus speaks thus of his "medicinal" utilization of sound:

> With music's melodies and rhythm he built remedies for men's disorders and passions, restoring the natural harmony

of their faculties, curing body and soul alike. . . . In the
evening, before his followers retired to sleep, he would by
means of music free their minds from the excitements and
perturbations of the day, purging their consciousness of the
flow of thought and exertion, assuring quietude of sleep, and
dreams both blissful and prophetic. When they arose in the
morning he would similarly awaken their minds from any
persisting drowsiness or lassitude, by the production of ap-
propriate chords or arrangements, using the lyre or the voice.
It was not the instrument or the voice equipment that enabled Pythagoras to obtain this effect, but the ability to project a thing divine and indescribable. Though it is difficult to
comprehend, he had rendered so subtle his powers of inward
hearing that he vibrated to the sublime symphony of the universe. He heard and transmitted the harmonious order and
consonance of the spheres, and of the stars that move in con-
cert with them, producing a melody fuller and more profound
than is possible without divine penetration. . . . Pythagoras
conceived that this music arose out of the central spring and
origin of the universe.

In this, of course, Pythagoras is quite un-Greek. One is reminded inevitably of the Oriental painter and of the Taoist æsthetic of a life-rhythm in the picture. The artist divines something
out of his awareness of, his identification with, the One, the centre
of life, the rhythmic universal order; and he communicates the
sense of that order to the listener or beholder. But, say Pythagoras
and Lao-Tse alike, we can all be artists in living, in "the art of
being in the world." We too can identify ourselves with the One,
can attune ourselves to the cosmic rhythm.

As Pythagoreans we begin by purifying our minds and bodies.
We vow a life of self-discipline, moderation, and rejection of
riches and fame. We know that only the most whole-heartedly
generous conduct toward our fellow men will express our consonance with divine movement; we abide by an ethic meticulous
and humane. We study, as friends of Wisdom, as philosophers, all
that leads to understanding of the central mystery of divinity.
We know the uses of silence, solitude, and contemplation. We
have faith in immortality, look forward to death as merely a
translation back to the soul's element. Above all we go about our
daily tasks, year in and year out, with a radiant awareness that

we are privileged to converse with God, and that every action, every impulse, is lighted from the transcendental Source.

Photius preserved a short biography of Pythagoras by an unnamed author, in which occurs this summary passage (though it is here shortened and rearranged):

> Man gains improvement in three ways. First, he converses with God — and to approach Him he must have stamped all evil out of the self, he must have followed the course of imitating the divine, he must even have identified himself with God. Second, he lives a life of good deeds, for all goodness binds one to divinity. Third, he will be finally improved in dying; for if by discipline of the body he has been able to lift the soul away toward God in life, how much more certain and rapturous will be the cleaving to God when the soul leaves the body altogether at death!

There is a story, sometimes branded apocryphal, of a meeting of Socrates with a Hindu sage who visited Athens to study Greek ways. The Hindu asks: "What, Socrates, is the substance of your teaching?"

"Human affairs."

"But," objects the Oriental, "can you know about human affairs if you do not first know about divine?"

Of all the philosophers of Athens — and there were innumerable "sophists" teaching there — Socrates would be the first to recognize and admit that the Hindu scholar had exposed a shallowness in Greek thinking.

Pythagoras had died in 496 B.C. During the following half-century, until the wave of popular fury broke over the brotherhood, his disciples conducted Pythagorean schools in many cities of Italy and the mother country. They had influence upon Socrates, who was born a quarter-century after Pythagoras' death; their effect upon Socrates' pupil, Plato, was profound.

Aside from the Pythagoreans, philosophy was following a course in which reason and science were claiming an ever-increasing allegiance. Egoism and utilitarianism, basic in Greek living, diverted philosophers from the search for wisdom in idealistic or spiritual realms. As always in utilitarian or so-called "realistic" eras, scepticism flourished.

Socrates came of age as a philosopher when the two streams,

Pythagorean or near-mystic and rationalist, were flowing side by side. On most matters he let himself be drawn into the stream of "believers in the soul"; but he did little to stem the stream of belief in reason, materiality, and expediency.

Socrates founded no academy; but every meeting with friends was a class. He founded no brotherhood, claimed no disciples; but in the end he was put to death because he had changed the lives and beliefs of those who went to the agora, the street corner, or the athletic field to hear him talk. Conversation was his method. He had a provoking, taunting tongue, and he was diabolical in his cleverness at leading a student or opponent into damaging admissions and contradictions.

He was least sparing of himself. When a petitioner asked "Who is the wisest man in Greece?" the Delphic Oracle (which had the motto "Know thyself" on the temple wall) answered "Socrates." And Socrates, pondering how this could be, came to the expressed conclusion that "I am named the wisest because I am sufficiently wise to know that I know nothing."

He was kindly and humorous. If a friend implied sympathy because he had the shrewish Xantippe for a wife, he put in a sufficient defence, then let on that he had married her knowingly, as a matter of self-discipline. And he took her outbursts as a philosopher should. He gave her cause enough for irritation with his casual ways, his improvidence (for he was above accepting money for his wisdom), and his absent-mindedness. If he ever worked for a living — and there is no undisputed record that he did — it was as a sculptor or stone-cutter. Physically he was under-sized and homely.

It may be questioned to what extent he was a mystic. That he enjoyed a sort of divine guidance is certain. That he gave himself up in the mystic's way to self-loss in God is less apparent. The truth seems to be — and there is no more evidence than can be gleaned from the imaginative Plato's writings and those of the hardly less fictional Xenophon — that Socrates had all the preparatory equipment and belief of a mystic, but that the culmination was generally lacking: his participation in the divine, his communion, was an intellectual's compromise. A true Greek thinker, an incorrigible reasoner, he came to the gates, perceived beyond them the divine reality, but could not enter because he could not divest himself of the intellect's questioning, the logician's unholy drag of thought.

On the one hand, these are the facts assembled when one undertakes to prove that Socrates was a spiritual innovator, mystically inclined:

(1) He put concern for the soul first in the conduct of individual life, before concern for possessions or bodily satisfactions or position or fame. In this his example was as eloquent as his theory. When he attended a market fair he speculated, not upon the means by which he might buy things, but upon how many things there were that he did not need or desire. He said that to want the least possible is to bring one the nearest possible to the gods. He said further that he had no other business than to go about persuading people to attend to the perfecting of their souls.

(2) From the desire to perfect the soul he inferred the necessity to conduct oneself decently, considerately, charitably — and in this he helped to establish the question of morality as central in philosophic study, opening one of the channels toward Christian thought.

(3) He believed in God, and that God's design is good. The universe or the world-mind is provident and benevolent — a view very narrowly held among the Greeks before him.

(4) He counted the soul a part of the divine essence; and though he disclaimed any opinion of what the after world is like, he endorsed the Pythagorean doctrine of immortality; it might be no more for the soul than an eternal night undisturbed, or it might be a place of eternal companionship and communion with the great and the wise — for "they will be immortal, if what is said is true." He adds that "No evil can befall a good man, either in life or after death," almost in the Buddha's words.

(5) He prayed not for the things or favours that are the objects of most men's petitions. His simple prayer was "Grant what is good for my soul."

(6) He experienced spells of raptness, during which he was oblivious to surroundings. One morning when he was away at the wars he took his stand near the camp, looking away in meditation. All day he stood immobile. At night the puzzled soldiers (who knew him for as brave a fighter as any among them) took up positions to observe him. Only when the sun rose did he break the spell, salute Apollo, and return to common affairs.

(7) He had also a link with the divine source of wisdom, a silent "voice" that prompted him to reject certain ideas or actions. It was something beyond thought or reason, intuitive, of the na-

ture of inspiration, not to be questioned. He said: "You have heard me tell of an oracle or sign that simply comes to me. . . . This sign I have experienced since childhood." And again: "The gods themselves give us this intimation."

But even with so much of the mystic's equipment, so well prepared by controlled living, selflessness, and awareness of signs from God, even recognizing the divine origin of the soul and its immortal destination, Socrates seems to fail of the mystic's ecstasy and absorption. Proof is lacking that his ceaselessly inquiring intellect ever let his intuition fully have its way. His rapt spells, his meditations, were — for all we know — mental, active, not thoughtless plungings into the ocean of divine consciousness. There is no description of the final act of union, of the state of being in God. His surrender is to the abstraction of thought, not to envelopment in the Absolute.

The oracle, the signs, that link him to a power which, as he said, "knows all things, what is done, what is said, and what passes silently in the mind, which is everywhere present" — those signs go not beyond divine guidance. They are out of Heaven; they fail to take him, before death, into Heaven. Socrates is typically the sage mystically inclined but held back by the temper, the drag, of his place and time. Greek rationalism defeats him.

And yet — there is the puzzling and the propitious way of his death. Certainly it is the death of one resting content in divine protection.

His attitude toward those who are, as they suppose, "legally" putting him out of the way is the chiefest evidence that he is guilty of the charges upon which he is tried — guilty of a faith, and of the teaching of a faith, at variance with that of the political-minded Athenian citizens. One is tempted to believe, in reading the testimony in his defence as so beautifully reported by Plato, that the man's serenity, his certainty, *is* born of faith, not reason. There is the vital ring of the voice of an initiate, of one who has committed all to God, who has known His nearness.

Perhaps — and not least persuasive are the historians who imply as much — the charge and trial came about because Socrates was suspected of being a Pythagorean and suspected of teaching, under guise of a mysterious, voice-guided personal faith, the beliefs of the heretical Sage of Crotona. That those teachings would include the strictest morality and non-interference would make no difference to the inflamed accusers of a vagrant philosopher in a city-state well-nigh torn to pieces in recent wars, rebellions, and political treacheries. Socrates in the light of martyr for his undeclared belief in Pythagorean morals and monotheism is a conception not too forced. Scholars have inferred even the existence of a cultish "school," with Socrates at its centre, and a doctrine drawn partly from Pythagorean and Orphic sources.

The philosopher, homely as always but with a kindliness lighting the satyr-like face, at the age of seventy years is brought before the Athenian supreme assembly on the charge: "Socrates is guilty of crime in refusing to worship the gods sanctioned by the State, and of introducing new divinities of his own. Furthermore he is guilty of corrupting youth." The judges are the members of the assembly, chosen for no better reason than the appearance of their names on the list of free citizens; alphabetical rotation has made them judges for the day. The accusation is made: heresy and teaching heresy to the youth of the city.

When asked before the trial if he had prepared a defence, Socrates had said simply that all his life he had been living what should be his defence. Now, in effect, he lays his life before his accusers and judges. He speaks calmly, confidently, even a bit scornfully. He believes that through the years he has spoken for truth and justice. Let them judge on that basis.

He is voted guilty. When he is asked whether he wishes to suggest a penalty, he refuses, as they see it, to be serious. It will be just, he answers, if they reward him not with the death demanded by his accusers, but with the honour of a place in the prytaneum; or if it must be a penalty, why not a nominal fine, say one mina? —he is, after all, practically penniless. A second vote is taken. This time the imposed penalty is death.

Permitted a response, Socrates is as unperturbed as ever, and he rises to new heights of clear speaking. The trouble in life, he says, is not to escape death; even a soldier can accomplish that, by throwing off his arms and begging mercy. "The difficulty, my friends, is not to avoid death, but to avoid evil; for it runs faster than death." At the condemnation his inner voice, his divine faculty, has given no sign, he says, that an evil has befallen him. "This is an intimation that those who believe death to be a calamity are in error." He paints the after life as either a single night of undisturbed rest or a continuing companionship with the souls of

SOCRATES. BUST BY AN UNIDENTIFIED GREEK SCULPTOR. NATIONAL MUSEUM, NAPLES.

the wise — "Assuredly it will be a world where they do not put a man to death for asking questions."

He is condemned to drink the cup of hemlock. Because of the incidence of holy days there is a month's delay. His friends bribe the jailers to release him. It is he who refuses to leave the jail, for law and legal justice, he insists, must be respected.

On the day appointed for the execution, Socrates converses with his friends and disciples as he has so often done, this time in the prison. He has talked most of the day, especially about the immortality of the soul. Plato tells of the end inimitably well. Socrates is speaking:

> A man of sense ought not to say, nor will I be very confident, that the description which I have given of the soul and her mansions is exactly true. But I do say that, inasmuch as the soul is shown to be immortal, he may venture to think, not improperly or unworthily, that something of the kind is true. The venture is a glorious one and he ought to comfort himself with words like these, which is the reason why I lengthen out the tale. Wherefore I say, let a man be of good cheer about his soul, who having cast away the pleasures and ornaments of the body as alien to him and working harm rather than good, has sought after the pleasures of knowledge; and has arrayed the soul, not in some foreign attire, but in her own proper jewels, temperance, and justice, and courage, and nobility, and truth — in these adorned she is ready to go on her journey to the world below, when her hour comes. . . . Soon I must drink the poison; and I think that I had better repair to the bath first, in order that the women may not have the trouble of washing my body after I am dead. . . .
>
> Now the hour of sunset was near, for a good deal of time had passed while he was within. When he came out, he sat down with us again after his bath, but not much was said. Soon the jailer, who was the servant of the Eleven, entered, and stood by him, saying: To you, Socrates, whom I know to be the noblest and gentlest and best of all who ever came to this place, I will not impute the angry feeling of other men, who rage and swear at me, when, in obedience to the authorities, I bid them drink the poison — indeed, I am sure

that you will not be angry with me; for others, as you are aware, and not I, are to blame. And so, fare you well, and try to bear lightly what must needs be — you know my errand. Then bursting into tears he turned away and went out. Socrates looked at him and said: I return your good wishes, and will do as you bid. . . .

Raising the cup to his lips, quite readily and cheerfully he drank off the poison. And hitherto most of us had been able to control our sorrow; but now when we saw him drinking, and saw too that he had finished the draught, we could no longer forbear, and in spite of myself my own tears were flowing fast; so that I covered my face and wept, not for him, but at the thought of my own calamity in having to part from such a friend. Nor was I the first; for Crito, when he found himself unable to restrain his tears, had got up, and I followed; and at that moment Apollodorus, who had been weeping all the time, broke out in a loud and passionate cry which made cowards of us all.

Socrates alone retained his calmness: What is this strange outcry? he said. I sent away the women mainly in order that they might not misbehave in this way, for I have been told that a man should die in peace. Be quiet then, and have patience. When we heard his words we were ashamed, and refrained our tears; and he walked about until, as he said, his legs began to fail, and then he lay on his back, according to directions. . . . And he said: When the poison reaches the heart, that will be the end. He was beginning to grow cold about the groin, when he uncovered his face, for he had covered himself up, and said — they were his last words — he said: Crito, I owe a cock to Asclepius; will you remember to pay the debt? The debt shall be paid, said Crito; is there anything else? There was no answer to this question; but in a minute or two a movement was heard and the attendants uncovered him; his eyes were set, and Crito closed his eyes and mouth.

Such was the end, Echecrates, of our friend; concerning whom I may truly say, that of all men of his time whom I have known, he was the wisest and justest and best.

Upon that execution day, while he was talking with his disciples and friends, himself happy if not radiant, trying to persuade them to his own view of the immortality of the soul and to the certainty that no harm could assail it, Socrates had said — and there is room for mystic interpretation here:

> I am quite ready to agree that I should be sad about dying if I were not persuaded that I am going to the company of gods wise and good — of this I am as certain as is possible in any such matter; and that I am going also, though of this I am less sure, to the company of men already departed, who are better than the company I leave behind. . . . Experience has proved that to have pure knowledge of anything we must be rid of the body. The soul in herself must perceive things in themselves. Only then shall we attain the wisdom we desire, of which we as philosophers are lovers: not while we live, but after death. . . . In mortal life, I believe, we approach nearest to truth when the body is least intruded, when we have not given way to the corporeal nature, having kept ourselves pure toward the hour when God pleases to release us. Rid of the foolish body, we shall be pure and we shall commune with the pure, and ourselves attain the pure light which is none other than the light of wisdom. . . . Therefore I depart with rejoicing.

He speaks then of "the mind made ready" and of "purification," and he adds the words that have echoed down the corridors of time, in the writings of Plotinus and the Neo-Platonist mystics of Christendom: "And what may purification be if not the disengagement of the soul from the body: the soul released and re-collecting herself, and then dwelling in her own estate, alone, as in another life — so also in this life if it can be accomplished. . . ." And:

> Were we not saying that the soul when using the mortal senses as instruments of perception is dragged by the body into the realm of the changeable, and acts uncertainly, . . . but when she collects herself, returning into herself, that is, entering into the realm of the pure, the eternal, the immortal, the unchanging, which are of her kind, when she is again herself, without hindrance, then the soul escapes from erring, mortal ways; absorbed into the unchanging she is unchanging. And that is the state of the soul called Wisdom. . . . That soul, I say, herself invisible, departs into the eter-

nal, the divine, the absolute. Arrived there she is secure of bliss. . . . Forever she dwells, as is true of the initiated, in communion with the gods.

Thus certain, thus happily expectant, Socrates shamed his grieving friends when the jailer handed him the cup of hemlock. Xenophon said: "Within the memory of man no one ever bowed his head more beautifully to Death."

The Golden Age in Greece came to an end almost at the moment of the death of Socrates. Plato was then twenty-seven years of age. Among the Hellenes the Golden Age had not been a time of divine intercourse of men and gods, a time of simple, serene living and spiritual enlightenment, as in the Orient. Rather, among the Greeks it had been the great age of expression in the arts, the time of expanding commerce and empire-building, of the appearance of systematic science and of reasoned philosophies.

But at the opening of the fourth century B.C. the Periclean tide of creation had spent itself. There were to be no further Parthenons upon which architects and sculptors would collaborate to achieve timeless beauty. Of the great tragedian poets, Euripides and Sophocles had died in 407 and 406. Athens was nearing the end of the thirty-year Peloponnesian War and the crushing defeat at the hands of Spartan armies, and was destined for further disorder and decline; was, indeed, in the last uncertain season of Athenian independence, before the capitulation to Macedon. Only philosophy and science were to continue to be grounds of expansion and advance. Yet Athens humbled, and in so many ways the scene of a degenerate life, was destined to be for several generations yet a centre of education in Europe, largely through Plato's founding of a university.

When Socrates had passed it was Plato who carried on in the mystical current. Devoted disciple of the great market-place philosopher, Plato was utterly different as a man: cold, reserved, aristocratic, literary. Yet he enriched the spiritual element in the Socratic belief, steeped himself in the Pythagorean sources, studied Oriental thought, and shaped in his writings the Platonism that has remained, in all ages since, one of the chief monuments of Western philosophy. Plato's was the most illuminated mind of his time.

Born about the year 427 B.C., of noted aristocratic families on both sides, Plato was educated as a noble. His father died early, and he was brought up in the home of a great-uncle who was prominent in the political life of Athens. Other relatives, the well-known Critias and Charmides, also were political figures. Plato at first was destined for a political career.

Socrates, a friend of the family, presumably was an influence upon Plato from an early age. At eighteen the youth became one of the old philosopher's followers, and for three or four years was closely associated with him. What other education Plato had was probably the standard training in literature, mathematics, rhetoric, music, and athletics. Probably he studied under other philosophers than Socrates, for Athens was a meeting-ground for sophists, popularizers of wisdom specializing in rhetoric, all willing to impart their learning for a fee.

Athens was seldom more chaotic politically than in the years of Plato's young manhood. He held off from participation because he was shocked by the violence of the rule of the oligarchic Thirty. Their obvious dishonesty and criminality, in which his close relative Critias was a leader, gave place, in 403 B.C., to a democracy dissentious and weak. When the democratic way of rule led to the execution of the wise and benevolent Socrates, Plato renounced politics for good. A rich man and an instinctive aristocrat, he could not stomach the practices of his own set while in power; and he thought democracy hardly better than mob rule.

He was absent, by reason of illness, from the group of disciples and friends present when Socrates drank the hemlock. With a number of them, however, he went to Megara immediately, to escape reminders of so great an injustice. There he stayed with the philosopher Eucleides. It is probable that only at this time did his mind turn to philosophy as a possible life work. He had written a great deal of poetry, but had, upon comparing it with that of Homer and the tragic poets, burned his manuscripts *in toto*. He had specialized in studying music for a time; then had taken up painting. Now the work of a philosopher, of a formulator and teacher of wisdom, called him from all other pursuits. It may be that the change was in the nature of a "conversion."

He travelled extensively in Greece, then went on to Egypt to study the religion and thought of that ancient land. Returned home, he found the Athenian atmosphere still uncongenial, and about 387 he proceeded to Italy. His inclination and his friendships took him to one of the Pythagorean communities. As Socrates had been deeply influenced by Pythagorean beliefs, so Plato absorbed a great deal that went into the shaping of his philosophy.

Before sailing for home Plato went to see the famed Mount Etna. He travelled on to Syracuse, where he greatly displeased, by his views upon good rule, the parvenu Tyrant of Syracuse. The ruler took revenge by betraying him into the hands of the Spartan ambassador. Put up for sale in the slave market in Ægina, Plato was recognized and bought in by an admirer. Freed, he made his way back to Athens. There a group of rich friends, hearing of his misadventure at Syracuse, had made up a purse to ransom him. When the admirer who had purchased and freed him refused to be reimbursed, Plato used the ransom money to establish a school of wisdom, partly on the pattern of the personal schools of the sophists, partly on the model of the Pythagorean communities.

For this institution of his dreams he established, about a mile from Athens on the road to Eleusis, the Platonic Academy, destined to be, during its nine centuries of service to learning, one of the greatest universities of Europe. The name was taken from the surrounding park or grove, which had belonged to an owner named Akademos — who thus unwittingly became the godfather to untold thousands of "academies" down the ages. The rest of Plato's life (he was now forty years of age) was given largely to teaching mathematics and philosophy at the Academy.

Twice he broke the continuity of his teaching work, in 367 and 361, both times to go to Sicily. Having expressed himself theoretically on the subject of the ruling of an ideal state, he was given the dubious opportunity of tutoring the young Dionysius II, successor as Tyrant of Syracuse. The experiment failed.

The Academy put less stress upon the spiritual life than did the persisting Pythagorean communes, but it was technically a religious institution, known as a place dedicated to the Muses. Religion, or the holy life, was taught to the students — women as well as men — as a part of basic philosophy. The other foundation study was mathematics. The students had the inestimable advantage of personal contact with their master Plato: the truest way of education. And yet there was lacking the spiritual fellowship and dedication to transcendental ideals known to the Pythagorean groups.

The atmosphere of the Academy was, in short, intellectual. Of the many distinguished philosophers and scientists who studied under Plato, none became a noted spiritual leader. Aristotle, the most famed of the graduates, turned scientific and realistic. Variously, others who absorbed Plato's teaching became famous as Cynics or Stoics or hedonists, as political economists or demagogues or logicians. (Hostile critics even attacked the Academy as a training school for tyrants.) Nevertheless Plato's written words lived on to inspire the most persistent train of mystic inquiry and devotion to be traced in the history of the Western world.

The only typical Greekness of his contribution is in the reasoned clarity of the prose in which he wrote his Dialogues; though it might be considered also a Greek trait, a result of the national glorification of citizenship, that he subordinated all his ideas, of religion, philosophy, æsthetics, and morals, to a conception of an ideal state as originally outlined in the *Republic* and modified in the works of his old age. There is no other idea of his quite so outstanding as this: that philosophers must become the rulers of men, or kings and princes take on the wisdom and power of philosophy.

At Syracuse he had tried sincerely and unselfishly to influence a ruler — to make over a tyrant. Not only had he failed, but his later years were disturbed by echoes of renewed strife in Syracuse. One of his own disciples, Callippus, gone to the Sicilian city on an idealistic mission, turned traitor and murderer, seizing the ruling power and becoming, for a brief interval, himself a tyrant. The Academy was thus brought into disrepute. Nevertheless there were serene and sunny years toward the end, with further teaching and writing. Plato died in 347 B.C. in his eighty-first year.

The heart of Plato's mysticism is in his tracing back of love to an eternal source, in the idea of the soul's turning from objective love to love of the Absolute. The archetypal values, the Ideas of Beauty and of Good, are oftener than not posed where God or Divinity or the One would be in cultures more God-centred than the Greek. But the passion for the essence of Good or of Beauty is a movement toward the centre, and it entails discipline, purification, contemplation, and entry into a spiritual communion. There is, moreover, when transcending Love has been attained, a return movement of the spirit, so that signs of the Eternal are detected in people and creatures and the manifestations of nature.

Here, indeed, is a framework adequate to a mystic interpretation of life.

Plato's faith is so much a flowering of the Socratic philosophy that no dividing line can be drawn between the expression of the one man's belief and the other's. The older man's words are preserved almost solely in the younger one's reports. But Plato lived more than a half century after the death of his master; and the spiritual beliefs that are so often repeated toward the end may fairly be considered his own — even though the most vivid expression of them be assigned to Socrates in the Dialogues.

The truth that is basic for both sages, the reliance upon the pursuit of wisdom as fundamental in the good life, and the sequent necessity of virtuous conduct or purification: this is asserted again and again — as in these words ascribed to Socrates in the *Phaedo*: "Is there not, my dear Simmias, one true coin for which all things should be exchanged, and that coin wisdom? Only in exchange for this, and in light of its value, is anything truly bought or sold, whether fortitude or temperance or justice. And is not all true virtue the companion of wisdom . . . ?"

Plato similarly reiterates that the soul partakes of immortality — this, it will be recalled, was still, in his century, outside the doctrine of the official Greek religion — and he sometimes used the figure so common among the Buddhists, of the body as the prison-house of the soul. In the *Phaedo*, putting the words into the mouth of Socrates, Plato speaks of the conception as one somewhat foreign, yet to be tested, in these words: "In one of the mysteries the figure is used that man is, as it were, held in a prison-house, and that he may not free himself and escape. This saying is too high for me. . . ." In the *Cratylus* he enlarges upon the idea: "Some say that the body is the tomb of the soul, as if the soul were buried in mortal life." There is also, he adds, among the followers of Orpheus, "the idea of the soul undergoing penalties, and shut up in the body as in a prison. The body is its keeping-place until the soul has served its sentence."

The prison-house idea, however, does not hold Plato for long. He does not emphasize it or permit himself to fall into a dark view of mortal life. Rather he believes that the sojourn of the immortal soul on earth has its place, even its pleasures. And, of course, the soul on earth has its duties, as the only true guide to living. "The soul of the philosopher will calm passion; she will follow reason; she will dwell in contemplation of the eternal, the divine, and the unchanging, and take nourishment therefrom. Thus she seeks to live while here; but she looks forward to release from human ills, to a return to her own kind, to that of which she essentially is."

It is in the *Phaedrus,* a dialogue of the middle period, that Plato paints one of his few pictures of the abode of the immortals — of Heaven or Paradise. "Of the Heaven which is above the heavens, what earthly poet has ever sung or yet will sing worthily? . . . There abides the ultimate Being, with which truth is concerned: the Essence, formless, intangible, colorless, visible only to Intelligence, the pilot of the soul." Of the manner of the individual soul's seeing in that Heaven, he adds:

> The intelligence of each soul capable of receiving the soul's inheritance is enraptured at beholding the Absolute, is fulfilled and rejoices. . . . She sees justice and temperance and absolute knowledge, not as these things are seen in the generative world, relatively, but with comprehension of their essential nature, in absolute existence. With that clairvoyant eye, she sees the truth of being, and glories at the sight, and so passes to the innermost Heaven and is at home. Such is the life of the gods. . . .

And Plato, aware of both the delights and the difficulties of the mystic existing among worldly, striving men, goes on to say:

> A man must have a sort of intelligence of the Absolute, . . . a recollection of those things which the soul beheld when it was in the company of God, an escape from relative being in the apprehension of true Being. In this, the mind of the philosopher alone has wings. To the extent of its enlightenment, it recollects those things in which Divinity abides. The philosopher thus experiences that which makes God divine. In the right use of such recollection he is continually re-initiated into the mysteries, and he alone among mortals takes on perfection. Because he is careless of worldly interests, being rapt in the divine, the crowds deem him mad; for they do not recognize inspiration.

There is a passage that links this conception of the philosopher as mystic to Plato's doctrine of the Idea of Beauty:

> He who loves the Beautiful is called a lover because he partakes of that inspiration. . . . Few men retain a real remembrance of the holy things they previously saw. Those few, beholding here on earth an image or reminder of that other world, are rapt in wonder, though they do not know what their rapture means. . . . We who are lovers of wisdom, in allegiance to Zeus or other gods, saw Beauty shining bright. We saw the blissful vision, and we were initiated into a mystery beatific and of primal innocence. We took part, purged of evil, untainted; we were admitted to see visions of the time of innocence, simplicity and happiness, apparitions in pure light — and ourselves no less pure, not enclosed in the prison that is called the body. Beauty, I repeat, we have seen shining there among the celestial forms. . . .

The beautifully reasoned and lucid dialogues of Plato are studded with "myths," poetic or imaginative interpolations in which the author escapes the limitations of argument and demonstration. There are, he seems to say periodically, truths that cannot be proved, experiences not to be sensibly explained. All that belongs in life to a man's faith, vision, and spiritual aspiration finds expression outside the routine of chain reasoning; and so he suddenly halts the logical discourse, abandons dialectic for creative picturing.

The Platonic metaphysic, the painting of an immortality of the soul, of an after life, of a fore-life of the soul, of a yearning toward the beautiful, is most richly revealed in the myths embedded in the *Phaedrus,* the *Symposium,* the *Phaedo,* and the *Timaeus.* Failing to make his points convincing by argument, he resorts therein to imaginative poetry, as spiritual prophets have been impelled to do throughout the ages. (Jacob Boehme was to say, twenty centuries later, condemning logic: "God goes clean another way to work.")

The myth in the *Phaedo,* a part of the discourse of Socrates and his friends in the hours just preceding his death, ends with the completest of Plato's affirmations of an immortal destination of the soul: "Those who have been exceptionally holy in their way of living are released from mortal limitations; they escape from the confinement of the body and rise to pure mansions above, and dwell as in a better land. If they have purified themselves by devotion to Wisdom they live thenceforward without the slightest bondage to the flesh, in still fairer mansions, indescribable even had I time to tell more. . . . The prize is fair and the hope is great."

Plato's "doctrine of Ideas," which is basic to his philosophy and a departing point for mystical speculation among countless Platonists down the ages, is especially shadowed forth in the myth of the *Phaedrus* (so far as the Idea of Beauty is concerned) and in the myth of the *Symposium*. The "doctrine of Ideas" posits the thought that there are universals or essences or absolutes — which Plato prefers to term Ideas — of every such attribute as beauty, goodness, and justice. The attributes may appear, incompletely and fleetingly, in the changing, fluctuating mortal world; their appearance is but the vague, relative reflection of the thing as it essentially is. The Idea, at the centre of life, in Eternity, is the reality; the manifestation is fragmentary, unreal, illusory. The cases or instances or examples of beauty or justice in the world are transitory, subject to decay and death. The Idea alone is unchanging, eternal. And of course the soul that knows its own immortality looks to the essence, the absolute, beyond or through the phenomenal manifestation. It is the part of wisdom to clear the way to that clairvoyant seeing.

Perhaps the Idea of Good should be taken as a sort of container or framework for all the other Ideas. Here the Good is not virtue or ethical conduct or a moral ideal, but Good in the sense of what is finally best for man's soul. The Idea of Good is Perfection, First Cause, even God. Its counterpart can be found in Oriental philosophy as the One, the Absolute, Infinity, the Source. As manifested in man it is at once the intuition toward God and the power that struggles against the lower cravings and passions, the power that steels man to renounce worldliness, to "re-collect" the soul and to build life around its needs.

In line with Socrates' benevolent universe, the Platonic Good is normal. "The world," Plato avers, "is the fairest of creations, and the Creator the best of Causes." And: "The Idea of the Good is the highest wisdom. All things are useful and helpful only when added to this. If we lack understanding of the Beautiful and the Good, though we learn all else to perfection, it profits us nothing;

for then we own everything but do not possess the essence, the soul. . . . That which gives reality to the known is the Idea of Good."

In the same discourse, the *Republic*, at the end of the famous allegory of the cave, Plato has Socrates say: "I believe that in the progression of knowledge the Idea of Good is apprehended last of all, and after effort. When at last attained it is discovered to be the animator of all that is beautiful and right, the creator of light and of that which sheds light upon our visible world, and the source of truth and reason. . . . The instrument of knowledge [the eye] together with the whole soul must be turned away from the world of becoming and toward the world of Being, until it can endure the vision of the most resplendent and highest of Being, that is, the Good."

Plato's mystical inclination is given freer rein in his writings upon the Idea of Beauty. The myth interpolated in the *Symposium* comprises one of the most imaginative and suggestive passages in all his books. It pictures the Beautiful as the object of all love and the Idea of Beauty as that immortality toward which the heart of the initiate yearns. The words here are spoken by the priestess Diotima to Socrates, who repeats them to his companions of the *Symposium:*

> He who would approach this mystery aright should begin in youth to have knowledge of beautiful forms. First, if he be guided aright, he will love one such form; this will engender thoughts of the beautiful. Gradually he will perceive without instruction that the beauty of one form is kin to the beauty of another. Then if beauty itself is the object of his search, it would be foolish not to recognize the beautiful quality in all forms as one and the same. Perceiving this, he becomes the lover of all beautiful forms, abating his passionate love of the one form, disregarding it now as something of a smaller sort. Then comes the stage at which he considers that inner beauty of the spirit is more to be honoured than outward beauty of the form or body, . . . and he is compelled to survey the beauty that is in institutions and laws. . . .
>
> He who has been led thus far by his instructor into the mysteries of love, who has successively surveyed the beautiful, in due order, at the end of his initiation will see suddenly

Beauty as essence — that thing, Socrates, which is a reward for all our labours — Beauty eternal, knowing neither birth nor decay, neither increase nor decrease; which is not fair in one view, foul in another, fair at one time, foul at another. . . . It is when a man ascends thus, under the guidance of love, and attains sight of Beauty eternal, that he reaches the goal. . . .

This is hardly less than a statement that immersion in the Eternal is the highest good of life. The disciples of Plato through many centuries after — though none during his lifetime — interpreted the passage as warrant for a life of mystic seeking.

But Plato himself is nowhere spoken of as a practising mystic. He had not the spells of raptness experienced by Socrates. Certainly he never instituted at the Academy any such training, in the nature of initiation, dedication, and revelation of secret wisdom, as was common among the Pythagorean communities. He seems to have been a theoretic mystic, an argued believer in the transcendental life, even a believer who occasionally visioned the rapture of immersion in the Absolute — whether called Beauty in essence or God or the Idea — but very little a participator in that disembodied rapture. He is a link in the historic chain of spiritual prophets, even one of the founders of Christian mysticism. But his personal life was little illumined in the mystic way.

Intuitively he yearned for the ecstatic experience, the union with the divine. But after the flights of poetic myth that express his longing and his vision, the trained, reasoning intellect takes control. He feels the passion for the Idea; but temperament and Greek reason hold him back. Ultimately it is the limits of the ideal city-state, as sketched in the *Republic,* that interest him more than the City of God.

There is one frequent softening or compromise of his ideas, however, that seems unfair. A misconstruction has come into currency, so common that it is to be found in the dictionaries — a misconstruction of Plato's passages about love. "Platonic love" is construed as mere affection, or as love without passion. As a matter of fact, Platonic love, in view of the philosopher's words, can mean only a love poured out at God's feet, an all-absorbing, all-consuming devotion. He himself speaks of it as "a kind of madness" — the very opposite of the sane and tame "Platonic love" of common currency — and he adds that even a glimpse of beauty in an earthly one leads to "recollection of Beauty itself," and to "transports" and to "being possessed." It is these words that the philosophers of the great ages of Neo-Platonism remembered, in connection with Plato and love.

Plato carried on the lines of mathematical research initiated by Pythagoras. Study of numbers, he said, was a way of approach to pure truth. The mysteries of number and of measurement have engaged the minds of mystics beyond counting, in both East and West, but no one of them ever put so much about the subject in so few words as did Plato:

> The knowledge at which geometry aims is knowledge of the eternal, and not of transitory and perishing things. Geometry leads the soul toward truth. It draws out the spirit of wisdom and it raises that which has fallen. There is in every man an eye of the soul, which, when it has been by other pursuits blinded or dimmed, is by this study restored and re-illumined. That eye of the soul is more worthy of preservation than ten thousand corporeal eyes, for by it alone is Truth itself perceived.

Iamblichus in the fourth century after Christ wrote, in summarizing the education given by Pythagoras to his followers: "He brought about for his disciples converse with the gods. . . . He purified and restored the soul. He revived and evoked its divine part. He directed to the centre of Being the divine eye, which, as Plato asserts, is more worth saving than ten thousand corporeal eyes, . . . for through it, we apprehend the one Truth."

That divine eye, more worth saving than ten thousand corporeal eyes, will be heard of again and again when, six centuries after Plato's death, the philosophy of Neo-Platonism is established. The Ideas, in a mystic interpretation and enlargement never quite foreseen or grasped by the founder, will be pushed into the battleground of religious thinking, influencing Christians and pagans alike, bringing clarification and hope to countless searchers for the centre of Being, even up to the twentieth century. It is Plotinus who will carry Platonism into that more spiritual phase.

Yet Plato *is* one of the prophets of universal spiritual religion, and a preparatory prophet of mystic religion. How much he sums up in a dozen words! "What comes to us from God looks back to God from us." And: "What if the man could see Beauty Itself, pure, unalloyed, stripped of mortality and all its pollutions, stains and vanities, unchanging, divine, . . . the man becoming, in that communion, the friend of God, himself immortal; . . . would that be a life to disregard?"

IV. The Tardy Flowering of Greek Mysticism: Plotinus

When the philosopher Plotinus had become a teacher of wisdom in Rome, he was urged by his friends to sit to a painter for his portrait. He declined. "Is it not enough," he asked, "that I must carry around this physical effigy in which nature has clothed me? Must I consent to leave behind, when I am gone, an image of the effigy?"

So little did Plotinus esteem the life in the body, to which "the soul has come down." So far had he advanced, to a philosophy God-centred, to an aspiration transcending reason and earthly ambitions. Not only did he shift the centre of Platonic philosophy to the realm of the spiritual, but he also repeatedly experienced complete deliverance from the mortal and assimilation in the Divine. Where Plato had an intellectual enthusiasm for mystic thought, Plotinus plunged for the mystical union with God. Life, Plotinus believed, should be lived in awareness of the Divine and in expectation of communion and ecstasy. Images of every sort belonged to the separative mortal world.

Plotinus was essentially the disciple of Plato; so much so that whenever he used, in his fifty-four treatises, the introductory words "We read that," he was understood to be discussing a passage from Plato's writings. Inferior to his master in clarity of reasoning and grace of expression, Plotinus yet achieved the higher place as spiritual prophet. Through the conviction and sincerity that lay behind his vision he became one of the world's great philosophers, perhaps the greatest Western philosopher in the mystical line. His books form the first imposing repository of mystical testimony and spiritual speculation written in Europe.

Between Plato and Plotinus six centuries had passed. They were centuries of turbulent and glorious and devastating history, in which empires flowered and decayed, in which religions died and were born. Alexander came and conquered and passed. The star of Rome rose and now was setting. The classic gods were becoming hardly more than a literary memory. Above all, Christianity had been born and had effected a spiritual union of men in a way that cut across territorial divisions and political aims.*

Immediately after Plato, philosophy had veered away from mysticism. His pupil Aristotle re-established scientific research as central to man's progress; he deserted Ideas and gave his allegiance to "forms," and after him for centuries a main line of philosophical development was scientific, empirical, and utilitarian. Other graduates of the Academy progressed along the variant roads of Stoicism and hedonism. It was the Pythagoreans rather than the Academics who kept alive the interest in philosophy as religion.

Alexander's conquering armies in Africa and Asia carried Greek learning over a vast territory. The nearer lands were Hellenized, and to the Hellenic centres were brought back the wisdom and the lore of Babylonia, Persia, and India. Alexandria in Egypt became a centre of learning more celebrated than Athens.

In the three and one-half centuries between the death of Alexander (and with it the break-up of the empire) and the preaching of Jesus, philosophy knew no leaders of the stature of Socrates and Plato. Eclecticism prevailed, and when seers rose high enough to claim a following they chose and pieced out their wisdom from the Platonic or Aristotelean or Stoic traditional store. Besides, there was the older, more spiritual heritage from Pythagoras, from the Egyptian seers, and from remoter Babylonian, Persian, and Hindu treasuries. The Jews were especially active at Alexandria; and one of the great figures between Plato and Plotinus is the Jewish Philo.

Philo Judaeus was a philosopher whose passion was the harmonizing of Plato and Moses. Born about twenty years before the birth of the Christ, he outlived the mortal Jesus by at least twenty years, but was little influenced by the inception of Christianity. Of a wealthy family, he was enabled to study as long as he willed, and then to spend his time writing at leisure. He was educated in the Jewish way, and went on to an extensive study of philosophy, mathematics, rhetoric, and the arts in the schools of

---

* In order to present the story of Christian mysticism in one sequence, from Jesus and John and Paul to the seers of the Middle Ages, it has seemed wiser to violate chronology at this point. The reader will be taken back to the beginnings of Christian development at the opening of the next chapter.

Alexandria. It is known that he was married, that he was considered a man of exceptional character, and that at the age of sixty he went as an ambassador of the Alexandrian Jews to plead their cause with the Emperor Caligula at Rome. Philo died at some time after A.D. 50.

An eclectic and a compromiser of traditional views, he was yet a thorough Jew, with pride of race and utter devotion to the Hebrew faith. He laboured to bring the Greeks and other pagans into Jewish orthodoxy. His basic endeavour was to show that Platonism, as well as sundry principles drawn from Aristotle and the Stoics, accorded with the law of Moses and with scriptural prophecy. In the course of his expositional writings he managed to combine elements of Plato's thought, especially the doctrines of the Idea of Good and of the immortality of the soul, with the God-centred Jewish philosophy. Going on to belief in the individual's power to rise, after purification and initiation, into ecstatic communion with God, he marked a further stage reached in the progression toward Neo-Platonism.

A single book by Philo, generally known by its Latin title, *De Vita Contemplativa*, deals with the mystic life. It describes a sect or community known as the *Therapeutæ*, resident upon the shores of Lake Mareotis, near Alexandria. Among the Therapeutæ a strict asceticism and monasticism obtained, varied by periodic festival-meetings, at which choral dancing and singing were features. The object of their life and devotions was purification and entry into spiritual union. Like the Essenes of Palestine and Syria (with whom they have been identified by some scholars) they were a communistic group of Jewish enthusiasts for the saintly life. They opposed the major evils of civilization, war, slavery, oppressive capitalism, and licentious living, and they were active in works of charity. Their devotional life was distinguished especially by the cultivation of solitude and meditation. They were, says Philo, "joyful with exceeding gravity."

Of the nature and quality of Philo's own "mounting into the Divine," there is not so much evidence in his writings as one would expect if he were an unreserved mystic. He considered that he had been accorded the privilege of rising into communion with the Deity, even that he had known divine madness; and he states that when he came to a difficult place in his writing "the living God" would unaccountably direct his pen. There is, nevertheless, an intellectual reserve about his reports, and it is likely that he gave himself but seldom and charily to the mystic experience. There is none of Plotinus's eager flooding of life with awareness of God and anticipation of being elevated into rapturous communion. Philo is a typical midway figure between the reasoning Plato and the self-abandoning Plotinus.

Philo's testimony of God's help as he sat writing is of special interest as a parallel to the saying of Fra Angelico that he painted his pictures wholly according to the direction of God; and to the insistence of Jacob Boehme that he was himself no author, but knew only how to act as the amanuensis of the Lord; and to Blake's cry that "The words are not mine." Philo's testimony is this:

> When I have come to my usual work of writing on the doctrines, sometimes I have found my mind dull and unproductive . . . and I have been amazed at the bounty of the living God, who at times opens, at times closes, the portals of the soul. Sometimes, coming to my writing thus, there has been showered upon me inspiration from on high. Because of this divine inspiration I have been kindled, knowing neither the place I am in nor who is near me, nor being conscious of myself or of what I am saying or writing. But afterward I am conscious of a wealth of thought, an illumination, and an outrush of energy toward whatever it is that must be done. It is as if my mind had witnessed the clearest working-out of the task.

A man's soul, says Philo, occupies in man the same place that God occupies in the universe. It is invisible although it sees everything. It ranges unlimitedly over land and sea and in the air. Of its elevation to Heaven and its approach to God he writes:

> Raised on wings it is borne into the upper spaces, to the company of the Heavenly bodies. In concert with the rhythm of the planets and the stars, in accord with the laws of pure music, impelled by love which is the handmaiden of wisdom, it rises above all that is intelligible to the mortal senses, aspiring to that which can be known only by the spirit. Perceiving then the Ideas or essences of those things which on earth had seemed endowed with surpassing beauty, it becomes seized with sober intoxication, like that of the cele-

brants in the Corybantic rites. It gives itself up to the madness, and possessed by a profounder desire and an inescapable longing, it is swept to the very heart of the spiritual realm, to the abode of the great King. It aspires to behold Him, immortal and undivided — and upon it like a torrent there is poured the light of Divinity, in a splendour blinding to the eyes.

Plotinus — after two centuries — gave more eloquent testimony about the same experience. But Philo had thus helped prepare the way for Plotinus's extension of Platonism; he had taken a step in the orientalizing of Greek philosophic mysticism. In his own time, too, Philo unwittingly affected Christian mysticism through another channel. In subjecting the Jewish scriptures to analysis and interpretation (this was his primary work as writer) in the light of Plato's thought, he more than any other insisted upon substituting "Logos" or "the Word" for the older Biblical conception of Sophia, Wisdom, as an attribute of God, as an intermediary between God and men. The writer of the Fourth Gospel, he whom we call John, opens his book, the most mystical in the Bible, with the statement: "In the beginning was the Word, and the Word was with God, and the Word was God. . . . In Him was life; and the life was the light of men." Or, in other versions: "In the beginning was the Logos . . ." It is easy to infer that the author was deeply influenced by the writings of Philo.*

There was a seer, Apollonius of Tyana, who even more directly inspired Plotinus by example. He was a more thorough Greek, a Platonist, and an inheritor from the chief sources of Plato's spirit-

* Although Philo's is the name oftenest heard in connection with Judaic mysticism, there is a Jewish mystical "system" that is widely known under the name cabbalism or Kabbalism. Its history can be traced back to the time of the *Talmud*, but its great period of expansion in Europe was in the twelfth and thirteenth centuries. The main stream had then absorbed strains from Gnosticism, from Neo-Platonism, and from the Asiatic religions. Cabbalism was always deeply concerned with symbolism and second meanings, and its secret character recommended it to that audience known as "students of the occult." The word "cabbalistic" became a term of reproach, as pertaining to something unduly esoteric — and, indeed, the cabbalists were not infrequently mixed up with the vogues for demonology, magic incantation, and the like. Recently the true core of mystic thought and mystic poetry in cabbalism has been uncovered by devoted scholars for all readers — though originally *Kabbalah* meant to the Jews *unwritten* tradition.

ual inspiration, the Pythagoreans and the Oriental sages. Apollonius was an ascetic, a mystic, and a philosopher. Born in or about the year 2 B.C., he is said to have lived exactly one hundred years. As a youth he was a brilliant student, and as a young man he became convinced that the saintly life is the only philosophic life. He gave away the vast wealth inherited from his father, embraced poverty, and adopted an ascetic way of living. He was known as a Neo-Pythagorean. He wore linen clothes, ate no meat, and condemned sacrifices. At one time he kept silence for five years.

After teaching for a time at Antioch he started those travels in search of wisdom that took him to Nineveh, Babylon, and the cities of India. For four months he discussed philosophical questions with the Brahmins. When he returned to the Western world there was hardly a Greek city that failed to invite him into residence. Indeed the entire Roman Empire seemed to be asking for him, so great was his reputation as philosopher, saint, and worker of miracles. He became adviser to certain of the Emperors, but was persecuted by others who disliked his way of speaking the truth in all circumstances and trumped up the charge that he had claimed to be a god.

And indeed his acts and prophecies seemed to many to prove his possession of divine powers. In his later years there grew up in Ionia a sect of Apollonians who had no doubt of their master's divinity. At Tyana a statue of Apollonius stood in the temple. But the seer himself was content to say only that he was a Pythagorean, and that all men could, by observing the Pythagorean precepts, attain purification and discover the divine within themselves.

Damis, a disciple and companion of Apollonius, wrote an admiring biography of the seer, with full credence to all the miracles and legends. The manuscript was reverently preserved until it came into the library of the Empress Julia Domnia. She gave it to Philostratus, with the request that he base a biography upon it. It was the newly written life of Apollonius by Philostratus that came into the hands of Plotinus, helped to kindle an ambition to live a similarly saintly life, and directed his attention back to Pythagoras, from whose wisdom Plato had drawn the more mystical of his doctrines. It affords a side-light on the religion of the times that Julia Domnia and her husband, the Roman Emperor Alexander Severus, had in their private chapel images of the

Christ, Abraham, Orpheus, and Apollonius of Tyana. A generation later the Emperor Claudius Aurelian, when he recovered Cappadocia by the sword, spared Tyana because of the universally honoured name of Apollonius.

It was Alexandria, in the third century, that was especially the melting pot of religions, as it was the city of museums and libraries and schools. Egypt was ruled by Greek kings, and in Alexandria there were temples of the Egyptian gods beside schools of Greek philosophy. Beside these again there were Jewish synagogues and Jewish colleges, and schools set up by Oriental spiritual teachers, and Christian congregations and preachers. To this beehive of religious activities went the youth named Plotinus, at some time in the first quarter of the third century. He had been born somewhere in Egypt, of Hellenized or Romanized parents, in A.D. 204 or 205.

It was when he was twenty-eight (according to the only substantial biography of him, written by his disciple Porphyry in A.D. 303) that Plotinus was "captured by the passion for philosophy." For a time thereafter he went from school to school, from master to master, in Alexandria; but he ended with a profound dissatisfaction and depression. Then a friend directed him to a philosopher-teacher named Ammonius Saccas. After hearing one lecture Plotinus exclaimed: "This is the man I have been seeking." For ten years he studied under his new instructor.

Ammonius, known as "God-instructed" — *Theodidaktos* — is said to have been born of Christian parents, though he became indifferent to Christianity, finding a sufficient spiritual philosophy in the wisdom of the Greeks. He adhered to Plato above all other seers. Sometimes it is he rather than Plotinus who is named the founder of Neo-Platonism, because he taught not only Plotinus but also Numenius. He wrote no books — he had once been a porter and was self-educated, except for God's tutelage — and his doctrines are rather hazily known through his pupils and through a reference in Hierocles, who says that he harmonized the ideas of Plato and Aristotle and thus handed on to Plotinus a purified and single philosophy.

Numenius, too, the fellow student of Plotinus under Ammonius, restored and clarified Platonism, rather than fused it into a religion with Oriental mysticism at its core. He was especially partial to Pythagoras; and he held, with Philo, that Plato had incurred debt to the old Jewish lore as well as to the Egyptian priests when he went to the country of the Nile to study.

When Plotinus had spent a decade with Ammonius Saccas, he felt the call to turn Eastward and study at first hand the wisdom of the Magi and the Brahmins; and it is possible that he had heard of the Buddha as well. The Emperor Gordianus, the last of the name, was just then starting on the expedition to recover Mesopotamia from the Persians. Plotinus, thirty-nine years old, joined the invading army. Although the Persians were defeated, mutinies and the murder of Gordianus wrecked his plans. He gave up his effort to reach India and made his way under great hardship to Antioch. In 244, when he was forty, he went to Rome. There he settled permanently.

During the next nineteen years Plotinus composed twenty-one short philosophical treatises. Very rough in form, misspelled, and hardly grammatical, they may have been little more than notes for his lectures. He had organized a school at which he taught a philosophical-mystical approach to life along the lines demonstrated to him by Ammonius, but modified by his own devotion to a saintly code and his passion for divine communion. His writings might never have been put into readable form had not Porphyry arrived from Greece in 263 to become his disciple.

Beyond his difficulties in writing Greek, Plotinus had remembered a pledge to Ammonius not to divulge his teachings except to those who could be considered serious initiates. But as he became a famous philosopher and saint, as much on his own account as through the wisdom gained from Ammonius, he yielded to the solicitation of his disciples and gave the manuscripts to Porphyry. Additional treatises were composed, and in the end the reviser had the texts of fifty-four discourses. These he arranged in groups of nine. For this reason the collection is called the *Enneads*.

Rome in the third quarter of the third century was harassed by enemies within and without. Wars, treacheries, and the plague made life precarious for the rich as well as the poor. The so-called barbarians of the North were stabbing at one front, then another. Emperors came and went in succession. In the midst of widespread suffering, political chaos, and unending alarms of war, Plotinus's little community carried on its search for wisdom undisturbed. The philosophy of the master was of a sort that admits no catastrophe as profound or final except the failure to live and act nobly, in accord with the spirit. This was a home of serenity and peace in the troubled and feverish capital of a disintegrating empire. At its centre was Plotinus, who when he talked "seemed to increase in beauty, the light of his soul visibly shining in his face."

To this school came an impressive assortment of public figures, philosophers, and children. Because Plotinus lived simply and honestly, the guardians of wealthy orphaned children were accustomed to place them in his care. His house was full of boys and girls, and although his gift was for unworldly things he bestowed meticulous attention upon the monetary accounts of each child; because, he said, "until they really get hold of philosophy, their moneys will be important to them."

As he paid attention to each of the children, taking seriously their problems, gaining their confidence and love, so Plotinus made his way into the hearts of all those about him, to the extent, says his biographer, that "he not once made an enemy of any citizen." So devoted to him were the Emperor Gallienus and his Empress Salonina that he was emboldened to ask a grant of land in Campania, where he proposed to found a City of Philosophers, to be known as Platonopolis. Although Gallienus seemed to approve, the project came to nothing, because of either the intrigues of jealous courtiers, as Porphyry states, or the Emperor's realization that so Utopian a community would with difficulty survive in a world hard-headed and murderous.

The Senator Rogatianus had greater faith, and perhaps he lived and died more happily than Gallienus, who was killed by his own soldiers. Rogatianus, swayed by Plotinus's teaching, gave away his property in order to live the life of a philosopher and ascetic. There were other prominent converts, among them physicians and political leaders and writers, as well as a band of students whose sole business was the pursuit of wisdom. Women were accepted by Plotinus as members of the community, as they had been by religious teachers since Pythagoras, in spite of their inferior place, socially and culturally, in all quarters of the Empire.

At the heart of this school community in Rome Plotinus lived out his life until its final year. As Porphyry puts it, he lived alternately an interior life within himself and an exterior life given to others. He had a genius for settling differences that arose among human beings around him. He was sought out no less by pilgrims who came to hear his lectures on philosophy. As a speaker he was inspiring, even illuminating, though sometimes difficult to understand. His mind was so fecund that he did not pause to fit the full complement of words to the idea. He spoke as he wrote, "all at one burst, after storing his mind." He was, says Porphyry, entirely unlike a professor.

Porphyry's own testimonial to the sweetness of Plotinus's character and to the oneness of his attachment to God is illuminating. "I found him to be gracious and good, and he was ever alert, ever zealous, toward the Divine, which he loved with all his being, and he laboured incessantly to free himself, and rise above the harassments of this sanguinary life. . . . The one aim of his life was to rise to God and become one with Him. Four times during the time I was with him, he achieved this relation, not as mere passive mergence, but by the ineffable act."

Plotinus was somewhat sceptical of medical science, and he was short with the doctors (who, he had observed, sometimes become so absorbed in physical symptoms and curatives that they forget the healing that arises out of harmony in the soul). Nevertheless the doctor Eustochius became one of his most devoted disciples and a beloved companion. When in his last year Plotinus fell seriously ill of a throat infection, he left Rome and went to an estate in Campania. He sent for his friend Eustochius, but the latter was delayed in arriving at the bedside, so that the saint, as it were, was obliged to put off dying. When the physician came Plotinus said only these words: "I have been waiting for you. Now I shall restore the Divine in me to the Divine that is All." And his spirit left the body. This was in the year 270.

When Porphyry had edited and published the *Enneads* — that is, when he had made them available for copying by the scribes of those scholars who asked for them — the Plotinian writings lived on to influence profoundly the course of both Greek and Christian philosophy. The greatest effect was upon the Christianized Western world through the medium of Saint Augustine; though Jerome, Gregory the Great, and other fathers of the Church felt the call of the prophet of Neo-Platonism.

It was Saint Augustine who fixed Plotinus's place as a new Plato, and a Plato inspired with God's spirit. "The message of Plato," Augustine writes, "the purest and the brightest in all philosophy, dissolving the clouds of error, has shone forth most clearly in Plotinus, who has shown himself so like his master that one might deem them contemporaries, did not the interim of years between them compel us to say, rather, that in Plotinus Plato lives again."

In *The City of God* Augustine echoes Plotinus repeatedly on the subjects of the nature of God, the divinity of the soul, evil as non-good, Providence, and other points upon which the African Saint had so determining a voice in the crystallizing of Catholic doctrine. Of Plotinus and the mystic experience he writes: "The beholding of God is a vision so beautiful and so transcendingly desirable that Plotinus does not hesitate to say that, failing this, he who enjoys all other blessings in abundance is nevertheless supremely bereaved." And in his *Confessions* Augustine tells of Plotinus's part in furthering his personal conversion, one of the most marvellous conversions (considering the Saint's training and his past life) and one of the most fruitful in the annals of religion.

Thus Augustine acted as a spiritual intermediary between Plotinus, last prophet of pagan philosophy, and the Church which was to become the guide of men's religious thinking in Europe for fifteen centuries after.

All the beliefs and doctrine of Plotinus grow like branches out of the tree of his mystical experience. His inner oneness with God is the centre, the trunk, around which are ranged the beliefs about life and immortality, about the world and cosmology, about ideals and happiness and morals. Plotinus was possessed with God: all else was incidental.

There is a characteristic passage in the fifth *Ennead* that indicates how far he had gone beyond any experience of which Plato, with his intellectual approach, was capable: "Those who are intoxicated with this wine, who are unstinted of this nectar, their souls suffused with this Beauty, cannot look merely at life's surface. Theirs is a profound inner vision, of the Divine Being. . . . Thus possessed of God, the man has only to look to the image of Divinity within and he sees himself uplifted, gifted with a nobler beauty. However beautiful that image may be, let him leave it aside, for it is of the world of separation; rather let him sink into identity with the Divine. Then is he one with God, experiencing in silence the Presence."

Philosophy, says Plotinus, begins in happiness, and the philosophic life is therefore the life that finds the Good; that is, finds God. Happiness is not in the things men do and the things they acquire, but in a habit of mind. "To hinge happiness on events, is to hinge it upon matters outside the Good and independent of the soul. The soul has its life not in events but in wisdom, in a contemplative experience of its own. This, this only, is happiness."

He goes on to warn that happiness is to be gained, not by withdrawal from life, but rather by detecting the opportunity to find all of Divinity here in the world. He insists upon "this beautiful world, which is a reflection and an image of the Original, the Divine Spirit." And once he exclaims: "If the transcendently beautiful, the Divine, did not exist, in a beauty beyond all thought, what could be lovelier than the things we see? Assuredly no reproach can be brought against this world save only that it is not That!"

Ethics or morals, he says, will take care of themselves once the man is embarked upon the adventure of living wisely; that is, in communion with God and in awareness of His beauty in daily things. Violation of natural decency can of course nullify happiness; but the very nature of the search for Divinity is such as to preclude lapses into evil conduct. "It is not by casting about here and there, outside itself, that the soul will understand morality and ethical conduct. It knows them of its own nature, as welling out of itself."

Plotinus himself, thus intuitively instructed as to what is "moral," came to a simple way of living, to a moderate and healthful asceticism. The picture we have of him in the descriptions of contemporaries is of a typical active saint. Having firmly in mind the image of Good, he spontaneously finds and attracts the good in the world. The Good is the normal thing, and it is ever present, even to those who are "asleep" as regards the presence of God. "In each of us there is something of this Entity. Wherever you may be, you have only to open to this omnipresent Good the faculty in you which is capable of drawing from it: your share flows to you." Evil is shut out, because "All who have possessed themselves of the Good find it sufficient." Therefore, "Essentially one's aspiration is less away from evil than toward the highest and noblest comprehensible to the soul; this attained, all has been won, and there is peace, the intended condition of life."

As if to sum up his attitude toward the Good as the positive factor in living, he adds: "The soul's true goodness is in devotion to its like; evil for the soul is in tolerating that which is strange to its nature. Let it cleanse away what is alien, and stand by its own — then a new phase begins. . . ."

Plotinus uses the word Good interchangeably with God upon countless occasions. And from discussion of the Good in us regulating our conduct to the thought of God as mystically apprehensible, he leaps in a single memorable line: "Our business is not merely to be sinless but to be God."

It is a basic Neo-Platonic belief that the soul has come down to this world — "Birth is brought about by the descent of the soul" — but that essentially the soul, even in the body, is "the high thing" implied in Divine birth. Without posing a perilous philosophic dualism, the Neo-Platonists accept the fact of the soul's stay in the mortal body and the separated world, and yet hold that its real life is with God.

There is a coming-down in the "couplement" with the body and the world; but "Not the whole of our soul sinks into our body; some part of her ever remains in the Divine sphere." That part of the soul which is in the mortal sphere often becomes confused, losing touch with the Divine part, especially when men give rein to their appetites. But the soul in the world will be at peace so long as it recognizes its origin and its Oneness with the Supreme Soul, and seeks what is, like itself, of Divine nature. Pain is the outward sign that the nature of the soul has been violated. Or, as Plotinus puts it again, "Pain is the recognition that the body is being deprived of its likeness to the soul."

The human soul is a sort of traveller for Spirit or Soul. It comes to mortals laden with the supreme gift. It is an interpreter between the higher and lower spheres. It invites the man to participate in the life of Divine Being. And, says Plotinus, "Our life apart from God is but a mimicry. . . . To hold aloof is loneliness and degradation. There with the Supreme is the soul's peace, away from evil, in a realm clean of wrong; there the soul has understanding, there it is free."

The Divinity to which the soul harks back is, according to Plotinus, at once a Unity and a Triad. The three grades of the Triad are The Good; Divine Spirit or Divine Intelligence; and the All-Soul or World-Soul. But as the highest, God or The Good, is all, and is in all, the divisions are no more than convenient devices for discussion, or as suggesting convenient steps between the realm of earth and the highest heaven.

There is, indeed, a series of steps well marked on Plotinus's journey to mystic realization. "This world must be a starting point of our pursuit. Arrived here out of Divine nature, we must inaugurate our effort by some earthly correction. . . . This means continence, self-restraint, holding firm against the sense-pleasures and ostentation, permitting no distraction of the mind. . . . Attaining freedom thus, we gradually bring to life within ourselves the Soul of All." But "Above this Soul, itself divine, there is a diviner still, its prior and source. For though so high a thing, the Soul is but an utterance and an image of Divine Intelligence, a stream of life sent forth by Divine Spirit for the increase of Being. . . . For its perfecting, Soul must look to Divine Spirit, which is as a Father watching over His child." And he adds: "You may now hold the faith that through the Soul you are nearing God. By the instrument of this faith, lift yourself toward Him. Soon you must attain. There are no great barriers between."

Plotinus is more Taoist than Christian (or Hebrew) in his conception of the universe in relation to God. God, he says, is not in the world; rather the world is in God, or the One. God, the Absolute, is so great that there is nothing that can contain Him. He is First, He contains all. He is not a figure that comes down, by favour, to help men. Men are, rather, intuitively of Him, of His nature, carrying on a separately created world in recollection of His wisdom.

"By derivation" there exists this lower universe, divided off, imperfection and discord introduced — by something not very different from the "fall" of the Hebrew-Christian scripture — but shot through with the divine element, and susceptible to redemption when the individual soul remembers its better part. Wisely he writes:

> It would be unsound to condemn this universe as less than beautiful, or as less than the noblest universe possible on the corporeal level. A majestic organism, complete within itself, the minutest part related to the whole, a marvellous artistry shown not only in the stateliest parts but in those of such littleness you would not have thought Providence would bother about them; and the wonder of the efficiency in each separate animal form, the exquisite design of fruits and leaves, the abundance and the delicacy and the diversity of flowers: all this issues not once, then ending, but is ceaselessly renewed as the Transcendent Life moves over our earth. . . . The Divine Spirit, in its unperturbed serenity, has brought

this universe into being by communicating from its own store to matter.*

But always the lovelinesses of the sense-world are catalogued with the intention of directing the attention to the Author of it all. "Seeing the beauty exquisitely mirrored forth in a human face, one turns to the Beauty of the Absolute. Perceiving the abundance of loveliness so grateful to the senses, and the marvellous orderliness of the spheres, and the glory of the stars, can one be so unmoved as not to recollect the Creator, and pause in reverent awe before this revelation of His greatness?"

Endowed with an all-embracing appreciation of the graces detected in nature, Plotinus could not but oppose those who found the world unlovely. It was at least in part his affection for the world that led him to take the road away from Christianity. For among the Christians, particularly among those Christians most mystic, this lower world was then considered evil and dark; the Gnostics even despised it as the creation of the inferior order of fallen gods or demons. There were, of course, more wholesome strains in Christian thought about mortal life and the earthly environment. But as yet to "admire this world of sense, its vastness, its beauty, its eternally ordered movement," even to admire it as the reflection of God, was more Greek, or Platonic, than Christian. Under later compromises and crystallizing of Christian thought, a great deal of Plotinian doctrine was approved and accepted. Augustine in particular agreed that "The beauty perceived in material things is borrowed," and that the man perceiving the beauty, knowing it comes through Soul, may be led back thereby to a consciousness of the Creator.

For Plotinus the universe is good and life is good; and both may be desired "for the colour cast upon them from the Good." That colour is the beginning point of the ascent to the Source. "The soul, caught up in that stream from the Divine, is awakened, suffused with a spiritual ecstasy, stirred by a new desire."

* Although my indebtedness and my thanks to translators are expressed fully in an appendix, I feel that in two cases, in connection with the chapters on Greek mysticism, I should make acknowledgment in this more conspicuous place. The extracts from Plotinus, as here, follow, with some paraphrasing, the translation by Stephen MacKenna as revised by Grace H. Turnbull in her excellent book, *The Essence of Plotinus*. In the preceding chapter the extracts from Plato are in general from *The Dialogues of Plato*, translated by B. Jowett (Clarendon Press, Oxford). The Oxford University Press has graciously granted permission for the quotations from *The Essence of Plotinus*.

The mystic need not study too deeply over the Plotinian theory that divides Divinity into an unknowable Power and a knowable Divine Intelligence or Spirit; nor need he remember more than that Plotinus says that "Both are of radiant beauty: and because Divine Spirit comes Thence and leads Thither, it, like the Good, is a magnet to the soul." But of the nature of the Good, the Supreme, the unknowable, it is necessary to learn more if one would feel the full impact of his call to participation in Divine rapture.

Porphyry, in his biography, speaks of Plotinus as "lifting himself often to the supreme and all-transcendent God," and of "God appearing to him, the God enthroned above Divine Intelligence and above all the Spiritual sphere." This God or Good of Plotinus is sometimes reminiscent of the Platonic Idea or Absolute, the Good in Itself, which is unattainable by the mind or reason. At other times it is nearer the Christian conception of God the Father, creator and comforter, accessible and comprehensible.

The naming of the Supreme as Beauty or First Beauty is Greek or Platonic. "The soul includes a faculty peculiarly open to Beauty, a faculty incomparably sure in appreciation of its own." And "It is fair to say that in the soul's becoming a good and beautiful thing lies its becoming like to God; . . . even that Beauty is the Real Being. . . . The soul is, as it were, a fragment of the Primal Beauty."

There is a contrast of mood in two other pronouncements about God as Beauty, the one calm, thoughtful, the other fervent, even ecstatic. "Everyone understands that the emotional exaltation which we attribute to 'love' appears in souls aspiring to the closest attainable union with some beautiful object. It is sound, I believe, to identify the first source of love in an inclination of the soul toward pure Beauty."

And, in contrast: "One who shall know this vision of God, the One Apart, the Pure, the Source — with what passion of love shall he not be seized, with what stabbing of desire, with what anticipation of delight, what longing to be molten into one with This! He that has never visioned this Being must hunger for It as for his very life; he that has known must love and exalt It as Beauty Itself. He will be filled at once with awe and with rapture. . . . Resting rapt in vision and in a supreme participation, what can the soul yet lack? For this, Beauty Itself, Primal, Absolute, shapes its lovers to beauty. . . ."

Yet un-Greek is Plotinus when he speaks of the Supreme as

God; at times he is near to the abstract conception of the Taoist Absolute, again in perfect harmony with the Christian belief. "The Source, having no prior, cannot be contained by any other form of being. It is the orb complete, possessing but unpossessed, holding all but nowhere held. It is omnipresent, yet there is nothing to which it can be present. . . . God is through it all, not something of God here and something there, nor all of God at any one spot; rather an instantaneous Presence, everywhere, everything fully held by Him, everything full of Him."

Within the Christian fold the Neo-Platonists have again and again brought alive the strain of Oriental mysticism existing since the founding of the faith (and implicit especially in the Johannine Gospel and the Pauline Epistles). They have regularly gone back for inspiration to the dual Greek-Oriental interpretations in the *Enneads*. For Plotinus most successfully held to the Oriental abstract, remote idea of the Highest, yet left open the way for a personal approach, even for a conception of God as One who comforts and aids:

> The One is, in truth, beyond all statement: whatever you say would limit It. The All-transcending has no name. . . . But if we do not grasp It by knowledge, that does not mean that we do not seize It at all. Those who are inspired and Divinely possessed at least understand that they hold within them some greater thing. . . . When the soul has suddenly taken light, we may be certain that we have experienced Divinity. For this illumination is from God and is God. We may believe that He is present.

Again he states: "The whole spiritual realm may be described as a kind of Light, with the One in repose at its summit, as its King." And finally: "We are always brought back to God."

The end of all ends, the ecstasy of living, is, Plotinus states, the mystical experience of the soul. "He that has the strength, let him arise and draw into himself, foregoing all that is known by the eyes, turning away for ever from the mortal beauty that once made his joy. . . . All our labour is for this, lest we be left without part in the noblest experience, which to fail of is to fail utterly."

Many are the passages in the *Enneads* that testify to Plotinus's overwhelming conviction in the matter. The one aim of his life, Porphyry said, "was to rise to God and become one with Him." Plotinus, out of his single-minded devotion, writes: "The soul is unlit without that experience. Lit thereby, it possesses that which it sought. This is the true goal set before the soul, to attain that light, to perceive God in His own radiance and not by any other light. . . . Let all else go!" This was one of the passages that haunted the memory of Saint Augustine when he was writing *The City of God.*

The freedom and the rapture felt by the soul in mystic attainment are suggested by Plotinus in words as specific as the nature of the experience permits: "The one who has experienced understands what I mean: how the soul takes on another life as it approaches God. Having come into His presence, it rests in Him, it merges in Him. It knows Him as the Dispenser of the only true life. Everything earthly is stripped away; bonds that fetter us are loosened so that we may adhere to Him, no part remaining in us but with it we may cleave to God. Then shall we be worthy to behold Him and ourselves in a single light: but it will be a self lifted into splendour, radiant with spiritual light, nay, itself become a light, pure, buoyant, incandescent, identical with Godhead."

The experience again is thus described:

> "The Supreme is close at hand, radiant, above the knowable. Here we may put aside all learning. At this stage, swept upward in beauty, suddenly lifted on the crest of the wave of Spirit, the seeker sees, never knowing how. The vision floods the eyes with light: but it shows not some other thing — the light *is* the vision. . . . Seeing and seen are one. Object and act of vision are identical. No memory remains of past seeing. Before, the consciousness had known. Now all knowing is drowned in the surge of love, in the intoxication of rapture. In this raptness lies profoundest happiness."

But the mystic experience does not last, is not continuous; that is, not before the moment of throwing off mortality. The initiate who goes up from this world returns inevitably. Plotinus puzzled over the reasons why the soul ever again should "come down" after knowing the ecstasy of rising to God. "Many times, swept out of the body, rising into my essential self, the world forgotten, I used to behold a marvellous beauty. Then, beyond cavil, I rose into a loftier communion, became ennobled, and merged in the Divine. I was translated into the Supreme. After this sojourn with God there comes the moment of descent. I ask myself, why must the soul come down . . . ?"

And he paints a picture of mortal life apparently drab in comparison, yet illumined with some reflection of that unearthly experience. "That all-sufficient life, primal, life in One, who can regard it without longing, disdainful of all else? Other forms of life are lightless, petty, poor, gloomy, unclean. . . . For evil is here, where life is a copy and mind a shadow. It is there that the Good is, holding all good, the pure Idea itself. . . ."

Yet because he "knows himself in likeness to the Supreme" he goes through life here with increased wisdom, unshakable courage, and faith that no catastrophe can befall him. "Once having sojourned There, the soul will barter for the experience nothing that the universe holds, no, not Heaven itself; for nothing is more exalted than this, nothing more blessed. . . . All that she welcomed of old, authority, power, riches, beauty, learning, the soul scorns, as she could not except she had found their better. With the memory of This, she no longer fears, nor can she know disaster. . . ."

No longer can the initiate, now become the Sage, demand equality in "matters of wealth and poverty." "He cannot believe that to own abundance of things is to be rich, or that the powerful have the better of the simple: all such preoccupations he leaves to another kind of man." And of course he frees himself of bodily desires, lives cleanly, and considers death natural and not to be feared. Above all he lives by a light brought back; he lives in a perpetual radiance of the spirit. His conduct is directed by that which his soul has refound in God's presence. "Spirit, God, This in action within us conducts our life: even here, and now, it is dominant. . . . The acting force of the Sage is the Divine Spirit."

The actual steps to the mystic experience, or to renewal of it, are not so much designated in the *Enneads* as suggested, haphazardly and incidentally. Plotinus offers no rules for the approach to God. Yet such is his conviction, even his enthusiasm, that his words are inspiring and memorable. "Disengagement means simply that the soul withdraws to its own place." And: "To know Divine Spirit, you must observe the higher part of your Soul, that part which is toward God. One certain method is to separate your consciousness from your body, resolutely closing the sense portals, ridding yourself of the cravings, inclinations and falsities that are set toward the mortal. Then you are left with only the Soul that is an image of the Divine Spirit. . . . "

Contemplation, however, is not always easy — and it must not be forced: "We must not run after It, but we should prepare ourselves for the vision and then wait tranquilly, as the eye waits upon the rising of the sun, which in its own time appears above the horizon and gives itself to our sight."

There is a curious passage in the *Enneads* upon contemplation, suggesting that, by a sort of inversion, creative contemplation begets the material or physical. Plotinus is ruminating over the existence of nature and mortal life:

> Let us suppose that all vital things are striving after contemplation, reaching after this as their one aim: not only beings endowed with reason, but even the unreasoning animals, and things that grow from the productive earth. . . . Who could tolerate so strange a thesis? Yet all of us, man or child, in play or in seriousness, are progressing only toward vision: our every act is an effort toward contemplation. . . . Nature, asked why she brings forth her works, might answer thus:
>
> "Whatever comes into being is of the silent vision that belongs to me by nature. I am sprung from vision, I am vision-loving, and I create by the vision-seeing faculty within me, create the objects of contemplation, as mathematicians imagine and draw their figures. I gaze within, and the figures of my material world take being as if they fell from my brooding. . . ."

This informs us that what we know as Nature is a soul, an offspring of an earlier, more mighty Soul; and that she possesses, in repose, a fruitful vision. . . . Human beings, when they are weak on the side of contemplation, cover their trace of vision in an over-active life. They hurry into action as their way to ends their vision cannot attain. . . . As the First exists in vision, all other things must incline toward that condition. All the failures among men, whether in being or doing, mark but the swervings of visionaries from the objects of contemplation.

Great spiritual teachers throughout the ages have preached the uses of silence and calm. On behalf of "men who have been hurried down the wrong path, losing thought of their origin in the Divine" — like "children wrenched young from home and brought up ignorantly at a distance" — Plotinus offers this prayer or invocation:

> Freed from deceptive activity, and from every guile, let the soul be collected, in silence. Let the soul that is not unworthy contemplate the Divine Soul.
> Calmed be the body in that hour, calmed be the striving of the flesh. Let all that is anywhere about be calm. Calm be the earth, the sea, the air, as the heaven itself is still. Now let the soul experience how into a silent heaven the Divine Spirit floweth in.

What may be called the accessibility of God when once the initiate has enjoyed the bliss of union is suggested in these lines: "Having known the Unity, when he returns to duality a certain purity clings to him, and he still is aware of the closeness of Divinity. He has but to turn the attention again, and God is there."

And finally, regarding the mystical life, as a sort of summary of Plotinus's conviction and of his instruction, there is this somewhat fragmentary passage, abridged from the discourse on Beauty:

> What is this rapturous joy that thrills through our being, this exaltation upward, this yearning to escape the body and live in the Divine Spirit? — This is the reaction that Beauty must ever induce, wonderment and a delicious aching, longing and love and a trembling that is all delight. . . . To attain It is for those who will enter the upward path, who will put off all that they have taken on in their mortal descent. For the initiate here, as for those who approach the celebration of the sacred Mysteries, there is required purification, and the laying aside of the garments worn before, and entry in nakedness. Then, having left by the way all that is other than God, each in the self's seclusion will know the Aloneness of Being, the Apart, the Undivided, the Pure, will know That from which all things issue, towards which all incline, the

Source of Life and Spirit and Being. . . . The Fatherland is There whence the soul has come, and There is the Father.

It is a journey not for the feet, which bring us only from land to land, nor for ship or carriage. Rather, close the mortal eyes, and arouse in yourself that inward vision, which is the birthright of all. . . . Withdraw into yourself and look about. If you do not find yourself beautiful yet, act as does the artist who is creating a beautiful statue. He cuts away, he straightens, he makes this outline less heavy, that one he purifies, until a lovely image shines forth. So should you do. Cut away what is gross, straighten out what is crooked, lighten the over-heavy, labour to bring forth one glow of loveliness. Never cease working until there shines out from the centre within you the Divine splendour, until you know that you have enthroned the Good in a stainless shrine. When you know that you have become this perfect work, nothing can keep you from the act of union.

The simile here, of man shaping his being, indicates an advance of Neo-Platonism over the æsthetics of Plato: an advance from Greek naturalistic idealism toward expressionism. The sculptor's primary goal is set forth as not reproduction of characteristic nature, or even of beautiful nature, but expression of the beauty or order that lies at the Source of life.

The apologists for Plato have been unable to explain away his seeming disdain for art and his exclusion of artists from the ideal commonwealth. There are obscure passages that hint that he recognized the existence of a profounder art, expressive of the Absolute, worthy of the Idea of Beauty (and he may have found and appreciated such an art, especially during his travels in Egypt). The art he disallowed was, the apologists note, specifically "imitative art."

Nevertheless the words of Plotinus indicate a revolutionary advance in æsthetics. Most impressive of theorists of art in the six centuries between Plato and Plotinus was Philostratus, he who wrote the *Life of Apollonius of Tyana* as well as a critique dealing with the pictures in a gallery at Naples. He definitely and uncompromisingly condemned imitation as the first principle of art — "Art is imitation," Aristotle had said dogmatically — and suggested that imagination, "a wiser creator than imitation," is the source of true art.

Plotinus, who had been so impressed by the biography of Apollonius, may have known Philostratus, who is supposed to have died in Rome in 245, the year after the founding of Plotinus's school there. In any case Plotinus completes the full swing from art by imitation to art expressive of that which the artist apprehends at the centre of life, art expressive of a felt rhythm or order or beauty inseparable from the Primal Beauty.

Remembering a line already quoted, "The soul includes a faculty peculiarly open to Beauty, a faculty incomparably sure in appreciation of its own," we may turn the pages of the *Enneads* and find, especially in the discourse on Divine Beauty, an outline of a mystic æsthetic, an outline containing an art derived less from nature than from the artist's identification with the Unity or the God at the heart of all things. The simplest statement is this:

> We are concerned to understand, if we can, how the Beauty attaching to Divine Spirit and to the spiritual realm can be revealed to sight. Let us suppose two blocks of stone side by side, once uncut, untouched by art, the other shaped into a statue, say of a god or a man, or a Grace or a Muse: a creation in which the sculptor's art has concentrated every expressiveness. Now the stone shaped by the artist to formal beauty is beautiful not as a stone — if so the uncut block would be as appealing — but in virtue of the form imposed upon it by art. This form is in the designer's being, before ever it enters the stone. He has it not by the seeing of his eyes or the skill of his hands, but by participation, as it were, in art. The loveliness in the work of art is an exalted one; though it is not the Beauty itself that is brought over but a derivative from it.

This neatly brings art into line with the Platonic-Plotinian theory of life as irradiated with beauty from a fountain that may be called the Idea, or Good, or Beauty, or God. It posits an *expressive art*, manifesting the Divine element within the objects shown, and suggesting a well of beauty above all nature; and this expressive visual art is as much superior to imitative art as poetry both musically and spiritually lovely is above prosaic statement. In declaring for art endowed with form-beauty, out of the central Source of creativeness, Plotinus becomes one of the earliest philosophers to lift Western art theory into conformance with Eastern; and one of the earliest Western theorists to become useful to twentieth-century Modernism.

The artist, says Plotinus flatly, should be a philosopher. He should be a sage and a mystic. He will be "exceedingly quick to beauty, drawn in a very rapture to it." But his wisdom will lead him to progress from appreciation of the beauty of the model, its harmony and shapeliness and patterns, to the centre at which all the components of art are unified in one Beauty, to the centre of Being. "He must be shown that what ravages him was essentially the form of Divine Spirit, the organic beauty of that realm: not one shape of beauty, but the Beauty-in-All, Beauty absolute. For this he needs fall back upon the truths of philosophy, to discover that which, all unknowing, he harbours in his inward self."

There are scattered in the modern world innumerable groups of believers in a positive philosophy of good, adherents of a faith of affirmation and trust. Plotinus might be considered a prophet of their cult of providence through prayer. Certainly the affirmation inserted in his discourse on Providence is the perfect prototype of those repeated daily by millions who believe in attainment by faith. He has been speaking of the wonders of the universe, the marvellous artistry of it, the active order that effects its continuance, and of its derivation from Divine Being. Then:

> Such is the organic cosmos; do but survey it and you will perchance hear something like this: "I am fashioned by a God. From that God I issued perfect, lacking nothing, fitted for that which I am to do. In myself I contain all that exists, every plant and every living creature, and all created objects, and all beings of the spirit realm, and risen souls, and all men who trust in the Good. . . . Everything within me strives toward the Good. Every part of my diversity, in its own measure, attains. From that Centre, that Good, the heavens depend, and my own soul, and the Divinity that is in my every part, and all that lives and grows."

It may be added that the thought was not entirely new when written down by Plotinus seventeen centuries ago; for he was renovating and enlarging a conception put into words by Plato.

But in the end Plotinus is most important as the whole-hearted philosopher of mysticism, explaining the liberation of the soul from the alien of mortal life, "the flight of the alone to the Alone," the attainment in the life of God. There is one further passage in which he summarizes the importance, the difficulties, and the culminating glory of that flight.

As philosophers we are in search of Unity, the Principle of all, the Good, the First. Rising from the world of sense, we must strike for the realm of the First. From many we must become one, ascending to Divine Spirit, renewing our soul in That. . . . The difficulty is that awareness of the One comes not by knowing but by a Presence passing knowledge. In knowing, the mind takes account of things: it departs from unity and becomes lost in multiplicity. This other way lies beyond knowing. We urge that you abandon discussion and heed the call of vision. . . . There the soul looks upon the fountains of Life and Spirit, the springs of Being, the well of Goodness, the root of the Soul. These fountains flow eternally, without diminishment. . . . Now the man is merged in the Supreme, molten into It, one with It. He is become the Unity, without diversity or separation. Once this ascent is achieved, there is no thought, no passion, no outward-looking desire. Reason is in abeyance, and will, and the life of the senses. Lifted away, God-possessed, in stillness, the initiate rests without movement: he is Rest itself.

There is, too, an unforgettable precept that has become a sort of motto of the Neo-Platonists: "Never did eye see the Sun unless first it had become Sun-like. Never can the soul see Primal Beauty unless itself be beautiful. Therefore let each man become Godlike and beautiful who aspires to see Beauty and God."

V. CHRISTIAN MYSTICISM, FROM THE FOUNDERS TO SAINT BERNARD

WHEN SAINT BERNARD of Clairvaux, after eleven hundred years of the gradual development of Christian mysticism, spoke these words: "The Lord, the Bridegroom, has entered into my soul . . . and I have known the loveliness of His beauty," he indicated a difference between Christian union with the Divine and Oriental types of mystical experience. The Christian mystic, while losing nothing of the sublimity of the abstract union with the Absolute as known to Eastern sages, is likely to substitute a "contemplation of the heart" — Bernard's phrase — for intellectual meditation. It is a love of the heart, channelled through the ineffably sweet experience of knowing Christ in the soul, that carries the initiate into the consciousness of immersion, of self-loss in the Eternal.

The Christian founders substituted, in place of the abstract One, a sympathetic God-Father. They further made Divinity engaging to the heart through the conception of a personal, indwelling Christ. Certainly it is the heart that is concerned when Bernard speaks of his experience as "an inpoured savour of heavenly sweetness" and "a taste of the presence of God." Again he is "'sweetly refreshed with delicious love." Love and beauty are of the texture of his song.

In a second matter Bernard is a perfect example of the departure of the Christian mystic from the Oriental type. He was, in addition to being a spiritual seer and an example of self-giving to God, a man of monumental energy, a statesman, and a great churchman of his time. Typically, the Christian mystic curbs the inclination to seclusion. He cultivates the uses of silence and withdrawal so far as may be necessary for serenity of mind and for occasional flight to divine union. But typically he follows contemplation with service, abstention with participation in active works.

From the incomparable preacher and organizer of churches, Paul, and from Augustine, most active of the "Fathers," to Saint Catherine, who interrupted her ecstatic devotion to Christ in order to sway kings and popes to her conception of an orderly church, and to Saint Francis and Eckhart and the baffled shoemaker Jacob Boehme, who hardly saw his visions out before snatching up a pen to inscribe God's message; from the first mystics among the Apostles to that latest Christian mystic poet whose hand never rested from "my endeavour to restore the Golden Age," to restore the Age when man finds "Eternity in an hour" — from first to last the great Christian mystics stayed out their lifetimes in the current of mortal occupations. As preachers, statesmen, writers, teachers, artists, they have returned from their contemplations, their flights, their rapturous sojourns with God, to illumine that corner of the earth about them, or it may be a whole nation or realm, with light from their visions and their understanding.

Mysticism in the West — that is, Christian mysticism — entails no denial of the warmth, the impulses, the humanity of the heart; involves, rather, a sublimation of the emotions. Equally, Christian mysticism implies less retreat from the world, a withdrawal into the light of the Divine, than an enlargement of the mortal horizon and a mission among men to reveal to them the joy of knowing Eternal Life in the midst of mortal affairs.

Buddhism and Christianity, the two most widely embraced spiritual faiths, were founded by mystics. In the one case the Buddha Gautama instituted for his followers a religion that induces a high personal holiness and an admirable social ethic, but only as incidental along a path of personal mystic experience. The end of the path is Nirvana, or extinction of selfhood in the ocean of eternal Divinity. There is a negative aspect to the Buddhist faith, a denial of the heart and of the importance of life in the world, which is fundamentally different from the message that can be read in the words, and the life, of Jesus. Nevertheless the Christian faith advances a way of life not unlike the Buddhist in its subordination of worldly and sensual interests to spiritual, its glorification of a transcendent Being (in the one case abstract, in the other God), and its positing of Divine immersion or communion as the highest good in mortal life.

Both faiths, in short, are essentially, profoundly mystical. The mysticism of the one is passive, impersonal, and a summons from life. The mysticism of the other is emotional, heart-warming, an active Guide.

The Roman Empire during the mortal lifetime of Jesus was already decadent. The Republic had given way to a monarchy, which alone seemed able to hold at bay the "barbarians" of the North and East and to check the disorders arising at home from the injustices suffered by a miserable and hopeless populace. A small minority, luxury-loving and cruel, joined with the military leaders to maintain a precarious stability of government in a capital city in which slaves outnumbered free citizens. The provinces that stretched from Spain in the West to Syria in the East, peopled by tribes and nations as different as the Britons, Gauls, Egyptians, Jews, and Dacians, were ruled by Roman governors and procurators, or in some cases (as in Palestine at the moment of the birth of Jesus) by native leaders invested with the authority to collect taxes and rule.

Herod the Great, named by Roman authority "King of the Jews," wholesale murderer and magnificent builder, ruled Palestine under the Emperor Augustus Caesar. The following Emperors, signalizing the increasing degeneracy of Rome, were the cruel Tiberius, the insane Caligula, the uncouth fighter Claudius, and the vicious Nero.

At this time Jupiter and the other sometime Roman gods had been all but forgotten. The Emperors were deified, and the only test of good standing within the official religion was willingness to take the oath of belief in the Caesars as divine. A hundred cults had crept in, largely corruptions from the Orient, and often enough were made to serve the bestial vices of a society more vicious than any other major one known to history. Nevertheless there were groups of sincere and holy worshippers in many parts of the Empire, many of them in direct line from the mystery religions of Greece. Judaism was the only united faith, and the only religion of the time destined to survive in the Western world.

In Palestine the air was doubly charged with confusion and despair, because the Jews had so long been a captive nation, subject successively to Assyrian, Persian, Greek, and Roman rule and persecution. For centuries Jewish literature had stressed the nation's woes and the apocalyptic note. An end of the old ways and the old sufferings was pictured as at hand. Faith in God's justice included expectation of reward and vengeance for the long-suffering.

When the Messiah came, saying that "The Kingdom of God is

at hand," the Jews as well as the Gentiles rejected Him. It was inevitable that influential Romans should act against Him; for He affronted officialdom by refusing to acknowledge the Emperors as divine, and He affronted the populace by condemning immorality and violence. On the other hand, the Jews failed to recognize in Him their promised deliverer. He wielded no political power, and He threw back on each man the responsibility of his own deliverance, revealing only a "way."

That his religion was a mystical one doubtless confused many who heard Him speak. He preached the experiencibility of God, the bringing of the joys of Eternal Life into the mortal sphere, the fellowship of a sacred communion. He spoke not of the freedom the Jewish prophets had so long envisioned and foretold, "the day of recompense," the riches shared, the oppressors put down. He offered no leadership in military glory. His message was that of a contemplative who walked in the presence of God.

It was the members of the mystery brotherhoods who were prepared to understand Him. Whether these were Greek or Egyptian or Roman, they were trained to the philosophy that begins with belief in the Kingdom of God within you, in a Divine indwelling light.

The great gift Jesus brought from Judaism, as contrasted with Hellenism, was the conception of a Father-God. There was also the strain of mysticism from the Psalmists and the prophets. The Jews had among them, moreover, certain groups of mystics who combined beliefs out of Judaism with others from foreign sources — Egyptian, Far Eastern, and, of course, Greek. The Essenes were the most famous sect within Palestine. They believed in One God, practical communism, and a moderate asceticism, were engaged in charitable works, and aimed at an ideal of holy living, contemplation, and Divine illumination. They believed in baptism, prophecy, the soul's immortality and resurrection, and the existence of angels. The Essene higher wisdom was carefully veiled from all but initiates.

The Essenes and the Neo-Pythagoreans, and the surviving members of the Orphic and Dionysian brotherhoods, would understand the message of Jesus because His life was essentially that of the self-abandoning mystic. The way of His own illumination, His self-identification with God, his retirement into solitary contemplation and prayer when mortal problems impended, and His casting away of self that a communion might be founded — this

CHRIST APPEARING TO THE APOSTLES AFTER THE RESURRECTION. COLORED DRAWING BY WILLIAM BLAKE. ROSENWALD COLLECTION, NATIONAL GALLERY OF ART, WASHINGTON. (PHILADELPHIA MUSEUM OF ART PHOTO).

is all in the pattern of the seer exalting the Spirit and bringing down the Life of Transcendence, of the Eternal, to the world of material and time. His own years he made an example of the "new" life, the "saving" life, of the man possessed of God.

His ethical teachings, even, are those of the mystic "mad with the Spirit." Poverty, compassion, pacifism, forgiveness, humility of the self toward the Divine — are not these attributes implicit in the lives of seers from Lao-Tse and the Buddha Gautama to Saint Francis and Brother Lawrence?

It is hardly necessary to remind ourselves of the visions Jesus experienced — how "He saw the Spirit of God descending," and "Lo, a voice from Heaven saying, 'This is my beloved Son' " — or of the characteristic periods of withdrawal for intercourse with God, from which He went back strengthened to His ministry among men, or, after the Agony, to make the supreme mortal sacrifice. His very way of meeting the world was that of the extreme visionary. "Take no thought . . . " and "Resist not evil." There is too the injunction to lay up treasures in Heaven, "for where your treasure is, there will your heart be also." There is, indeed, in all literature no statement of the way of life of the mystic who has committed all to God that surpasses in rich suggestiveness the Sermon on the Mount.

But it is the deified life as a whole that so shines forth as a model to all Christian mystics after, so that the phrase "the imitation of Christ" carries an import of perfect holiness, continuous communion with God, and the illumining of mortal environment with a joyous Heavenly light. This is the avatar in perfect example. This is the Son of God conscious in every mortal act of His Divine being and Divine responsibility.

Jesus did not escape, nor has any committed mystic altogether escaped, the dark night that precedes the day of Light. He experienced temptation and frustration and the disappointment that came with the inability of common men to grasp His message. He felt that He had failed of His mission — in life. But unfalteringly He persevered, selflessly, knowing that in death He would triumph. And, indeed, then the message was made clear to those who had faltered, denied. Upon the cross, as if to emphasize the humanness of his being, he cried out (if Mark is to be believed) in desperation of suffering. But the end is in glory: being disappears into Being, and the faithful ones see Him triumphant in the vision of the Ascension.

Jesus wrote down, so far as is known, not one word. Nevertheless books of the sayings of Jesus were in common currency in the century during which Christianity took shape. From these and from personal recollection the several framers of the Gospels drew, and the wisdom of the Christ was given to the wider world.

"This is the Life Eternal, that they might know Thee . . ." is but one of the sayings that are essentially mystical. The words fix the basic metaphor by which He was to present His message of attainment. To know God, to live a life of consciousness of His presence, to feel oneself a citizen of His joyous Kingdom, is to partake of Life Eternal: such is the essential Christian revelation.

The figure He used most frequently in His preaching was that of the Kingdom. Before taking thought of things, "Seek ye first the Kingdom of God." And "I must preach the Kingdom of God to other cities also: for therefor am I sent." The Sermon on the Mount opens with an enumeration of those who shall be blessed, who shall "see God" and know "the Kingdom of Heaven." The parables oftenest begin with the words, "The Kingdom is like unto . . ." whether it be "like unto treasures hid in a field," or "like unto leaven," or "like unto a grain of mustard seed."

When the Disciples ask why He speaks to the multitude in parables, Jesus answers: "Because it is given unto you to know the mysteries of the Kingdom of Heaven, but to them it is not given." He thus touches upon a mystery of the secret life: that, though it is appointed for all, initiates only are ready for it. Its wisdom must be somewhat veiled. Yet it must be preached, even though the one preaching die for it.

Patiently, when He meets lack of comprehension, the Master explains that "The Kingdom of Heaven is within you." He is explicit: not here, not there, "but within you." The millions who pray daily, "Thy Kingdom come," are petitioning — if the words of Jesus signify — for entry into His Eternal Life, for inward union with God in the mystic's sense. It is within, not without, that a portal opens upon God's presence. The one who believes experiences a new birth, enters, "rests" in Him.

But at the time of the ministry of Jesus the road to that consummation has been obscured. The Christ's own preaching fails to reveal the way for numbers of men. Even the example of Divine living is not enough; they will not believe fully, passionately, until His mortal life is done, until the dénouement of a death-sacrifice makes clear the significance of his story.

Then the ones who are ready recognize that He has lived the life of the invisible in the visible. He has known the one Reality, has been conscious of the one Kingdom. He has brought down Divinity, as Son of Man and Son of God. He has interwoven the mortal with the Transcendent order. In the supreme act of surrender, the bodily crucifixion, the end of the sacrificial life is made clear: the final issue is ascension, joy.

Among the sayings of Jesus are a few that suggest practical steps by which other men may approach the road into the Kingdom. Among the parables and the metaphoric figures and the oblique references — hardly less indirect and cryptic than the body of literature concerning the Greek Mysteries — there are phrases and directions patently calling the believing ones to participation. "If any man will come after Me, let him deny himself, and take up his cross, and follow Me. . . . For what is a man profited if he shall gain the whole world, and lose his own soul?" And: "Except ye be converted, and become as little children, ye shall not enter into the Kingdom of Heaven."

Upon the nature of His own Sonship he is specific. Then: "Where two or three are gathered together in my name, there am I in the midst of them." At the Last Supper He specified the symbols, the sharing of bread and wine, that would witness his "covenant," that would mark the communion of those who had entered, through belief in Him, into the Kingdom.

Even in these sayings, nevertheless, the meanings are veiled. The "way," as indicated in "self-denial" and "conversion" and "communion," the mystic meaning of entry into the Kingdom, of His presence in the community of holy ones, of the nature of the bread and wine as His actual Being — all this was destined to remain a mystery in most men's minds until there came interpreters and builders of a church.

Fortunately the disciples of the Christ included in their number both vivid historians and men of mystic vision. It is the author of the Gospel of John especially who adds perfect visionary understanding and imaginative poetry to his account of the life and ministry of Jesus. Paul too, hostile and callous and legalistic until he is accorded, unaccountably, an ecstatic revelation and is converted, takes up the work of interpreting, preaching, organizing. It is he who recognizes the significance alight under the mystery-words and, more than any other, sets Christianity in the mould of a Christ-fellowship. It is he who speaks of the attainment of the

Kingdom as "putting on Christ." It is he who places peace and serenity of the spiritual life, through mystic attainment to the Presence, first among Christian aims.

For many decades after the death of Jesus it was not Christianity that was at the heart of religious controversy in the Western world. The liveliest conflict was between Greek thought and Judaic faith. The Jews of the Western Dispersion had developed at Alexandria a community second only to Jerusalem as a centre of Jewish life and culture. Their scriptures had long since been translated into Greek in the Septuagint Bible, and a considerable literature had grown up around the question of a possible reconciliation, if not marriage, of Greek philosophy with the faith of Judaism.

In the time of Jesus the great philosopher Philo marked the culmination of the attempt to Platonize the religion of Moses. He more than any other teacher achieved a synthesis of Jewish and Greek ideas about God, the universe, good and evil, and man's spiritual nature. These compromises, more liberal than Eastern Jewish orthodoxy would tolerate, nevertheless were discussed at Jerusalem and wherever Jews congregated in the Roman world. In so far as they created an atmosphere of liberalism and open-mindedness they helped prepare the way for the triumph of Christianity. The idea of a fusion of philosophies and religions led also to the founding of Gnosticism (which drew upon Philo, the mystery religions, and many other sources, including the revelation of Jesus); and Gnosticism had to be fought by the early Christian founders.

Paul and the author of *John* found the way somewhat prepared for Christianity by the Alexandrian Jews. They took, especially from Philo, some enlarged framework conceptions. They even incorporated certain Greek philosophic truths within the structure built according to Old Testament Jewish prophecy. It is probable that Christianity would have preserved less of the mystic form of the message of Jesus, had not Paul and the writer of the Fourth Gospel known Philo's books.

The one who wrote in John's name gave to the world a mystical poet's account of the ministry of Jesus. His is the most beautiful and perhaps the truest story of the life and death of the Christ. It is profound, moving, and spiritually illuminating.

The Apostle John had been the best-beloved of the disciples of

Jesus, the most understanding and the most spiritual-minded. He apparently had given himself to the sort of companionship with God that was exemplified in his Master. The later writer who composed a gospel under John's name, emulating him, was enabled to transmit the revelation of Jesus as Matthew, Mark, and Luke could not. We have every reason to believe that he speaks as the Christ spoke — with the mystic's love and certainty and raptness.

The opening lines of the Johannine Gospel are like an announcement that this is to be an interpretation through an initiate's mind: the story told by one who has known the Christ as the mystic Logos, the Word, by one who has tasted Everlasting Life:

> In the beginning was the Word, and the Word was with God, and the Word was God. . . .
> In Him was life; and the life was the light of men.
> And the light shineth in darkness; . . . but as many as received Him, to them He gave the power to become the sons of God.

Thus John prefaces his history with the assertion that the life in God is the light of men, that most men live in darkness, but that for the initiate the light shineth. The initiate, reading the Evangelist's preface, would comprehend second and third meanings in the term "Word" or "Logos." For among mystics and philosophers since the time of Heraclitus, "Logos" had meant the immanence of a higher Spirit in human life, a sort of intelligence or Divinity that fathered the soul; and but recently Philo, in harmonizing Hebrew, Platonic, and Stoic conceptions, had glorified the Logos as the unknowable Supreme God come down to the knowable range of Creation, and again as the agency or expression of God entering into the consciousness of man, rescuing the soul from the darkness of mortal illusion.

John takes the decisive step of naming the Christ as the Logos. It is one of the determining steps in Christian history. Jesus is portrayed as the redeemer of a mankind lost in an illusion of reality, recalled by His presence to Oneness, in the only true Reality, that of God, of the Holy Spirit. "The Logos was God. . . . The Logos was made flesh and dwelt among us. . . . As many as received Him, to them gave He power to become sons of God." And John ascribes to Jesus the promise: "He that heareth my word, and believeth on Him that sent me, hath everlasting life, and . . .

is passed from death to life." As if in summary of His own mission as guide into the mystic life of knowledge of God, Jesus adds: "I am the Way, the Truth, and the Life: no man cometh unto the Father, but by Me."

John lights up the Fourth Gospel with this special seer's illumination, portraying and interpreting Jesus as the mystic, but there is no point at which he pauses to expound, as it were, the philosophy of Christian mysticism. He takes it for granted that the message of Jesus is that of a redeemer sent to save mankind from the unillumined life. It is in John's report that Jesus, raising his eyes to God, speaks the words: "This is life eternal, that they might know Thee, the only true God, and Jesus Christ whom Thou hast sent." The chapter, the seventeenth, is the nearest approach in the Christian Bible to what may be conjectured as the final rite of the mystery religions: the solemn appeal in the Holy of Holies for God's entry into the souls of the initiates and for their participation in His Eternal life. Toward the end occur the telling words: "I in them, and Thou in me, that they may be made perfect in One."

Such, in the words of John, is Jesus' own exhortation for Divine living for all those who receive Him. Just before speaking thus to Heaven, He has said to the Disciples: "Behold the hour cometh that ye shall be scattered, every man to his own, and shall leave me alone: and yet I am not alone, because the Father is with me. These things I have spoken unto you, that in me ye might have peace. In the world ye shall have tribulation: but be of good cheer; I have overcome the world." The world overcome, peace within, God in the soul: it is as simple and true a statement of the mystic's aim as any in the world's literature.

There is a surpassing love in John's own heart toward Jesus; and in his testimony to the glowing personality of his Master — echoed a thousand years afterward in Bernard's veneration of "the loveliness of His beauty" — there is a beginning point of the digression of Christian worship and Christian mysticism from the abstract ideal. Of all the Gospel-writers, John spoke most of love, and found love in the words of Jesus. "We love because He first loved us." And: "If a man love me, he will keep my words: and my Father will love him, and We will come unto him and make our abode with him."

The loving intimacy of the soul and the Redeemer is beautifully suggested in John's allegory of the vine and in its refrain, "Abide in me, and I in you."

John's mysticism is Christ-centred, though not with Paul's insistence upon "Christ in me." John's emphasis, unlike that of many a later Christian writer, is on the possibility of redemption now: not saving from a dire fate after death, but a lifting out of death into life *now*. Salvation is a present matter. Similarly John has less to say of the Crucifixion and atonement than of God brought down among men, revealing the way, establishing the One among those who believe, giving "of His fullness."

Central too is that other thought, "Ye must be born again." To escape from the darkness of uncomprehension, conversion is necessary. "Except a man be born again, he cannot see the Kingdom of God." We have been born of the flesh: we must be reborn of the Spirit. Taking on the Spirit, God, we overcome, with Christ, the world.

It is John, finally, who explains the mystic significance of the sacrament of the bread and the wine: the forming of a Christian fellowship of those who are One — "I in them, Thou in me," and "they also One in Us" — because they have taken on the Christ. "The bread of God is He which cometh down from Heaven, and giveth life to the world. . . . I am the bread of life: he that cometh to me shall never hunger; and he that believeth on me shall never thirst. . . . He that believeth on me hath everlasting life. I am that bread of life."

There was yet a third beside the Master and the disciple John who helped fix Christianity in the mould it had during the primitive age. And again, with Paul, it is a personal, heartfelt, loving experience that is at the centre of the interpretation of the Christ's words.

Paul is at once interpreter and organizer. The practical nature of his interpretations, his way of restating and universalizing the Christian principles, grows out of his experience in founding churches. His writings are exclusively letters, to fellow disciples or to congregations. Nevertheless the Pauline Epistles are vivid, convincing, wise. Incidentally they form the earliest body of Christian literature, for the Four Gospels were not written in their surviving form until after Paul's death in the year 67.

But if he is practical, Paul is nevertheless both dreamer and mystic. From scoffer at the Christ and persecutor of Christians, he turns to mystic devotion and to a dream of a universal Christian brotherhood. He gives his life in service to that dream. His name lives on as that of one of the greatest spiritual leaders of all time.

Born Saul of Tarsus, a Jew, in the year 1, he was educated in Jerusalem as a rabbi. He became a fanatic upholder of Judaism and one of the bitterest persecutors of the Christians. It was while he was travelling toward Damascus upon a mission to uproot Christianity there that he experienced a conversion so vivid and so miraculous that he was instantly forced to accept Jesus as the Messiah. After three years in retirement he took up his Christian work; and it was he who determined that the religion of Jesus should be put before the world as a universal religion rather than as a variant sect of Judaism.

As a rabbi he had been lawyer as well as minister, and his devotion had been overwhelmingly to the Law of God. His conversion taught him to put Christ and Christ's love first. As a student he had been conversant with Greek philosophy and with the efforts to reconcile Platonism with scriptural Judaism. He knew of the mystery religions of Greece, and doubtless of the Essenes in Palestine. He was thus prepared in mind to understand the revelation of Jesus; and he threw himself unreservedly into a mystic relationship with "the Christ within."

For more than thirty years Paul preached, at first to the Jews, then especially to the Gentiles. He founded churches, travelled as missionary, wrote long letters of direction and exhortation. He succeeded in establishing Christian congregations in key cities of the Roman Empire, including Antioch, Ephesus, Philippi, and Rome, although he failed in Athens. In addition to suffering "the care of all the churches" he suffered persecution and imprisonment. One has a vivid picture of his troubles in his own words in the Second Epistle to the Corinthians. "Thrice was I beaten with rods, once was I stoned, thrice I suffered shipwreck, a night and a day have I been in the deep; in journeyings often, in peril of water, in peril of robbers, in peril of mine own countrymen, in peril of the heathen, in peril in the city, in peril in the wilderness, in peril in the sea, in peril among false brethren; in weariness and painfulness, in watchings often, in hunger and thirst, in fastings often, in cold and nakedness."

But he persevered, and went on founding churches and advising other missionaries and preaching. Going as an old man to

SAINT PAUL. PAINTING BY EL GRECO.
CITY ART MUSEUM, ST. LOUIS.

Rome, where he had once been acquitted after imprisonment, he arrived, accompanied by Luke, when Nero was exterminating the Christians there. He was condemned by Nero and beheaded.

The success of Paul's life is in the joy that he could draw upon at any hour, the unfailing Presence from which he could take courage. He made of the Christian religion, not a hope, but a way of living, a salvation accomplished. He knew the Christ in the heart, by experience. He had visions, too; but it was the continuous realization of the Divine One within that seemed to him central. Because one possessed Christ, one possessed Sonship, one was with God, one was sustained from within by a fountain of joy that nullified every tribulation, every affliction.

The intuition of Christ, the sense of community in the Divine, the ever-present feeling of "Christ in me": it is this that is Paul's essential contribution to the determining of the "way" of Christianity. To live life as illuminated by the Christ's presence, that is the ideal — to live as He lived mortally, in forgiveness and love and purity, and thereby to know the glory of the Everlasting Spirit; to love the Christ, for in loving Him you will be uplifted, and you will have only His divine impulses. Bitterness and anger, sensuality and covetousness will be impossible to you. Once we find the Christ in this total sense, "in Him we live and move and have our being."

In Paul's interpretation, one does not really belong to the Christian faith unless one thus holds personally to the Christ-identity, embraces the Christ in the heart. "Only faith working through love is of importance." Faith in Christ implies utter selfless reliance upon Him, a giving of one's consciousness to Him, a resting in Him. It is the sort of "rest in God" that the mystic knows as the profoundest peace — and the ultimate blissful rapture. Paul described it as "the peace of God, which passeth all understanding."

This inner love of the soul for Christ is the perfect incentive to a holy life, the spur to continual service of others and sharing with them; for when one can say with Paul, "It is no longer I that live, but Christ lives in me," one knows the sense of holiness and is impelled to enrich existence, to uncover in every mortal procedure or thing its eternal and divine aspect. One is then the true "God-seeing man." Arguing conversely, Paul writes that "He that doeth evil hath not seen God."

In acting always as the Christ in the heart impels, men become as brothers in His image, in "a vast family of brothers, and He the Eldest." This is the true Church. It is to be entered by experience, by a way of living, and not by profession. The Church is indeed, in Paul's view, a fellowship of those who have known mystical union with Christ. It is the body of those who have experienced His Being.

Beyond the taking of God into the soul Paul adds that the initiate must, in a very true sense, live again Jesus' life of ministry, suffering, and redemption. Only thus will he attain "the riches of the glory of this mystery." A sharing of His afflictions, a travelling of His way through sorrow into glory, is a part of the soul's "abidance in Him." Yet there is in Paul's letters no unhealthy obsession with affliction, sorrow, and death. As in John, the crucifixion and the idea of atonement by sacrifice are less stressed than the life divinely lived and the illumination brought into men's consciousness. "For if we have died with Christ, we believe that we shall also live with Him." And "Be ye therefore followers of God, and walk in love. . . . Ye were sometimes a part of the darkness, but now ye are light, in the Lord; walk as children of light."

Paul was converted swiftly, ecstatically, in a vision. He speaks of visions as normal manifestations, as any convinced mystic must. He tells his own story by indirection, as of "a man in Christ . . . caught up to the third Heaven. . . . How that he was caught up into Paradise, and heard unspeakable words, which it is not lawful for a man to utter." But he does not expect all men to have specific visions; though all mankind must be converted. Sometimes he speaks of conversion as the raising of the soul out of darkness or out of death. Oftenest he speaks of putting on "the new man." Thus he exhorts the Ephesians: "that ye be renewed, in the Spirit, in your minds; and that ye put on the new man, which, after God, is created in righteousness and true holiness." This rebirth in the Spirit results in a total change in the man's outlook: "If any man be in Christ, he is a new creature: old things are passed away; behold, all things are become new." This is "the life-giving change in the inner man," "the re-birth in Christ," which is the mystical conversion and the true entry into the Christian Church.

Thus was fixed by the Founder, and by two visionary disciples, the "way" that is Christian. They did not state, at length, any philosophy. Rather they revealed in snatches, and incidentally to parable, narrative, and letters of counsel, an art of life that is spiritual, profound, and mystical. Other prophets and seers were to come, to reinterpret and enrich, and to make easier of access for common men the profundities and the gracious humanness of the Christian message. Yet in the course of ten centuries there came hardly more than two or three seers who both understood Jesus' intuition of God and themselves possessed the gift of philosophic prophecy. There is but the smallest body of Christian mystic literature as a heritage from the millennium ending A.D. 1000. Certainly there was no mystic writer within the faith to compare with the non-Christian Plotinus.

Happily there were many men and women who grasped the message to its profoundest implications and lived the Christ-centred life. Hermitic and monastic mysticism flowered among the monks of the Egyptian deserts. Saint Anthony, fleeing a life of riches, sought solitude in desert ruins, persisted through distractions, hard work, and temptations, and came to believe that mystic union with God is "the only perfect prayer." His follower, Saint Macarius the Great, his soul alight and afire with the love of Christ, became one of the earliest inspired writers in the Johannine tradition. He especially set the pattern, in his *Homilies,* for the Christian mystic's life that alternates between "peace and activity"; for, he says, "at times the holy man puts on the armour of the Spirit, and attacks and crushes the enemies of the soul; but again he sinks deep into silence, and silent his soul rests in profound peace, and savours ineffable delights."

In the second and third centuries there had been that other sort of mystic faith, a self-giving and a spiritual certainty, which had armoured the martyrs against surrender of their beliefs and against fainting under torture. There is no more moving and uplifting story in the martyrology than that of Perpetua and Felicitas, who went to the arena with a band of fellow-Montanists, to be pitted against wild beasts, in the year 203. The twenty-two-year-old Perpetua and her serving-maid Felicitas, a slave, were tortured and killed before the crowds. Felicitas, who had shown outwardly her suffering at childbirth, when asked during the days before going to the amphitheatre how then she could bear the pain of an attacking animal, answered: "There I am to suffer for Him; there He will be in me, He will suffer for me." And in the arena she fully bore out her promise to rely on Him; for when she had been gored once, she called for her brother and said to him: "Stay fast in the faith, and all love one another; and do not be distressed by our sufferings." Tertullian, who tells the story, speaks of Perpetua's joy as the little band marched to the amphitheatre: she went "with a shining mien, as if fully the spouse of Christ, beloved of God."

Thus had their souls so come into the Kingdom that uncounted thousands of martyrs marched joyously into the Roman arenas, suffering torture, degradation, and mortal death, untouched in the spirit. It was a sort of mystic exhilaration lifting them above every mortal consideration that thus shielded them. But it marked a phase of Christian mysticism far from the normal, lasting, contemplative type.

During the first five hundred years of Christianity the new faith swept amazingly across the Roman world. Having no political aims, the Christian leaders proceeded without organized opposition to any government. They scrupulously practised Christian non-resistance. What brought the martyrs into conflict with authority was their refusal to declare openly an allegiance to the Emperors as divine. But the persecution was fitful, and as the Church took form a succession of great spiritual leaders lived, organized, strengthened the structure, wrote books, and passed on.

Among the Greek Fathers particularly, the work of universalizing the faith continued, and since Greek thought was pre-eminent in the Mediterranean cities there was a continual process of reading Platonic ideas into Scripture. Clement of Alexandria, who lived during the latter half of the second century and the opening decades of the third, brought elements and something of the terminology of the Mystery faiths to his interpretation of Christian theology and mysticism, holding especially to "purgation" as a necessary preparation for illumination. He moved in a line parallel to that of the early Neo-Platonists, though without ever giving himself unreservedly to the experience of divine union.

Origen, too, a generation younger and a devoted student of Ammonius Saccas, interprets Christian ideas with an unmistakable Neo-Platonic emphasis. At the very moment when Plotinus is erecting the structure of Neo-Platonism in his lectures at Rome, Origen is both borrowing from and opposing that pagan mystical faith (and opposing also the more dubious Gnosticism). He succeeds in reconciling elements out of the Greek and the Hebraic traditions. Of mysticism he makes something considerably more sober and brooding and God-centred than does Plotinus; something at once less abstract and less ecstatic.

It was a century later that Victorinus, a Neo-Platonist philosopher and lecturer in Rome, was converted to Christianity, bringing a fresh wave of Greek influence into the current of Christian teaching. As a Christian he was soon forbidden by the Romans to lecture, and he closed his school, but not until he had instructed Jerome, thus profoundly influencing later Church thought. Nor was he without influence upon that greater contemporary of Jerome, Augustine. In this same generation there was the recluse Cassianus, who gathered all the materials about the life and mystic practices of the desert monks and wrote the *Dialogues,* a much-prized treatise on the life of the soul and on the form of exalted prayer that opens the doors of the heart to Divine communion.

When the fourth century opened, the time had come when all institutions in the Roman world were forced to cast up their accounts with Christianity. Persecution by successive Emperors had merely proved the mettle of the believers and had increased the number of Christians. The old Roman faith, the classic gods, had died of neglect. The attempt to deify the Caesars and to exact worship by force had failed to make of the worshipped anything more than ambitious overlords; had certainly failed to unite the worshippers in holiness. Christianity had grown steadily, had expanded, had fired the minds of those men who might be least expected to give themselves to a religion of self-immolation and divine communion: slaves and patricians, soldiers and philosophers, even the prison attendants who tended the martyrs and the gladiators who sometimes had to kill them when the beasts were not wholly effective. Finally an Emperor was won over.

It was in A.D. 312 that Constantine, as the result of a vision, placed the Christian insignia upon the shields of his soldiers and, when he had been successful, legalized Christian worship. As emperor he presided over the Council of Nicaea in 325, a historic meeting at which Church leaders from East and West healed certain divisions among the faithful, clarified the Creed, and started the Christian polity upon its momentous way. The occasion was of such import that to this day historians speak of Ante-Nicene Christianity and Post-Nicene Christianity.

Of the Post-Nicene Fathers of the Church there came in this century one who served memorably to reinforce mystical interpretations of the Gospels and to fix yet more firmly in Christian thought the Neo-Platonic philosophy of Ammonius Saccas and Plotinus. Augustine, Bishop of Hippo in Roman Africa, was personally a mystic; but he came to occupy so eminent a place in the Church and was so busied with sermons, letters, tracts, and exegetical works that he seems to have found time seldom for entry into the higher and serener ranges of divine communion. His most personal published work, the *Confessions,* is lit up again and again with joyous praise of God's goodness in granting to the soul the boon of identification with the Holy Spirit. But the indications of an utter self-giving to the Christ experience are less evident. Saint Augustine was a restrained mystic, a believer in the ecstatic experience but one not fully committed to habitual contemplation and entry into rapt union.

Born a Numidian, in the year 354, of a Christian mother and an indifferent father, Augustine was educated at Carthage and became a teacher of rhetoric. Sceptic, irregular in morals though periodically contrite about it, he was anything but Christian in his early years. In Rome he was deeply affected by Victorinus' translation into Latin of the *Enneads* of Plotinus. Then, partly through the influence of the great Ambrose of Milan, he was converted, though the actual occasion of his spiritual awakening had something of the character of a swift and peace-bringing illumination. He returned to Africa for years of study and writing, and at the age of forty-two was consecrated Bishop of Hippo. Of the numberless works he wrote in the following thirty years the most important is his monumental *The City of God,* an extraordinary exposition of Christian doctrine and an idealistic prophecy of the fellowship of Christians as a world-community.

Saint Augustine takes a great deal of his mysticism from Plato and Plotinus, while reconciling Christian thought with theirs regarding the soul, Providence, good and evil, and many other matters. But in the end he is more Christian than Greek. His way of integrating his mystical life with his career as a churchman is directly in line with Paul's compromise of vision with the worklife. And his later pronouncements upon the experience of rapture were tinged with memory of the personal experience of Christ, of a communion born of love.

In one of the tenderest and most thoughtful passages in the

AUGUSTINE RECORDING HIS VISION OF THE CITY OF GOD. MINIATURE PAINTING, ENLARGED. FLORENTINE, 15TH CENTURY. SPENCER COLLECTION, NEW YORK PUBLIC LIBRARY.

Confessions he tells of talking with his mother, the gentle Monica, just before her death, about the nature of the eternal life and of approach to the state of perfect spiritual understanding. At that time he was newly a Christian, and his words and images are tellingly those of his Neo-Platonist teachers.

> We were discoursing then together, alone, very sweetly; and we were inquiring, in the presence of Truth, which Thou art, of what sort the life of the Saints might be, which eye hath not seen, nor ear heard, nor hath it entered into the heart of man. Nevertheless we panted with the lips of our soul after those heavenly streams of Thy fountain, the fountain of Life, in order that, receiving waters thence according to our capacity, we might in some sort penetrate so high a mystery. Brought to the conclusion that the very highest delight of the mortal senses, in the purest corporeal life, was, as regards the delight of that life, not only unworthy of comparison but unworthy of mention, we raised ourselves with a more glowing love towards the inward Eternal; and passing by degrees through all things constituted, we were soaring higher yet by inward thought and discourse and marvelling at Thy works. We came to our own minds, and went beyond them, that we might come into that realm of never-fading plenty where "Thou feedest Israel" for ever. . . . And while we were discoursing and panting after her, we slightly touched on her with the final leap of our heart; then we sighed, and left enshrined the first fruits of the Spirit. . . .
>
> We were saying then: if the tumult of the flesh were hushed, hushed the impressions of earth and waters and air, hushed also the poles of heaven, yea, the very soul hushed to herself, . . . if we might hear His Very Self, without intermediary — as now we reached forward and in a flash of perception touched on the Eternal Wisdom that enwraps all — if then this could be prolonged, and other visions of unlike kind be withdrawn, and this one ravish, and absorb, and wrap its beholder in inward joys, so that life might be eternally that one moment of understanding, were not this "entry into the joy of the Lord"?

The dispassionate air and the dispensing with intermediaries are signs of Augustine's dependence still upon Plotinus. In other cases he actually echoes, even quotes, the great Neo-Platonist: never more so than when he praises, in *The City of God*, that other face of mysticism, the finding of the signature of the divinity in common things:

> Plotinus the Platonist proves by means of the blossoms and leaves that from the Supreme God, whose beauty is invisible and ineffable, Providence reaches down to the things of earth here below. He points out that these frail and mortal objects could not be endowed with a beauty so immaculate and so exquisitely wrought, did they not issue from that Divinity which endlessly pervades with its invisible and unchanging beauty all things.

To this passage Augustine appends the thought: "This is proven also by the Lord Jesus, when He says: 'Consider the lilies . . .'"

Of the mystic experience as a foretaste, permitted to chosen and prepared mortals, of the beatific vision to come, Augustine writes in the *Confessions:* "Where hast Thou not walked with me, O Truth, instructing me what to beware, and what to desire? . . . Thou art the abiding Light, which I consulted, and I heard Thee directing and commanding me; . . . nor in all these matters can I find any safe place for my soul except in Thee, to Whom I am gathered, and nothing apart. And sometimes Thou admittest me to a wondrous love, in my inmost soul; rising to a strange sweetness, which, if it were perfected in me, I know not how it might be different from the Eternal Life."

The special Christian mysticism of the heart, alight with love, is epitomized in another passage of the *Confessions:* "What do I love when I love Thee? Not the loveliness of bodies, nor the brightness of light, gladdening the eye, nor the sweet melodies of various songs, nor the spices, nor manna and honey, not limbs inviting bodily embrace: not these do I love when I love my God. Yet it is an illumination I feel, and melody, and fragrance, and a sustaining food, and an embrace that possesses my soul — when I love Thee."

Nevertheless Augustine goes back often to the Plotinian idea of the Absolute, and especially of the Absolute as the unchangeable: "The Light unchangeable," and "That which unchangeably abides, namely God." He goes back often, too, to the thought that however ecstatic the pleasure of divine union may be, it is attained in quietness and lingers in solitude. He speaks, from what depths of feeling only the mystic can know, of "such an absolute enjoyment of the supremest and truest Good, such a breathing of serenity and eternity, as is indescribable."

There is a point near the end of the seventh book of the *Confessions* at which Augustine tells how he has gained everything essential to a Christian mystic's understanding except the central taking on of the Christ. The passage signals a main juncture of scriptural and Greek ideas, a synthesis of enormous significance to Western mysticism. He sums up his gain from the Neo-Platonists in these words: "Thus in the flash of one trembling glance my soul arrived at That Which Eternally Is." But the experience was not complete: "I was thrown back on my wonted habits, carrying with me only a loving memory thereof . . . until I embraced that mediator between God and men, the man Christ Jesus." Thereafter he is the Christian mystic, in the line from Paul to Bernard and Francis, gaining his entry into "the inward sweetness of God" by the way of love and of "contemplating His beauty."

By the time of Augustine's death in the year 430 Christianity had dominated men's minds over most of the Western world. No rival religion had vitally survived. Judaism alone remained strong, and it was intensely racial and patently could not sway more than a small minority. Manichæism and Gnosticism had dwindled in stature from rivals of Christianity to inferior sects; though in early life Augustine had professed the one, and in later life he could not have been other than sympathetic with many tenets of the other. The Church had been consolidated and united, and the major heresy of early times, Arianism, had been put down. That is not to say that the progress of Christianity as a religious and social institution was no longer stormy. But the rise toward the Church's peak of influence and power, to be attained early in the sixth century, was continuing.

Before the year 500 there came into Christian literature a body of writings that had more influence upon the mystics of the Church than any other composed before the *Theologica Germanica* of the fourteenth century and the works of the German mystic divines of that century. The writings generally ascribed to "the False Dionysius" are a fountain-head of Christian mystic doctrine and a sort of final mingling of the waters of Palestinian wisdom and Greek philosophy. Seemingly from the pen of a Syrian monk writing in the second half of the fifth century, the Dionysian treatises present for the first time an orthodox philosophy comparable in scope and clarity to the Plotinian *Enneads*.

The tradition of pseudonymous writing went back centuries to the era of Jewish prophecy. In the three hundred years before the ministry of Jesus, when the Jews were struggling valiantly to preserve their faith inviolate, book after book of prophecy and apocalyptic promise had been composed and sent on its way under the name of Enoch or Daniel, or it might be Noah or Solomon or some other traditional spiritual leader. The authority of an earlier prophet was thus invoked for a contemporary message — and the local prophet without honour was cloaked in an honoured pseudonym. After the Christian revelation it was an unknown poet-prophet who put the name of John over the Fourth Gospel.

Now, in the fifth century, a churchman so obscure as to have remained untraceable in fifteen centuries since wrote under the chosen name Dionysius Areopagiticus. His books on Christian history and doctrine bulk incomparably larger than his lone work on the mystic life (and it may be this fact that led to the Church's blanket imprimatur upon his works, where the single book alone might have been suspect, for its patent Greekness or its mingling of Greek and Oriental thought with Jewish and Christian).

Biographically, then, there is nothing to be said of the False Dionysius. The biography of the little tract, *Concerning Mystical Theology*, is brief. It was written in Greek, and doubtless it was enthusiastically circulated in its own time and through the succeeding "Dark Ages." But it was only after its translation into Latin, at the hands of Erigena or John the Scot in the mid-ninth century, that it blazed a path across the sky of mediæval Christian thought. The triumphant rise of the Dionysian doctrine is then marked by the enthusiasm of a succession of great philosophers and theologians: Saint Anselm, Saint Bernard, Hugo and Richard of Saint Victor, Saint Thomas Aquinas, and many another.

John the Scot thought that Dionysius had marked more clearly than any other writer the path of mystic belief from Saint Paul through Plotinus and Proclus and Iamblichus. To put it in light from the Christian point of view, Dionysius had redeemed Platonic mysticism from its pagan estate, had adopted the truth and wisdom in it, and showed it out as a thing identical with the attainment of the Kingdom of Heaven preached by Jesus. Indeed he had, in his books on *The Celestial Hierarchy* and *The Ecclesiastical Hierarchy*, provided a framework for the mystic life in unassailable statements of Christian belief about God, the world, and the Church.

Yet the False Dionysius reverses some of the familiar symbols and figures of the earlier mystical writers, and he falls somewhat short of painting the experience of communion as an experience of love. For him, to live is to be conscious of God; all that is evil proceeds from lack of that consciousness. God is transcendent and unknowable, yet He is immanent in everything that is. The soul by purification rises to illumination and union. But the final union with God is described, not as attainment, but as entry into darkness. It is the darkness of unknowing, "Divine Darkness," the darkness that is at the heart of light. In other words, light is a thing created; there is a "beyond light"; and with the cessation of mental consciousness, the cessation of knowing, the soul is immersed in that "beyond," that darkness.

Unlike other leading Christian mystics, Dionysius tends to an Oriental abstraction, minimizing the rôle of the indwelling Christ. There is more of the unapproachable, the remote, than of the humanity of Jesus and of a "taken on" Redeemer. More is made, too, of symbols and of the offices of the Church. Yet no one ever put more simply and systematically and convincingly the mystic interpretation of the Christ revelation. There is, for illustration, this passage:

> You should, in the purposive practice of mystic contemplation, escape the senses and lay aside the guidance of the intellect, leaving behind, indeed, all that belongs to the sensual and the intellectual spheres, escaping alike what is and what is not, and rise upward toward union with Him Who is above all knowing and all being. By a continuous and total abandonment of your self, and withdrawal from all things, relinquishing all and freed from all and thus purified, you will pierce to the region of Divine darkness transcending all essence. . . . Then one is free and unhampered by things that are seen or by seeing, and one enters into the essential mystical darkness, the cloud of unknowing, from which knowledge is shut out, abiding in that which is intangible

and invisible, absorbed into Him Who is beyond all things. Now one belongs no longer to any, neither to the self nor to any other, but is united at the highest point to Him Who is above knowing. The soul, because of its complete unknowing, grasps Him in a manner above mind or understanding.

Dionysius, like all writers who set out to explain experiences for which there are no words, falls into apparent contradictions. He speaks, for instance, of "this luminous darkness, which is above sight and knowledge"; and again he says that "The divine darkness is the inaccessible light surrounding God." In one of his letters he parallels a familiar paradox of Lao-Tse's regarding the *Tao:* "If any one, seeing God, knows what he sees, it is by no means God that he sees, but something created and knowable." Nevertheless the obscure writer who is known only as the False Dionysius did more than any other toward Christianizing the Plotinian conception of a Divine ecstasy to be attained by purification, contemplation, and illumination. He laid the foundation for the structure that became mediæval Christian mysticism. John the Scot is no less indebted to him than is Eckhart, Saint Bernard than Ruysbroeck.

The centuries that fall between the fifth, when Augustine and the False Dionysius wrote (also the century when the Roman Empire finally dissolved, and a Goth became King of Rome), and the ninth, when John the Scot translated the treatises of Dionysius into Latin, are known as the Dark Ages. Doubtless in that era many men knew the incomparable joy of walking with God. Nevertheless it was a period of halting progress for Christianity, perhaps most important as preparation for the great mediæval surge forward. Philosophic writers were plentiful but unoriginal.

In the sixth century Boethius, a belated Roman noble, while in prison waiting to be put to death, wrote *On the Consolations of Philosophy,* a work widely prized during the Dark and Middle Ages, as witnessed by numberless translations and imitations. While somewhat less than a classic of mysticism, it is lighted with flashes of the wisdom of Neo-Platonism.

More directly in the line of mystic theologians was Gregory the Great, Pope and Saint, of the second half of the sixth century. A great teacher and a great Christian administrator, he wrote no treatise directly on the mystical life, but his books contain innumerable scattered references to apprehension of the Eternal Being by contemplation. He believed that "The soul is admitted to a certain unwonted sweetness of inward savour." But he warned that for a mortal it is impossible to attain the beatific vision as known to the blessed Saints; that is, to look upon God's face "and the unencompassed Light." Indeed, all the mortal can hope for is "to attain to somewhat of the unencompassed Light by stealth and scantily." Yet even this little is a sort of ecstasy, in which "the flood of the Holy Spirit in exuberant outpouring is gathered in the soul."

It was only a few years later that Maximus the Confessor, an ascetic of the Eastern Church, wrote his mystical works, including a commentary upon the works of Dionysius. But it was John the Scot, Erigena, translating the Dionysian treatises from the Greek into the language of the Western scholars, Latin, who is the pivotal figure during the dark half-millennium. He translated the commentary of Maximus along with the original texts, and elaborated the thought of the whole in tracts of his own.

An intellectual by nature, Johannes Scotus Erigena leaned to Greek abstraction rather than to Pauline or Johannine traditions of apprehension of the Kingdom through the Christ-consciousness. Nevertheless he fired the thought of all the men who contributed to the mystic tradition in the mediæval centuries; and he handed on to the Scholiasts — who in the end gave allegiance to Aristotle rather than to Plato and Plotinus — a structure of Christian theology and doctrine that preserved a special chapel for mystic devotion. It is beside the point that when reason, as opposed to authority, claimed an increasing place, especially with Abelard, Albertus Magnus, and, above all, Saint Thomas Aquinas, when scholastic rationalization and dogma tended to minimize the experiential aspects of religion, Erigena's works were banned by the Church. In any case John Scotus formed a bridge to the Christian mysticism of the mediæval saints from the combined Palestinian and Neo-Platonic mysticism of the Church Fathers.

As yet, and even as late as A.D. 1100, more than two hundred years after the death of John the Scot, there had been no major philosopher of Christian mysticism — only those early founders who had taken the philosophy for granted, and minor prophets, and commentators, and statesmen-seers whose services to the Church in other directions overshadowed their devotion to the mystic life. Before the mediæval flowering there was to be one of these active churchmen who, without being a prophet-philosopher in the fullest sense, would put forward Christian mysticism as had none before him: Saint Bernard.

In the early part of the twelfth century the Monastery of Saint Denis in Paris had succumbed to those temptations to worldliness that had carried monastic life to one of its lowest points. Even some years after the famous Suger had become Abbot, the monks of Saint Denis were engrossed with pursuits shameful in men vowed to poverty and holiness. It was another French Abbot, Bernard of Clairvaux, who wrote: "I have heard that this cloister is filled with petitioners and intriguing courtiers, and that it echoes with the tumult of worldly affairs, even that women find free admittance there. I ask how can the mind remain absorbed in God amid such disorders?" And it was Bernard who brought about the conversion of Suger and through him the reformation and purging of the Abbey.

The changes wrought at Saint Denis were but one example of the influence toward holiness exerted by the young Bernard from his monastery at Clairvaux — literally a Valley of Light, from which the illumination of a primitive monastic spirit shone out into the lives of numberless men in the Catholic world, laymen and bishops, soldiers and kings and common men, saints and sinners. Bernard, who had been made Abbot of Clairvaux when he was twenty-five years old, became within two decades the foremost churchman in Europe — and perhaps the most active mystic in the history of the Church. He is sometimes called the last of the Fathers; certainly he is worthy to end the line of organizers of the faith that began with the Apostolic founders.

To the mind of the ascetically inclined contemplative there is no tragedy greater than that of the man who comprehends the rewards that lie at the end of the mystic way, who has the inclination to surrender the self and live wholly in the mystic pursuit, yet lets himself be drawn into the business of the world, to the virtual exclusion of serene meditation and intuitive communion with the Divine. There are those who believe, on the other hand — and they are in the majority in the Christian community — that complete withdrawal and exclusive devotion to attainment of the sense of God's presence are less admirable than a balanced spiritual life; a life in which one knows at intervals the supreme joy of Divine union, yet at other times takes active part in the affairs of community, Church, and state. From Paul, who at first, upon conversion, was inclined to seek retirement and indeed withdrew into the Arabian desert for years of study and meditation, then embraced the active life, to Augustine and Gregory and John the Scot, the great Christian mystics are men of affairs. Each of these leaders, instead of retiring into monastic solitude or merely preaching or writing about the mystic life, entered into the work and the controversies and the propagandizing activities of a confused and often stormy Christendom.

Bernard carried on the tradition, and perhaps he felt more than any other the deprivation involved in abandoning the contemplative life for an active career. Few men have so nobly combined statecraft and a priest's devotion. Few have so lighted up a life of busy service with an awareness of the joys to be attained by flight from cares into the "embrace of God."

Bernard knew, indeed, mystic ecstasy, and he longed for the ordered life and the leisure from official duties that would permit frequent surrender to the soul's longing. But he was so sought after, and so efficient as organizer and founder, director and adviser, healer of schisms, debater of the doctrine, charity worker and writer, that his personal devotional life was all but sacrificed. He exclaims: "How often does holy quiet give place, even from a pious motive, to the tumult of business affairs!" He may begin a passage with a prayer — "O holy soul, remain alone, preserve thyself for Him alone . . ." — but he ends it with the thought that it is also Christian to enter the life of practical service to men.

He reverts to this difficulty often, and he sums it up in one of his sermons on *The Song of Songs:* "The seeker desires one thing but receives another. He longs for the repose of contemplation, and the laborious office of preaching is laid upon him. He thirsts for the Bridegroom of the soul, and the task of caring for God's children is instead given him. . . . We must leave aside the embrace of Divine contemplation, for the labour that supports others, because none may live for himself alone."

It is a question not yet answered, and perhaps unanswerable except by each holy one in the recesses of his own mind and soul. Certainly Bernard's view is that of the great ones in the first twelve hundred years of Christian mysticism. He is essentially the last of the organizing, constructing Fathers. He writes no treatise directly on the thing that is closest to his heart, no expositions comparable to those of Eckhart the Catholic mystic of the high mediæval time, and of Boehme the half-articulate Protestant seer of the seventeenth century. And yet his writings, though they deal mostly with theological questions, administrative regulations, and political controversies, strangely clarify the stream of Christian mysticism as it had formed up to his time. He brings clear the central current as flowing from the Christ. He marks mysticism as an experience of the heart. He stresses the creative issue of it: the heart, having returned, blissful, from the Divine experience, will not rest until it has nourished other men, until it has shown them the way of love, the way to the Divine embrace.

Scholasticism had hardly yet been born, but the threat of its rationalism may have pushed Bernard the more fully to the side of intuitive faith and mystic fervency. He was unswerving in his loyalty to Church tradition, but his temperament was that of one who surrenders to God in utter self-forgetfulness. When the unhappy Abelard, first of the Churchmen to advocate the claims of reason as a searchlight upon the body of Christian doctrine, was condemned and brought before the Council of Sens in 1140, it was Bernard who confronted him and upheld the traditional opinion. And perhaps he more than any other determined that Christianity, endangered by the too great intellectual certainty of the Scholastics, in danger of systematization under realism and reason, should retain its radiant mysticism.

Bernard's mission was, he conceived, to restore contemplation as the central activity of devotion. As he was in the Christo-centric line of seers, he counselled contemplation upon the redeeming Christ. Finding abstractions less than adequate, either for stirring other men to comprehension or for expressing the feelings of his own heart, he fell into the habit of speaking in terms of the marriage of the soul to Christ. The Saviour is "the Bridegroom of the soul"; the soul enters into "a spiritual union with the Bridegroom" and is "granted an embrace" of surpassing sweetness and serenity and power. In elaborating the figure — which is (as one would expect) especially evident in the *Sermons on the Song of Songs*, eighty-six talks originally delivered before the monks at Clairvaux — Bernard speaks of "the kisses of contemplation" and "the mystic kiss," of the "inward embrace of the soul" and of the "rapt joy" and "transport" of "this sweet intercourse."

The language of physical love in descriptions of mystical union was not a novelty. The Church had approved the interpretation

SAINT BERNARD OF CLAIRVAUX.
PAINTING BY EL GRECO.

of *The Song of Songs* as an allegory of the marriage of Christ and the Church, and Bernard uses the figure thus at times; though the more striking passages are those depicting the individual soul as desiring and seeking the Bridegroom.

Saint Paul had opened the way with the words: "He who is joined unto the Lord is but one Spirit with Him," and their context concerning bodily union. By the time of Origen the imagery of the spiritual marriage was well developed. Saint Augustine had turned gradually from the abstract conceptions of his Neo-Platonic period to the imagery of a consuming love for Christ, a contemplation of the beauty of God, and the embrace of the Eternal. Thenceforward there is increasing use of the terms "the spouse of Christ," "the spiritual marriage," and "the Bridegroom of the soul."

Bernard, whose every thought seemed to be conditioned by a flow of love from the heart, fell naturally into this sanctioned usage and carried it on to wide acceptance. Had so free an indulgence in physical imagery been suspect in his time — as it was in later Puritan eras — his own patent innocency, his immunity from any possible charge of erotic association, would have cleared him. He simply and devoutly loved God with all his soul and heart, and he sublimated all his emotions in his one longing for the Divine embrace.

In Bernard's time, Richard of Saint Victor even more fervently glorifies the final stage of mystical activity, the ecstasy beyond contemplation.* In *The Four Degrees of Burning Love* he indulges an almost Oriental fancy: through the "transforming union" the soul attains a "divine fecundity." In later centuries Richard and Bernard are recalled in the writings of the German mystics and Ruysbroeck, in Saint John of the Cross and his "rapturous marriage," and, with a pathological overtone, in Santa Teresa.

In Islam the poets of Sufism had but recently, in Bernard's time, introduced the imagery of love and earthly beauty into their exaltation of the mystical life. The literature of Sufism is the richest, not to say the lushest, in the field of spiritual speculation.

---

* The Monastery of Saint Victor in Paris, founded about the year 1100, had long been a centre of mystical study and practice. The Victorine school was known especially for its systematic teaching of the way into vision by the graded means of recognition, meditation, and contemplation, and for its glorification of the culminating rapturous ecstasy. The two outstanding figures are Hugh of Saint Victor, who died in 1141, and his pupil Richard, who lived until 1173.

The devotion to the metaphors of desire, marriage, and intoxication is pressed far beyond the limits observed by Bernard. Unfortunately the books of the poets, and the Mohammedan mysticism of which they are the literary flower, have been obscured in an era and a part of the world too conscious of the body to accept its pleasures as symbols of divine experience.

At one of the assemblies of the monks at Clairvaux Bernard told of his own experience of the coming of the Bridegroom, in this fashion:

> I confess that the Word has visited me, even very often. But although He has frequently entered into my soul, I have never at any time been sensible of the precise moment of His coming. I have felt that He was present; I remember that He has been with me; I have sometimes had a presentiment that He would come; but I have never felt His coming or His departure. By what means He has made entrance or departure, I confess I know not to this day. . . . How then could I know that He was present? He is living and powerful. When He has entered into me He has quickened my sleeping soul, has kindled and softened and incited my heart. . . . Only by the stirring of my heart was I enabled to recognize His presence; only by the amendment of vices and the strong restraint put upon all carnal affections did I know the might of His power.
>
> His goodness and kindness have become known in the amendment, whatever it may amount to, of my life. In the re-formation and renewal of my spirit, of the inward man, I have known in some degree the loveliness of His beauty and have been filled with wonder at the immensity of His greatness. . . . As often as He shall leave me, so often shall He be called back by my voice. Nor will I cease to cry out after Him as He departs, expressing the ardent desire of my heart for His return, that I be saved to Him, in joy, that He restore Himself to me. I confess that I take pleasure in no thing until He again is present, He who alone is my joy.

In other of his writings Bernard may be sober, reserved, even terse. He once summed up the "way" to mystic experience in these few words: "Contemplation must seek; prayer must ask;

holiness, merit; purity, obtain what words cannot express." Of the difficulty of telling others about the mystery of Divine experience he writes: "Can I explain what is unspeakable? It is not the tongue, it is the gift of grace that teaches these things. They are hidden from the great and the wise of this world, but God reveals them to babes."

But the one unforgettable truth about Bernard's relation to these mysteries is that he entered into them, and wrote of them, in terms of love. In that, he fortified a Christian way that had been foreshadowed by Paul, outlined in the Gospel of John, and progressively made clearer by Augustine, Gregory, and their followers. Of them all he is the one who most fully and ingenuously gives himself to the love that his heart dictates. He longs for the experience of union with God. His soul "like a bride in purity" yearns for the coming of the Bridegroom.

Bernard guards against misconstruction of the words he uses, stressing the preparation or purgation of the soul for so holy and solemn a consummation as the mystic embrace. "He will not present Himself, even in passing, to every soul, but only to the soul that is prepared to be His bride, by profound devotion, desire and love: the soul worthy that the Word in all His beauty should be her Bridegroom." And: "Every soul to which He is to come must show such an ardour of sanctified longing as to burn away every impurity of thought and deed, in preparation for the Lord. Then He comes, and the soul feels itself consumed. . . ."

It is in the passages about spiritual love that Bernard is the most eloquent and most the Christian initiate. Of the spiritual marriage of the soul to Christ he writes:

If this love be perfected the soul is wedded to the Word. What can be more replete with joy than this union? What is more to be desired than this love? . . . This is the contract of a marriage spiritual and sacred. It is more than a contract — an embracing. It is an embracing in which a perfect joining of desires makes one spirit of two. Let it not be feared that the inequality of the two will render the union imperfect, or impede its consummation. Love waits not upon reverence. Love proceeds from loving, not from honouring. Love is filled with itself, and where love has come it inundates and transforms all other feelings. Love is sufficient of itself, a self-contained joy, worthy for its own sake. It is a merit, it is its own recompense. Love, then, is a great reality. . . . The very being of the soul, the Bride, is love, and love is her only hope. With this the Bridegroom is content. . . . Happy is the soul granted the blessing of a rapture so great. Happy the soul experiencing that so-sweet embrace; for it is a love holy and chaste, a love harmonious and delightful, a love serene and profound, a love mutually felt and intimate and binding, not in one flesh but in one spirit joining two together, making of them one, as Saint Paul said, "one spirit."

Finally, there is a passage in the *Sermons* that at once holds out the hope of the mystic embrace to each one of us and reminds us that, so long as we retain mortality, the experience will be fleeting:

> If one among us feels that it is a blessing to draw near to God, if he longs for that meeting, if he desires to be dissolved and to be with Christ, such a one, thirsting for it ardently, dwelling upon the thought of it ceaselessly, shall receive the Word. This visitation will be the Bridegroom come to the soul. That is, he shall feel himself inwardly embraced, as it were, by the arms of Wisdom, and then he shall receive an in-pouring of the sweetness of Divine Love. Thus is the desire of his heart granted him, though he is still in the body, a pilgrim on earth, and though it be only for a brief time. . . . For suddenly when he is thought to be held, the Bridegroom will glide away. He allows himself to be regained, but not to be retained; anon He passes away. . . . Thus, even in this body, the joy of the presence of the Bridegroom may frequently be felt; but not the fulness of His presence, because though His visitation gives joy to the heart, the alternation of His absence brings it sadness. This the beloved must, while in this life, endure.

Thus, while he wrote no treatise on the mystic life, Saint Bernard capped a progression of Christian thought that can be traced through eleven hundred years. The mysticism interpreted from the sayings of Jesus by Paul and John, with a special love in their hearts, had grown fuller and richer through a millennium, until Bernard gave it this emphasis upon love and longing and

SAINT BERNARD

spiritual intimacy. When he dies in 1153, the stage is set for entry of the prophets who will make a life and a philosophy of mystic devotion: Francis, inarticulate in words but eloquent in works, and Meister Eckhart, the first literary philosopher of the mysticism of the indwelling Christ.

VI. The Mediæval Flowering:

Eckhart and the Friends of God

Fifty years ago there were many Classicists who believed that the Mediæval Age in Europe had constituted a continuation of the Dark Ages, a sort of twilight prolongation of the darkness of the "barbarian" centuries. The light of the world had gone out with Classicism and there had been this thousand years of eclipse, after which the lamps of culture were relighted at the inception of the Renaissance. Western art and Western learning were, in the view of the Classicists, a natural continuation of the Greek-Roman-Renaissance form of civilization. European life from the fall of Rome to the Florentine rebirth had been an interruption of the normal course of Western development.

Within the half-century critical opinion has shifted, especially in the field of art. Mediæval art and culture have been elevated to a ranking among the supreme achievements of mankind. The monuments of Romanesque and Gothic architecture, sculpture, and craftsmanship are held up as models of originality and beauty. The Mediæval era is seen as a flowering of the arts hardly less lovely than the Greek, and indubitably superior to the Roman.

In the history of religion, which so often parallels the history of art, mediævalism has been less contemned; and yet few historians have ventured to mark the Gothic centuries as the peak of Christian civilization. A historian of mysticism, nevertheless, cannot escape the conclusion that the Middle Ages constitute an unrivalled era of great spiritual philosophers and great saints. In the course of Western religion this is a summit. It is the Golden Age of Christian mysticism, and therefore of Christian holiness. The twelfth to the fourteenth centuries give us Saint Francis, Saint Bonaventura and Saint Catherine, Meister Eckhart and Tauler and Suso, the Friends of God and the Admirable Ruysbroeck, and England's one distinctive and wide-spread blossoming of the mystic spirit.

Toward the end of the era the Church lost a good deal of its power over common men's minds. Intellectual enlightenment and religious scepticism — sometimes hardly to be distinguished — were spreading. The monastic orders, enjoying one of their propitious and favourable enlargements, yet harboured increasingly the moral ills that were to end in the purging by Reformation and Counter-Reformation. The Church was losing its hold as mother of all the arts and culture. As science was growing up outside the ecclesiastic walls, so philosophy was beginning to sigh for the freer speculative air of courts and secular universities. Learning was hardly yet ready to escape the restrictions put upon it by a growingly inflexible Church, but its more creative minds foreshadowed the freedoms and the defiance of the pagan Renaissance.

Mediæval learning blossomed in the incomparable scholarship of Roger Bacon, Albertus Magnus, and Saint Thomas Aquinas; and partly by way of reaction to an excess of intellectual and worldly learning, there emerged in Italy Saint Francis, and in Germany those Friends of God, inspired by Meister Eckhart, who were to give to Christianity its most wide-spread acceptance of the mystic life and its most treasured body of mystic literature.

A contemporary philosopher has ventured the thought that Christianity lost its opportunity to unite the Western world in one active faith when the Church departed from the teachings of Saint Francis. The Saint of Assisi was the essentially Christian figure at a time of crisis in the Church's political career; but he was so Christ-like that the rulers at Rome could not visualize a harmony of his religion and their own mortal pretensions — nor could they believe that his asceticism and his mysticism, though moderate and sunny, would win the masses of men. He founded an order of "penitent" monks and left the example of his own selflessness, charity, and gentleness. But he failed to transform the Christian structure or to initiate a general return, among common men, to the mystic and simple holiness of Jesus.

Francis was born in Assisi in the year 1182, only twenty-nine years after the death of Bernard. His family name was Bernardone and his given name Giovanni. But his father, a wealthy cloth merchant, returning from a business trip to France enamoured of the northern country, called the boy Francesco, a name which through the Saint was to become one of the most honoured and prevalent in Christendom.

As a youth Francis was high-spirited and a leader among the merry-making young men of his city. But a division in his loyalties was already evident. He was giving money freely to beggars;

and indeed he was animated by a sort of unlimited charity that was to be a part of the Franciscan philosophy ever after. He went to war against the Perugians and was captured and held for a year in prison, where his cheerfulness, even radiancy, was especially remarked. Upon his return he was stricken with illness and with discontent over the prospect of spending a life in business. He had visions or dreams, and he began to see vaguely a mission totally unconnected with his father's plans for him.

His conversion was signalized in a meeting with a leper who was begging by the roadside. Fastidious by nature, Francis had conceived a horror of leprosy beyond all other evils. Now, confronted by the beggar, suddenly recognizing his own fear, he conquered his aversion and not only gave alms but embraced the diseased one. From then on he devoted himself to charity among the lepers. His father had him brought before the local Bishop for discipline, but before any action could be taken Francis dramatically threw off his clothes as a sign that he was through with his family's protection and wealth. "Hereafter," he said, "I am the servant only of God, our Father in Heaven."

The voice of God had told him to repair a ruined little church known as Saint Damian's, and he had gone some way with the project, partly by use of his father's money. Now he saw that God meant him literally to build the walls himself. He begged stones and mortar and set about restoring the walls with his own hands. His sincerity and conviction were such that a few of his one-time companions joined with him. Soon he had twelve fellow-workers — and he recognized that in a second sense he had begun the rebuilding of God's Church.

While Francis was working on the walls of another ruined chapel, the Portiuncula, he heard a priest recite the lines spoken by Jesus, beginning: "And as ye go, preach, saying, the Kingdom of Heaven is at hand. Heal the sick, cleanse the lepers, raise the dead. . . . Provide neither gold nor silver." Francis asked the priest to repeat the passage. When he had heard it again he said: "This is what I have been seeking." The revelation was complete. He would found an order based on the poverty that Jesus had enjoined upon His followers. "If any man will come after me, let him deny himself"; and "Give to every man that asketh of thee. . . . Sell all that thou hast, and give unto the poor."

And so the Franciscan Order came into being, the brotherhood

SAINT FRANCIS RECEIVING THE STIGMATA.
PAINTING, OF THE SCHOOL OF GIOTTO.
FOGG ART MUSEUM, HARVARD UNIVERSITY.

of God's servants pledged to poverty. Francis' own vow was celebrated thereafter in poetry and in art as "the marriage of Francis to Lady Poverty." When there was danger that the Papacy would fail to sanction the founding of an order upon a premise that seemed to many quixotic, it was Cardinal John of Saint Paul who swayed the mind of the Pope, saying: "All that these men ask is that they be permitted to live in accordance with the directions in the Gospel. Let us beware lest, in averring that this cannot be done, we offend against the Gospel, and thus against Jesus the Christ."

For the rest of his life Francis was drawn alternately to a life of prayer and contemplation on the one hand, and on the other to a career of humble service and of increasing administrative cares as director of the Order. He strove endlessly to discipline himself out of any possible infraction of the rule of poverty and self-denial. But he combated the idea of mortification or self-torment, and he remained the most sunny, considerate, and radiant of the mediæval saints. Everyone knows how marvellously his Order spread, until its charitable works were witnessed in all parts of the world.

The mysticism of Saint Francis was that of a man of utter compassion, of an inborn gentleness, of a passionate desire to serve others. He was not a mystic of the speculative type, and there are no undisputed writings of his that tell of his way of living in consciousness of God. But no one ever more clearly demonstrated a way to divine awareness. He stripped himself of every worldly possession and distraction, that his soul might be open to God. Everything else he subordinated to that self-purification, that self-opening.

He accepted explicitly Jesus' mapping of the way to the Kingdom. He took on utter meekness, utter poverty, utter faith. He gave universal love. He excused and forgave those who made life a selfish struggle, even those who had introduced selfishness and evil into the Church and the Christian orders. He believed only in setting an example, as Jesus had done.

His example was the more winning because his sunny-mindedness never failed. If he seemed to ask God for an ever more rigorous poverty, even for misfortune and suffering, it was only in order that his blessing in knowing God's presence might be the more realized by contrast. The more destitute the mortal life, the more complete and glorious and suffusing the experience of God's immanence.

As evils had grown up in the Church, so that Francis as a beggar was sometimes rebuffed where charity should be most honoured, so a dark view of life had developed among many Christians, an opinion that all rewards were to be paid after death, and life to be endured as a misery; even that a life of suffering would better please God. Francis asked for his share of suffering, but only that it might increase his consciousness of the presence of the Christ, that he might pay one more cost for the overwhelmingly joyous boon of a life lived in divine communion. Certainly he never thought of poverty as an evil. Poverty, he said, is "that virtue which enables the soul, while she is still on earth, to enter into converse with the blessed in Heaven." He would begin an admonition with the words, "Where we have poverty and joy . . ."

Jesus had said: "Love your enemies." Francis loved everyone and everything. He had cast off the clothes given to him by his father partly in order that the last hindrance to the love of that worldly-minded one might be removed. He loved his old friends who made fun of him when he was converted, and he won them to his order by love. His love was universal, and it grew out of the mystic's awareness that all that exists is one, and that God is in all, is All.

The Church, forgetting a little the awareness of nature that Jesus had shown — one remembers immediately His sayings, "I am the vine . . . " and "He sendeth rain on the just and on the unjust," and His parables of the seed, of the fig, of the fields, and of "the reed shaken with the wind" — the Church had permitted the view of nature to become objective and insensible. The Christian mystics before Francis had lost the sympathetic understanding of the animals and the birds, the woods and the mountains, the waters and the stars, that had animated the Hebrew Psalmists, that had provided Jesus with innumerable parallels of the natural and the spiritual life. But Francis instinctively felt his kinship with all that is. He sang to "our brother the Sun" and "our sister the Moon," to "our mother the Earth" and to Brother Fire and Sister Water and Brother Wind; he prayed to the Father of all, saying, "Praised be my Lord God with all His creatures." He is important in the history of Christian mysticism because he brought this natural universality back into it when it had been obscured for centuries.

He made his kinship with the animals unforgettable ever after, by dramatizing it. There occurred two incidents especially that became favorite themes in art and literature. He delivered, out of a full heart and a perfect understanding, a sermon to the birds, reminding these brothers and sisters of men how much they were beholden to God their creator, and bidding them rejoice and sing the praises of the Lord. His greeting to the birds as to all creatures was always the same: "My brothers, God give you peace." And once when the people of Gubbio were panic-stricken because of the depredations of a savage wolf, Francis, using his love of all creatures and his faith in God as a shield, met with the animal and turned him from his savage ways, not neglecting to remind the townspeople to look after their trespasses and develop more of Christian understanding. Once when he and his companions had set out their few scraps of food on a ledge of rock by a spring, he was moved to exclaim: "How can we be worthy of such treasures?" The monks being puzzled, he asked what table could be more beautiful — did not the rock and the water both speak of God?

This is the mystic's instinctive and constant detection of the Divine in common things. It is one of the reminders that all are one, united in One, in divine fellowship.

In the absence of extensive writings from Francis' own hand, there has been some questioning whether he actually entered into those ecstatic, trance-like periods of communion with God that are described by the more fervent mystics. Among the prayers attributed to the Saint are ones that lack nothing of the ardour and the self-abandonment of the initiate. "I beseech Thee, O God, that the flaming yet sweet power of Thy love may wrest and absorb my soul from all things that are not Heaven's; that I may die out of love of Thy love — as Thou didst descend to die for love of my love."

In the life of Francis by Saint Bonaventura there is a passage in which Francis is represented as asking counsel as to the superiority of the life of prayer (his word for contemplation) or the life of preaching. "In prayer there is the union with the one true and highest Good. . . . In prayer we converse with God, and hear Him speak, and we live the life of the Angels. . . ."

Bonaventura describes, not without Platonic overtones, the two directions of Francis' quest for God, in the world around him and in a dedication that ended in raptness: "In all fair things he beheld Him who is most fair, and, through the traces of Him which He has implanted in all His creatures, he was led on to reach the All-loved, constructing of these things a ladder whereby he might ascend to Him who is Loveliness itself. . . . The Christ lay, as a bundle of myrrh, in his heart's core, and he yearned only to be consumed into His fire by his own unremitting love. With such glowing love was he moved, and with so intimate a love did the Bridegroom repay him, that it seemed to the servant of God himself that he felt the almost continuous presence of the Saviour."

It is to be inferred that the attainment was a continuous awareness, a constant sense of Divine presence and love, rather than the occasional ecstatic immersions in bliss described by the extremer mystics. And certainly Francis was true to the Christian type in being faithful to his vow to service, even at cost of shortening the periods of withdrawal and prayer.

It was in the year 1226, at the Portiuncula Chapel near Assisi, that Francis died. After his going the Franciscan Order knew controversy and division. Those who insisted upon holding strictly to the rule of poverty, called Zealots or Spirituals, were the smallest of three groupings that developed within the Order. Following the extreme Franciscan "way," they served notably, but they lost control to the parties that wanted a relaxed discipline and a spread of the society into distant fields and varied service, for which an un-Franciscan accumulation of wealth was necessary. Between the Spirituals and the extremists who desired to cancel the obligation to poverty, a third party of moderates grew up, and the main work of the great Franciscan Order developed under their guidance.

It was chiefly among the Spirituals that the Franciscan mystics appeared. There was the visionary Pier Pettignano, who dreamed of a procession of the Apostles, and of unnumbered saints and martyrs, all walking with eyes anxiously downcast to perceive the guiding footsteps of the Christ — and the magnificent figures were followed by the barefooted Francis, who alone walked easily and naturally in the way marked by Jesus. And there was Jacopone da Todi, who also saw Francis as a sort of second Christ on earth; who was a true *Penitente*, carrying disdain of self to mortification, and asking God for ever more punishment. "What evil comes from

MEETING OF SAINT FRANCIS AND SAINT DOMINIC.
PAINTING BY FRA ANGELICO. KRESS COLLECTION,
NATIONAL GALLERY OF ART, WASHINGTON.

Him," he said, "is sweetness to me." He was one of the great mystic poets of Italy. But he wrote some bitter verses about the worldliness of the Pope and the Church, and was imprisoned and cruelly humbled until his spirit broke.

There was, too, the great Bonaventura, known as "the Seraphic," who became head of the Franciscan Order when divisions threatened to destroy it. A true mystic, he yet was ready to listen to those who counselled relaxing of the rule of poverty, and he ultimately diverted Franciscanism to the side of the Church and of expedient Christianity. He was in the line of the Christian mystics influenced by Neo-Platonism, a follower of Augustine and the False Dionysius and the seers of Saint Victor's. He was sainted by the Church more than a century after his death.

Among the myriad men and women whom Francis loved in life the dearest to him was Clara, the high-born woman who adopted his rule of poverty and founded the order of Franciscan nuns. Beside the original order, sometimes known as the Friars Minor, and beside this other group known as the Poor Clares or the Clarisses, there was a third Franciscan order, the Tertiaries. The members were not monks and nuns, but laymen and laywomen sworn to observe rules of charity and service. Without leaving their usual walks of life they joined a spiritual fellowship animated by the memory of the saintliness of Francis.

Two of the mystics mentioned above, Jacopone da Todi and Pier Pettignano, were of the Tertiary Order. A third member who wrote of the mystic life was Angela of Foligno, who left an illuminating account of her road from worldly indulgence to self-imposed poverty and spiritual attainment, and finally to ecstatic union. The Tertiaries seem often to have been loosely organized in groups for the purpose of studying the mystic life, and there may have been a connection with the groups in Germany known as the Friends of God. In Italy other Tertiaries who became famous for their expressions of mystic truth were Dante * and Giotto.

Angela of Foligno was not the first woman who took important place among the Christian mystics, or the first to write mystical

---

* The *Divine Comedy* of Dante is, of course, the most celebrated "epic" in mystical literature. If it wanders far afield, in its business of portraying, judging, and rebuking a myriad of sinners, it does begin with something approaching a spiritual conversion and end with the protagonist's entry into the highest Paradise and his experience of God.

tracts that are still read. Contemporary with Saint Bernard and Richard of Saint Victor in the twelfth century there had been the German contemplative and poet, Saint Hildegard, who seemed to those who knew her to reflect upon the world the "Living Light" that she recognized as God. At the end of a long life of service to the Church and to common people, she said that her soul had often seen the Light within Light, and that "when and how I see this living radiance I cannot say — but then all of misery and sorrow evaporate, I am as a simple girl again, and age has fallen away."

In the thirteenth century Saint Mechthild of Magdeburg wrote a treatise entitled *The Inpouring Light of God* which became a favourite among the German Friends of God. She was but one of three nuns known as inspired mystics at the Convent of Helfta in that century. Saint Gertrude the Great, who lived until 1302, found in the Sacred Heart a symbol of the mystic love of her soul for Jesus, thus initiating a cult of devotion.

There is, perhaps, a special emotional note in the mysticism of these women-saints. But their devotion of the heart in no way unfitted them for administrative, even political, service in the Church. Hildegard and Mechthild especially corresponded widely and threw their weight against the corruption and depravity that had grown up even in the houses of God. They rivalled Saint Birgitta of Sweden, author of a unique book entitled *Revelations,* who is less known as a mystic than as a castigator of the powers in Rome; and with her they are sometimes cited as forerunners of the Reformation. But the unrivalled one among the women who were mystics, who became Saints, who aided in bringing purgation to a tragically desecrated Church, was Catherine of Siena.

Born in 1347, a visionary as a child, dedicated to God at sixteen, Catherine perfected her mystic life as a recluse. But at twenty she felt a second call, to go out and exercise her spiritual wisdom for the good of all men. She served humbly and menially at first, but in the end she wielded an extraordinary authority over high churchmen and politicians and princes; it was her planning and diplomacy that especially served to bring the Popes back to Rome from their "Babylonish" exile in France.

As a mystic she was an extremist, given to penance and ecstatic visions and trances, but neither the sincerity of her self-giving nor her extraordinary spiritual and intellectual powers can fairly be questioned. She experienced a vision of her soul's marriage to the

Christ, reminiscent of the legend of the mystic marriage of Catherine of Alexandria.

She lived in surroundings peculiarly suffused with memories of mystic attainment, for here Saint Francis had preached, and the Sienese had built a church in his honour; here a school of artists had spiritualized and etherealized painting, even while restoring melodious composition and entrancing colour; and here a local tradition of humble service combined with mystic devotion had flowered in the founding of the Society of the Gesuati. The Society, under the guidance of Giovanni Colombini, demanded that its initiates should die as to all the attractions of this world, in order to be reborn to the spiritual life.

In "embracing the riches of poverty" Catherine thus was following in the steps of many high-born men and women of her community. But she outdistanced them all in the fervour of her ecstasies, and she composed the one most valuable document among those of the Sienese spiritual writers. Characteristically it is a treatise on Divine Love, dictated to her secretaries while she was "rapt out of her corporeal senses," and described on the title-page of some editions as "dictated by God the Father." It is a dialogue between Catherine — or, it may be, the typical loving soul — and God. It includes revelations of her ecstatic visions, telling how she was "by desire and affection and loving union transformed into Christ"; but it adds speculation, and burning denunciation of the corruption of the times, and spiritual admonitions.

In England too, in that century which saw the flowering of Christian mysticism, there were worthy advocates of the contemplative life; and the one among them most to be remembered in later times was a woman, Julian of Norwich, an anchoress. Spiritually Britain was a part of the Roman Empire in those days, and all the currents of Christian thought flowed to the islands. Franciscan influence was strong, especially through the writings of Bonaventura. And the cloistered life was exalted.

Three mystics stand out from among all others. Richard Rolle, not a professional churchman, nevertheless embraced poverty, turned hermit, and, when he was not seeking solitude, acted as a spiritual teacher. A distinctive characteristic of his ecstasies was that he, a poet and musician, felt and described the experience of divine attainment in musical fashion, as joyful song and "inshed melody." A homely, pastoral note to be heard in Rolle's descriptions is sounded also in the writings of Walter Hylton; but he was more learned in the wisdom of Augustine and the false Areopagite and Bernard. His book *The Scale of Perfection* became one of the most popular spiritual treatises, not only in his own century, but through generations after.

Julian of Norwich, born a gentlewoman in 1343 — sometimes called Lady Julian — experienced a conversion, with visions and revelations, at the age of thirty. She wrote of her experience in a book that shows familiarity with the writings of the great Christian mystics from Augustine to her own contemporaries, but she adds her distinctive note as an Englishwoman. The *Revelation of Divine Love* is a candid, vivid, and inspiring account of the circumstances of her visions and of the lessons she drew from thinking of them. Although she is one of the glad saints, not dwelling unduly upon sins and suffering, and quite frankly discounting God's wrath, she concludes one of her chapters with a memorable picture of bliss "after woe": "At the end of woe suddenly our eyes shall be opened, and in clearness of light our sight shall be full; which Light is God. . . ."

But her knowledge of the sublime does not blunt the edge of her common feeling. "A child when it is a-hurt or a-dread, it runneth hastily to the mother for help, with all its might" — and so should we run to God. And once she writes that "Our courteous Lord willeth that we should be as homely with Him as heart may think or soul may desire."

Besides these three there was a fourth, an anonymous writer on mysticism in England of the fourteenth century. The author of *The Cloud of Unknowing* was a Churchman who carefully distinguished between the true and sober mystical life and the activities of those who lost themselves in emotional fantasying, or those who by presumption of will would force the doors of Heaven — types he described not without humour. He is supposed to have written an English version of the *Mystical Theology* of the False Dionysius. But *The Cloud of Unknowing*, wherein he shows how the mist of unknowing around God can be pierced by "a sharp dart of longing love," is an original and sincere exposition of the way to mystic atttainment, with typical homely English touches. And indeed throughout this late mediæval period, whether in England or Germany or Italy, the spiritual leaders are writing in the vernacular instead of the Latin of the scholars, in common phraseology and homely imagery, out of the feeling of the heart.

When Meister Eckhart was brought before the Archbishop's Court in Cologne on a charge of heresy in January 1327, more saintly people, it seems likely, prayed to God for his release and vindication than had prayed for any other Christian suspected of heresy in all history. Certainly no mystic since the time of Paul and John had attracted such an immediate following, among Churchmen and among laymen.

Eckhart is best known for his sermons and his "Talks of Instruction" as Prior of Erfurt Monastery, and his most famous followers were the two preacher-mystics, Johannes Tauler and Heinrich Suso. But he inspired the unnumbered thousands of holy ones who attempted practice of a primitive Christian communism under the name of the Friends of God, and, only less directly, the Beghards whom the Church eventually condemned and persecuted.

Eckhart was a Churchman and a stout defender of the authority of the Roman establishment. But he was intuitive and, when he was in the pulpit, spoke what an inner voice prompted — and his immediate apprehension of God led to statements too independent for the liking of his less flexible-minded colleagues and superiors. Unfortunately the Franciscans, who should have been the first to understand his praise of poverty and self-giving and identification with God, had hardened and had drawn away from the mysticism of their founder; they, having found Eckhart, a member of the Dominican Order, pitted against their chosen leaders at the universities and church councils, judged him too liberal and self-reliant and determined to brand him a heretic. The controversy, however it may have saddened the seer in the final years of his life on earth, in no way affected his influence upon the lay mystics of Germany and the Low Countries. He was above all a people's leader, warmly human, direct and vivid in statement, prophetic, sympathetic.

It is not always easy to distinguish between the original writings of Meister Eckhart and the versions of his sermons or talks set down afterwards by his hearers, or legendary retellings of the sermons. There are characteristic simple fables that could hardly be ascribed to any other advocate of the mystic life. This is one:

Meister Eckhart met a lovely boy who was naked.
"Where do you come from?" he asked.
"From God," the boy said.

"Where did you leave Him?"
"In all understanding hearts."
"Where are you going?"
"To God."
"Where shall you find Him?"
"In departure from everything worldly."
"Who are you?"
"A King."
"Where is your kingdom?"
"In my heart."
"Be careful that no one takes it from you."
"I am careful."

Then he led the lad to his cell, and he said, "Take for yourself whichever coat you will."

The lad said, "But then I should not be King." And he vanished.

Then Meister Eckhart understood: it was God Himself, who had left serious matters for a while.

Thus simple and direct, even naïve, was Eckhart in his preaching and conversation in the troubled Rhineland of the early fourteenth century.

It was his life in God that mattered to Meister Eckhart, and he never bothered to set down his mundane biography. He was pretty well forgotten for centuries after his immediate disciples died — during that time his sermons were sometimes printed with Tauler's, under Tauler's name — and only the scholarship of the nineteenth century uncovered the basic facts of his life on earth.

Johannes Eckhart was born about the year 1260 near Gotha in Thuringia, his father being steward of a knight's castle in that forest land. As a youth he went to the monastery of the Dominicans at near-by Erfurt and spent nine years as a student there. Cologne was at the time a famed seat of learning. Thomas Aquinas had taught there, but had been away for some years when he died in 1274; Albertus Magnus, however, was a teacher until some later date, and Eckhart, taking up his theological studies at Cologne, could hardly have escaped the influence of the two incomparable scholastics. He was to develop in quite another direction, but in absorbing the fundamentals of theological learning at so high a source he doubtless put the solidest sort of foundation under his mysticism.

He returned to the monastery at Erfurt, and at the end of the century he was Prior there and "Vicar of Thuringia." From his talks to the brothers at Erfurt dates his first known book, usually entitled *Talks of Instruction,* in which he discusses the problems of the devotional life with a constant mystical inclination. "One should be so penetrated by the Divine Presence, so in-formed with the form of the God of love within, that one unconsciously radiates that Presence."

When he was about forty years of age he went to the University of Paris for graduate study, and in 1302 he received the degree of Meister — that is, *Magister* or Master of Sacred Theology. Thereafter he was known universally as Meister Eckhart. At Paris he not only studied but taught, and it was there, in debate, that he earned the dislike and the distrust of the Franciscans. He kept up his end of the controversy, putting into one of his late sermons this gibe: "I stated when I was preaching in Paris, and I repeat it, that with all their learning not one man at Paris can perceive that God is in the least of creatures, even in a fly."

In 1303 or 1304 he was sent to be Provincial of the Dominican monasteries in Saxony, and shortly afterward he was made Vicar-General of the Order in Bohemia also. For years he led a busy life as travelling administrator and preacher. He found time to write — he was almost the first German to write of these deep matters in his own language, instead of the scholars' Latin — *The Book of Divine Comfort.* The immediate purpose of the treatise was to solace Queen Agnes of Hungary, who had suffered unusual mortal bereavements, but its deeper significance is in the restatement of Eckhart's spiritual beliefs.

He was back in Paris, on what mission we know not, about 1312, and there he wrote a treatise in Latin. But a year or two later he is found in Strassburg, where his preaching is renowned. He is a favourite teacher in the monasteries and convents (it is from the nuns' reconstructions of the sermons that many of the texts have been recovered); and when he preaches publicly the churches can hardly hold all the common men and women who flock to hear him. Without willing it consciously, he is starting many on the mystic way as Friends of God. About 1320 he is called to one of the highest posts open to a priest, as teacher in the college at Cologne.

Just when the increasing tide of suspicion and dislike broke in a wave of public charges is unknown. Eckhart's new superior, the Archbishop of Cologne, was a Franciscan. He had been worried over the growth of unauthorized mystic societies in the Rhineland. He might well have remembered the one comparable phenomenon, the spread of lay groups of Franciscan Tertiaries, partisans of the Spirituals who believed in practising Saint Francis' way of poverty, mystic devotion, and universal love. But the Archbishop judged that his brilliant assistant at the college, instead of advocating a spiritual life sanctioned by Church tradition, was leading his hearers into notions of a mystic living that could dispense with priests and services. He called for an investigation by the officers of the Inquisition.

Whether political manœuvring had to do with it or not, the investigator turned out to be a Dominican. Eckhart was cleared. This may have been as early as 1325. The nature of the defence is not known.

The Archbishop did not rest easy under the acquittal, and shortly he contrived that a second investigation be put under way. This time two Franciscans were chosen to obtain the evidence, and they preferred a long list of charges. Late in 1326 Eckhart submitted a written defence, at the same time denying the right of the inquisitors to attribute falsehood or heresy to him or to bring him before the Archbishop's Court. Nevertheless he was forced to the Court in January 1327. He appealed his case, as his right was, to the Pope. The last reported step, during his lifetime, was the dispatching from Rome of a denial of his appeal. His death is recorded as occurring simply in 1327.

No one will ever know what might have been the outcome of the trial, or what punishment might have been put upon the great seer. In 1329 the Pope issued a bull in which twenty-six points in Eckhart's writings were posthumously condemned. Seventeen were said to be heretical, the others dubious and indiscreet. They showed, the Pope said, that he "wished to know more than he should." It was an old, old story, the mystic knowing, out of the certainty of intuitive experience, a thing which his literal-minded accusers and contemners could not know; the mystic knowing, and telling of his knowing, and therefore persecuted.

In the end Eckhart was technically cleared, so far as the Church view went, in that the papal bull announced that he had retracted his heretical views. In his defence he had said that many of the statements quoted from his sermons and writings could be understood in more than one sense, that the inquisitors were reading error into them, and that he would be the first to repudiate those strained meanings. He admitted that he might even be in error in interpretation and would be glad to "yield to a better understanding." He noted that "It is possible that I err, but impossible that I am a heretic, for the one is a matter of intellect, but the other is a matter of will." Nevertheless he defended vigorously the interpretations that bore on his central doctrines of a divine, uncreated part in man, of the essential unity of man and God, and of the nothingness of life unless lived in consciousness of Divine being.

When he died in 1327 he was under the cloud of the heresy charge, and he must have seen before him the prospect of condemnation as a heretic — the most terrible fate a believing Churchman can contemplate — or retraction of those basic Christian beliefs in which his very being was involved. Perhaps death was merciful in coming at this juncture.

Meister Eckhart was the father of German theology, and he is sometimes put down as the father of German philosophy — Hegel especially was indebted to him — but the greater distinction is that he was the highest figure among all the mystics of the northern countries, towering above even Suso and Ruysbroeck and Boehme. There is in him an unexampled combination of scholar and intuitive, of traditional wisdom and personal experience. He shows his indebtedness to Augustine and to Dionysius and to Bernard; and he exhibits a special affection for the Gospel of John. He has felt the influence of the Arabian mystics, of both Persia and Spain, especially Avicenna, al-Ghazali, and Averroes.

There is just here an illustration of a phenomenon recurrent in the history of Christianity. The Plotinian stream, already effective in modifying the course of orthodox thought through Augustine and many others, is again re-absorbed into the main current of Christian mysticism. The flowing-in from Arabian sources is part of an enriching process that continued through more than a millennium.

The Arabs of Islam, who did so much to keep alive and enlarge science during the so-called Dark Ages of the West, also built up their own mystic philosophy, enlarging it with materials salvaged by their scholars out of the wreck of Greek learning. They not only had copies of Aristotle's treatises when they were practically unknown to the Latin West, but they had also a book that made Aristotle appear a mystic of the first water. It was in fact a copy of the *Enneads* of Plotinus which a scribe had mislabelled as from Aristotle's hand. When the Islamic philosophy and mysticism began to seep into a reawakened Europe, a major puzzle was the source of spiritual ideas which, though ascribed to Aristotle, bore the unmistakable impress of Neo-Platonism, and thus a likeness to the mysticism of Augustine and Erigena and the others. The Arabian mysticism had itself been affected, and students such as Eckhart found the beliefs and even the imagery of the Sufi poets and especially of the later Arabian philosophers not incompatible with the thought and expression of Bernard and the Christian mystics of Saint Victor's.

Thus Meister Eckhart draws together mutiple threads of spiritual philosophy; and indeed, his writings are rich in quotations from and allusions to earlier advocates of a life lived in companionship with God. He tempers his enthusiasms, too, by constant reference to his scholastic masters, Albertus and Thomas Aquinas. But in the end it is his own personal experience of the mystical life that lends conviction to his words. He is a participator in Divine life, an initiate who feels the presence of God, and therefore there are warmth and certainty and wonder in his preaching.

The hold of Eckhart upon the minds of listeners who had, presumably, no deep knowledge of theology and of philosophic subtleties is to be traced in part to his use of common illustrations and images, even in the most recondite sermons, and to a telling of simple stories that harbour deep meanings. There is a deceptively simple tale, preserved by Tauler but bearing all the marks of the Meister's method, which sums up a great deal of his spiritual belief. (It is here somewhat abbreviated.)

> There was a learned doctor who prayed for years that he might encounter someone who would teach him the way to Truth. One day when he especially longed for this guide, a voice out of Heaven bade him go to the front of the Church, where he would find an illuminated one able to point the way to blessedness. He found there only a beggar, worn and tat-

tered, all his clothes being hardly three pennies' worth. The scholar greeted him, saying, "God give thee a good day."

"I never had a bad one," said the beggar.

"God grant thee good fortune."

"I have never had anything else."

"Then may Heaven bless thee."

"I am ever blessed."

The learned doctor then asked the poor man to explain his answers.

"Gladly. You wish me a good day, and I tell you I have had no other — for if I am freezing I praise God. Whether it be rain or snow or hail, or fair weather, I praise God, and so it is a good day. You wish me good fortune, and I tell you ill fortune is unknown to me — for I learned to live in God's presence. What He gives or ordains for me is best, be it pain or pleasure. I accept what He lays up for me, and therefore I know no adversity. You call upon Heaven to bless me, but I have never known any lack of blessing — for I gave my will to God. My desire is only to do His will. In doing that I am blessed."

"But what if God were to cast you into Hell?" asked the scholar.

"Cast me into Hell? That is not in His nature. Yet should He, I would embrace Him with my two arms. The one arm I would place beneath Him, for it is Humility. The other arm, being Love, would rise about Him. I would sooner be in Hell with God than in Heaven without Him."

"Who are you, then?"

"A king."

"King of what?"

"My kingdom is my soul. All that I am, body or being, pays homage to my soul. It is a kingdom greater than those on earth."

"How did you reach this perfection?"

"I silenced my five senses, and looked with all my being to Heaven, and I came to union with God. I could find rest nowhere short of God. I have Him, and I possess eternal peace and joy. Is there any kingdom to compare with that?"

Eckhart used the same gift of simplicity of expression in coining terse and memorable sayings about the spiritual life. "Have God ceaselessly in your heart." And: "Where your mortal self ends, there God begins to be. God asks only one thing of you: that you dethrone the creaturely self and let Him be God in you."

There is hope for common mortals in many of his aphorisms. "Every creature is on its way to the highest perfection. In each there is movement from mortality toward Being." And: "When God lights the soul with wisdom, it floods the faculties, and that man knows more than ever could be taught him." Once, in the midst of a disquisition on suffering and its disappearance in God's goodness, he pauses to exclaim: "Just think what an amazing life a man might have on earth, a life exactly that of God in Heaven!" Immediately he adds one of the deepest and knottiest thoughts developed in his writings: "There is a marvellous comfort to be had when adversity serves as well as fortune; then pain is like pleasure."

Meister Eckhart is firm-set in the line of Christian mystics who balance the life of detachment with a life of works. At the beginning of his career he was blunter about this than in the later years when, perhaps, he felt the privation due to overcrowded schedules. One of his earliest recorded sayings is: "If some one were in a rapture like Saint Paul's, and there were a sick man needing help, it would be better to come out of the rapture and exercise practical love by serving the one in need." Immediately afterward he adds that one is not thereby robbing oneself of grace, for did not Jesus say that "He who forsakes anything for my sake shall receive an hundredfold"? He will again know the rapture that is perfect consolation — especially if he remain cheerful and trustful through the whole matter.

Elsewhere he writes that "He is blessed who shares himself usefully." And: "In this life no man reaches the point at which he can be excused from practical service." To this he appends the statement that no thought of deeds to be done should be permitted to intrude during the hours of contemplation; but that "active life is to alternate with contemplation."

Contrary to the accepted meaning of the story of Martha and Mary, he marks Martha's as an equally commendable rôle. "The life in work is necessary and the life of contemplation is good. In service the man gathers the harvest that has been sown in contemplation. . . . God's purpose in contemplation is fruitfulness in works. Activity is a further part of the Unity seen in the vision. . . ." Nevertheless there is at other times an almost jealous guarding of the preciousness of the contemplative life. And to the monks at Erfurt he gave this advice: "Saintliness does not come from occupation; it depends upon what one *is*. However sacred a calling may be, it is a calling, without power to sanctify. Rather, as we are, and to the extent that we have Divine being within, we bring blessings to our task."

The beginning of Eckhart's mysticism is in the belief that the soul in each of us is God. Or, if the statement seem extreme — and the charges of blasphemy and heresy arose partly over interpretations of his language identifying the human soul as "the Father dwelling within" or "the living Christ within" — if we say only that he pictured the soul as essentially divine and a spark of the Light that is God, we hold the key to his spiritual philosophy. "God made man's soul so like Himself that nothing else in Heaven or earth so resembles Him." And: "Between God and man alone is there no difference, no separation, but Oneness."

Again and again he speaks of a faculty of the soul that is above time and mortality, knowing the perfection of Eternity; and of a soul-foundation that is Divine. "Here the core of God is my core, the ground of my soul is God's ground. . . . In all you do, act from this core." Sometimes he adds a sly warning: "God is with us on that ground, provided He find us within and not gone out on the business of our five senses."

He describes the attachment of the mystic's soul to God as "an indivisible union" and as "the true possession of God." "When the soul rests in God in purity, it takes all its life and being from the core of God, yet it is not conscious of any knowing, or loving, or whatever else. It rests, utterly and at one, in Divine Being, knowing naught else but that absorption. So soon as it becomes conscious that it beholds or loves or knows God, that is in itself a departure out of the purity of the experience, back into the natural order." Elsewhere he writes: "There is a capacity in my soul which is unreservedly open to God. Of this I am as sure as that I live. Nothing is as close to me as God. He is nearer to me than I am to my self. His presence is my being."

Meister Eckhart, for all his theological erudition, discounts, as do so many spiritual leaders, learning and reason as against intuition and direct experience. "The less theorizing you do about God, the more receptive you are to his in-pouring." And: "True possession of God lies in the heart, not in thinking about Him. A Divinity theoretically conceived will not do. For then God goes when thought goes. Rather, grasp the God that is Being, above all thinking and all creaturely activity."

Harking back to Plotinus, Eckhart makes a distinction between God and Godhead — for God is expressed and is apprehensible, but there is a higher Divinity that is ineffable and unrevealed. Between the God that came down to man and the hidden Source there is an unbridgeable chasm. "God and the Godhead are as different as earth is from Heaven." But the soul of the mystic craves entry into that holy of holies. There is, indeed, in this view, a scale of experiences, each more wonderful. "When the soul first breaks into the Kingdom it possesses God, beyond truth and goodness. It penetrates deeper and possesses him in Oneness, in Essence. Still unsatisfied, it goes on in quest of the mystery of His Godhead, the unknowable nothingness of His Being."

In summary of the sermons on the soul in relation to God, Eckhart wrote this paragraph: "When the soul lives in its own secret inner chamber in such way that it images God, then it enjoys the oneness that is mortally indivisible. Nothing celestial or earthly can divide this soul from the image of God. This constitutes true Unity — and true blessedness depends upon it."

Meister Eckhart puts upon each man the burden of gaining entry to the Kingdom by purification and preparation — especially by annihilation of self-interest. He discounts conventional rites and prayers, and he condemns mortification. But the road to rebirth is by way of a purposeful freeing, a detaching from and indifference toward worldly living, an opening of the faculties to divinity. In a sermon on "Eternal Birth" he said: "To experience this noble birth you must get back to the centre, the ground of the soul, departing from all crowding activities and agents, even from memory and knowing and willing and all their multiple entanglements. You must escape them all, whether sense reports or romancing or reasoned plans. After that preparation you may experience this birth, but not otherwise. . . . If the divine birth is to occur in a man in all its shining reality and clarity, it must flood up and out of the soul in which God is indwelling — and that will be when all the man's own efforts are suspended, and the soul's ground left receptive to God." *

Because Meister Eckhart derived his mysticism from so many sources, incorporating anew the Greek and Oriental ideas and methods into his conception of "the way," he is the less in the succession of Christo-centric mystics. There is little of the language and imagery of mortal love as known in the writings of Saint Bernard and Richard of Saint Victor: little recourse to picturing the Christ as the Bridegroom of the soul, or to the mystic kiss and spiritual embrace. He is, nevertheless, in a reverently dignified way, eloquent in describing the Christian rebirth as attainment of the Kingdom through the manifestation of the Son within the soul. He can rise upon occasion to noble expression of his certainty in possession of the Christ-spirit:

> Even should I be emprisoned in the flesh until the day of judgment, and subject to the torments of Hell, it would be of no matter, since I possess my Lord Jesus Christ. He has given me the certainty of never being parted from Him. So long as I am here He is in me; in the after life I am in Him. All things are possible to me, for I am one with Him to whom all things are possible.

In describing the preparation for the coming of the Son into the soul, Eckhart speaks most of detachment or self-negation — his word is *Abgeschiedenheit*, and its exact meaning is untranslatable — an idea that includes both seclusion and the forsaking of self.

What one must do to escape into detachment is suggested in one of Eckhart's often-quoted aphorisms: "If you would have the kernel, you must break the shell." (The same idea is expressed, and never better, in William Blake's symbol of "the mundane shell" enclosing man, to be breached before "infinite life" can be re-attained.) Once you achieve detachment, you can "relax and let God operate you — this birth is His, your being is His: you have

---

* Again I wish to supplement my thanks, as recorded in the Appendix, with a notation of my gratitude to two translators. In preparing this and the preceding chapter I have had the privilege of drawing upon Raymond Bernard Blakney's excellent book, *Meister Eckhart: A Modern Translation*, and, for extracts from Saint Bernard's writings, upon Dom Cuthbert Butler's enlightening study, *Western Mysticism*. The publishers concerned, Harper & Brothers and E. P. Dutton & Company, have graciously authorized a somewhat elastic use of the translations — at times verbatim, oftener in my own paraphrased versions.

surrendered to Him, yielding all your faculties and functions and will. You are like a desert, cleared of all that grew out of self. . . . Be as a desert." Again Eckhart put the thought more succinctly: "Unmovable disinterest brings man into likeness of God. . . . To be full of things is to be empty of God; to be empty of things is to be full of God."

The idea of the man relaxed, the self emptied out and desert-like, leads into the thought so frequently expressed by the mystics, that the consciousness of divinity comes only with quietude. A saying of Eckhart is one of the most memorable on the subject: "Nothing in all creation is so like God as stillness."

Sometimes he tucks the recommendation of silence into a sermon unobtrusively — though the mystic will know how profoundly it is grounded in his thought. "You need seek Him neither below nor above. He is no farther away than the door of your heart. He stands there, His readiness waiting upon yours, until you open the door for His entry. Do not call as if He were far away. . . . Be quiet — and do not waver, lest, turning away from God, you never return."

The attainment of detachment or seclusion, the getting away to "the silent wilderness that harbours nothing," is not to be achieved, he avers, by the road of mortification or penances. Nor is prayer "for something" of any avail. There is a paradoxical saying of Eckhart's about this: "When I pray for something, I do not pray. When I pray for nothing, I really pray. . . . To pray for anything except God's will might seem idolatry, or injustice."

Saint Gregory and Saint Bernard had made the point that the beatific vision could not be attained by human beings on the mortal plane. Eckhart, however, draws no distinction between the mystic's possession of God and the blessed state of Being and of Vision in Paradise. "Many people imagine that there is a creaturely side to Being here, and only Divine Being there. It is not so. A man beholds God in this life in perfection as in the after life, and the experience is beatific in the same way."

Eckhart is, however, far more restrained than the Victorine mystics and Bernard in his descriptions of the actual experience of divine union. He seems more fully than any other Christian mystic to live in a pervading consciousness of God's presence and to enjoy uninterrupted spiritual bliss. But he describes not at all the sort of sudden ecstatic flight and inundation in rapture known to, say, Suso or Saint Catherine. Eckhart's is a steady, continuing communion, an experience habitual and calm.

It is none the less intense, illuminating, and intimate. There is even a passionate note in his praise of it: "Jesus unfolds Himself in the soul in unmeasured wisdom. . . . He also reveals Himself in boundless sweetness and plenitude. The soul that is prepared is inundated in unsearchable riches and delights. When Jesus thus enters, the tide of Being floods all things, claiming the soul as its own, sweeping it back to the Source."

How far this unfolding of Jesus in the soul is from an exceptional or miraculous occurrence is suggested again and again, sometimes in flaming words, in Eckhart's sermons: "I have said often that there is a part of the soul that is untouched by time or mortality: it proceeds out of the Spirit and remains eternally in the Spirit and is divine. In this part or faculty of the soul God Himself unfolds perpetually, in all the bliss and glory that are His. Here is felicity so ravishing, so inconceivably intense, that no one can describe it. . . . Here God glows and flames without ceasing, in all His abundance and sweetness and rapture."

In a treatise on "the Aristocrat," which is one of Eckhart's names for the spiritual part of man, or for "the Heavenly man," he lists six grades of living through which the spiritual initiate passes. "In the sixth grade he is transformed and dissolved in the divine, eternal Being. He has entered perfection. Having escaped all things of temporal, mortal life, he is caught up in the nature of God. There is no further ascent, nothing beyond this. It is rest in Eternity, and eternal bliss — the last aim of the spiritual or reborn man: Eternal Life."

There is a fragment about Eckhart, preserved by his disciples, which runs like this: "A hearer made complaint to Meister Eckhart that no one was able to understand his sermons. To this he answered: 'He who would understand my preaching must have accomplished five things. He must have put behind him all mental disturbance and temptation. He must have turned his intention toward the highest good. He must have let his will go in order to obey God's will. He must have studied to become a beginner among beginners. And he must have obtained mastery by conquering anger and overcoming self.'"

There seems to have been a fascination about the preaching of Meister Eckhart for both the learned and the untutored, for the unprepared and for those few prepared according to the specifications in the lines above. Perhaps it was the way in which the saintly man opened, with a bit of homely language, vistas into the depths of Paradise. "If you care to, you can have God." And: "As soon as He finds you ready, God is bound to act, bound to pour Himself into your being, just as, when the air is pure and clear, the sun must pour into it without holding back."

Remembering the saying that "Every creature is on the way to highest perfection," and remembering the iteration of the thought that a part in every person *is* God, a hearer might easily feel that preparation for continuous union need not be too arduous or difficult. A man need not be disturbed in his work. "Since one in this life cannot exist without work, one learns to possess God in all things, not the less in work and its conditions."

He was not very specific in some of these matters of the preparation for union, but he evaded no question put to him by his hearers. There is one passage about the conflict of the soul and the flesh that is particularly representative of both his thought and his method. At first it seems that he is recommending penances, but the transfer of emphasis to a better solution brings him back safely to his main theme:

> Fasting, praying, keeping watch, undergoing disciplines, wearing hair shirts, sleeping on boards, etc., were all invented because there is continual opposition of the flesh to the spirit. The body threatens to overcome the spirit and there is unending conflict between them. Here on earth the body is confident and fearless, for the world is its element. The earth is its fatherland, and it is at home among its own kind, abetted by food and drink and all the unspiritual pleasures. On the other hand the spirit is alien on earth. Its kind and its kin are in Heaven, and all its friends. In order to help the spirit in this unequal conflict with the body, a man puts penances upon the flesh, to weaken it so that it cannot overcome the spirit. He curbs or bridles the flesh so that the spirit may be able to conquer.
>
> This is one way to subjection of the body. But if you wish to make conquest of it a thousand times more certain, let *love* be your curb. With love you conquer the flesh quickly and beyond any danger of revolt.
>
> In just the same way God uses love to draw us to Him.

> Love is like a fisherman's hook. . . . He who is caught by it is held by the strongest of bonds — yet the being drawn in by it is pleasant. He who takes this sweet restraint of love upon himself will come nearer his aim than if he employed any man-devised curb. . . . Therefore look only to this hook, for in being caught you will be blessed. The more you are caught the more you are made free.

As with Saint Francis, so with Meister Eckhart, the attainment of universal love is not to be achieved without fullest embracing of poverty. He does not urge privation of the sort practised by the Saint of Assisi and the Zealots after him. But he is precise in his mapping of the territory of poverty. There are two sorts, he asserts. One is the outward poverty of those to whom the world assigns the word poor. The other is a profounder sort, more important to salvation, alluded to in the Sermon on the Mount when Jesus speaks of "the poor in spirit" — a phrase shockingly misinterpreted by numberless churchmen and philosophers.

"The poor in spirit" are those who, to prepare their souls for the entry of the Divine Spirit, have divested themselves of selfish wants, selfish thinking, and selfish possessions. "External poverty is good, and praiseworthy in men who take it upon themselves willingly, for love of Our Lord, for He practised it in the earthly sphere. . . . But a man should be poor in will, willing as little and desiring as little as when he did not yet exist. . . . A man should be as empty of all knowledge, as unburdened by human opinion, as when he came from God, in order to open the way to His will. . . . The third poverty is most inward and most actual — that a man *have* nothing." At this point Eckhart expounds one of the subtlest and extremest doctrines in all his philosophy. This not-having, this emptying of the self, must constitute so great a renunciation that the desire for God, even the place for God to come into, is to be driven from consciousness. Only utter nonbeing is an intimate enough sort of poverty. "What I am as a temporal creature is to die and come to nothingness, for that being came with time and will pass with time. . . . Here God is identical with the spirit, and that is the ultimate poverty."

To the sermon that ends with those words Meister Eckhart adds a thought for listeners who may have been puzzled. "If any man here does not comprehend what I have been saying, let him not worry. It is simply that he has not that special capacity for truth in him — all this is something that God put into my heart to say at this moment, without reflection." And somewhere he put the thought that those who did not follow him would do well to "hold by the common faith."

He laid his treasures of spiritual thought before all who came to him. But he knew argument and exposition and pleading to be a small part of that persuasion which turns man from simple, reasoned faith to illuminated living. He recognized the truth in the ageless paradox: to turn to holiness one must be holy.

Nevertheless he went on spreading his wisdom before rich and poor, before learned and ignorant, before initiates and the unawakened, as had no mystic seer before him. And it would be unfair to conclude any summary of his beliefs and teachings with other than sayings about the part of God that is in every soul, and about the ease of emptying the self of all that is not divine — once the paradox is understood. "If a man owned a kingdom or all the riches of the world and renounced it all for God's sake, becoming the poorest of men, if then God gave him suffering, and if this man persisted through suffering to his death, if then, even for one moment, God let him comprehend the way He is there in the man's soul, all his loss and suffering would seem a trifle in comparison with the glory of that moment. . . . For God Himself is in that soul-part, and the moment embraces Eternity."

And, as a final reminder of the necessity to be empty, in exactly the sense employed in the poems of Lao-Tse: "The good man will feel shame before God and himself if he discovers that he does not harbour God, that the Father is not working through him, that he is living and acting by the inferior creature self. . . . A perfected person will be so cleared of self, so wrapped in God, so obedient to His willing, that his joy will be in the escape from himself and from mortal concerns, and in consciousness of nothing but Divinity. . . . He wants only what God wants, and wants it God's way."

Meister Eckhart, worthy to stand beside Saint Francis and Saint Thomas Aquinas in the inmost circle of mediæval spiritual leaders, was not beatified, much less canonized, by the Church. At the time of his death he was under the cloud of the charge of heretical utterances. He is not venerated as a saint, and no monastic order carries on devotion and works in his name. Yet it is doubtful if any one of the Saints inspired more men and women to seek God's companionship and to live in what they conceived to be God's holy way. Certainly no other saintly man ever so effectively praised and promoted the mystic Christian life. No other had a group of disciples so gifted and original as Tauler, Suso, and Ruysbroeck, or a popular following such as that constituted in the Friends of God. In the northern countries Eckhart was the fountainhead of mediæval mysticism, from which in turn the seers of the Reformation and the Counter-Reformation drew their sustenance.

Meister Eckhart is the soberest, steadiest of the mystical philosophers. Many another in the Christian line is more picturesque, more dramatic, more vivid. But for depth and common sense and understandability his writings are unsurpassed. There is, too, a freshness, even a naïve childlikeness, in his thought and his expression, not unlike that to be detected in the German art of the period. For never elsewhere was Teutonic art so harmonious and fresh and serene as in the paintings of the School of Cologne. Then especially artists planned their pictures "to kindle men's minds toward God."

Johannes Tauler was a Dominican Brother and a famous preacher in the Rhine Valley. He was born at Strassburg, probably a few years before 1300. Educated at Strassburg and Cologne, he had opportunity to imbibe to the full Eckhart's ideas and he became especially the link between the Meister and the wide-spread groups of lay Friends of God.

For a time, in middle life, he was stationed at Basel, but before and after his service there he preached at Strassburg. A loyal churchman, he was caught in the dilemma created by the interdict laid upon Strassburg by one of the French Popes. He is said to have solved his personal problem by declaring his faith in the Church and the Pope, while at the same time averring that there exists a supreme spiritual union of the soul with its Bridegroom, a union that cannot be disturbed from without so long as the individual sincerely "waits upon God."

Tauler was a sympathetic, homely preacher, close to the brothers and sisters of the monasteries and humanly close to the lay audiences of *Gottesfreunde*. He pointed out the way to a life of Christlike service and of spiritual communion, and he showed how this might be attained without travelling the path of scholastic learning and without too much regard to churchly routine and direction. For a long time it was supposed that he was the author of *The Book of the Master,* the treatise entitled *Imitation of the Poverty of Jesus Christ,* and other famous German documents describing the mystic life. But recently scholars have ascribed these to unknown authors who, as Friends of God, wrote anonymously, being averse to show and fame; or to the mysterious "Friend of God from the Oberland."

The Friends of God did not aspire to an organization of their own, though they banded together informally in many places. They were in and out of the Church, some loyally faithful, others insistently independent. Their name sufficiently indicates the basic tenet of their religion: a friendly, heart-felt reliance upon God, whose presence in the soul actuated their every thought and deed. Looking at the corruption about them, they felt that most men, in their way of living, had become, often unwittingly, enemies of God; and so they set out, in one of the most remarkable revolutions in religious history, to be friends of God.

In Germany and Switzerland and the Low Countries the informal fellowship grew until no one knows how many individuals or "centres" entered into the movement. Sometimes monks and nuns took up the spread of the mystic doctrine, sometimes tertiaries were the animating spirits; but the most remarkable thing about the *Gottesfreunde* in the end is the essentially lay character of its devotion. Uncounted thousands, scattered over a large part of Europe, met together informally, attended sermons by mystic preachers such as Eckhart and Tauler, built up an amazing system of education and inspiration by correspondence, circulated the famous treatises on mysticism, along with many lesser contemporary accounts of conversion and attainment, and in general promoted individual "flight to the One." As they accepted literally the injunctions of Jesus regarding poverty and charity, they became known as practical saints in their communities.

The Friends of God, without rules of membership and without accredited leaders, attracted many a dubious character too, and in the end it is difficult to draw the line separating them from the Beghards and other sects that the Church found it expedient to persecute. The Beghards were communities of men ostensibly retired to live holy lives. The pattern for them had been set by the Beguines, lay women who banded together and established "God's Houses," did charitable work, begged alms, and sometimes estab-

THE GARDEN OF PARADISE. PAINTING OF THE SCHOOL OF COLOGNE. GERMAN, ABOUT 1400. STÄDEL ART INSTITUTE, FRANKFURT-ON-MAIN.

lished centres of study and pious work not far from the ideals of the Friends of God.

But the Church, concerned with the salvation of all souls in every community and having orders and convents of its own, could not tolerate an unauthorized and sometimes definitely heretical movement. It had laws passed against the Beguines and Beghards, and when that method did not suffice it took action through the Inquisition, not stopping short of burnings at the stake. A part of the charges against Eckhart had arisen out of the suspicion that he was sympathetic toward the Beghards — as well he might have been, since many of them professed a poverty and a holy illumination growing out of "annihilation of self that God might be in them."

A multitude of spiritual sects, indeed, was born in the thirteenth and fourteenth centuries, and one might trace lines from the Friends of God to some of the lay or tertiary Franciscan groups in Italy and France — the *Fraticelli* or *Frerots*, though originally Franciscans professing extremest poverty, were later disowned by the Church and forcibly exterminated — and to such sects as the Waldensians and the White Brothers. Especially close, and indeed a thoroughly mystical sect, was the fellowship known as the Brothers of the Free Spirit.

Apparently this sect developed out of an earlier society known as the Brothers of the New Spirit, which the Church had suppressed in Strassburg about 1317. In that year a letter was forwarded by one John of Ochsenstein to the inquisitorial office, containing charges that throw light upon the varied elements in these "societies" and upon the reasons for the Church's hostility toward them. "Some persons who call themselves begging Sisters and Brothers have among them, to our great sorrow, monks and priests and married persons. We condemn all the doctrines and ceremonies of this sect. . . . They claim to be God in virtue of their nature, because they claim that a man can be so united to God that his powers, his will and his activities are not different from God's. . . . There is no Hell, no Purgatory, no last judgment. . . . All property is common to all — so it is no sin to steal." Pointing out further extreme beliefs — even that each perfected man is a Christ — the informer recommends that "these heretics be chased from their habitations," that their houses be sold for the profit of the Church, that their books be turned over to the priests to be burned.

Nevertheless the groups of both the Friends of God and the Brothers of the Free Spirit multiplied through the rest of the century; indeed, both their activities and the hostility of the Church were to continue up to the time of the Reformation. A passage written about the "Brethren and Sisters of the Free Spirit" by Hannah Adams and published in *A View of Religions* in Boston about 1790 affords a succinct view of their belief. It indicates how they accepted the mystic doctrines of Tauler and the Friends, yet went on to extremes that gave substance to the charges of heresy and lawlessness. Incidentally it describes, in admirably simple language, the groundwork that is common to the mystic structures of many faiths:

> The sentiments taught by this denomination were as follow: That all things flowed by *emanation* from God, and were finally to return to their divine source. — That rational souls were so many *portions* of the Supreme Deity; and that the universe considered as one great whole, was God. — That every man, by the power of contemplation, and by calling off his mind from sensible and terrestrial objects, might be united to the Deity in an ineffable manner; and become one with the Source and Parent of all things. And that they, who, by long and assiduous meditation, had plunged themselves, as it were, into an *abyss* of the divinity, acquired thereby a most glorious and sublime liberty, and were not only delivered from violence of sinful lusts, but even from the common instincts of nature.
>
> From these, and such like doctrines, the *Brethren* under consideration, drew this conclusion, viz. That the person who had ascended to God in this manner, and was absorbed by contemplation in the abyss of Deity, became thus a part of the Godhead — commenced God — was the *Son of* God in the same sense and manner that Christ was, and was thereby raised to a glorious independence, and freed from the obligation of all laws, human and divine.
>
> In consequence of this, they treated with contempt the ordinances of the gospel, and every external act of religious worship, looking upon prayer, fasting, baptism, and the sacrament of the Lord's supper, as the first elements of piety, adapted to the capacity of children, and as of no sort of use to the *perfect man,* whom long meditation had raised above

all external things, and carried into the bosom and essence of the Deity.

They rejected with horror every kind of industry and labor, as an obstacle to divine contemplation, and to the ascent of the soul towards the Father of spirits.

Extreme as this statement is, it indicates, in the earlier portions, how close these people came to a literal application of Eckhart's ideas; and, before the end, how easily the practitioners might slip over into licentiousness, laziness, and false piety. The truth seems to be that under the name of Friends of God — and Brethren of various sorts — one of the greatest and most admirable mass developments of spiritual-mindedness and mystical attainment occurred; but that at the fringes the "mystical associations" slipped over into being dubious and often heretical cults.

Among those who, in that time, drew a distinction between the Friends of God on the one hand and the Beghards and the Brothers of the Free Spirit on the other, was the preaching brother Heinrich Suso. A sensitive, brooding, imaginative boy, he entered a Dominican monastery at Constance when he was thirteen. At eighteen he had something approaching a conversion and an illumination. In an ecstatic vision he tasted "the bliss of Eternal Life."

Unlike Eckhart and Tauler, who spoke soberly of the mystical experience and counted the constant mindfulness of God's presence a greater blessing than ecstatic flights into union, Suso was emotional and passionate and rhapsodic. He was by turns tormented by the miseries of his mind and transported to a region of indescribable spiritual joys. He was not a great preacher, but his sermons and particularly his personal counsel were greatly valued by the monks and nuns of the monasteries and by lay disciples who sought the mystic "way."

Suso was much more intensely the lover of God and dedicated "adventurer in glory" than was Eckhart. He had a vision of Heavenly Wisdom (the idealized Sophia of the Gnostics) as a glorious maiden who became his spiritual bride. And once, looking into his inmost being, he beheld the lovely form of Heavenly Wisdom beside his own soul, within the arms of God. His *Autobiography*, produced late in life with the help of a devoted nun who was one of his "spiritual daughters," and his *Book of Heav-*

enly Wisdom are filled with lyrical, not to say sentimental and lush, accounts of the mystical life. He toured Germany, Switzerland, and the Netherlands as a flaming evangelist for the life of Christian communion with God — and like a troubadour he sang the praises of his incomparable spiritual bride.

It was perhaps Eckhart who curbed Suso's imagination and vehemence, during a period when the younger man studied in Cologne between 1324 and 1327. At any rate Heinrich Suso seems never to have been disciplined or suspected by his superiors except when, after Eckhart's death, he told of seeing the Meister in a vision, perfected in union with God in Heaven.

Suso was afterward beatified. Doctrinally he paralleled Eckhart and Tauler, but emotionally and imaginatively he was at the opposite pole from them.

A disciple of Eckhart even greater than Tauler or Suso was Jan Ruysbroeck, a Fleming, who lived from 1293 to 1381. Born in a village near Brussels, he is said to have run away at the age of eleven to dedicate himself to religion. An uncle at Saint Gudule's Church in Brussels undertook to supervise his education. Later he studied at Cologne, but whether Eckhart was then teaching there is unknown. In any case, when Ruysbroeck became a priest and returned to be an assistant at Saint Gudule's he was thoroughly grounded in the mystic doctrines of the Christian writers from Augustine and Dionysius to Bernard, Bonaventura, and Eckhart.

For a quarter-century he discharged his duties as priest at Saint Gudule's. But at the age of fifty he decided to act upon his own counsel of withdrawal, left the active Church, and retired, a virtual hermit, to a retreat at Groenendael in the Forest of Soignes, near Brussels. For thirty-eight years he lived there, and his retreat, at first an abandoned hunting lodge, turned into a centre to which mystics came as pilgrims.

While at Saint Gudule's Ruysbroeck became famed for his saintliness, and already he was known as a visionary and a seer. He then wrote at least the first draft of *The Book of the Kingdom of God's Lovers*, one of his most famous works. He took an active interest in the lay sects, especially the Beguines (to whom his mother became attached) and the Friends of God. He strove to curb heretical tendencies among the free associations of mystics and spirituals, and he wrote in the German-Flemish dialect of the time instead of the Church Latin, in order to reach the common people. But it is in the life at Groenendael — Green Valley — that the interest of later mystics centres.

With him from the church at Brussels had gone his uncle and a third priest, Franc van Coudenberg. The three formed a "mystical community," built their own chapel in the forest, and settled down to a life of poverty, manual labour, and meditation. Pilgrims came and went. A few decided to stay. Ruysbroeck and his fellows soon saw that this would be a monastery, with need for rules and direction. They became Augustinian monks.

Ruysbroeck, while never shirking any arduous labour, avoided administrative duties as far as possible. He communed with nature, meditated, talked with pilgrims, and wrote books on the spiritual and mystical life. Among his writings were *The Adornment of the Spiritual Marriage*, *The Spiritual Tabernacle* (an autobiography of his own soul), *The Book of the Sparkling Stone*, and *The Seven Beguines*. These books belong on the shelf of foremost treatises upon the Christian mystic life. They are commonly known as the works of "Ruysbroeck the Admirable."

As Eckhartian mysticism is the standard in his time, so that one encounters the Meister's conceptions and even his phrases in the writings of Tauler and Suso and in the correspondence and tracts of hundreds inside and outside the Church who devoted themselves to the mystic quest, so too it seems to afford the basic structure of Ruysbroeck's doctrine. Nevertheless the great Fleming was more original than either Tauler or Suso. He broadened the base upon which Eckhart's conception of an immanent Divinity rested; and he added his own versions of the discipline necessary before attainment, and of the way in which the soul is a part of God. He was a nature-lover, and he sought God's signature in the natural world as the Strassburg mystics did not. He also trimmed his sails a little, as Eckhart scorned to do, in view of the storms of protest sweeping from the Church over the lay mystic associations.

But most of all there is a gentleness, a compassion, over Ruysbroeck's life and writings that carries him a little of the way toward the sweetness, the fresh simplicity, and the humanness of a Francis — or a Jesus. Indeed there are disciples of Ruysbroeck who would place him rather than Meister Eckhart at the peak of mediæval mysticism, because of the simple saintliness and warm sympathy of the man, beyond the erudition and felicity of expression of the philosopher.

And indeed it was at once a Christlike holiness in the man and a warmth of feeling in his writings that brought about his influence in so many directions in the century following his death. It was after visits to Ruysbroeck at Groenendael that Gerhard Groot founded the Brothers of the Common Life, a sort of Church-sponsored counterpart to the lay societies of the Friends of God. The Brothers lived in houses communally and in dedication to a holy life, but not as members of orders. Gerhard Groot was at the time a lay preacher, loyal to the Church but independent. He was an evangelist for "the New Devotion" — his name for the spiritual life as outlined especially by Ruysbroeck.

Church-sanctioned monasteries were, however, erected by his followers, and it was at one of these that Thomas à Kempis wrote, or compiled and edited, *The Imitation of Christ*, that classic of Christian devotion which, without being intensely mystical, is one of the loveliest survivals from the literature of mediæval mysticism. It argues especially the feasibility of living an inward life in spiritual awareness of the Christ, and an outward life in harmony with His ethical and social teachings.

While Ruysbroeck's influence worked upon the religious communities of Flanders and Holland, it worked too upon the German communities of the Rhineland from which the Hermit of Groenendael had gained so much. Tauler is supposed to have visited at Groenendael, and perhaps it was he who took copies of Ruysbroeck's writings back to Strassburg. There a rich merchant who had come under Tauler's influence and had reformed, one Rulman Merswin, had bought an abandoned church and convent on an island close to the city and had founded the Green Isle Community to further the life and the work envisaged by the soberer members of the Friends of God. At first primarily a retreat for lay mystics, served by four secular priests — that is, priests unordained though approved by the Church — it later took refuge under the Knights of Saint John. But its chief claim to the everlasting gratitude of students of the spiritual life is the literature that was there collected and preserved, and in some cases composed. Ruysbroeck's *The Adornment of the Spiritual Marriage* was but one of many manuscripts that found their way into the scriptorium at Green Isle, to be incorporated into one or another of the books "produced" there. To this day no one knows how much Merswin actually wrote of the mass of material associated with the Green Isle name.

In any case the treasury of books with which Merswin's name is connected contained a cycle of treatises purporting to be by "the Friend of God from the Oberland," a figure as mysterious as the False Dionysius of nine centuries earlier. For long he was identified as Nicholas of Basel, again as the "other personality" of Rulman Merswin. Several of the books now ascribed to him appeared for centuries under the name of Tauler. All that is certain is that the literature compiled at Green Isle affords the initiate, in *The Book of the Nine Rocks*, *The Book of the Master*, *The Spark in the Soul*, and a dozen other treatises, some of the most enjoyable and inspiring reading in the entire library of Christian thought.

Mystics as writers have often preferred to be anonymous; and in the Rhineland of the fourteenth century mysticism had taken the road of suppressed personality and withdrawal. It is fitting therefore that the final flower of spiritual writing of the era is by a churchman whose name and station are hardly guessed at by the scholars. The *Theologia Germanica* is a simple, profound, and beautiful presentation of the idea that one loses the life of the self to attain the life of God, that Christ is in each of us, and that the most real thing in life is the tasting of Eternity or Divine Love through Him.

It was Martin Luther who edited the first printed edition. And he said of the *Theologia Germanica* that it taught him "more of what God and man and all things are" than any book except Saint Augustine's writings and the Bible. The experienced mystic goes back to it again and again as one of the supremely helpful expositions of the "way," which it charts from purification to enlightenment to union. He finds in it an engaging and calm epitome of the wisdom of the mediæval Christian mystics. It is the last and one of the choicest blossoms in that incomparable flowering that occurred between the conversion of Saint Francis in the year 1202 and the gradual dispersion of the Friends of God after 1450.

VII. Fra Angelico, the Saintly Painter and Tool of God

If there is a land close to Heaven, where the climate is agreeable to the soul, where saints should be a little more at home, it is the realm of Tuscany. Here there is a spot where the hills and plains are disposed like a vast amphitheatre spreading fanwise out from the Valley of the Arno, with Florence at its heart. The landscape has about it a tranquillizing rhythmic order, not too smoothed and clipped and trimmed as some attempted northern paradise might be, nor yet partaking of the sharpness and irregularity that obtain just beyond the Apennines. Rather, the rounded, breast-like hills, the terraced orchards, and the plotted valley fields are composed with a sort of musical order, harmonious and temperate, yet cadenced and inspiriting.

The olive groves are clouds of silvery grey clinging above villa gardens. The low lines of the farm-houses echo the vineyard rows and the smooth-ploughed meadows. The shadowy gardens are rich with legendary fig and laurel, ilex and myrtle, and groves of chestnut and pine. At intervals, erect black cypresses, like exclamation marks, correct the otherwise too lazy aspect. Beyond are the mountains, seemingly as rhythmically disposed.

One feels, when one comes to Tuscany as a pilgrim, that a special sort of clear-seeing is here entrusted to man. If the land is opulent, generous, colourful with flowers, fruits, wine, and grain, the riches of it seem the more natural because a transparency of atmosphere blends all things together, as in one harmony. Of Florence and Fiesole and the valley of the Arno it is commonly said that, as nowhere else, an utmost clarity of light obtains. The sunniness that lies over the plains and hills shades off into the Apennine purple-blue haze; but even distant objects, too distant it seems for the unaided eye, come to sight clear-cut and defined. There are many who go on to belief that the inner eye, the eye of the soul, may similarly enjoy increase of seeing in this favoured land.

Tuscany has its magnificent place in the history of the Christian mystics and prophets. And in a realm so close to the spiritual that no one may say where the one ends and the other begins — the realm of art — there has been as much of deeper seeing and of inspired revelation here among the Tuscan hills as anywhere on earth. The noblest of the Christian painters, from Duccio and Simone Martini and Giotto to the giant Michelangelo, were Sienese or Florentine.

It is in another art, however, that the sunny, rhythmic quality of the land seems perfectly echoed and immortalized. In Florentine architecture the rhythmic order is set out precisely and fittingly. The arcades, the serene, symmetrical façades, the low-roofed hospitable buildings are of a fitting unison, a conforming spirit. As religion was basic to the greatest painting art of the time, so an odour of religious seclusion clings to the purest examples of Renaissance building; for nothing else so well epitomizes the style as the colonnaded cloister. If the two great Renaissance innovators, Brunelleschi and Michelozzo, Florentines both, borrowed their detail and their accent from exhumed relics, striving to re-create a vision they had formed of Greece, they nevertheless moulded their expression to fit the sunniness, the clarity, and the tranquil loveliness of the countryside, even while the persisting spirit of a sequestered monastic life as the highest ideal entered as a third shaping factor.

Italy had tried and rejected the more sombre Gothic architecture of the North and was destined to return unreservedly to the adapted classic as the truly Christian style. At this period — when Fra Angelico was externalizing his spiritual devotion in his most appealing pictures, in the second quarter of the *quattrocento* — at this period, Renaissance architecture was classic, Tuscan, and to a degree monastic.

In the cloisters and on the terraced hills, then, one may imagine the soul at rest, in harmony, surrounded with a quietude contrived jointly by God and man. It is a land, and a moment in history, when saints and mystics, and inspired builders and painters, may well appear among common beings.

At Siena there had been, a half-century earlier, a revival of piety and mysticism. Giovanni Colombini had founded the Gesuati, and the incomparable Saint Catherine had joined her clairvoyant seeing and mystic inspiration with service to the international Church. At Florence the spirit of man had expressed itself less through the pure contemplatives and religious figures than through men of letters and of the arts: Dante and Petrarch and Boccaccio, Giotto and the Giottesques and Lorenzo Monaco, and that greatest of early Renaissance sculptors, Jacopo della Quercia. It was in Florence, or its *contado*, that there appeared that artist-saint, known first as Guido of Vicchio, then as Fra Giovanni of Fiesole, then universally as Fra Angelico, who combined a rare and radiant holiness with the genius of a born painter.

While the time was ripe for the birth of this saint among artists, the times, in broader perspective, would seem to have been inauspicious for either serene and chaste devotion to God or sober, exalted artistic expression. Politically Italy was divided, and the picturesque war-lords and fiery citizens of the city-states had waged savage battles, each town against all others. The histories of Siena and of Florence during the *trecento* had been chronicles of almost incredible factional strife and civil wars, of intrigue and corruption and murder, of treason and hysteria and assassination; and to these disorders the pestilence had added a horrible chapter. The Catholic Church had never fallen so low in power and prestige; the Pope had been for years a prisoner of France in Avignon; the monastic establishments had permitted unspeakable evils to grow up, so that the monk's habit and the nun's veil were no longer infallible signs of a holy seclusion and a chaste personal dedication, but as often reminders of cloaked profligacy and degeneration. The world of the mind, too, the world of learning, of dawning science, and of historical research, was disturbed, divided, and without directive centre. Because the old learning had been so possessed by the Church, the New Learning took on a bent toward scepticism, if not atheism. Innumerable able scholars were led unaware into being not only anti-clerical but anti-spiritual. Though politicians were corrupting and dividing the Church, and the Churchmen shamelessly playing corrupt politics, and each side meddling into learning, chasms were being opened between government and religion, between religion and education, between Christianity and social progress. Those ideas were emerging, of an exclusive humanism, an aggressive individualism, and a personal materialism, that were to deprive the Western world of a sustaining faith and a spiritual unity down to the twentieth century.

Yet here was this Tuscan land, hospitable to the spirit, giving birth in the midst of violence and corruption to arts so genuine, so gracious, so inspiring that no like manifestation was to be known for five centuries after; fostering, too, in the midst of a break-down of faith, a genuine revival of spiritual devotion and a wide reformation of the monastic orders; and reviving a mediæval mystical philosophy that is counted by some the innermost substance of Christianity.

Fra Giovanni was given by his contemporaries the name Fra Angelico — "The Angel-like Brother." Ultimately the Church beatified him, so that he went thereafter by the doubly blessed name Beato Angelico. But to the world he is known less for his holiness than for his immortal paintings. It is easily overlooked that his created world of lovely colour, serenely contrived groupings of figures, and affecting devotional sentiment reflects a mystic's inner life. This is, nevertheless, Christianity's supreme exhibit of a revelation, in terms of art, of a saintly man's meditations upon his religion.

Fra Angelico was heir to the mediæval Italian tradition of painting; that is, to the Byzantine manner, now modified by the innovations of Duccio, the Lorenzetti, Giotto, and his other predecessors (who are spoken of sometimes as the last flower of the Middle Ages, again as heralds of the Renaissance). Of this Italian manner — the Byzantine manner softened, enriched, and rendered rhythmical by those Tuscan dreamers — he became the perfect master.

Living at the moment when classicism stirred again, when Brunelleschi and Michelozzo were experiencing a dream of Hellas revived — and digging for relics that would serve as models of the new building art — when Ghiberti and Donatello were establishing in Florentine sculpture a classic realism and pictorialism, Fra Angelico in this revival found sound precedent for his own love of serenity and clarity; and he adopted the new tranquil architecture into the backgrounds of his pictures, and, possibly, a traceable rhythm of composition. Nevertheless, with these two influences accounted for, the old Byzantine-Italian tradition and the new classicism, it is the third factor, his life in religion, that is conclusive, that most essentially makes his art what it is. Certainly he could not have been so great an artist if he had not been a man of religion first.

Few painters in history have been so individual, independent, and single-minded. But it is no repeated style-mark or mannerism that proclaims as his own Fra Angelico's least painting. It is the man's soul expressed, made manifest in "The Annunciation,"

"The Nativity," or "The Coronation of the Virgin." The holy man, the man who loved quiet, the man who chose to love chastely, the *frate* who won extraordinary amounts of gold for his Order but elected to live in poverty, is here in these pictures.

It is not the devotional subjects only — there are no paintings from Fra Angelico's brushes except religious ones — nor the atmosphere of quiet and naïve charm that lies over so many of them. Rather it is that this painter, saint, and mystic learned ways to carry over into his fresco or panel some oblique revelation of his experience of God's presence, some reminder of a world of the spirit. They speak of a cosmic architecture or a celestial scene familiar to the soul but lost to most men in the process of — as they say — "living."

In expressing so much of a hidden life in his fresco or panel Fra Angelico, unlike modern painters who try to isolate a geometrical order in "abstract" pictures, or those who speak of revealing "form" without serious regard to subject, was able to wed perfectly the formal side of his art and the subjective. For it was meditation upon these same subjects that led him to experience of a higher world. He had followed all the steps of the Christian mystic: dedication to a life of selfless devotion, of chastity, obedience, and poverty; austere discipline; adoring contemplation; a placing of one's consciousness in Christ; and, final consummation, experience of God's presence. There are painters in great number who acceptably illustrate Bible stories and Christian legends. Fra Angelico is of that small company that paint the story and at the same time reveal the realm of God. Of them all he is perhaps the purest Christian, the most feeling of God's painters.

Fra Angelico, speaking to his fellow-workers, said that an artist should cultivate quiet seclusion, and that if he made it his business to deal with the stories of Christ, he should then see to it that he lived "in Christ." In his own life he not only obeyed this injunction, but believed that in being a painter devoted to religious expression he was completely a tool of God. He never, he explained, retouched a picture, or even so much as corrected a line, because the original had been put down at God's will. He worked, we know, in the mystic's strange state of combined humility and confidence, in devotion and at times in rapture.

There is tenderness, almost patience, in each of his works; so

THE ANNUNCIATION. PAINTING BY FRA ANGELICO. SAN MARCO MONASTERY, FLORENCE.
(ANDERSON PHOTO).

PORTRAIT OF FRA ANGELICO. BY CARLO DOLCI.
ACADEMY, FLORENCE.

that it is believable when one reads in Vasari that Fra Giovanni was never known to show anger. There is tenderness of a particular sort in his treatment of women in his pictures. The celibate monk reverences womankind. Mary is never, in any other artist's interpretation, so fragilely lovely, so girlish, so chaste. As the artist matures, the Madonna may appear more maternal, and saddened in the "Passion" series, but there is no departure from the blond loveliness and the innocency of the original type. As the colouring is harmonious, almost golden, so too the figure composition, its line and mass and ordering, is simple, melodious, and chaste. And as holiness seems to surround the Madonna as an aura, so too all the other women, whether known Saints or anonymous attendants, are depicted as sweet-faced, exquisite, and saintly. It is, one knows, a part of the Brother's own innocency and devotion, of his purity and lovingness. He is the tool of God; God has created woman to be fair, has revealed to him her fairness and her delicate loveliness as a part of the Divinely ordered world; he has observed how often the heavenly ideal is reflected among the women of Florence whom he, if only distantly, meets; he places her in the picture as God would will, as womanly but as holy and touched with immortal beauty.

As this sort of reverence and revelation arises from the silence and the meditation of the monastic life, so too does a quality or aspect of *repose* that distinguishes almost the full body of Fra Angelico's paintings. They are quietly composed, tranquilly adjusted. They do not lack movement, are not static; that is, the eye moves about in them; they are plastically alive. But the movement is gentle, melodious; the pattern is closed. The achievement comes not only out of the gift for formal organization, which even the form-conscious moderns of the twentieth century might envy, but from a quietude of the spirit, mystically attained.

In the valley of the Mugello, above Florence, somewhat below the ruined bastion known as the Castello Vicchio, in the year 1387 a boy named Guido was born. His father has been identified only as one Pietro, whose family presumably belonged to the farming or artisan class. For the first seventeen years of his existence Guido lived the life of that favoured countryside, knowing its riches, absorbing into his own nature, apparently, something of its sunniness. He had a brother, Benedetto, two years younger, who can be pictured as a beloved companion and confidant; for both chose art as a field of work, and together they were to renounce the world and enter the Dominican Order of Friars Preachers.

Benedetto was later an illuminator of manuscripts and an illustrator, and Guido, when he became a painter in tempera and fresco, obviously spent some years outgrowing the idioms of the miniaturist. It therefore seems not unlikely that the two youths attended together an apprentice school in Florence dedicated to the arts of illumination, possibly the one maintained by the friars of Santa Maria degli Angeli. This would have been in the years 1406 and 1407. Florence at that moment was alive with new or revived ideas in the field of the arts; the commission for the door panels of the Baptistry had been given to Ghiberti, and Donatello and Brunelleschi were just returning from their epochal study of classic monuments in Rome.

It was in 1407 that Guido and Benedetto made their decision to enter holy orders. They went as postulants to the Dominican monastery at Fiesole, up on that hillside which commands so glorious a prospect of the valley of the Arno and the City of Flowers. Vasari records that Guido chose to become one of the preaching friars "in order that he might have tranquillity and quietude in his life, and to assure the salvation of his soul." Whether he was thinking also of his gifts as an artist, desiring to consecrate them to God, does not appear from any record; but the first entry in the chronicles of the monastery at Fiesole, naming him as "Brother John, son of Pietro of Mugello and Vicchio," speaks of him as one "who has excelled as a painter, having decorated tablets and walls in various places."

The Monastery of San Domenico at Fiesole was famed for its strict observances and the exceptional worthiness of its Brothers. It had been founded by Johannes Dominici, who but recently had preached the necessity of reform of the holy orders, enjoining stern self-discipline and obedience to vows upon all those who followed him. He was carrying on, too, the tradition of mystical communion, if not mystical living, handed down by his saintly and inspiring master, Fra Raimondo of Capua, and the inspiration of that master's other, more famous pupil, Saint Catherine. Johannes Dominici also succeeded in taking his followers back to the ideals of the thirteenth-century founder of the order, Saint Dominic, who had enjoined a Christlike way of life, even to utter poverty and evangelical preaching.

The zeal and the piety of Johannes Dominici had not greatly influenced the members of the Dominican order at Florence; but somehow his spirit touched the youthful Guido and led him to the portal at Fiesole. So great was the youth's reverence for the reformer-preacher that he took the name Giovanni, from Johannes, becoming Fra Giovanni of Fiesole; though it is added in the records that he was thinking too of Saint Francis, who had been born Giovanni Bernardone.

Novices were not trained at Fiesole, and the two brothers were sent to the Monastery of San Domenico at Cortona, also of the reformed type. There Fra Giovanni spent the year of novitiate, in an atmosphere still Tuscan but away from the intellectual-liberal exposure of Florence. Again the young man found in his surroundings the inspiration nature is able to give, for the monastery looked away over a fair valley centred upon Lake Trasimene. Even more notable was the rich spiritual legendry of Cortona itself, for here Saint Francis had walked the streets, and on an island in Lake Trasimene he had fasted.

It is likely that Johannes Dominici, now charged with state matters and near to elevation to a cardinal's seat, was only infrequently a visitor at the Cortona monastery; but his gifted pupil Fra Lorenzo Ripafratta was in charge of the training there. Both he and Fra Antonino, the second of the direct spiritual influences upon Fra Giovanni, were to be lifelong friends and companions to the painter. All three, so holy and so helpful were to be their lives, were destined to be sainted or beatified by the Church. There was, moreover, a local tradition of self-giving to God; for in Cortona Frate Ricardo had written *The Little Garden of Devotion,* and Johannes Dominici had composed *A Counsel of Love.* A young art student and religious novice, amid mementoes of Saint Catherine and Saint Francis, already resolved upon consecrating his life, may well have received into his soul, in this air and this company, the impress of gentleness and repose and the sense of garden-like ordered beauty in the world that were to characterize his paintings throughout his career.

Christendom was disturbed at this period by a schism almost as grave as the one that had exiled a series of Popes through seventy years in France. Two rival Popes, to whom a third was presently added, had claimed election, and even an order so important as the Dominican found itself divided, and certain of its monasteries were disrupted. In 1409, a year after Fra Giovanni professed and returned to Fiesole, the chapter there fled, refusing to compromise, Florence having declared officially for the unacceptable Alexander V. Some of the monks went to Cortona, but the younger ones took up their abode with their brothers at Foligno, in Umbria, not far from Assisi.

Again Fra Giovanni found himself placed where impressions and influences were exactly calculated to develop the two central trends of his spirit: toward mystical holiness and toward the purest Christian expressiveness in pictorial terms. This was Saint Francis' own land, rich in mementoes of the most appealing of Catholic saints, and, too, of that Saint Clare, "Princess of the Poor," who had so aided Francis. Angela of Foligno, author of *The Book of Divine Consolations,* had been a mystic of extraordinary powers. In the Assisan churches, moreover, were the fitting and lovely devotional paintings by Giotto, to which had been added many works of the Sienese painters, most spiritualized of all *trecento* artists, and others by the Giottesques, who formed a golden bridge down to Fra Giovanni's time.

It has been inferred that the young painter was trained in the studio of one or another famous painter; some say Gherardo Starnina; others Lorenzo Monaco, a more logical inference on stylistic grounds, and because Lorenzo was a monk connected with the monastery of Santa Maria degli Angeli in Florence, and, like Fra Giovanni, given somewhat to the employment of a miniaturist's technique. But the only well-marked current of influence is that which can be traced back through the Giottesque religious painters to Giotto and the Sienese. So strong and obvious is the descent of certain qualities, both of manner and of spirit, that the mature Fra Angelico is often accounted the final figure in the progression of mediæval "unreal" painters.

This much only is certain: the youthful friar-artist gained the knowledge of an apprentice illuminator, he added something of the broad training in goldsmithing that went into the average Florentine painter's equipment, and he somewhere picked up an adequate knowledge of tempera painting on panels and of fresco. Thus equipped technically, he devoted himself to painting along the lines of the Byzantine-derived tradition, the tradition in which the simplicity, the colourfulness, and the formalism of the ikon were still implicit, rejecting to a large degree the gains in naturalism and picturesqueness made by the scientific realists of his generation.

The plague that was the scourge of Europe in the fifteenth century drove the monks of Fiesole from Foligno in 1414. The disorders resulting from the papal schism being not yet fully resolved, the Fiesolans went to stay with their brothers at Cortona; and for three or four years Fra Giovanni made his devotions and worked at the monastery above Lake Trasimene where he had once been a novice. He may at this time have gone to Siena, to add further inspiration and memories to those shaping his way of expression.

The fraternity returned to their monastery in Fiesole in 1418. Even then the ill-feeling among churchmen had not wholly passed, for the brothers were obliged to buy back their home from the local Bishop, they having technically forfeited the property by absenting themselves. They had been away almost a full decade.

The saintly Antonino, vowed to poverty, fell heir at this moment to a considerable patrimony. This, increased by a gift from a Florentine patron, not only served to bring the property back into the brothers' hands, but permitted new buildings and improvements. The friar who had come to the monastery portal as Guido of Mugello, Fra Giovanni, now thirty-one years old, naturally settled into the position of mural painter and decorator of the monastery, while his brother Benedetto worked at illumination and illustration.

The stay at Fiesole lasted eighteen years. The monastery was known again as the abode of men of exceptional saintliness and benevolence. Gradually it became known too as the abode of the most spiritual of painters, of Fra Angelico. He decorated panels and spread frescos on the walls, aided by assistants robed as he was in the Dominican black and white habit. He began to go afield. For it is no part of the Dominican purpose that the brothers shall retire from the world; rather they are encouraged to go out among men, to disperse their good works. Fra Giovanni was soon painting reliquary panels for Santa Maria Novella in Florence; and he executed one of his most celebrated works, the Altar of the Linaiuoli, with its central "Madonna," for the Florentine Guild of Flax Workers. For the church of the Dominicans at Cortona, also, he painted a "Madonna," and one for the Church of San Domenico at Perugia.

The artist had no interest in payment for the pictures he created, but the Dominican Order profited richly by his labour. It is said that when donors of pictures approached the brother, asking him to produce a panel or to decorate a wall, he invariably assented provided they could arrange for it with his prior. And the prior, since he was bargaining for the good of the holy fraternity and in no jot for himself, could ask a good round sum. The contract for the Altar of the Linaiuoli stipulated that one hundred and eighty gold florins were to be paid for Fra Giovanni's "pains and handiwork . . . or less in accordance with his conscience."

The banker, art patron, and uncrowned ruler of Florence, Cosimo de' Medici, commissioned many a work from the hand of the friar. It was accepted in those days that an international financier and virtual tyrant, a patron of the profane arts and the sciences, a lover of luxury if not a sensualist, should be also a patron of the Church and a student of divine affairs. It was to become apparent presently how deep and sincere was Cosimo's regard for the friars of Fiesole. In the early 1430's he was already ordering panel pictures from the artist who was being spoken of as Giovanni Angelico, not only as a rubric befitting his life, but because he had made himself *par excellence* the painter of angels and saints.

Fra Angelico did not mature early. It was about 1433, when he was forty-six years old, that he arrived at the height of his powers. He had only gradually outgrown the technique of the illuminator. He was destined always to retain something of the simplicity of presentation of the miniaturist, a characteristic chasteness and exquisite sensibility. Nevertheless he now gains in breadth and command. He outgrows also a somewhat cramping allegiance to Gothic idioms in the backgrounds of his picturing. The classic influence is evident; and indeed the rounded arches of Michelozzo's and Brunelleschi's architecture become his melodious composition better than had the pointed windows and tabernacles of the mediæval style of the north.

Fra Angelico goes on with the moderns of his time, learns the intricacies of the new science of perspective drawing, puts sufficiently correct anatomical structures under the clothing of his figures. But he does not abandon certain conventions that seem to the young realists to be archaisms. He is still primitively simple, direct — and, at will, heedless of scientific reality. It is the special charm of his work that it should be so. If he had filled in his spaces with the wealth of detail of those who followed him, if he had paused over each face or figure to endow it with photographic

THE NAMING OF SAINT JOHN. PAINTING BY FRA ANGELICO. SAN MARCO MONASTERY, FLORENCE. (MUSEUM OF MODERN ART PHOTO).

THE VISITATION. PAINTING BY FRA ANGELICO.

light and shade, he might easily have forfeited the simple, reposeful freshness that adds a note of other-worldliness, almost of enchantment, to his painting.

The fact that he uses shadow arbitrarily, as his plastic composition demands, without regard to the sources of light, has been an affront to the realists (who complain that "he never mastered the science of chiaroscuro" — as if his visions of Heaven, his ways of illumining the saintly life on earth, were dependent upon this materialistic detail). He remains in this matter a naïve, a Giottesque if you will, a pre-realist. He is unsophisticated, even unlearned, preserving a freshness that is childlike — perhaps angelic.

Certain it is that the method, the knowledge, is perfectly fitted to the religious, the sacred, painting that he undertakes. Masaccio had already painted his epoch-marking pictures in the Brancacci Chapel, with Adam and Eve shown forth as impeccably anatomical, and the lighting as correct as if a photographer had contrived it, and thus had loosed the naturalism that was to devour talent after talent down to Leonardo and Raphael; but in the face of excessive devotion to scientific accuracy Fra Angelico holds tight to the conventions of a Byzantine-derived, ikon-like art. He accepts the melodiousness that comes with revived classicism, incorporates it into his manner. But he recognizes the dangers as well as the mind-freeing aspects of the science that is mistakenly taken as the New Learning's most precious gift. To science and to the analytical reasoning that is its human tool he opposes his own method of intuitional divination, of mystical apprehension.

When one speaks of Fra Angelico as unlearned, the word needs qualification. The good friar was obviously a penetrating student of that subject which seemed to him, and has seemed to the majority of human beings of both Occident and Orient in many periods of history, the subject most important to mankind: that is, the life of the spirit. The themes of his painting and the figures he introduces show Fra Angelico to have been conversant not only with the two Testaments — no less with the legendry, prophecies, and imagery of the Old than with the answering realities, symbolism, and hope of the New — but also with the history of the Church and with the commentaries and imaginative literature of ecclesiastic writers. When he painted series of pictures dealing with the life of Mary or the life of Jesus or the stories of the saints, his interpretations were authentic, yet personal, original.

In his studies he had the example of the erudite Johannes

Dominici. He had the companionship of the learned Fra Antonino, soon to be his prior in Florence, and of Fra Tomaso Parentucelli, the scholarly librarian of San Marco, keeper of the richest collection of manuscripts in Italy. We may believe that his reading went far beyond the bounds of "the Scriptures and the Fathers."

But a Fra Angelico "Annunciation" or "Coronation of the Virgin" or "Madonna" is so profoundly true that one knows all talk of learning to be beside the real point, which is that this painter expressed understanding, a wisdom of the spirit. He sufficiently observed nature, he quite exceptionally knew the historical substance of the stories he chose to re-create; but gloriously he revealed an inward light, a radiant personal outlook upon spiritual events. It is from no sentimental limitation that he excludes the harsh aspects of human existence from his pictures. (The one point at which he failed was in giving reality and movement and agony to his limning of the damned in "The Last Judgement" — if indeed his own brushes touched that part of the work.) Because his own mind had arrived at illumination and tranquillity, he revealed the gay, the luminous, and the harmonious aspects of living in terms of serene and lovely beings, of gardens and flowers and dancing and adoration.

There is a sense of everlasting golden youth about his Madonnas and angels, a transcending sadness in the face of his "Christ," a visionary rapture in the faces of saints gazing up at the Madonna or at their Redeemer. The subjects are, after all, of the sort that might be thought unpaintable (except as any illustrator can arrange a scene with figures and entitle it "The Annunciation" or "The Nativity," as indeed a thousand artists have done); Fra Angelico nevertheless paints the wonder of the Annunciation, the *feeling* of the Nativity, the unearthly loveliness of Paradise. His is a world of grace, of exaltation, of still wonder. His colour is fittingly fresh and lovely, with an all-over golden tone and fields of ultramarine and olive green, crimson and vermilion or rose. Over all is a shadowless celestial light.

In 1436 the Dominican monks of Fiesole moved to a more extensive but dilapidated group of buildings known as the Monastery of San Marco in Florence. It was a major change for the brotherhood and for Fra Angelico. It was effected by Cosimo de' Medici. We are not told what arguments persuaded the Prior and the brothers to give up their country retreat in favour of an urban home — probably the greater opportunity for service, and perhaps promises of gifts that would make their chapter a centre of learning and influence: promises amply fulfilled, and amply to be repaid by the Dominican chapter to Florence, in the services of the Archbishop Antonino and of Pope Nicholas V, of Savonarola (a century later), and of Fra Angelico and his pupils.

Cosimo, having conceived the idea, quickly arranged matters with the Pope. San Marco was currently the home of a fraternity of Benedictines, regrettably carrying on the idleness and luxury, not to say the debauchery, of the worst period of the Church's decline. They were ousted and the worthy Fiesolan brothers given their home.

At first the removal brought trouble. The condition of the buildings, then a disastrous fire, made security from the weather impossible. Many of the brothers were ill and a few died. Cosimo then commissioned his favourite architect-retainer, Michelozzo, to rebuild the monastery not only usefully but magnificently. Antonino and his brothers, feeling a sincere aversion to worldly show, stipulated that a certain simplicity and austerity obtain; and Michelozzo beautifully solved the problem of contriving a building monumental yet monastic in atmosphere. In all, Cosimo spent 36,000 florins on the project in the years 1437–43. In 1442 there was a ceremonial dedication, and the church and the unfinished monastery were consecrated by Pope Eugenius IV.

As soon as Michelozzo had completed the first of the new walls Fra Angelico took up what was to constitute a great part of his life work, the decoration of the various halls — church, chapter room, dormitory, refectory — and, above all, the Cloister of Antonino and its more than forty cells. There is hardly anywhere in the world a treasure-house of the work of a single painter comparable with San Marco. No longer a monastery in the twentieth century, it is an art gallery of an exceptional sort, a shrine of the spirit as well as a display of noble paintings. In it one can submit oneself to the visioning, the revelation of the spirit, of Fra Angelico as in a specially shrine-like library or study one might read *The Imitation of Christ* or Brother Lawrence's *The Practice of the Presence of God.*

Fra Angelico put the best of himself, one may believe, into the simple unframed frescos on the walls of the tiny cells and the mural of the corridor outside. One may enjoy them not only for their spontaneity and utter unpretentiousness, but because one knows that the artist painted them wholly for love of his brothers. They would be seen by no others, so far as he knew. If, as he believed, God guided his hand, this was opportunity not only to lighten each cubicle with what joyous embellishment and grace art may bestow on its decorative side, but to afford to each brother a reminder of devotion, of God's plan, of legendary holy service; to provide, perhaps, a bridge to meditation, to communion, to saintly resolution.

The rooms are cramped, ill-lighted, rude; but each one has its picture, simple, eloquent, holy. The display attests that at least one artist of the Renaissance worked wholly unmindful of public approbation or monetary reward or fame, that he gave his best in a spirit of consecration and of service to the Christian commune of which he was a part.

In the cloister and cell frescos Fra Angelico is the most himself, for here the treatment is at once rich and simple, luminous and reticent. There is nothing in the whole range of his work more sensitive and chaste than the "Annunciation" of Cell 3; yet it is full-bodied and rhythmic (only less melodic than the incomparable treatment of the same subject on the corridor wall outside). Almost naïve is the simple story arrangement of "The Maries at the Holy Sepulchre" in Cell 8; and there one sees that variation of rhythms, through marshalling of figures and playing with linear directions and with planes, which adds a sort of counterpoint to the deceptively simple melody. It is both a compositional device and a reinforcement of the story that the figures of the saints are grouped in a drooping design, inexpressibly mournful and sad, whereas the heraldically opposed angel forms an open figure, radiant, pointing outward and upward. There are naïve touches in the little masterpiece of "The Nativity." Such are the lowered heads of the ox and the ass — because they, like Mary and Joseph, are kneeling in adoration of the Child.

At the end of the row of bare cubicles designed for the monks Michelozzo constructed a somewhat larger cell, devoted by agreement to the uses of the patron, Cosimo de' Medici. He was sincerely a student of divine affairs, not a little worried at times about the destination of his soul, and doubtless occasionally penitent and solicitous of quiet and sanctuary. Possibly he felt something of the nostalgia for the country of the soul which many busy men experience, a sort of haunting recognition of a lost world of the

THE ANNUNCIATION. PAINTING BY FRA ANGELICO. SAN MARCO MONASTERY, FLORENCE. (ALINARI PHOTO).

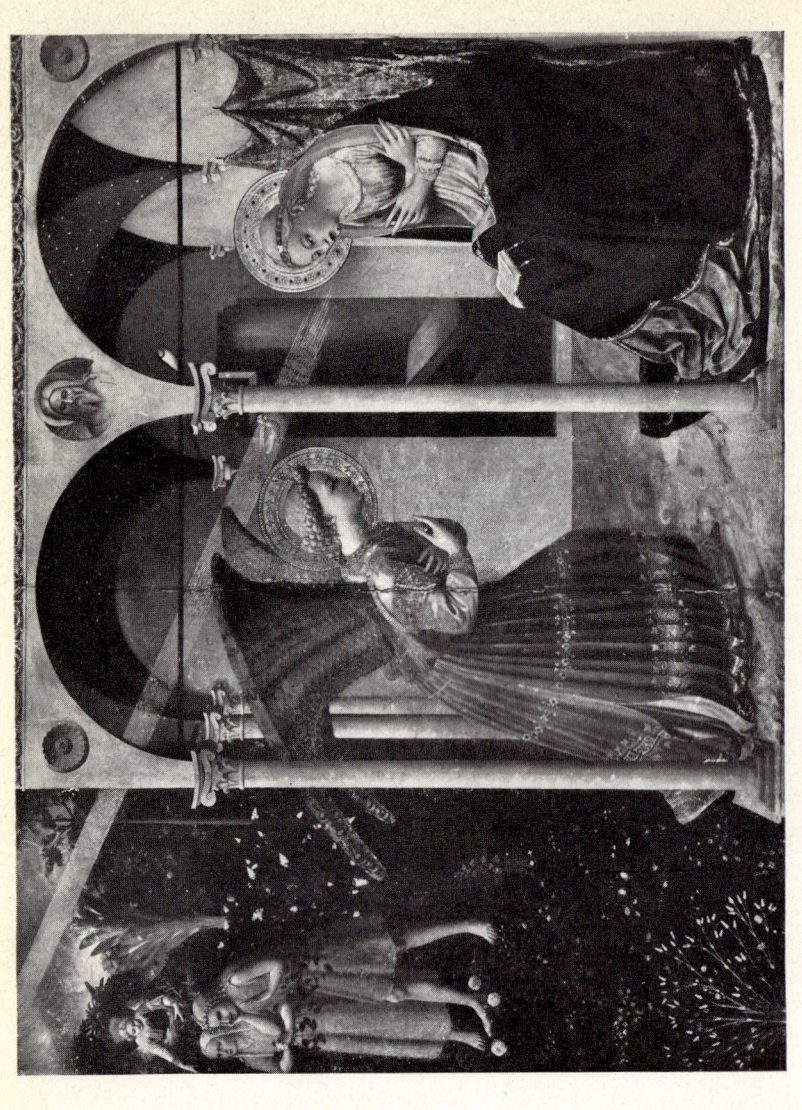

THE ANNUNCIATION, WITH THE EXPULSION. PAINTING BY FRA ANGELICO.
PRADO, MADRID. (ANDERSON PHOTO.)

spirit. Perhaps he longed the more for light after exploratory talks with the Prior Antonino, or after the inspiration of seeing Fra Angelico go about his tasks selflessly, in rapt devotion, knowing divine illumination. For Cosimo's cell the painter chose the subject "The Adoration of the Magi," an obviously fitting allusion, for here the virtual ruler of Florence retired for contemplation and humble adoration; in this cell, too, the Pope had slept when he came to consecrate the monastery.

Of his brothers in religion, Antonino, now Prior of San Marco, had long been Angelico's most respected and cherished friend. A convert to the eloquence and holy example of Johannes Dominici, a postulant at Fiesole not long before the arrival there of Guido and Benedetto, a counsellor and friend to Fra Giovanni during the period of his novitiate, Antonino seems to have followed the same changes of residence. A man of erudition as well as saintliness, he would find in the painter-mystic a perfect companion and co-worker. The Prior had attracted to his chapter an exceptional number of enlightened and able brothers, who also were Fra Angelico's constant companions. Among them were his own blood brother Benedetto and the librarian of San Marco, the scholar Tomaso Parentucelli, who was to be the first "Humanist" pope not many years later.

The activities of both Fra Tomaso and Fra Benedetto were sponsored by Cosimo de' Medici at this time. For five years from 1443 Benedetto was employed upon the task of inscribing and illuminating a monumental series of choir books for San Marco (which can be seen in the church there to this day). Cosimo donated fifteen hundred ducats toward the work. Whether Fra Angelico may have aided his brother, among many assistants, is a question upon which critics and historians are divided; but certainly the bulk of the miniatures comes from less inspired, though competent, hands.

In an even more munificent gesture Cosimo commissioned Michelozzo to incorporate into the monastery buildings a spacious library; and he presented the celebrated collection of manuscripts, the finest in Italy, formed by Niccolo Niccoli, so that automatically San Marco became one of the centres of scholarly study in the learning-mad Florence of the mid-*quattrocento*.

For the monastery church Fra Angelico painted an altar-piece, an elaborate panel of "The Madonna and Child with Saints," and in fresco he painted a simpler mural of the same subject in the corridor leading to the upper cells. In the backgrounds of both pictures he utilized fluted pilasters and Corinthian capitals, evidence of the influence of his Neo-classic architect friends. He showed also a perfect knowledge of the new scientific perspective (over which, at this time, Paolo Uccello was going, quite literally, mad). And he fell momentarily into a literalism of detail that carried him, disturbingly, toward the ideals of Donatello and Luca della Robbia, of Masaccio and Filipino Lippi. But gradually he reverts to the more primitive virtues, to his own sort of simplification. The tendency toward naturalism is soon ended, though a typically Renaissance ease or grace is gained. During the ten years that he resides, almost without a break, at San Marco, he paints many of his most moving works, including the cell and corridor frescos, the "Great Crucifixion" of the chapter-hall, and panels for outside churches in Florence and elsewhere.

In 1445 he is summoned to Rome. The Pope, Eugenius IV, whether impressed by the growing reputation of Fra Angelico or, as seems more likely, already a friend of the monk artist after extended visits to Florence, commissions him to decorate the Chapel of the Sacrament, otherwise known as St. Peter's Chapel, at the Vatican. The frescos dealt with incidents in the life of Jesus. It is one of the irreparable losses that the Chapel was torn down to make way for "improvements" during the sixteenth century.

At this time the Pope (if Vasari may be believed) conceived so high an opinion of Fra Angelico's saintliness and wisdom that he asked him to accept the Archbishopric of Florence, the seat being in 1445 vacant. The artist, alarmed, content with his own work — and preferring a certain solitude, not to say obscurity, obtaining in it — pleaded to be excused. He explained that in all matters he was satisfied with little, and that to rule men seemed to him less estimable than to practise obedience. He presumed, however, to recommend his companion, Fra Antonino, the Prior of San Marco, for the appointment. It was thus that Antonino was elevated to that archbishopric to which he did so great honour, being sainted not long afterward for his pious works.

Pope Eugenius died in 1447, when the commissioned frescos were hardly begun. His successor was that Tomaso Parentucelli who had been for several years a friend and companion of the painter at San Marco Monastery and librarian there. He ascended the pontifical throne as Nicholas V. He not only desired to see the series of pictures completed in the Chapel of the Sacrament, but embarked upon a vast scheme of improvement for the Vatican and the whole of the capital city.

It is of the relations between Nicholas V and Angelico that a slight but illuminating anecdote is told by Vasari. Being invited by the Pontiff to breakfast with him one morning, the good Fra was dismayed to find that meat was put before him. "You see," he explained, "I have no way of getting the permission of my Prior" — he totally forgetting that the higher power of indulgence and forgiveness lay with the Sovereign Pontiff.

A very few months after Nicholas V became Pope, Fra Angelico left Rome, perhaps to escape the excessive summer heat, and went to work on a commission to decorate the Cathedral at Orvieto. There he is given every honour, is termed "the Master of Masters" and "most famous of Italian painters," and is promised two hundred ducats for three months' work each year, together with payment to his assistants and "what bread and wine are called for." The subject is "The End of the World," including a "Last Judgement"; and perhaps it is this uncongenial theme that determines the master painter to quit Orvieto at the end of the first summer, never to return. His imagination simply cannot compass the gestures and the tortures of the damned — and there are commissions enough awaiting him elsewhere to engage his brush through the too few years left to him. He is now sixty years of age.

The Church authorities at Orvieto wait hopefully for two years, then release him from the contract. Fifty years later Luca Signorelli, adapting the original plans, in keeping with the spirit of the times, fills the empty spaces at Orvieto with vigorous and astonishing depictions of the contortions of the wicked and the damned; but in his treatment of the blessed he is sentimental and wooden, losing all feeling of the other-worldliness that had guided Angelico's hand. From being in essence devotional, out of stillness, adoration, and illumination, painting had then become scientific and "real," out of learning and clever observation of the physical.

Probably it was a summons by the Pope in the autumn of 1447 that took Fra Angelico back to Rome; though his movements and the order of his works during the last eight years are to be traced but sketchily. He finished the frescos in the Chapel of the Sacrament. He seems to have been in Florence, or Fiesole, in 1449. The Pope asked him to decorate his own study at the Vatican, later known as the Chapel of Nicholas V, though Angelico may not have begun the series there before 1452.

He had asked in 1446 that he be not appointed Archbishop of Florence, but he became, in 1449 or 1450, Prior of San Domenico at Fiesole. Whether from a sense of duty or partly for personal reasons, he then took up work that must have seemed less fruitful, and less directly a service to God, than his painting. It may have been an escape from the somewhat worldly and political atmosphere prevailing in Rome — escape back to the beloved and still halls in which he had spent happy years as Fra Giovanni of Fiesole. There were other sentimental considerations. His brother Benedetto, after serving as Sub-Prior of San Marco, had returned to Fiesole as Prior and had died there, a victim of the plague, in 1448. Antonino was at near-by Florence.

Summoned to Rome again in 1452, with his assistants, he seems to have spent the major part of the following three years in the capital city. In the Chapel of Pope Nicholas V he painted one of his most ambitious mural series, dealing with the lives of Saint Stephen and Saint Lawrence. Although some panels painted for the doors of the silver cabinet of the Santissima Annunziata Church in Florence, about this time, revert to the simplicity, even the naïveté, of the artist's early work, the frescos at Rome indicate a singular drift toward the manner and methods of the new realists.

Fra Angelico had ever been an explicit story-teller; but hitherto he had chosen, elided, omitted when it served his primary purpose of conveying a feeling or creating an atmosphere. His pictures are atmosphere and feeling incarnate. They breathe simple holiness, quietude, adoration. The Nicholas V frescos are (in general) illustrations in the other sense. They are weighted with detail, they are precise, almost hard, in drawing, they are secular in effect. The last of the archaisms, Angelico's way of depicting without shadows, is almost abandoned; although not quite, for the uncertain chiaroscuro of each individual face and figure is accomplished with no logical regard for a single source of lighting.

To account for the change in "style" some critics have made much of the influence of Masaccio's naturalistic innovations. Some have put the differences down to the increasing part taken by the aged Fra's assistants, and especially to the consideration he would accord to so talented and beloved a helper as Benozzo Gozzoli. Still others attribute the whole series to the pupils, allowing the master only the first sketching and superintendence and a stroke here and there — though the virtues of the series seem too outstanding for that. The commentators who are realists at heart hail the Roman murals as an advance upon earlier work, considering it a fitting climax to a career not sufficiently actuated, previously, by the advances made in the name of the New Learning. They note a gain in strength, dynamism, and physical reality.

But obviously the Fra Angelico of the cell frescos at San Marco is absent from the series at Rome. The freshness of aspect, the radiant tenderness, the chaste simplicity of conception, the occasional naïvetés — these are gone. Moreover there is lacking that happy manipulation of compositional intangibles, of formal organization, which adds to all other factors a revelation of universal order, which gives second meaning, a mystic significance, to the story-telling. In short, the spiritual elements have been pressed out for increase of literal truth and physical vigour. Perhaps the holy painter felt that this was right for political Rome, which was so different from Florence, from idyllic Fiesole, from the country of the Mugello.

It was in Rome that he died early in 1455, at the central convent of the Dominican Order. His body was entombed in the convent's church, Santa Maria sopra Minerva. He might better, some think, have been placed at rest in the monastery church of San Marco; or at Fiesole, where the gentle sunniness seemed to have entered into his very soul, where he experienced his stillest moments and found readiest access to God. There is one consoling thought. His earthly remains were placed close to those of another Dominican saint, Saint Catherine of Siena. She too had found God in the mystic way and had served man and her Church immortally. It is fitting that the two foremost Tuscan mystics should lie for ever under one roof.

The Pope wrote an epitaph. The words commemorate Fra Giovanni's Christlike way of life first, his eminence as an artist second. Later the Catholic Church beatified the friar-painter.

A century after the death of Beato Angelico his holiness was as much a legend in Florence as his skill in painting. Vasari observes: "This master might have secured for himself the richest enjoyments of the world, and more, merely by the exercise of the arts of which he was already a master when a young man. But being naturally disposed to unselfishness and piety, and desiring quietude and serenity, as well as the salvation of his soul, he entered religious orders." He writes also: "This excellent Fra Giovanni, worthily called Angelico, gave his whole life to God and laboured unceasingly for the good of others. . . . He was a man of simple living, guileless, holy in every act, . . . and as modesty and humility entered into his intercourse and his works, so his paintings were simple and pious. The saints he depicted have more the air and semblance of saints than any others."

All the scant records before Vasari agree in describing one who was a saint in actuality, one who worked among men but had his being in God. His self-discipline is complete, his selflessness sincere.

He is ascetic as compared with those millions who set their eyes upon the world's comforts and pleasures, but his abstinence and austerity of living never border upon mortification. If he thought of himself as humble and a penitent when he spoke to God, there was no infirmity or morbidity in his attitude. Rather he is depicted, as one would guess him to be from his paintings, as healthy, whole-minded, radiant, and smiling. He put his faith in God and therefore feared no man, evaded no confronting of circumstance, faced difficulties confident and firm. No life lived in the period of the Renaissance illustrates more clearly "the imitation of Christ" or the joy of the Christian reborn soul.

Living a life of exemplary holiness does not necessarily mean arriving at mystic enlightenment. One may come to saintliness by arguing that the holy life is the best life, forcing oneself to it by intellectual will, without intuitive self-giving. One may even give oneself to works conceived to be Divine, devoting oneself to God's plan, without arriving at communion with God. How, then, know that Fra Giovanni came to illumination, arrived at understanding? How know that he habitually walked with God?

The evidence is comparatively slight until one looks at the pictures, perhaps until one learns to read in them a language of form and order and feeling — of the pictorial intangibles. The paintings are this mystic's record of contemplation, participation in divine content, and communion. Nowhere is there a written document from Angelico's hand that attempts description of the mystic experience. There are, however, many disconnected lines in Vasari's essay, quoting what the Fra was "accustomed" to say, that perfectly characterize the practising mystic. At the heart of the matter is the report: "He was accustomed to say that he who sets out

CORONATION OF THE VIRGIN. PAINTING BY FRA ANGELICO. SAN MARCO MONASTERY, FLORENCE. (ALINARI PHOTO).

THE NATIVITY. PAINTING BY FRA ANGELICO.
METROPOLITAN MUSEUM OF ART.

to interpret Christianity must live in Christ." It is the central precept, the prime symbol, of Christian mysticism through the ages. Other "sayings" afford perfect background or reinforcement of the idea: "He was accustomed to say that the practice of art should be born of repose and peace, and that a painter should take no thought of the world"; and: "In his painting Fra Giovanni never altered a stroke once it had been put down. He said that it came so from the will of God, and therefore he left it as it was."

There is, too, that so common saying of the saint East or West, so essentially Christian, but so denied in the thinking of the Christian millions: "He was accustomed to say that the only true wealth consists in being content with little." And as for wielding power and attaining fame: "He might have commanded many . . . and he might have held positions of authority and prominence, both within his order and in the world outside, but he let all that go, saying that he wanted no tribute or recompense, but only to work in such way as would assure the saving of his soul from torment and a drawing near to Paradise."

These few sayings are practically all we have of the saint's own words, even at second hand. But shadowed forth in them are the chief steps commonly trod by the mystic: the yearning toward God — or toward God's symbolic garden called Paradise; renunciation of the world and its so-called "goods"; self-dedication; disciplined seeking of repose and serenity; and attainment of the sense of God's immanence, of the consciousness of knowing God's will and acting as His tool. It is not a great deal by way of "testimony"; doubtless Fra Angelico too thought of his paintings as the true record of his way of life and of his intercourse with God.

In his æsthetic — if the name may be given to so slight a body of sayings — Angelico is closer to the Orientals than to his fellow-Florentines or fellow-Europeans. He aspires to paint states of the soul, to translate transcendental visions and essences and intimations. He asks of the painter that preparation which the Western artist so seldom knows, a soul arrived at peace through meditation, and a mind in repose. The typical Chinese painter, it will be remembered, does not depict any specific landscape as it is "seen" (as we say). He may go into the mountains to enjoy inspiration and contemplation, even for weeks or months, but when he returns his picture is painted out of his feeling about mountains, woods, and water. It is a distillation of experience, a translation of mood and fleeting aspect and spiritual import, never a portrait of physical, accidental nature.

It is a more difficult sort of painting, for it demands clairvoyance and the intuition of a seer. It means attunement to the rhythmic courses of the universe. Of Western artists who have painted in that spirit, out of meditation, out of the clear-seeing of the inner eye, out of the soul's rapture, Fra Angelico is pre-eminent.

For all the implied impersonality of his way of living — renunciation of riches and position and fame, renunciation of any will of his own, abandonment to God's will — it is in a higher sense *himself* that he paints. It is his life transformed by a consciousness of Divinity, his mind conquered, cleared, tranquillized, then filled with other-worldly light. It is the artist elevated to Understanding. It is this man, Giovanni of Fiesole, risen to a height from which he sees the world illuminated with divine radiance, in a purity of light, a fresh joy of colour. It is his temperament, his faith, his being.

The subjects, the labels, are those of a thousand other artists: "The Annunciation," "The Maries at the Tomb," "The Nativity," "The Birth of Saint John," "The Crucifixion." . . . He does not construct his own legendry, his own theology, his own martyrology. He accepts, as do ninety-nine out of one hundred Christians in his time, the terrestrial world and man in the terrestrial framework, traditional through the Church. God the Father, Christ the Redeemer, the rewards of Paradise, the punishments of Hell: these are norms to which he conforms without thought. Nevertheless a civilization turned materialistic and a Church too frequently political had lost a light once immanent in that structure. It is his mission to illuminate the holiness that is fading from the structure, to restore the simple wonder of the adoration of the Child, or the Annunciation, to suggest the purging holiness and joy of the Communion, the rapture of understanding of the pilgrim at the feet of Christ.

A divinely inspired painter does not *depict* wonder or joy or rapture in a countenance. He suffuses his picture with the emotion. His own chasteness, purity, and selflessness open the way. His experience of God's presence endows him with powers unknown to the imitational painter. He actually brings into being reflections of his own experience of grace, his own joy in mystic union.

Fra Angelico, we are told by Vasari, invariably made his prayers before taking up his brushes. So wholly did he consecrate himself, so deeply realize being in Christ, that "the tears streamed from his eyes" as he depicted Jesus crucified. And we can see him kneeling, silent, humble, his heart filled with love, as he painted those golden Madonnas. It is thus that the story-telling becomes so much more than illustration. Angelico's belief lies over it like an aura. There is an emanation of freshness, of harmony. As his belief is in divine goodness, in a great compensation, in a transcending bliss, so his pictures breathe holiness, beatitude, an unearthly lustre. They are simple with a childlike simplicity. They are flower-like. They are glad and open and innocent.

That pervading fragrance is one side of the mystical revelation that the sensitive observer feels in them. There is also the subtler, still mysterious, almost unexplainable form-manipulation, the intuitive design of intangibles that speaks to a sense of order within the beholder. There is in the arts a power to move men's souls without regard to thought, story, reality, or emotion. The disembodied arts, especially music, are more powerful, more effective, in carrying this impact to the spirit. Music at its highest purges, delights, transfigures our consciousness.

But painters too — a very few of the masters — have attained that magic. They have known how to manipulate the abstract elements of their art, the solids, the planes, the lines, the colours, so that there is the impact of a rhythmic order upon our souls. They create within a sort of celestial mathematics, beyond our minds to explain. They implant in the canvas a movement structure, a plastic animation, a rhythmic synthesis. They endow the picture with a second life, a soul of its own, that speaks to the observer's soul, outside the bounds of the known elements of illustrational picturing.

Fra Angelico was of the company of painters utilizing that magic, speaking mystically — not in the sense of something hidden as an abstruse riddle, but as a joyous second language, a code known to the spirit. One need not have special learning to recognize it; only an open mind and a soul awakened. It is the most precious element in the arts, it is the most difficult for the painter to master — being wholly of the intangibles, woven of abstractions — and it speaks most surely to the inner faculties of men, call them æsthetic or spiritual.

It is not to be overlooked that this special animation or plastic synthesis in the picture has oftenest been introduced by the religious painters. As it is a thing both solemn and joyous, purging and radiant, it yields itself, it would seem, to men who approach their art in the spirit of communion with God, of revealing some detected hidden movement of the spirit. Your student of art will tell you that the early great masters of the plastic synthesis (after the unknown Byzantines) are the Sienese painters — Duccio and Simone Martini and the others — Giotto and the Giottesque little masters, and Fra Angelico. The magic of it is largely lost in the following era of scientific materialism, though Michelangelo restores it grandly and movingly. The Venetians, Giorgione, Titian, Tintoretto, adapt it to profane ends, gorgeously, but their pupil El Greco again uses it in religious picturing, at its intensest power, with a mastery still unsurpassed and still mysterious.

As if to suggest the universality of this mystic element, this intangible power in painting, a second outstanding example of it occurs in Oriental painting. In the dark ages of Europe and of Christianity, the eighth to the twelfth century, Chinese artists sought to attain this revelation beyond all other objectives. Their paintings are holy, spiritual, evocative of the adorational response. They are pure, simple, chaste in the sense in which Angelico's pictures deserve this description. They may be Taoist or Buddhist or beyond identification with any stated or statable religious belief; but they are born of the religious spirit, redolent of a religious calm, of peace and communion and a super-terrestrial understanding. In any of our museums a gallery of Chinese paintings is likely to have the aspect of a chapel or a shrine.

The Chinese were hardly more successful than the Western artists in describing or naming the elusive form-quality or vitality that they recognized as being the first requisite of spiritually effective art. One of them spoke suggestively of "the life movement of the spirit" and of a "rhythmic, spiritual animation" which endows the picture with "a life of its own," beyond the depicted life. No one has come nearer to explaining the mystery of the work of art that is an experience rather than an informer or a reminder.

There are mystics who are lifted to so exalted a plane of impersonality, of selflessness, that they seem to have soared above every activity and every necessity of common man. There are seers who believe that it is possible to rise so high that the soul's consciousness of God is enough; that all things realized or received through

THE FLIGHT INTO EGYPT. PAINTING BY FRA ANGELICO. SAN MARCO MONASTERY, FLORENCE.

the senses — including the aural and visual arts — fade, at that height, from importance. They are the exceptional ones who renounce all, abandon all, give over the activities of the mortal world.

Fra Angelico was not of that extreme company. Nor need we foresee that mankind, in recovering mystic insight, in restoring to the individual the whole life in place of its materialistic half, will in great numbers consecrate itself to that austerity, that extreme purgation.

The realm of art is illumined at its best with spiritual light, with a heavenly splendour. The fugue or the picture may evoke the consciousness of the immanence of God. The senses provide the channel; but in the end the sensuous delight is merged, is drowned, in the silent understanding, the spiritual feeling. Sense-delight is a part of the mood; but the whole experience is by so much greater than this part, partaking of a timeless rapture, that art here becomes sacramental. It transports the soul into the mystical Presence.

Fra Angelico achieved in his paintings exceptional sensuous loveliness. But he transcended mere decorative picturing because he had the genius that enabled him to put this other vitality or power or feeling into his pictures: this element that we call holy or spiritual because we cannot find other words to suggest its balm to the spirit, its profound quietude, its evocative sweetness.

Human experience is his material. But the material is in-formed by divine knowledge. There is a mystical second unfolding. How else explain the truth that one experiences a wave of delight sweep over the soul when one comes before "The Annunciation" in the bare corridor at San Marco, or "The Transfiguration" in an adjoining barren cell? How explain that one feels impelled, in a crowded gallery in a teeming city four thousand miles away, to kneel down when one confronts the little panel-painting of "The Nativity," as if the one picture made about it a silent sanctuary?

VIII. Jacob Boehme, The Shoemaker-Illuminate of the Reformation

One of the most individual, modest, and persuasive of all the favoured mortals who have walked in the presence of God was Jacob Boehme, the Illuminate of Goerlitz. He is the most artless and unpretending of those who have left records of the mystic "way." There is even a touch of homely humour in his admonitions. "Beloved reader," he writes, "if you want to understand the high mysteries, you need not first put a university upon your nose, or any such spectacles."

Perhaps Jacob never quite grew up. At any rate he stayed near the country from which the soul of each child is borne. A child-like directness and trust were in his faith and in his evangelism. "My writings," he once wrote, "are those of a child. Their power comes from the Father who directs the child. . . . To understand them is child's play too if only you will let the Spirit illuminate your coming." If he had his way, we should all make simple work of turning back toward the home of the soul, of changing our lives, of finding peace of the spirit.

Had Jacob Boehme lived in a period other than that between the sixteenth-century civil wars and the Thirty Years' War, he might have altered the main courses of Christianity. His visions, his faith, and his writings have repeatedly convinced world leaders of his authentic speaking for God. His character was of the sort around which legends accrue. His innocence, with a Franciscan other-worldliness about it, his humility among the humble-born, and his noble bearing among aristocrats and scholars, his record of struggle against grievous odds, of dedication to God, persecution, and final vindication — all this is of the stuff that makes, in normal times, for elevation to religious leadership.

As it was, caught in the chaotic cross tides of war, and equally in the tides of bitter struggle within the churches, he fought resourcefully for his visions and his beliefs. In the last year of his life he saw his message accepted by princes and theologians and scholars, then died while his converts were still scattered and impotent. A Europe reeling and bleeding under physical disasters all but forgot him.

JACOB BOEHME

A harmonist, seeking solution of all problems in the attainment of personal spiritual peace, Jacob Boehme spent his life on earth in the midst of strife. The very air of his land seemed poisoned against peace. His native Lusatia lay along the shifting borders of Germany, Silesia, and Bohemia. The Lusatian towns were on the through trade routes of northern Europe and were meeting-grounds for every public evil, for decimating plagues as well as the armies of contending states. German in language, culture, and religion, Lusatia was, in the time of Boehme's youth, a possession of Bohemia. Later in his lifetime it became a helpless pawn in the imperial games played by German, Bohemian, and Austrian rulers and adventurers (a rôle resumed, as Sudetenland, in the twentieth-century wars).

Spiritually Jacob Boehme was heir to the truths bequeathed by Eckhart and Tauler and the Friends of God, and by the unknown author of the *Theologia Germanica*. He was heir also to the half-truths of pseudo-science and pseudo-mysticism, to alchemistic lore and Paracelsian "magic." His land, his people, his way of expression were northern, Gothic, and mediæval. He knew little of the fruits of the Renaissance that had lifted Italy out of mediævalism; nor would the intellectual and worldly yield of that rebirth have seemed to him so profitable as one spiritual revelation — by a Francis, an Eckhart, or a Ruysbroeck — lighting a way to the experience of God.

Jacob Boehme set up his revelation and his small peasant-like voice against the established churches and against all political parties, and lost. Sweet-tempered, tolerant, devout, he was called by his own community a heretic, and he was repeatedly accused to the higher Church authorities as a false prophet and a disturber of the realm. He was once imprisoned and twice exiled. At the end he had found powerful friends, even at the courts and in the higher Church, but after his death their influence and power were sucked down with all else in post-war anarchy. Rediscovered by later mystics and philosophers, by poets and scholars, by artists and scientists, he came to enjoy the fame of a remote genius, of a sweet but hidden spiritual fountain.

In beliefs, and especially in reliance upon illumination direct from God, the Quakers, or Society of Friends, took much from Boehme. But all the followers who organized in his name — the Angel Brothers, who republished his books, and the Behmenists and the Philadelphians — disappeared at last, leaving Boehmian marks only (except for Quakerism) upon some minor or digressive sects. Through George Fox, William Penn, and the Quakers, and through the influence of greater numbers who rejoined the larger communions, he brought warmth and joyousness to the religion of many men. But it is an individual hold, a personal master-and-disciple relationship that distinguishes, still, the attitude of most readers toward the Illuminate of Goerlitz.

Jacob's kindliness and his simplicity, his tenderness and his lovingness, are revealed again and again in his writings — between, it is true, very difficult and abstruse passages — until one feels the little man, a cobbler and a pedlar, at one's side, holding a light as one reads. As he rose from humble station and unlettered estate to understanding of the most baffling mysteries of God and man and the human spirit, so he seems to say to his disciple: "If only you will come disarmed, without knowing too much, artless and candid, you too may attain to the bliss that the theologians have obscured."

If, indeed, one disarm oneself of adult defences, if one forget the forests of complexities conjured up by philosophers, theologians, and scientists, one may find imaginative splendours and a magical place of rest — and perhaps the way to God's presence — through the guidance of the cobbler-mystic of Goerlitz. All along the way there will be the sense of his sweetness of spirit, his selflessness, and his childlike confidence. He is the most companionable and homespun of the major prophets.

Jacob Boehme was born in the village of Old Seidenberg, Upper Lusatia, in November 1575. His people, like most of the German-Bohemian peasantry of which they were a part, were self-respecting, frugal, and pious. His father owned the farming land upon which the large family made its living.

The child Jacob received no more of formal education than a knowledge of reading and writing. The influences that moulded his character and determined his conduct, education in the fuller, warmer sense, issued from religious training. The community was God-fearing and devout, and schooling was largely within the province of the Protestant church. Home life, under a father religious-minded if not definitely mystical, served to support the influences of the church school. The one book that became a companion to Jacob was the Bible, in Luther's translation.

The boy enjoyed an unaccountable second sight, and he began

early to have visions. The village children, Jacob among them, were accustomed to care for the cattle in the fields and on the surrounding hills. One noonday Jacob wandered to a ridge known as the *Landeskrone,* and there a vaulted cave was disclosed to his eyes. Making his way to the entrance, he gazed in astonishment at a vessel overflowing with gold. Judging the whole occurrence to be a work of the devil, he turned and fled. When he went back to the ridge with other boys the cavern had vanished, nor did repeated search ever uncover it.

Such incidents, and a bent toward meditative solitude — as well as absolute devotion to religious services — tended to separate Jacob from the other boys of the community; and there settled upon him a certain spiritual loneliness, which was to obtain through life. Detachment and introspection made him aware of forces not detected by others. It is said that he never questioned the validity of fairy tales or the truth of miracles.

Jacob's constitution was accounted too delicate for a life of farm labour, and he was therefore, in his fourteenth year, apprenticed to a shoemaker of Goerlitz, the nearest large town, a few miles to the north of Seidenberg. As before, he read his Bible zealously. He became known in Goerlitz as an exemplary youth, perhaps too dreamy to promise outstanding attainment as businessman or artisan, but honest, willing, and attentive, and of modest bearing. The cobbler's one complaint arose because the youth corrected or reproved others; he even rebuked the master himself for cursing.

One day he had been left in charge of the cobbler's shop and the house was empty, when a stranger entered, a man of unusual and grave appearance, whose eyes seemed to Jacob to emit light. The stranger wished to buy a pair of shoes, and the apprentice, without authority to put through a transaction so momentous, placed a high price on the chosen shoes, thinking thus to temporize. The man nevertheless bought them and left the shop. From the street he called back, "Jacob, come out!" And Jacob, marvelling that the stranger knew his name, went forth, and was further surprised to hear these words:

"Jacob, you are little as yet, but you will become great, and you will become a man so uncommon that the world will marvel. Be dutiful to God and reverence Him. Especially read His word in the Holy Scriptures. There you will find instruction, and consolation for the poverty and trials you will endure, and for the persecution you will suffer. Be brave, be persevering. God holds you in His love and will be gracious to you." With a hand-clasp and a glance from his piercing eyes, the stranger was gone.

Thereafter Jacob "much more frequented the public worship," and he was so devout and so actively pious, remonstrating with all who broke the Commandments or talked with a loose tongue about God, that his master the shoemaker discharged him. The indignant man said that he had no need of a house missionary.

The youth was seventeen years old when his craft training was thus ended abruptly and prematurely. The seeming catastrophe fitted into the system of interposing *Wanderjahre* between the period of one's professional training and that of one's life work. For two or three years Jacob wandered over the neighbouring German states, making his living as an itinerant shoemaker. No doubt his experiences as a journeyman worker taught him about the ways of his trade; but he was the more eager to learn of the ways of men in their relationship to God. While not faltering in his faith that the Church is the gateway to God's realm, he yet saw enough of jealous, factional congregations and bigoted pastors to realize that the Reformation had brought in grave evils, and that the Lutheran Church was criss-crossed with battle lines and filled with the confusion of intrigue and dissension. He ever afterward employed the symbol of Babel in referring to the shortcomings of the Church.

Babel had entered into his own mind, too. At no other period of his life was he to be so troubled, confused, and depressed. His own country, and indeed all of Bohemia and of Germany, was filled with tumult and distress. Civil wars had been intermittent for more than half a century. Everywhere Jacob Boehme found poverty and hardship. The battling Catholic and Protestant factions were led now by political pretenders and adventurers rather than Churchmen, but their bitterness and dissension, and their drafted and mercenary armies, were no less destructive of spiritual peace. War with the infidel Turks, too, was renewed in 1593, and repeated draughts were being made upon the resources of the German states. Wherever the Lutherans were entrenched, as in Lusatia and adjoining Saxony, a special bigotry and rigidity of life obtained. The Church seemed to find the destitution of its members of less concern than foreign quarrels and the enforcement of rigorous laws of moral conduct.

Jacob thus returned to Goerlitz, after his wander-years, profoundly depressed. He knew that destitution and injustice ruled in the lives of the people. Intrigue and force determined the fortunes of members of the upper class. Many of God's representatives on earth were as self-seeking, as little Christian in spirit, as the princes and politicians and landlords. He was to find at Goerlitz that the local pastor was despotic, fanatic, and petty-minded like those he had encountered in Germany.

A severe melancholy settled upon him, and for a time he could not find comfort, even in reading the Scriptures. But a native sweetness of character and an intuitive trust lifted him finally above his depression. Shortly he was enabled to look out patiently upon a universe in which evil had its part and corruption its station, but not, he believed, beyond help. He was aided by God in a direct way. Again he experienced a vision. After a severe struggle by which he sought to be rid of self-seeking, after contemplation and prayer for divine guidance, he entered into God's presence.

> When my spirit, so filled with affliction, as if in a storm of sorrow, rose up toward God, conveying with it unreservedly my heart and mind, dedicating to Him all thought and all willing; when I resolved not to cease asking for God's love and mercy until His blessing should descend upon me, then did the Spirit break through, . . . then were the clouds broken away and the illumination of Spirit was shed upon me. Thus in my zeal I beat down the portals of Hell and hazarded my whole life . . . until suddenly my spirit burst through the last barriers and I stood in the Presence, apprehending the very essence of Divine Being I was there enfolded with love.

Thus the unlettered shoemaker described his first memorable entry into the presence of God and the loving welcome "as when a bridegroom receives the bride." In his first book, *The Aurora*, he further described his feelings thus: "I cannot find words to express the exaltation and sense of victory I then experienced. I can compare such a spiritual triumph only to a miraculous birth in the midst of death. It was like resurrection from the dead. It was then that the eyes of my spirit were opened. By a miraculous light I saw God. The interior of all was illumined. Thenceforward I was able to recognize God in each separate thing, in the creatures, and in plants and grasses. I understood what God is, and how He is what He is." But he adds that for a whole year the glory of the experience was too moving and too blinding for complete mortal understanding of it.

In 1595 he had set up as a master cobbler, with a stall or shop of his own. About the same time he had married. His wife was a girl of solid character, one Katharine Kunshmann, the daughter of a master butcher. Jacob was a steady, affectionate husband, in spite of the burdens put upon him by the call into God's service. And Katharine was faithful to him and solicitous for his health and comfort. She is known to have borne to him four sons, and possibly there were two daughters of the union. Until the day of his death, thirty years after their marriage day, she was his mate and helper, and she seems never to have wavered in her loyalty — though perhaps her patience gave way — even under the persecution that ultimately drove him from home, or the poverty that his attention to his studies brought upon them.

From 1595 sixteen years were to pass before the Spirit would command Jacob to write down his experiences. That term of years is a period of study, absorption, and gestation. From confusion and concern over injustice and wide-spread destitution he goes on to faith that there is an answer to all problems, even a way of common salvation.

Once convinced that the universal order is harmonious and constructive, he passes on to the search for a key to earthly concord. Not a student by temperament or training, he yet probes into abstruse writings, going painfully from theological books to treatises upon alchemy and astrology. The vocabulary of the alchemists, especially of Paracelsus, is to remain a part of his equipment when he too becomes a writer of treatises; but, strangely enough, what he takes of the substance of alchemy seems only to enrich his theology. He has read and reread his Lutheran Bible until all the treasures he finds, in places orthodox or pagan, clean or unclean, range themselves around the central truth of God as Father, Christ as saviour, and the world of humanity as a realm to be redeemed.

A milestone was marked in Jacob Boehme's spiritual growth when, in 1600, he experienced the most striking of all his visions. Ordinarily he needed no objective instrument, no bridge to contemplation, but this time it was outward seeing that led to revelation. His eye had been caught by a brilliant, not to say a blinding, reflection of the sun in a burnished pewter dish. As he watched, ordinary sense left him. He seemed to see into, to be admitted to, a world transformed. His inner mind and the hidden forces beyond nature became as one, pulsing, radiant, divine.

Startled by so much of splendour, he thought to break the trance by going into the open. But there he was amazed to see similarly into the heart and essence of nature, detecting the harmonious forces pushing up through the herbs and grasses, feeling creation at work. He noted the harmony between living and objective things. Thus were the wonders of God's purpose revealed to him.

He thanked God mightily in his soul, but was outwardly silent about the experience. From the time of this event he feels that he knows about God, the universe, and nature; but he is not ready to speak, because he cannot yet reconcile the existence of misery and evil, especially of human depravity, with the illuminated harmonious world revealed to him.

The wisdom of silence was upon him for twelve years, during which he made no attempt to enlighten the minds of those blinder than himself. He carried on his craft without interruption, cared for his family, and was in outward seeming the normal, diligent cobbler and citizen. He went to church regularly, and covered up the antagonism and pity he felt toward the particularly limited and bigoted pastor who instructed and threatened the Lutheran flock at Goerlitz. He was busy in his mind, nevertheless, with the problems of his fellow-men, busy particularly with the squaring of mortal ways of living with divine plan and order.

If he was starved of spiritual sustenance when he attended the town church on Sundays, he was abundantly nourished at his cobbling bench by the memories of Divine goodness to him. He was sustained by the thought of the companionship of God; and periodically he was taken up "as in a flash" to experience illumination anew. In nature he saw the "signatures" of divinity, and the qualities and essences of all things were laid open to him. He read, too, in the mystical works of Franck, Schwenckfeld, and Weigel, divines who had variously opposed, during the sixteenth century, the formalism and literalism of the Lutheran Church.*

---

* These German mystics of the sixteenth century were inheritors primarily from Eckhart, the Friends of God, and the *Theologia Germanica*; though they doubtless absorbed influences from the revived Neo-Platonism of the time. While they were carrying on, as links between the Eckhartian seers and Boehme, the Catholic Church was experiencing one of its greatest revivals of mystical devotion. In Spain there appeared an extraordinary group

In the dozen years between the primary illumination that came in 1600 and the call to write down a record of his spiritual experiences in 1612 there were trials and doubts enough, but gradually an invulnerability to disaster, an innate sense of well-being, grew upon Jacob Boehme. The Saxony and the Bohemia of the period were disordered, and the flames of war burst forth at intervals. Boehme seems never to have been enlisted in any one of the armies that marched back and forth, attacking or retreating, conquering or losing, destroying and pillaging always. His attitude toward war was that of the Christian pacifist who interprets literally the Sermon on the Mount. One of his few expressed opinions on political conditions and the wars indicates his separation from "causes" and parties:

> Everything for which these men are competing and fighting, the while they devastate lands and slaughter peoples, is only an empty skin without its fruit, and the whole belongs to the world of fire and separation. Not one of these parties has truth or understanding on his side. All contend in the name of God but none does His will. They fight for their own personal glory and to secure their carnal pleasures. If they were truly Christians, there would exist no question or quarrel between them.

Boehme was, however, concerned for the peasant and artisan classes, upon whom the burden fell the heaviest; who were, indeed, close to a condition of slavery. Yet Boehme himself prospered in those years. In 1610 he was enabled to buy a home and stall on a busy street in Goerlitz. Life was nevertheless insecure in a different way, since complaint to the right authorities that a man's views were heretical and his influence subversive might lead to his being put away permanently, even without trial.

If the waspish Evangelical pastor, one Gregorius Richter, had known at this time how Jacob's mind was ranging through ideas and even books that smacked of brimstone — the "magician" Pa-

---

of advocates of the inward finding of God. Not wholly the dedicated mystic, but celebrated as founder of the Jesuit order, was Saint Ignatius of Loyola. Most fully the self-abandoning mystic, and a vivid writer about visions and the "way," was Santa Teresa, who lived from 1515 to 1582. Her book entitled *The Castle of the Soul* is a classic of mystical literature. Santa Teresa's follower, Saint John of the Cross, wrote two books well known to all initiates, though hardly serviceable as introductory works: *The Dark Night of the Soul* and *The Ascent of Mount Carmel.*

racelsus and the cabbalists contributed to his development — there might have been an end then of the cobbler's studies and a stopping of his pen before he began composition of his first book. But he kept silent until God should give him the word to set down in ink the revelations vouchsafed to him. His activity did not become known until he had composed practically all his first "memorial," so that when it was taken away from him it was already so near completion, and so potent, that it started trains of thinking and action not yet stayed, three centuries later.

The "books" of Jacob Boehme were not books in the accepted sense, nor did the author intend that they should be. How should a nearly illiterate shoemaker compete with writers who had education and the advantages of study in libraries and association with scholars? Only one of his manuscripts was made into a printed book within Boehme's lifetime, and then without his consent and only in the last year of his life. But in those matters that render literary art excellent and inspiring, in the basic clarity and pungency and vividness of his speech, he outran in innumerable passages most of the writers of his age. The disproportion between his achievement in the literary field and his education is not unlike the contrast in his ways of meeting the world, at the one extreme the humblest of men, self-depreciating and submissive, at the other confident with the assurance born of faith, ready to meet with scholars, divines, and rulers upon the one ground of philosophical discussion.

At such meetings, he believed, God spoke through him. No man who had been chosen as an instrument by God could be self-effacing or lax or servile. Boehme's familiars in Goerlitz expressed wonder and astonishment when their cobbler friend began to receive noblemen and scholars from afar, who took seriously his visions and his opinions; and later they were amazed, and the Pastor Richter stirred to bitter envy, when Jacob was invited to courts and universities. He took it all simply, unemotionally, with dignity. On some grounds he knew more than the men from the universities. He explained in this way:

> I am not versed in literature, nor in the arts that belong to this world, nor have I desired to learn the sciences. But from boyhood I have striven for salvation of my soul, taking thought how I might come into the kingdom of heaven. Even within myself I found powerful opposition to this in-

tent, in the desires of the flesh, and I had to undertake a mighty battle against my own corrupted nature and the serpent's seed in me. I resolved with God's aid to overcome and destroy that evil, and to enter into the love of God. . . . I resolved, moreover, to regard my inherited form as dead in me, so that the Spirit of God would make a new form within me, to the end that I might conduct my life through Him and in Him. I said to myself that I would will nothing except that which I knew to be His will. He would thus be both my will and my doing. This I could not wholly accomplish, but I persevered and fought a fierce battle against myself. . . . Finally the portals of the deep broke open, I attained to the very centre of being, and a wonderful light arose within my soul. It was a light wholly foreign to the man I had been. Therein I first apprehended the true nature of God and of man, and of the relationship existing between them, a thing which I had never before understood.

And in a letter he sums up the struggle and the gains of this period of trial: "I earnestly prayed God to be wrapped in His holy Spirit, and asked for his mercy. I asked that He would bless and instruct me, and deliver me from all that might separate me from Him. I asked that I might live not in my own will but in His. It was in answer to this seeking that sometimes the gate to His Mystery was opened to me. Then in a quarter of an hour I understood more than if I had been many years at a university."

For twelve years, Jacob says, this life went on, a life that seemed to his neighbours and patrons the normal one of an obscure cobbler. To him it was a life of seeking, petitioning, and periodic answer from above.

Finally it came to him "with commanding power" that he should write down with pen and ink an account of the revelations, "for a memorial to myself — albeit I could hardly express or even contain what I had seen." At another time he wrote: "I am not educated in these matters, but I do make clear things which the schools and universities have left obscure. . . . So long as the hand of God rests upon me I *understand.*"

And so, in 1612, Jacob Boehme sat down to the writing of *The Aurora*. Composition was not easy for him, and his confusion and lack of words were often enough reflected in the manuscript.

Nevertheless this first report is amazingly comprehensive, and it has passages both of poetic beauty and of profound import. It is Boehme's testament of faith and his first account of God, the cosmos, and the drama of life. He is anxious that no reader think of it as an abstract from other men's writings; nor does he wish it to seem an invention of his own. It is, he believes, God's work.

"I have written," he explains, "neither out of book-learning nor from other men's opinions or their science, but out of a book opened within myself, as a reflection from God. This alone it has been vouchsafed me to read. It is there that I have studied, as a child in its mother's house, repeating what its father does."

The title *The Aurora* was bestowed on the work by a friend. The author happily adopted it because the word *Aurora* had for him a desirable classical look. His own title had been, as variously translated, *The Rising of the Glowing Day* or *The Morning Redness* (*Morgenröthe im Aufgang*); or, as certain of his Rosicrucian disciples have it, *The Rosy Dawn*. He makes it clear that he had in mind the symbol of a new and glorious day dawning for man. In his own outlook the new world was most often symbolized by a glow of light — "Light, which is the heart of God."

The scheme of *The Aurora* is grand beyond compare. After telling all about the created world, and man and the angels, and Heaven and Hell, he turns to philosophy. Years later he wrote for a friend this summary:

> I saw and comprehended the Being of all Beings, the Byss and the Abyss; and the generation of the Holy Trinity. I saw the original and primal existence of this world and of all creatures. Within myself I perceived creation entire, in its order and movement; I saw, first, the divine world, of the angels and of paradise, second, the darkened world, the fiery realm, and third, this world around us, visible and tangible, as an issue and expression of the two inner, eternal, hidden worlds. Moreover, I comprehended the whole being and reason of Good and Evil. . . .

And all this he endeavoured to explain, in one scheme, in explicit and sometimes painful detail. Not Aristotle or Mohammed or Dante tried to put more into a book. It is a marvellous confusion of inspired grandeurs and dull commonplaces, of spiritual gold and slag.

Jacob never quite completed the manuscript of *The Aurora*, and after the original was taken from him years passed before he saw a copy of it. When he again perused his first treatise he did so with interest, and he remarked not only upon its unfinished condition, "missing thirty sheets," but also upon his inexperience as a reason for certain crudities in it. The circumstances under which he gave up the script and was forbidden to write further were these:

A nobleman, Karl von Endern, came to the cobbler's shop one day and chanced upon the written pages of *The Aurora*. He glanced through enough of the material to perceive that it treated of matters that he, as a student of philosophy and mysticism, held close to his heart. He prevailed upon the shoemaker to lend the manuscript to him. He was so struck by the originality and truth of the treatise that he took the doubtful liberty of having copies written out. Without consulting the author he circulated sets of the papers among friends who were interested in cosmology, theology, and the occult sciences. Thus Jacob Boehme found his name suddenly become familiar among a company of notables whom he would not have thought to approach. He felt surprise that his writings were being circulated as if they had been a true book. He foresaw that there were dangers in being brought out of obscurity into the light of public interest. He was more distressed than pleased.

The storm broke over him in the way that he least expected, at a religious service. One Sunday in the summer of 1613 he took his accustomed place in a pew well forward in the Evangelical Church at Goerlitz. The Pastor Richter entered the pulpit and announced his subject as "False Prophets." It became evident that the attack on falsifiers and deceivers was to be a personal one, and shortly every eye in the church was upon the unhappy and unprepared cobbler. The pastor attacked him with the ferocity of an enraged animal. He accused, he vilified, he shouted.

At a time in the recent past Jacob Boehme had crossed the pastor in a small matter. In aid of a relative who had been accused by the irascible Richter of not settling a debt, he had gone to ask consideration for the youth on the ground that the whole matter had been one of misunderstanding, which reasonable talk together could easily put right, asking also that the older man make allowances for the youth's inexperience; at which the pastor turned his wrath upon Boehme, called him a Godless fool, and

GLAD DAY. POSSIBLY SUGGESTED BY BOEHME'S *AURORA*. ENGRAVING BY WILLIAM BLAKE. ROSENWALD COLLECTION, NATIONAL GALLERY OF ART, WASHINGTON. (PHILADELPHIA MUSEUM OF ART PHOTO).

bade him be gone without further interference in other people's business.

Now, as Richter thundered from his pulpit, it became evident that a copy of *The Aurora* had come into his hands. The crimes of blasphemy, heresy, and false prophecy had been added to the catalogue of the humble shoemaker's misdoings. He was abused as a very monster of a man, a tool of Satan, and a disturber of the Christian realm. The whole city of Goerlitz, the minister said, would incur divine wrath if this heretic and criminal were not scourged from the parish. If he remained, the community might expect to be dropped whole into the pit of Hell.

Boehme faced out the storm, and after the service he did the manly thing, going to the pastor to protest against this persecution, asking that he be permitted to talk the issue over reasonably. The only answer was a theatric exclamation: "Away from me, Satan, away to Hell!" Richter then formally called upon the City Council to banish Boehme. The civil fathers, themselves afraid of being consigned to the flames by the all-powerful Pastor Primarius, consented. When they conveyed their order of expulsion to the cobbler, he agreed to leave, saying only: "My friends, since I cannot do otherwise, I shall go content." He requested that he be permitted to return to his home to put his small affairs in order and to take leave of his family, but this slight grace was refused him. He was escorted outside the walls and left alone. The rest of that day he walked among the fields and hills beyond the town. No one knows where he found shelter that night.

The following day, however, new forces were brought to bear upon the Councilmen. They refound their leadership and cancelled the order of banishment. Jacob was sent for and returned to his home. He was forced to agree not to write again and to keep to shoemaking, leaving spiritual interpretation to the appointed and competent authorities.

Thus lightly punished, as everyone thought, the shoemaker took up his routine and tried faithfully to fulfil the spirit as well as the letter of his promise to Richter and the City Fathers. There is, however, evidence that either at this time or in a similar crisis Boehme was briefly imprisoned. The Burgomaster of Goerlitz, in whose diary the incident is recorded under the date 1613, notes only that the shoemaker "living at the gates behind the hospital smithy" was brought in, accused, and listened to. Placed in prison, he was detained only until the authorities had looked into a manuscript of *The Aurora*, when they adjudged him harmless if deprived of his pen.

Richter in return for Jacob Boehme's promise undertook not to attack him further, an undertaking not fully honoured. But, in general, life went smoothly in outward seeming for several years. The cobbler sold his stall and entered a business that permitted more of freedom, the buying and selling of woollen gloves. He had to attend markets as far away as Prague, and therefore he gained the widened contacts and the view of current history — this was at the opening of the Thirty Years' War — yielded by travel. It is likely, however, that he returned to cobbling at least for brief periods in later years.

In his relations with God he knew this to be, afterward, a period of timid uncertainty and trial. Eventually he came to feel that his promise not to write had been an act against God, and he conveniently laid the prohibition to Satan. Gradually it became clear that, despite all he could do, the seeds of other books were germinating within him. He began again to pray for guidance and inspiration. He knew well that he could now write a fuller, clearer exposition of cosmic and mystical truths than he had been able to compass in his first literary effort.

The great men who travelled to Goerlitz to seek out Jacob Boehme had something to do with his decision to write again. During the six years that he held his silence there occurred a series of meetings with occultists and scholars of various sorts, mystics and theosophists, alchemists and astrologers. From the pseudo-scientists, and especially from the followers of Paracelsus, he adopted ideas and elements that sometimes consorted uneasily with his essentially Christian theology and legendry. Within the vision he had gained by revelation there were details to be filled in and conceptions to be named; and having a gift for perceiving meanings in symbols and "signatures," he poured into his cosmography and his vocabulary a stream of newly met ideas and terms.

To some adopted words he gave meanings all his own, or only vaguely relative, and it was for this reason especially that he became known later as a difficult writer. His grasping at "scholarly" phrases at other times helps his meaning and sharpens his image. Altogether, the association with students of the occult and men of letters both enriched his store of knowledge and served to make more certain his eventual return to his writing.

Boehme possessed an intuitive feeling for words, often knowing, his associates declared, what a Latin or Greek term signified the moment he heard it pronounced by one of his learned friends. They even brought collections of wild flowers to him, spoke the Latin or Hebrew name for one or another, and marvelled at his unerring sense of sound-values when he picked the flower to match each name. Once when the scholarly Dr. Balthazar Walther enunciated the word *idea* in the Greek pronunciation, Boehme leaped to his feet in excitement; the very sound of it conjured up a vision of a heavenly virgin — to be identified ever after with his soul-companion Sophia, who was also a symbol of divine wisdom, and of spiritual purity.

It was Dr. Tobias Kober, a physician, who was closest to Jacob Boehme. He had settled in Goerlitz the very year of the shoemaker's official disgrace. Already interested in scientific and supernatural knowledge and a student of Paracelsus, he found in Boehme an interesting companion and a remarkable proof that understanding can be attained by other paths than intellectual learning.

The most distinguished of those who counted themselves friends, not to say disciples, of the humble Jacob was Dr. Walther. He had mastered the deepest books and had consulted with the greatest living scholars, and he had travelled far in hope of discovering new clues to magical knowledge. He had consciously sought the philosopher's stone. Neither in Egypt nor in the Holy Land, neither in India nor in the farthest corners of Europe, he averred, had he discovered so much of spiritual or real understanding as in Jacob Boehme's first manuscript, *The Aurora*. He visited Goerlitz, and he spent three months in the Boehme household, that he might enjoy daily meetings with this natural philosopher. When he went eventually to Germany to become director of the Chemical Laboratory at Dresden, he kept in touch with his humble friend, and so well did he advertise Boehme's powers that when, some years later, renewed persecutions drove the illuminate from Goerlitz, he found refuge in Dresden, was honoured at the Saxon Court, and was received by scholars and high Church officials with respect.

It was Kober and Walther and their friends who kept asking Jacob for further writings. The Pastor Richter had been irked by the sight of his victim in the companionship of celebrated visitors to the city and had reopened his campaign of defamation. Boehme thus in a way felt himself released from the promise to abstain from writing. The renewed persecution was less depressing on his own account — for he was big enough in spirit and outlook to get the Pastor Primarius into perspective, knowing the matter to be one of envy — than on account of his wife and children, who were on every side ridiculed and even threatened with ill treatment.

In 1618, six years after the *Aurora* manuscript had been taken away from him, he began, at the age of forty-three, to write again. During the remaining six years of his life he was to compose urgently, almost feverishly, producing in a half-dozen years what for most authors would be, in bulk, a lifetime's writing. Of his importunate friends he said: "Many learned men, including not only priests and doctors but noblemen, both counts and princes, corresponded with me, and some came to me in person to demand more of my gifts and knowledge. But I dared not accede, for the Pastor Primarius had seen to it that I was forbidden. These friends suggested that God might withdraw my gift and bestow it upon another who would make real use of it. They urged that I obey God rather than man."

He was already trying to get light upon the matter direct from God. If his writing had been taken from him at the instance of the Devil, he must be very sure to listen to any urging from above to resume the work. Yet he would, despite the glory of his mystic experiences, feel a relief and contentedness if the gift were taken from him. He wanted only what God wanted.

But, though the light of grace had been withdrawn from him for considerable periods, there remained a smouldering within, as of a fire that is not out but only covered. Finally, "With all my prayers earnestly put before Him, I found that the fire did but revive and burn the brighter; and in the glow of that fire, in that illumination, again I wrote."

His manuscripts, which followed one another rapidly from 1619 to 1624, show that the illuminate had lost none of his humility or his simplicity through talk with the most learned of men. "I own this gift only in the measure vouchsafed me of the Lord. I am His instrument, with which He does as He wills. I declare this, my friend, once and for all, in order that no one may think of me as other than what I am, believing me a man of talent or intellect. . . ."

The Three Principles was completed in 1619, no fewer than

seven treatises in 1620, and from three to six in each year thereafter until his death. He permitted his manuscripts to be copied, and shortly he was enabled to increase his scant income by taking fees for the privilege of making copies. Some of the wealthier of his disciples, uneasy over his self-sacrifice and poverty, were accustomed to make gifts of food to his sometimes neglected family. Not until the last year of his life, 1624, was one of his manuscripts put into type. This step, like the first copying and circulation of *The Aurora*, was without his authorization or knowledge, and brought him no profit.

The Three Principles was designed to be a clarification of his position on all questions, divine, cosmic, and natural. He called it his ABC book. But it was as grand in scope and as thorough as *The Aurora*, though at points simpler in language and more lucid.

The sweetness of temper of Jacob Boehme held steady now through years of renewed persecution at the hands of Richter and the local authorities of Goerlitz. They were years also of war and pillage by invading armies. Lusatia was a pawn between Saxony and Bohemia, had been ravaged by Polish Cossacks, mercenaries of the Roman Emperor Ferdinand, and had suffered defeat and occupation by Saxon and imperial troops. The churches, at a time when the bitterness and strife born of the Reformation and Counter-reformation persisted, when politically ambitious rulers used one religious party or the other for their own imperial designs, were seething with factional animosity and intrigue. Boehme, nevertheless, writing of fundamental religion, rose above quarrels, censure, and fighting. Taking the highest possible grounds of cosmic monotheism and primitive Christianity, he was outside the field of sectarian feuds, and he ignored the challenges and abuse of Churchmen, such as Richter, who were incapable of ascent to disinterested heights.

When he wrote his third treatise, *The Threefold Life of Man*, he had apparently experienced a fresh surge of God's goodness and was enjoying an increased measure of spiritual peace. The theme of regeneration, of a man's power to reach God by a new birth within himself, enters strongly. In its promise of "inexpressible joy in the love and mercy of God," of personal participation in "glory, strength and majesty beyond all powers of description," it is one of the most mystical of his works. In the preface he wrote of the book as "a memorial to ourself, and a stay to uphold us in these distracted, miserable times."

He did not hesitate to criticize official Christianity and man's departure from the religion of Jesus. "O Antichristian World, how have you exalted your own ceremonies, setting them in the stead of God!" And: "All the Apostolic ordinances and virtues have been left aside and our precious Christendom laid in bondage to human opinions and institutions. In sham reverence Christ's kingdom has been made a show of pomp and vanity. . . . It is men who have introduced *ceremonies*. Oh, had they only instead kept simple faith, and shown the way to regeneration. If they had only shown one another the clear countenance of God . . ."

Jacob Boehme often deplored the glorification of the empty church buildings — "stone houses, called churches." They have, he said, "no more holiness than other shelters, since they are built of the same stone, and God is no more powerful there. But a meeting there of the congregation in union and prayer, lifted by communion into one holy body in Christ, is a true church, a holy temple of Jesus Christ."

The force of *The Threefold Life of Man* lies in its own simple faith and certainty of regeneration. It reiterates that the Kingdom of God is within, that the soul can speak to God, and that the reborn man reopens the gate beyond which are found illumination, spiritual nourishment, and peace.

Boehme was at this time showing the final proof of greatness: he preserved sweetness of character under adversity, an imperturbable temper under persecution. In *The Threefold Life of Man* especially he holds out to mankind the wisdom that steels against despondency or surrender, the wisdom that is part of the sweetness of Jesus, of the Buddha Gautama, of the saints among men.

In that same busy year 1620 Boehme was led by Balthazar Walther to answer categorically the questions concerning the soul of man then agitating the minds of the theologians and philosophers of Europe. Walther had the idea of pitting his humble friend against the sages of East and West. He was confident that the intuitive powers of Jacob Boehme were outrunning the best-trained intellects of the time. So he busied himself for months travelling to the university cities of Germany. There he interviewed scholars and churchmen and scientists. With their assistance he compiled a list of forty questions regarding God, man, and especially the human soul, its source, its seat, its nourishment, and its final rest.

He transmitted the questionnaire to Jacob, and he anxiously awaited the sheaf of answers.

Nor was he disappointed, for after a few months there came to him the manuscript of a book, fully answering the queries. It was entitled simply *The Forty Questions of the Soul*. For three months the author had given himself to the task, and out of "meditation and prayer" had written down some of the soundest theology and science of the period. Characteristically he prefaced the composition with an *apologia:* "Respected Sir and my Beloved Friend: The mind or reason of man could not answer all the questions you have put to me, for they compass the chiefest and greatest Mysteries, which are known to God alone." But "seeing you seek so earnestly after such things, you become thereby even the cause of finding them. . . . To forestall the boastful, God sometimes employs very mean men to unfold His Mysteries, in order that it may seem the more to come from His hand alone. . . ."

The Forty Questions is a sort of handbook of the soul according to Jacob Boehme. It answers such queries as "Whence came the soul in the beginning?"; "What is the soul in its inmost essence, substance and nature?"; "How and what is the illumination that comes to the soul?"; and "What is the source of the conflict between the flesh and the spirit?" Never faltering, Jacob put down answers to all, not calling upon learning or consulting books, but asking God to illumine each matter for him. "Neither might I write it at all, except I did set it down as the Spirit did say it."

The Forty Questions spread his fame more rapidly and more widely than any other of his books, and it became the most popular of his treatises. It was the first of his works translated (1630) into Latin, the language of scholars throughout the Western world, from his High German, and it thus attained circulation among students at the churches and universities abroad. It was *The Forty Questions* that brought about the naming of Jacob Boehme as "The Teutonic Philosopher," or "Teutonick" as the early editions have it — or again, in learned circles, *Teutonicus Philosophus* — and it is by that name that he has been best known since 1630. A flood of writings came after the *Forty Questions,* five additional "books" in 1620 alone, four in 1621, and six in 1622. It was in 1622 that he wrote to a friend that he had "put aside trade in order to serve God and his fellow men." It was then, doubtless, that his family came to realize fully what it means to have a "philosopher" as the head of the house.

With Jacob Boehme theology and philosophy are hardly to be dissociated, so entirely is the wisdom of life identified with the understanding of and allegiance to God. Certain of the treatises, nevertheless, are to be put on the one side, as primarily spiritual counsel and affirmation of Christian truth — such was *The Incarnation of the Son of God*, of 1620 — whereas others, such as the *Signatura Rerum*, are rather to be set over toward the other side, as attempting more of systematization of knowledge.

The Signature of All Things, as the English title goes, covers some of the ground of the earlier writings, but Boehme had in view a special approach to life. Everything, he said, belongs to the inward or the outward realm, the one spiritual, close to God, the other tangible, "natural." The outward is meaningless without reference to the inward; is, indeed, its "outbreathing or pouring-forth." Everything in the tangible world, men included, is a reflection of the spiritual, bears its signature in form, shape, inclination, and property. And, he admonishes, the true meaning of outward life is revealed only to him who goes to God, gets understanding of the Signer, and thus is able to read the world in its divine revealment.

If two men have the same understanding, their own signatures alike, then they can speak fully and lucidly to each other. "Then," says Boehme, with his knack at analogies, "I may understand him really and fundamentally . . . he has the hammer that can strike my bell." If this be the true significance of the *Signatura Rerum* — no two students return from the reading of a Boehme book agreed as to its contents; it is like going to Russia — the author hid it under some of the most difficult language written into any of his books.*

There is reason for the difficultness. He was trying to explain a faculty of man seldom used, too little recognized — and unnamed. It is something like intuition, or spiritual understanding, or clairvoyance, and yet is none of these or all of them. Boehme had the faculty, developed phenomenally. He was manifesting it when Dr. Walther and Dr. Kober would speak an unfamiliar word to him and he would, as in a flash, image its true meaning from the sound and way of saying; or when they spoke a plant's Greek or Hebrew name and he would unerringly choose the flower from its

---

* *The Signature of All Things* is unfortunately the only inexpensive, easily attainable book by Jacob Boehme available in English. It is to be had, with an excellent brief introduction by Clifford Bax, in Everyman's Library.

properties or looks. It is the faculty of recognition by a hidden spiritual signature. It is insight of the sort displayed by the cobbler-mystic after his second illumination, when he looked out to see nature's forces of creation, growth, and order unveiled to him. Dr. Walther called it, in the original sense of the word, "magic," as something proper to a Magus, a wise man or seer.

Unfortunately Boehme here larded his High German with many terms taken from the devotees of magic in a less reputable sense, especially from the alchemists. Without a key the reader stumbles over the Divine Mercury and the poisonful Mercury, over the tinctures and the temperature and the spalt, over sulphur and salnitre. But if he persists he is sure to find his awareness of inner significances and essences heightened, his detection of God's presence easier. The ultimate idea is clear: each reader who is a true seeker may find God's signature in himself by treating this book as his mirror, and, as the author says in an afterword, "create him much profit and joy, and even be helped in all natural things." The final words of the book are typical Boehme: "A lily blossoms upon the mountains and vales in all the ends of the earth; he that seeketh findeth."

In that same year, 1622, Jacob Boehme wrote four monographs known collectively as *The Way to Christ*. Transparently he composed the successive essays, on Repentance, Regeneration, Resignation, and the Supersensual Life, as a dramatization of the way or road of spiritual salvation as he had experienced it. Perhaps he was exaggerating the obstacles in his own path to regeneration and magnifying his own lapses and sinfulness, for he had found God years before, and had since continued in grace. But there is in his writings a strong sense of nostalgic longing, a feeling of the prodigal degraded, lost like a child, then returned home; and finally a feeling of the glory and rapture of the experience of mystic union with the divine. *The Way to Christ* is one of Jacob's noblest writings, a key work. At the opening he writes: "In this the author gives thee the most precious jewel he hath."

He would have liked to bring the message and the way of regeneration to simple men like himself. But he was blocked from directly influencing his neighbours and his peasant-born friends, blocked and discredited through the defamation of his character by the Pastor Richter. The townspeople, like the City Fathers, were ready to take the Pastor's word for it that the seemingly inoffensive little man was inhabited by a devil and given to heresy and blasphemy. Nor did the lesser clergy of the neighbouring districts fail to inflame their parishioners against the heretic. There is, too, the truth that Boehme's evangelical message is obscured, for all but persistent readers, within his grandiose discussions of the cosmos, the estate of God, man's origin, and the nature of the soul. The jewel is deep-hidden; one must work to it through difficult ore.

Predestination was the most controversial topic under debate in northern Europe, and in 1623 Jacob Boehme determined to write a book about it. He rose above the current bitterness and contention. The Reformation, which had seemed to so many the hope of Europe and the salvation of Christianity, had itself fallen victim to many of the church evils that Luther had revolted against. (The sale of indulgences and the low moral average of the clergy were only pegs upon which hung a network of corruptions.) Bigotry and despotism were rife in the new Church. The chasm separating the Protestants from Rome was hardly greater than that now dividing the Lutherans from the Calvinists. The overharsh interpretations of the Calvinist doctrine of "election of grace, commonly called pre-destination," would not attract a man so kindly, so charitable, so certain of God's goodness, as Jacob Boehme. But he does not, in his book *On the Election of Grace*, take up a position *against* the Calvinists. Characteristically he tries to draw both parties with him to a higher ground whence all can see Christian doctrine alike. He disputes with no one. He shows the grounds for harmony and points out the foundations for one united Church. He speaks with the utmost reverence, and yet his writing is everywhere touched with warm human feeling. Through it all is that special simplification of speech, that directness of statement, so typical of this unlearned man.

The introduction of the book is notable for its reasonableness, logic, and clarity of expression. Here an author who spoke often of "man's deluded reason," who mistrusted intellectual processes — "for God goes clean another way to work," he said — strikes directly to the heart of the subject and proceeds down a path of argument with extraordinary balance and acumen.

> There has arisen contention over an opinion, regarding men, that God has elected one part of mankind to the kingdom of Heaven, to enter into His holy bliss, and elected the other part to eternal damnation . . . so that every happen-

ing occurs by necessity; and the part of mankind chosen for damnation are said to be so stamped in God's purpose and so reprobate therein that God's grace is wholly inaccessible to them, while to the others there is no possibility of damnation. . . . In certain passages the Scriptures speak almost in such a manner, and creaturely Reason, not understanding God on the highest ground, assents; while on the other hand the Scriptures also seem to say the direct opposite. . . . With good intent and affection we will employ our talent . . . not in the spirit of attacking or despising anyone for a formed opinion, but to advance a Christian and fraternal union of all our gifts, which we have together by the divine grace.

Before Boehme was finally exiled from the city that had been his home since boyhood, one more work was completed and put into circulation, during the year 1623. Although he had spoken of his treatise upon the election of grace as "determined upon the deepest ground," he described the *Mysterium Magnum* to a friend as "still more deep." It is an amazingly complete commentary upon Genesis — and more, for each verse of the original serves as point of departure for an allegorical or speculative essay. In his very involved but sometimes magnificent treatment of the subject Boehme embedded those ideas that led to acceptance of him as first in the line of German philosophers, to whom Hegel, Schelling, Schopenhauer, and the others were to be frankly indebted.

Late in 1623, for the first time, one of Jacob Boehme's manuscripts found its way into the hands of a printer, and early in 1624 copies of *The Eternal Life* were circulated with a celerity impossible to the painfully copied script versions. The author himself knew nothing of the business and would have prevented it if he had known. He had reason for caution, for the book was to cause his expulsion from Goerlitz and Lusatia.

The Eternal Life was not a newly written book, but a portion of *The Way to Christ*. When it appeared publicly Richter had at last the evidence he needed to bolster his charges. Before, in the years since the exile and swift recall of Boehme in 1613, the City Councilmen, reluctant to injure a citizen who seemed honest, humble, and inoffensive, had only passively supported Richter. Now it was shown beyond doubt that his opinions — which were contrary to the teaching of the recognized Church, according to the Pastor, and the Pastor should know — were being actively circulated. All the dignity of a printed book witnessed that there was an audience for them. Richter did not hesitate to rouse the portion of the public that enjoys witch-hunting. He even added charges of personal vice against the upright little man. He conspired with the pastor at the neighbouring city of Liegnitz so that the latter also brought accusations of heresy and disturbing the peace before the Councilmen at Goerlitz, thus giving the impression of a united action of churchmen against Boehme. Richter's own charges as well as his actions were intemperate and fanatic. He goaded the reluctant City Fathers into action.

Jacob at this time had gone for a period to stay with a nobleman in Silesia who had become a disciple and patron. When he returned to Goerlitz he was summoned to a session at the Rathaus to answer "numerous complaints regarding his alleged pernicious teachings." On March 26, 1624, he made his defence before the Council with dignity and resolution. But, according to the official record, "Jacob Boehme, the shoemaker and confused visionary, admits that he composed the book entitled *The Eternal Life,* but did not have it printed. . . . He was directed by the Council to seek his fortune elsewhere, or in default be reported to the illustrious Prince Elector. He promised to leave Goerlitz as soon as possible."

Determined not to give up again his liberty to write, sick of the whole business of proscription and persecution at the hands of the local churchmen, and sick of the insults and threats of a rowdy element of the populace — indeed, he was waylaid and insulted by ruffians on his way from the Council chamber — he saw no course open but acceptance of exile.

In an *Apologia contra Richter* Boehme reviews the events that had led to Richter's enmity, points out his own blamelessness for the circulation of his works and the spread of his fame (which, indeed, he notes ironically, Richter had done much to further), and reaffirms his reliance upon the Divine Spirit for the materials of his writings and for guidance in living. He is, he avers, neither a drunkard nor a vagabond, and neither a despiser of the Church nor a heretic. On the contrary he derives his very sustenance from Jesus Christ and obeys to the best of his understanding all Christian tenets.

He put this further defence and profession of faith before the

Councilmen, but they merely affirmed the decree of exile. They added that since he had such fame and so many important friends in distant places, he might easily find an abode more suitable and pleasant. They frankly wanted peace, and they could not have it while he and the Pastor both remained within the city walls. They even entreated him "that in love to the city's quiet" he would go. Boehme answered that "Since they will not listen to my defences, that I may discover my innocence, or grant me any support, due to the slurs and recriminations from the Pastor Primarius, I will commit the matter to God, and await how He will lead me to a place among spiritual men, where I shall be clear of the Primarius."

Once again, however, he was to cross lances with the Pastor, and this time his reserve and sweet-temperedness partially gave way. Richter published a fresh attack, libellous and transcendingly violent. Writing in Latin verse, he gave an extraordinary exhibition of hatred borne upon scurrilous language. "Antichrist," "villain of a shoemaker anointed with offal by the Devil," and "whisky drinker" were phrases applied to the saintly man. It was then, between the issuance of the order of expulsion and its execution, that Boehme momentarily forgot his saintliness and his poise. He composed a detailed answer to Richter's blast, pointing out that the Pastor was intemperate not only in his accusations and language but in his drinking — "as witness the wine-blossoms upon his face" — and suggesting that "it may be taken as a sign that the road of repentance that leads to Christ smells to you of offal." But his lapse into anger and name-calling is slight and fleeting; the whole of it occurs in an uncirculated manuscript discovered among his papers after his death. In June 1624, soon after composing and suppressing it, he writes to Dr. Kober concerning Richter's anger: "This is a fire to be quenched by divine love and humility. We must not in any way add fuel to its burning."

Jacob Boehme had long since been invited to visit Dresden, where Balthazar Walther had wanted him to expound his ideas, and where it would be well to resolve the doubts raised by the trial in Goerlitz and the decree of expulsion. Dresden was the nearest large city (closer than Prague), and the mystic had been assured that high officials there, even high churchmen, would listen to him appreciatively and open-mindedly. Nor was he disappointed. The last half-year of his life was brightened by the reception accorded him in the Saxon capital, and even the boorishness and intemperance of Richter toward him were somewhat atoned for in the respect and praise accorded by the German high clerics.

Boehme had never considered himself to be in opposition to Lutheranism or the Evangelical Church, albeit his frequent references to Babel were aimed transparently at all churches and churchmen serving to lead men away from the spirit of Christianity and into conformance with one or another narrow interpretation of the letter. He recognized the failure of Protestantism to rise above destructive quarrels and its failure to lead congregations back to the simple piety and kindly fraternalism implicit in the teachings of Jesus. It must have been in his mind that a new, a true Reformation was called for, and that the message he brought to mankind — direct from God, he was convinced — would afford a sound basis for recovery of Christ's way. Three years earlier he had experienced a vision in which it was made clear to him that a new Reformation impended — though his connection with it was left vague.

His humble position and his unaggressive character precluded immediate spread of his doctrines and his fame. The section of Europe in which he lived and worked was still at war. The churches were against him because their very existence seemed to depend upon loyalty to established interpretations of truth. He could not work within them, and he was ineffective without them. He could only put down in writing the revelations that came to him, hinting at the unutterable joy attained with understanding of them, and then leave the fulfilment to those who would come after. Yet there was possibly in his mind, as he travelled from the now inhospitable Goerlitz to a welcoming Dresden, the thought that a new Reformation might follow his participation in the coming meetings.

On the ninth of May, 1624, Boehme departed from Goerlitz. He left behind the faithful Katharine and their sons, until he might know definitely where their future home would be. He had travelled no farther than Zittau, hardly twenty miles away, when he encountered a different and friendly atmosphere. The leading men of the learned professions met with him and paid him honour, assuring him that Richter's actions were understood for what they were, as proceeding out of bigotry and envy. These new friends not only showed every sign of valuing sincerely his ideas and his writings, but contributed money for the easing of his journey; and one of them went on with him to Dresden.

The Prince Elector's physician and court alchemist, Benedict Hinkelmann, took Boehme into his own house in Dresden and acted as host. Thus the unassuming little man met naturally the scholars and the clergy, and finally the high state officials, of the court. All seemed friendly and desirous of taking part in the discussions that the physician arranged. Doubtless the alchemical-minded were hopeful that this magician would give them clues to the transmutation of baser metals into gold. Doubtless the clerics had a mixed interest. If there were heresy or blasphemy behind the affair at Goerlitz, they should inform themselves of it. If, on the other hand, as Walther (no longer in Dresden) had claimed, the man were a true illuminate, a mystic who had walked with God, now reverently reporting the experience, even aiding his fellow-men by teaching the way of repentance and regeneration, they should, as open-minded divines, encourage and honour him.

While Boehme went from meeting to meeting, his new friends read copies of his published book, and they seemed uniformly to approve it. The Lutheran high priests discovered in it only a strangely moving account of one man's finding of God by the path of repentance and rebirth, written simply and praisefully — obviously the work of a noble mind and a reverent hand. If the ideology went back to the mystics Eckhart and Tauler and to the *Theologia Germanica*, had not Luther himself drawn generously from those sources?

The Eternal Life seemed to the higher clergymen of the Lutheran establishment in Dresden — and they were Richter's own superiors in the church hierarchy — pious and helpful. If, in the conferences that followed, the author mixed into his theology some tincture gained from the alchemists and some explanations of the cosmos that were more suitable to the discussions of scientists and astrologers, there was no mistaking the truth and sincerity of his central message and the man's freedom from deceit or self-seeking. They made it clear that Richter had blundered.

Under the friendliness of the liberal churchmen and of the scholars and court notables, Boehme's spirits brightened, and he wrote hopefully, even jubilantly, to his friends and family in Goerlitz. Finally the Prince Elector himself, who had been away, returned to Dresden and interested himself in the conferences. He appointed two theologians to hold an examination and report their findings to him direct. A meeting of the Supreme Council was arranged to conduct the inquiry. Thus Boehme, recently threatened by the Goerlitz City Council with exposure to the Elector, now appeared before that great ruler in circumstances just and favourable because the Elector's friends and advisers believed in the importance of his gift and his works.

The Court Council's decision cleared Boehme completely. It seemed, moreover, in the permission to "return home in favour," to imply an overruling of the Goerlitz Councilmen. One of the examining theologians exclaimed that if all the world were offered him to do so, he would not condemn such a man. The second examiner, pressed by the Prince Elector for light on the questions discussed at the trial, confessed that Boehme had brought up conceptions that were beyond his comprehension. And he added: "How can we condemn that which we have not understood?"

Jacob returned to Goerlitz to find that vindication in Dresden had little effect upon the people of his home city. Richter was still fulminating, and he had stirred up such bitter feeling that whenever Boehme appeared mob violence against "the heretic" was threatened. The windows of his house were broken and his family threatened with personal outrage.

He himself stayed only briefly. His nobleman friend, Sigismund von Schweinitz, the one who had committed Boehme's book to print, was begging him to visit again in Seifersdorf, Silesia. He held out the inducement not only of further friendly conferences but of probable advantageous contacts with other noblemen of the neighbourhood (and indeed Boehme's works were destined to enjoy a special popularity in Silesia and adjoining Moravia). He was to visit also Abraham von Frankenberg, destined to become his first biographer. Frankenberg was a wealthy Silesian scholar and writer, a student of theology and the occult sciences, and a mystic over on the vague side. He had been drawn to Jacob Boehme because the latter had attained that illumination and that saintly character which he could approach only intellectually, outwardly.

Boehme again for several months enjoyed the companionship and the adulation of cultured and appreciative men. While at the castle in Silesia he began to compose *Theosophical Questions*, a question-and-answer review of his beliefs, designed to be complete in 177 sections; but he was taken ill while on the fourteenth. An abdominal sickness developed alarming complications, and he asked to be returned to Goerlitz. His friends agreed, and he was transported to his own home. There Dr. Kober did everything possible and called other physicians from neighbouring towns. But Jacob knew that he was close to the end of his mortal path. On a Friday in November he spoke to friends who came to wish him a speedy recovery, saying: "You will see that three days hence God will have made an end of me."

He asked that the last rites of the Christian Church be administered to him. The intemperate Richter had died during Boehme's visit to Silesia. One Nicholas Thomas was now pastor of the church Boehme had considered his, despite differences of interpretation and almost intolerable persecution. Thomas, trained by Richter and perfectly fitted to fill his shoes, decided to place every obstacle in the way of the dying man's desire. With an eye upon the favourable attitude toward Boehme among the clerics of Dresden, he could not refuse the Church's offices outright. He declined to officiate himself, but authorized a subordinate to administer the rites if "the heretic" would re-subscribe to the full Lutheran confession of faith.

The underling acted in the spirit of Richter and Thomas. He not only examined Boehme on all the points of faith — which indeed were not different from the mystic's own beliefs if only one interpreted words liberally — but also demanded that the sick man in case of recovery "would keep to our church and doctrine, and give up everything in opposition." He lectured him on the uncertainty of visions and seeming revelations and the difficulty of detecting the Devil's hand in such matters. He insisted that he again renounce all writing of books.

Noting in the sick man's answers a special cleaving to the New Testament, which Boehme had considered the real foundation of Christianity, he pointed out the necessity for keeping strict allegiance to the Old Testament also. He asked whether Boehme earnestly repented, whether he had customarily partaken of the Lord's Supper, whether he realized that, though he might deceive men as to his innermost feelings, he could not deceive God. To all these questions Jacob Boehme answered in the affirmative.

The priest wrote in his report of the examination: "These matters taken care of, I prepared for the final act. But before absolution and administration of the Lord's Supper, I once more questioned him, even to superabundance. . . ." During the renewed interrogation Boehme elaborated one answer: "Yes, with his whole heart he forgave everyone who had injured him, and he besought of others a like forgiveness. He prayed insistently that this should be said publicly in his name; but he passed away before it could be carried out." But the sick man was absolved of his sins and partook of the Lord's Supper.

The way of Boehme's passing was this. On the Sunday night as he lay in his bed it seemed to him that he heard strains of sweet music. He asked his son Tobias if he too could hear that melody. Receiving the answer "No," he asked that the doors of his chamber might be opened "to let in more of that music." He inquired what the hour was, and being told two in the morning, he said that his time would not come for three hours yet. To Katharine he gave final instructions regarding his manuscripts and other small properties. He told her that she would soon follow him. Twice he prayed audibly. At six o'clock, while the city of Goerlitz was still dark and quiet, the hour arrived for the soul of Jacob Boehme to leave his body. He asked to be turned about, so that he might face away from his loved ones, because their love seemed to bind his spirit to earth. Saying aloud: "It is time to go into Paradise," he parted company from his body tranquilly and joyously.

Within a few hours of the death of Jacob Boehme the Church again proved its unfriendliness. The Primarius Thomas forbade a church burial or service. The City Fathers were appealed to, but side-stepped the issue. Friends of Boehme made arrangements to inter the body privately in unconsecrated ground in the country. Just then the governor of the province, Count Karl Hannibal von Dohna, came to Goerlitz, took stock of the situation, and frightened the churchmen and the Councilmen into rescinding the prohibitions. He forced the Church to arrange a regular and solemn ceremony and to allocate a grave in the churchyard. He insisted that the Council show its respect by delegating two members to attend the services. The Primarius, rebelling, took medicines to induce a seeming illness and thus was able to excuse himself from delivering the funeral sermon. A subordinate fulfilled the other offices acceptably, but prefaced his sermon with the statement that he was preaching it under orders and with the greatest feeling of aversion.

After the burial some of Boehme's many Silesian friends sent to Goerlitz a memorial cross, an elaborate affair with inscribed mottos and sentiments and painted with pious pictures. It was placed over the grave, but was promptly destroyed, some say by a mob, some say by vandals in the service of the priests.

Boehme was in his fiftieth year when he died. His faithful but not always patient wife Katharine followed him to the grave within the year.

"God is silence rather than speech," say the Oriental mystics. The aphorism is understandable to every initiate. Yet Western seers and Western students are apt to depart from the austere, silent way of the East. They commonly retain the impulse to go on from spiritual immersion to intellectual understanding; from there it is but a step to instruction of other men. The Reformation mystics especially partake of the burning evangelical spirit of their time. Jacob Boehme is the most zealous and vocal figure among them, the farthest removed from the type figure of Oriental recluse. He knew the value of "innermost Quiet" and of "doing in quiet love"; but he could not stop there, without speaking.

Of one of his early visions he said: "I was enwrapt in the Divine Illumination for a space of seven days; I was then possessed of the supreme beatific wisdom of God, in the kingdom of His ecstasy." Thus, in the most resplendent of his visions Jacob lost himself utterly. He knew fully the glory of mystical union. He experienced the transport, the joy, the bliss of immersion in Spirit. But his "illuminations," as he called them, were not usually those of the practising, the absolute, mystic.

Toward the after life, he was intent upon salvation for his soul. He yearned, moreover, to make clear to other men the way to both illumination and salvation. He entered into the presence of God not as a seeker of personal favour, not as an adept in contemplation, surrender, and absorption, but as a supplicant for "the light that is God."

The progressive road he travelled was one of infrequent attainment of light between dark periods of conflict, doubt, and struggle, then arrival at an overwhelming experience of God's goodness and mystery, and finally a settling into a tacit relationship with divine power. In the later, writing years he enjoys an almost continual communion with God. It is a sort of permanent sanctification combined with an active working discipleship. Reliance upon God becomes instinctive and habitual, but the resplendent visions are fewer.

The endless hours of composition, when he felt that he was acting as a privileged amanuensis, were not, indeed, times of blissful forgetfulness. To pierce to the centre, to apprehend the very being of God, each time he took up his pen would have meant abandonment of his purpose to instruct or guide other men. At times his soul "sees the Godhead like a flash of light," or again "The soul itself is clothed in the substance of God." But oftener the process is one of bringing his mind into "a godlike state," raising his consciousness to the voice of the dictating Spirit, and writing down the "inexpressible words" so far as he is enabled to apprehend them.

In one of his letters he set down a picture of himself hurrying to inscribe God's message. Obviously his agitation is of a sort inimical to joyous partaking of the illumination of Spirit. He is shown everything "in a wonderful clearness." But he cannot inscribe the thoughts fast enough, and he falters in his style, even in his grammar. "The fire rages within me and I am driven on. My mortal hand and my pen can only follow the words haltingly." Having in mind his shortcomings as amanuensis, Boehme invites the reader "to follow the flights of my soul rather than those of my pen."

Against Eastern withdrawal, in short, Boehme opposed the Western ideal of making all things, even the highest, practical and useful. He believed that an inner bliss, a soul-contentment, could not but be more profitable for the world if repeated in the lives of a thousand men. He must break into the quiet even of his companionship with God in order to bring back the completest transcript possible of the Spirit's words. He undertook not only to render divine illumination practical and outward, but to reconcile the vague mystic "way" with the path to salvation as prescribed by the Lutheran Church.

Jacob Boehme found in illumination and revelation no bar to laborious cobbling. The flexibility that enabled him to bring down the mysteries of Heaven and God and of mystic participation into workaday life and an imperfect society enabled him also to remain within the Church, yet oppose its errors. However limited its keepers, however cramped its dogma, he saw no reason to deny the magnificent concept of God's mystic Church on earth. He looked back through the long vista of church history and envisioned even so rigid a communion as the Lutheran as being, at heart, devoted to the evangelism of Jesus and Paul and John.

JACOB BOEHME

In his inmost being he knew the religion of the Founder as one centred in mystic union. If the Church concerned itself more with dogma and conventions, reward and punishment — especially punishment — it yet held to the Eucharist and was the earthly symbol of a fellowship of men bound in mystic fealty to Christ. He knew too much about the depraved side of man not to feel the need of authority and management. If the Church was imperfect too, then one should dwell upon the imperfections in the hope of doing away with them; but, he counselled, do not cast away the institution that alone can reunite men in the faith of Jesus. His impulse to speak and instruct brought him into conflict with the churches at Goerlitz and certain neighbouring towns, by reason of the stupidity and envy of the Pastor Richter. But he dreamed of bringing the Protestant Church back to simple surrender to Christ, back to the simple morality of the Sermon on the Mount, back to ideals of personal regeneration and selfless living, and to religion as mystic experience.

"Let no man wonder," wrote Jacob Boehme, "if I write about the creation of the world as if I had been there and had myself witnessed it." He felt that he had known the event. He explains in surprisingly modern terms the consciousness — "spirit" — that is the race-inheritance of each one of us, that has lived through all the generations from the beginning, remembering all that has existed or happened. He also enjoys direct revelation from God. In writing of the cosmic drama he astonishes with the vividness, directness, and assurance of his reports.

Boehme was content with nothing less than offering an entire schema of creation, cosmology, and natural phenomena. He visualized clearly the processes of beginning, evolution, growth and decay, fall and redemption, and the nature of God, the angels, the devil, and man. Like the great imaginer and seer he was, he paraded glorious protagonists and inspiring scenes upon his cosmic stage; but he failed often as playwright-craftsman, neglecting dramatic order and transition and motivation.

He did not lack for unity of conception. He perceived all history and all processes in one Unity, and he apprehended the whole in each separate part of nature's expression. He owned the mystic's true sense of the macrocosm in the microcosm. In sensing the cosmic processes in the growing grasses or the tree vital with sap — favourite symbols — he did not, however, fall on the side of pantheism, which is so small a part of mysticism. His cosmos is God-centred and God-illumined. But the awareness of nature's orderliness and vitality affords a special livingness to his picturing of the universe.

As he wrote and rewrote his descriptions in book after book, his ideas sometimes changed and clarified. But the greater wonder is that the story of creation, of the heavenly and earthly realms, and of all nature is practically complete in the first book. The one scheme persists, with minor modifications, through the author's major treatises and into his last attempt to systematize knowledge.

"Spirit" may be said to be the leading character in the drama of the universe as it unfolds in Jacob Boehme's writings: Spirit as the essential part of man, Spirit which is at once the substance of the universe before creation and the Being of God; Spirit which is the light of God. It is the element of being. It is the Biblical Word. It is also, more humanly and understandably, the "Wisdom" that Boehme visualizes and dramatizes as the Eternal Virgin Sophia.

The processes by which Spirit or Will brings about creation, and the cardinal events of Lucifer's fall, the creation of Adam and then Eve, and their fall, the conflict of good and evil, and the coming, the supreme sacrifice, and the triumph of Jesus — these are the materials of the narrative-expository books. The climax is in the regeneration of man, the reclaiming of his soul and his life by Spirit, his return to rest in God.

A thousand details are woven into the pattern behind the events, often obscuring the drift and structure of the design. There are multiple meanings in the words and images. Man is the microcosmic image of the universe, and every element and figure and event of cosmic history and natural evolution is implied in the life of man. Each major motive or figure carries a double meaning or a host of meanings.

Thus the simplest activity of nature implies the story of Lucifer and Adam, of man fallen and reclaimed. The tree blossoms, and in Boehme's mind it symbolizes the rebirth of the individual man. For him everything had its "signature," signalling to him its properties, its nature, and its place in the kingdom. Into his mind would flash all the analogies, in Heaven, Hell, and earth — and often he expects from the reader more of this second seeing than average comprehension warrants.

JACOB BOEHME

Out of the Abyss, the Deep, came the first movement, or light, or existence. Essentially the universe unfolded out of God, when the Virgin Wisdom held up a mirror to His desire for manifestation. Conflict arose in the working of the Seven Properties (or Qualities out of God) upon one another, but was resolved when the contraries existing in six of the forms or forces fell into harmony in the Seventh. The Seventh Property became perfect union, Paradise, and "eternal nature."

Lucifer set himself up in opposition to God — "He wanted to be an artist," Boehme explains succinctly — and was cast into Hell. When Adam was created, life was still paradisaical, but he was led astray and went out of the orbit of the light of God. It was then that life on earth ceased to be harmonious and angelic. Eternal nature became temporal nature; time came alive; imperfections, iniquities, pain, and decay were thenceforth the lot of terrestrial man.

As a result of Adam's fall, death became the common price of the return to God, to the orbit of Spirit. Jesus made the supreme sacrifice and manifested the "way" by which man, in life, may destroy the corrupt self and open the soul to the light of God. By resignation, by faith in the Kingdom, by devotion to the Christ-Spirit, one rises out of the prison of temporal circumstance. Effacement of the vanities, of aggressiveness, of self-will, permits return to the paradise that is harmony, love, plenitude, to the estate of eternal nature.

It is here that man redeemed may enter into "the play of love and life," into the blissful activity of the Spirit. At last he is the mystic, experiencing the *Mysterium Magnum* which is the manifestation of all the processes of union, harmonization, and rest initiated from the time of the Abyss. At last he is in the light that is God. He is liberated, he is in peace.

A warm human feeling is sensed throughout the drama of the cosmos as Jacob Boehme writes it. He loses himself at times in splendours and grandeurs and magnificences. But he straightway returns and explains the stupendous in terms of growing trees and running streams and ripening fruits, with homely touches that put the reader at ease. The Kingdom of God is within; it is as readily approached as one's bedroom or garden. The God whose light the wise man seeks above all else is a glorious God, in Boehme's noble descriptions, but he is the God of one's heart, a

God of love and sympathy, desiring the soul's return as it, reborn, desires Him. The return from darkness is a home-coming to a loving Father.

Boehme loses nothing of attractiveness in destroying the myth of Heaven as a tangible place, for he makes the everywhere of God's light so inviting that all "localities" fade in significance. He cleverly transposes from time-conditioned existence to timelessness, and he transcends all described heavens with his boundless one. In his last book he wrote: "There is no place prepared for God, where He dwells apart. Rather, He is in, with and through us. Wherever He becomes active with His love in a life, there His place is revealed. . . . Heaven is in the ground of the soul." And in *The Aurora* he wrote:

> If you fix your mind upon Heaven, desiring to understand what it is, you need not project your thoughts thousands of miles away, for that distant place is not your Heaven. . . . The true Heaven is everywhere, in the very place where you stand or go; you need only push through outward earthly surroundings until your spirit apprehend the Being of God, then you are clearly in Heaven. . . . Then an immaculate, glory-filled Heaven, in which God is, and all the sanctified angels, takes form in purity, radiant beauty and joy.

All this, man may return to, may comprehend, by looking into his own being, by purifying himself, by uncovering the Christ within. In returning to Heaven he is going back to his native country. Within himself, moreover, is the mother element that will bring about rebirth. He must only, says Boehme, "be at one with himself." For originally man is a *microdeus*, a god in little, formed in the image of, as an expression of, the God that is All.

To bring the inner, holy self into ascendancy an awakening is necessary, an awakening that is at once a realization of the inadequacy, restlessness, and futility of worldly life (the message perfectly parallels Oriental teachings here) and a desire for return to Divinity. "The soul in its essence is a miraculous torch of fire from the flame of God. It is a burning desire toward the Light." How to release this desire, how, in the divided self, to grant dominion to the Spirit — that is the question of cardinal importance for the individual. Boehme's message begins with reiteration of the ageless injunction, "Know yourself." Know, moreover, your two selves, the Christ-self and the self that fell with Adam. Know then the two worlds of manifestation. Recognize your false position in relation to God so long as you hold to the selfish, worldly, intellectual materialism of the outward life. (Boehme wrote at the opening of *The Threefold Life* a marvellously clear statement of the necessity to face these two worlds and to make one's choice.) Having chosen, it is necessary only to turn to the Christ within; for Christ, who died on the tree, yet lives in every man. One must die as to oneself and live as to Christ, and all else will follow. It is this that is meant by the phrase "Christian resignation"; and herein is the truer meaning of Christian humility.

Boehme's favourite motto was "Our salvation is in the life of Jesus Christ within us." It is to the Christ that he goes, as the way and the life. Nor will all the prayers to God for forgiveness of sin avail if the Christ-consciousness be not aroused and sustained. For it is He who has "opened a way through death and wrath to the Splendour that is God. You must turn round and go in by that path."

There is no insistence in Boehme's writings upon the cross man must bear in following Jesus. Jacob Boehme had known temptation and struggle, and he recognized that sacrifice is necessary. But the rewards of conversion so outweighed the price that he was inclined not to linger over the relinquished values. He once wrote of his early period of confusion and despair: "My soul became distracted within me and I was in anguish as a woman in travail. I found no way out until I followed Christ's words when He said: 'Except a man be born again, he cannot see the Kingdom of God.' At this my heart was stopped because until then I had thought I could not be born again in this world but only when I depart this life." Having followed, he felt no longer the importance of the sacrificed things, so great were the joys.

As to help from the books so precious to some mortals he wrote: "If I have no other book than only the book I myself am, yet I have books enough. All of the Bible is in me if only I have Christ's spirit. In reading myself I read God's book. You my brothers are the alphabet to be read in me, for my spirit discovers you within me." Then he adds: "From my heart I desire that you too should find me in *your* reading."

Collectively it is all part of the one change crucial for humankind: "God must become man, man must become God; Heaven must become one with earth, the earth must be returned into Heaven. Give then to the earth Heaven's food. . . ." And he describes the joy obtained by partaking of Heaven's food. "If a man here on earth is illumined with the Holy Spirit from the fountain of Christ, so that life from the Source is kindled in him, then there arises a bliss in his heart, spreading through all his veins, until his whole being trembles with it; then the victorious soul rejoices as if it were in God — a thing understood only by those who have been guests in that house."

The birth of the new man: this for Jacob Boehme constitutes at once entry into blissful mystical experience and the very practical business of saving one's soul from affliction and restlessness on earth and from the flames of the after life. The message is repeated again and again in variations of the statement "Christ is the temple whereinto we must enter." He elaborated those few words to their full significance thus: "The man who enters unreservedly into the state of spiritual rest in Christ attains the perception of divinity. He finds God in himself and he apprehends God everywhere. God speaks to him, he converses with God. He is granted understanding. . ."

The regenerated man, however, does not, in entering into the world of light, go out of the natural world; rather, it too is revealed to him as divine. He sees both ways, into Heaven and into earth, and he brings the quality of Heaven from the one seeing to the other. He discovers Heaven as his realer home — "Home is rest in God" — but, conditioned to life on the terrestrial level, he looks upon nature and men with new eyes, recognizing the divine properties he had overlooked while unregenerate. "Empty" nature is revealed to him as filled with the life, the order, the beauty, that arises from God. Man, degenerate though he be, still holds latent all the divine powers. In him may be roused the desire, the will, that sets in motion "the process of Christ." This is the meaning of man's dominion on earth, of his estate as master of all its powers and potencies: that he is able to "rise up among his thoughts and direct his consciousness toward the divine," and to "go in through Heaven and apprehend the very heart of God."

If the regenerated man comes to inexpressible bliss thus, it is no less his for eternity. Boehme in that way adds the history of the future to his all-inclusive report of creation and evolution."

JACOB BOEHME

A guardian spirit attended Jacob Boehme, an angel guide, a beloved soul-companion. Wisdom, known also as Understanding, an abstraction at first, became his adored Sophia, the spouse of his soul, his comfort in hours of trouble.

Usually impersonal and self-depreciatory, Jacob Boehme here bows to the common need for objectification and takes to himself the love and protection of one of the company of Heavenly beings. He lacks nothing of respect and seemliness in his adoration, but he descends to the emotional plane. Occasionally he is romantic, rapturous, even fervid in the vein of the sensuous and amorous symbolism of Saint Bernard or the Sufi mystics of Persia. (Some of his intenser passages seemed "not permissible" to staid Victorian readers.) He let his heart take precedence over his soul in worship and in glorification. In general, however, his is a sober and a magnificent portrait of Wisdom.

"The Virgin has promised to be faithful to me and not to forsake me in my need," he writes in his second book, *The Three Principles*. ". . . I am strengthened to persist through thorny ways, through mockery and disdain, until I arrive back in my own native country, from which my soul has wandered, back in the land where my dearest Virgin dwells. She appeared to me, and I rest upon her promise then that she would turn my sorrows into joy. I lay upon the mountain at midnight, the trees fell about me, the winds of the storm beat upon me, and Antichrist was baring his teeth to devour me; then she came, and she comforted me and married herself to me."

Sophia is, in Boehme's cosmic and theological scheme, Divine Wisdom, or, as some translate it, Divine Imagination. At the time of the Abyss she is the mirror of God's properties and potentialities, of His Glory and His riches. "She moves before God to reveal His wonders" — thus leading Him on to self-manifestation. She is the pattern or model of creation.

The Eternal Maiden Sophia is also "the playmate of God in honour and joy." She is the feminine wisdom answering, innocently mating with, the masculine will. She seems in some descriptions to be almost the equivalent of the Great Mother-Goddess; yet always she derives all from God, is but the reflection of one side of His Being.

A special note of tenderness comes into the Illuminate's writings when he speaks of Sophia. Even in the works tinged with the hardness of the alchemists, she is accorded properties and symbols that are femininely attractive and insinuating. She is "the water spirit"; and Boehme adds: "This water is true humility, the soul of the light according to love."

Sophia becomes the symbol of love in its mystic aspect, because love is implicit in wisdom. She is the harmony and gentleness of eternal nature, as contrasted with the harsh conditions of temporal nature, of the earthly environment.

When Adam fell, Boehme explains, Wisdom no longer was his light and companion, a part of himself. He was divided, and his interest centred upon Eve. Mortal love, sexual love, too often held the place of heavenly love. Light remained in Adam and Eve only as a potentiality and a mystery. But "The soul that has become pure as clear gold, tested in God's fire, is rightly the husband of the saintly Sophia, the spirit of light. . . . Adam will receive back the majestic bride taken from him while he slept." In other words, the terrestrial substitution of Eve for Sophia holds only so long as men perpetuate Adam's lapses. When one is reborn, Sophia is again one's bride.

In Boehme's picture, the Virgin Mary "put on" the heavenly Sophia; that is, to her mortal virginity she added Sophia's eternal virginity. "The soul of Mary received the Heavenly Virgin and the latter covered Mary with the holy garment of the Spirit." Thus in a mystic sense Sophia, as Wisdom, Light, became the spiritual mother of Jesus, through Mary, "the star of the morning." She is in the Christ; in being reborn, the individual embraces her through his devotion and cleaving to the Christ-spirit. There is a warmth in the presentation of the idea of Wisdom in-living in the Christ, as of something shining, beautiful, star-like, and infinitely desirable.

When the seeker becomes wholly and unreservedly the mystic, forsaking the attractions and distractions of the outward world, it is the image of this angelic and blessed figure that makes easy the following of the way — which is sometimes thought of as bare, austere, and impersonal. It is Sophia, the holy man's ideal, his saintly guide, who welcomes him, comforts him as mother, cherishes him as bride, and unfolds before him the incomparable glories and riches of the spiritual life.

Many seekers of truth or holiness before Boehme had personalized and depended upon a second self in the heart. The second-century Gnostics, while only imperfectly distinguishing her from the Mother-Goddess inherited from the Babylonians, called her by the same name, Sophia, and considered her a mediator between the lower mortal environment and the heaven of light and revelation. They were influenced, of course, by Plato, who had, more vaguely and abstractly, attributed some of Eternal Wisdom's properties to the Ideas of Beauty and Good.

Nor is Wisdom's name as that of guide absent from the books of the Old Testament. Philo, drawing upon both Jewish lore and the Greek philosophers, had postulated a more abstract representative of man before the heavenly tribunals. With the cabbalists she was again personalized, and emotionally as well as mystically celebrated. Nor was she unknown to the Neo-Platonists.

Jacob Boehme goes beyond all these in his personal feeling for his idealized Virgin. She is warmly, almost ecstatically, the bride of his soul. She is his genius, a part of himself, the torch of celestial light burning in the inmost chambers of his being. She is rare and beautiful and not to be apprehended while one holds to the restless courses of the sense-world. She is the mother of the reborn, companion of the mystic pilgrim. In *The Three Principles* he writes:

> In the realm in which the body is not at home, when an unaccountable fire of eagerness burns in our minds, then the precious maiden who is the Wisdom of God comes forth to us in a radiant mien, saying, I bring the light, the means, the glory, and mine is the gateway to understanding. I am your bride in the hour of illumination, and your desire and my fulfilment are one.

The state of virginity, the unsullied, is dear to Boehme in his meditations upon regeneration. "It is necessary to be reborn out of the virginity of which Christ was born." And: "We must attain to the virginal essence wherein is God's only dwelling, and so come into the presence of God." And indeed it is in the aspect of guide on the way to the mysterious, virginal, and joyous chambers of Divinity that Sophia becomes man's dearest companion and hope. She speaks to us of the wonders of God in sweet feminine terms, and all our vision, our idealism, our Christ-spirit, yearns toward her. She is herself purity, rest, and harmony. She leads us to the Source — this incomparable Maiden from Paradise.

When Jacob Boehme died he left, toward the future spread of his ideas and inspiration, a great pile of manuscripts. One book from his pen had been put into print. The others had been circulated by means of laboriously inscribed copies among a few devoted and believing friends. Little groups of these followers were to be discovered in the cities and towns of Saxony, Lusatia, Silesia, and Moravia. Some of them attempted to found Boehmian congregations or societies. But the times were desperate for so many, and the manuscripts and printed books so costly, that all hope of founding an original sect in eastern Europe faded.

Doubtless some of the devotees were only intellectually interested. More were fanatics without ability to organize or instruct. One of the believers who sincerely tried to advance the fame and inspiration of Jacob Boehme was a son of the Pastor Richter who had so shamelessly persecuted the Illuminate. In no fewer than eight books the younger Richter paid tribute to the "shoe-patcher" who had been hounded out of Goerlitz as a devil's disciple and heretic.

Johann Georg Gichtel, who was born fourteen years after Boehme's death, was the most successful of the evangelical-minded followers. Driven from Germany — for neither established Church was of a mind to sit by idly while Boehmians got a foothold — Gichtel gathered a group of fellow-spirits around him in Holland. He and the Angel Brotherhood actually put into practice a religion of self-denial, contemplation, and illumination, a sort of Quakerism with emphasis on withdrawal and ascetic living. It was they who succeeded in having Boehme's writings, which Gichtel described unreservedly as a gift from God, printed in German.

A contemporary of Gichtel, the founder of Pietism, Philip Jacob Spener, aided in spreading the fame of the mystic in Germany. Remaining within the Lutheran Church, he effected reforms toward toleration, personal devotion, and stress upon regeneration that would have pleased Boehme; and his followers, particularly Count von Zinzendorf, implanted even more of the Illuminate's creed of holy living, redemption, and quietest devotion in the doctrine of the Moravian Church, founded in 1727 — whence an influence spread over Germany, England, and America. Spener himself after years of study abandoned as impossible the effort to arrange Boehme's thoughts logically, in easily apprehensible order. One Quirinus Kuhlmann was less moderate and less fortunate. After a stormy career as advocate of Boehme's ideas, in opposition to established governments and the established churches, he was burned alive in Moscow in 1689.

A Hollander began before these others the work of preserving Jacob Boehme's writings systematically in printed books. By chance Abraham Willemsoon van Beyerland came upon a Boehmian treatise in script, and thereafter he made a life work of seeking out as many as might be recovered of the "books" and printing editions of them. Thus it was at Amsterdam, beginning in 1634 and ending in 1675, that the complete *œuvre*, excepting one treatise never recovered, was set in type and made widely available.

In Germany, although Boehme's religious influence was dispersed into many channels, becoming effective in several churches rather than one of his own, later philosophers accorded him historic importance as the first notable figure in the German philosophical line. Schopenhauer, himself directly influenced, spoke of Schelling as a vendor at second hand of Boehme's thoughts. Hegel, less indebted because an enemy of mysticism, strangely found in Boehme's writings some of the outlines for his rational universe.

The German poets who drew upon the cobbler-mystic were even more notable than the philosophers. At the height of the romantic movement Tieck, grudgingly giving time to a book of Boehme's, found himself overwhelmed; and Friedrich Schlegel named Boehme prince of the mystic writers. The poet Novalis frankly avowed himself a disciple, and he could think of no better way to honour the great Goethe than to call him "the Boehme of Weimar."

The honour done to the memory of the cobbler-illuminate by internationally famous men was so great that even in Goerlitz the traditional picture of him as blasphemer and heretic faded. In 1875, three hundred years after his birth, a commemorative statue was unveiled in a public square and provoked no disorder. At the tercentenary of his death, in 1924, the City Fathers issued medals and sponsored commemorative books.

In England and therefore in America the influence of Jacob Boehme was more immediate and more direct. The Quakers, establishing a religion in which contemplation and inner illumination are central, went to the very heart of Boehmian doctrine. George Fox, born in the year of the Lusatian mystic's death, was educated in a time when England was seething with nonconformist ideas, when the "Behmenists" were but one active mystic sect among many. Practically all of Boehme's books had been translated into English by 1660 and had been accorded an importance among spiritual leaders, scientists, and laymen not then achieved on the Continent. One of Fox's friends, Durand Hotham, wrote a life of Boehme, and the whole atmosphere of dissent in England was coloured by "Behmenistic" thought.

Hotham believed that Boehme transcended all Greek philosophers, that whatever "Pythagoras spake by authority or Socrates debated or Aristotle affirmed, yea, whatever divine Plato prophesied or Plotinus proved," all this is in Boehme's writings — "or a far higher and profounder philosophy." He advocated that the calendar of saints be amended so that the truly saintly "Teutonicus" might be placed high in it. He spoke rather slightingly of some "who have termed themselves saints" — "What shift God may make of them in heaven, I know not (He can do much)" — and of "those who claim also to hold the bunch of keys to the bigger Heaven." He decided that it might be fairest to "begin a new roll of Civil Saints" with Jacob Boehme in first place.

Without discounting Fox's originality or detracting from the credit due him for founding the Quaker Church, it is possible to agree with Henry More, who spoke of Boehme soon after 1660 as "the Apostle of the Quakers." Boehme's mystic ideas had influenced also those other sects that fed into the Quaker movement, not only the Seekers but also the Platonists and, later and less directly, the Philadelphians. Eventually the societies that took the name "Behmenist" were widely attacked by leaders of the Friends. And it may well be that the Quakers had understood the heart of the message of the Illuminate of Goerlitz better than the avowed Behmenists had.

In America, New Jersey and Pennsylvania became "Quaker colonies" when George Fox and William Penn introduced the Friends' unique type of religious community and communion among the settlers. In Pennsylvania, especially in its capital city named for brotherly love, the experiment of establishing a government upon Quaker-Christian principles, which is to say substantially Boehmian principles, was tried. It failed only after achieving one of the most heartening records of fraternal progress in recent history.

Along with the Quakers in Pennsylvania were groups of Pietists and other immigrants even closer to the source of Boehmian mysticism, pacifism, and fraternalism. German congregations, especially those of the Moravian faith, persecuted at home, had emigrated to the land in which William Penn pledged freedom of worship. These pilgrims not only imported the books of Boehme but printed American versions of his lesser writings. Discipleship of a more intellectual sort was to be discovered in the nineteenth century in New England. There the writings of Boehme deeply affected the Transcendentalists. Emerson counted the shoemaker-mystic's books a valuable part of his library. He had the Sparrow and the Law translations, as well as an abridgment entitled *Theosophick Philosophy Unfolded*. In England the poet Milton echoed Boehme's descriptions and characters in *Paradise Lost;* and William Blake as poet and as painter was stirred to expression of mystic ideas traceable to the Illuminate.

"The outward personage of the man," wrote Durand Hotham in a biography of Jacob Boehme, published in 1654, "was not such as was amiable among the children of men." Every extant description adds to the impression of a person physically insignificant and indifferently formed. Abraham von Frankenberg, probably the only one of the biographers who actually knew Boehme, saw clearly that the outward flesh was little touched by the spiritual fire and grandeur within. He pointed up the truth that physical handicaps and drab, even sordid surroundings have little relationship to illumination of the spirit and the emission of spiritual light. Frankenberg found Boehme himself unwilling, on the plane of common meeting, to seem other than a homely, artless man. "Do not mistake me for an angel," he wrote. ". . . I am surely the fullest of all men of infirmity and error." He asked that the reader accept his texts as the writings of an inconsiderable child, whose only importance lay in the adeptness with which he transmitted the words of God.

"The outward form of Jacob's body," says Frankenberg, "was almost of no personage; he was lean and plain, and small of stature, with a forehead very much inbowed, high temples, somewhat hawk-nosed; his eyes were grey, toward azure, and lighted up like the windows of Solomon's temple; he had a thin beard, and a small, low voice, but an amiable, pleasing speech; he was modest in his behaviour, humble in his conversation, and meek in heart."

Immediately from the description of so ill-favoured an exterior

Frankenberg leaps to a statement about "his spirit, highly illumined of God, far beyond nature's invention." And he goes on to speak of "his writings out of Divine Light."

Light! That is the key. Jacob Boehme's first book was of the Aurora — of the coming of a morning light, a spiritual dawn. All his life he stayed by the primary metaphor of enlightenment, of illumination. As the sun is the light of the world, he said, so God is the light of the soul. Christ is the sun in the consciousness of the reborn man, dispersing darkness, illuminating the place of divine rest. And he sums up the tragedy of Lucifer thus: "His light went out."

When Jacob Boehme comes into the presence of God, he experiences divinity as a sweet radiant glow through all his being. On the way to that consummation he has known the Christ-light as beacon and guide. And his cherished companion, the Virgin Sophia, has been to him the mirror of the resplendence of God and is herself termed "love light." He tells us that when we postpone our day of repentance and rebirth we "conceal, defile and violate the light." Very simply he avers that any one of us may come out of the darkness of worldly living by tending the flame of the divine that has been kindled in each human being, that yearns back toward home in God, toward a Paradise that is a glowing, luminous realm.

Curiously, what has seemed to so many men dim and mysterious and shadowed, what has been called occult and obscure, is discovered in the report of Jacob Boehme to be clear, lucent, radiant. Above all else he lights the "way" for other men. "My whole work on earth," he once wrote, "is nothing else but an instruction how man may create a Kingdom of Light within himself."

His own lustre will grow, for he is one whose example of living by revelation, by direct illumination from God, will increasingly find followers as the darkness of materialism and self-indulgence is — as we all know it must be — dispelled.

Let Jacob himself, however, have the last word to the reader. "But open your eyes," he said, "and the world is full of God."

IX. Brother Lawrence, the Lay Monk Who Attained Unclouded Vision

The most amazing fact about Christianity, for those who do not credit to God the major operations of history, is the expansion of the faith throughout Europe in the centuries just after the mortal Jesus lived and died in Palestine. The second most amazing fact might well be considered the decline of the faith during the seventeenth and eighteenth centuries.

Of the decline in the belief in God, Francis Bacon observed in 1612 that "A little philosophy inclineth man's mind to atheism, but depth in philosophy bringeth men's minds about to religion." Bacon was writing at the beginning of the age of "Enlightenment." He could hardly have foreseen the extent of the flourishing about of the torch of learning among common men during the three centuries following, the spread of the light of superficial education, and the negligent lapse of millions of minds, if not into the full dark of atheism, then into the twilight of scepticism.

In a companion essay Bacon commented upon unity in religion, reprehending "quarrels and divisions." Therein he touched upon a second cause for the growing ranks of "atheists and profane persons," saying that "nothing doth so much keep men out of the church, and drive men out of the church, as breach of unity."

Already in his time for a hundred years the breach in the Christian structure had been growing. At last it was apparent that the idea of a united Christendom in the Western world had collapsed. Britain afforded the spectacle of Englishmen established in a State church half-catholic, half-Protestant, and of Scotsmen defiant in Presbyterianism, while the Irish remained defiantly Roman Catholic. Nor was the actual bloodshed past in the quarrels between "divisions." Charles I would soon be at war with the Covenanters of Scotland; in the end he was to be beheaded by the Puritans, being suspected of leanings toward Romanism.

Even so, England had been spared something of the horrors of Christian division. It was in Germany that religious bitterness, disorder, and civil war were at their worst. The almost continuous century-long strife was leading on to the Thirty Years' War of

1618–48, a struggle that was to leave Germany (and bordering Bohemia) spent and prostrate for three generations — even while it ended the Catholic Emperor's dreams of patching together the Holy Roman Empire. In France, officially Catholic still, but with grave divisions between Rome and the Gallican church order, there were to be persecutions, though no repetitions of the riots of 1572, when tens of thousands of Huguenots had been massacred because they professed the Protestant faith.

In all these areas of terror and devastation the cause of religion was at the heart of the matter. The breach within Christianity, the epochal schism of "reformed" churches from the Catholic body, was central. But almost equally the strife resulted from the separation of civil and religious power. Civil rulers still claimed divine right and (like Louis XIV of France) insisted upon political supremacy in their own branches of the Church; while Church officials, popes and cardinals, became shrewd and sometimes unscrupulous politicians in the effort to perpetuate a Roman hierarchy superior to the kings. How many people were burned at the stake, sent to the galleys, or variously murdered, will never be known; from France some millions of Huguenots escaped to join the Protestants of Germany and Holland, the emigrants to America, or the Reformists of Switzerland (whose foremost leader, Calvin, had been an exiled Frenchman). The sixteenth century had been the century of Reformation and Counter-Reformation, and of disorder enough. The seventeenth was, however, pre-eminently the century of Christian wars, of a continent finally and bloodily divided, of the Mother Church broken and henceforth powerless alone to affect the Western world for peace or war.

In such a century it would be a miracle if the faith of millions of men were not chilled; a miracle if a Saint Augustine or an Eckhart or a Saint Francis appeared. Nevertheless, in the midst of so much disorder and strife and devastation isolated mystics attained to tranquillity and peace, and seers looked beyond the temporal confusion and affirmed God's order and constructive goodness. There were even movements and organizations inspired by the idea of living only for the will of God.

Such an organization or association, in France, was the Port Royal group, sprung miraculously out of the corruption of the times, disciplined into a model of Christian holiness by the inspired Mère Angélique, finding its mystic spokesman in Blaise Pascal. All the followers of the Christian way at Port Royal Monastery were — mistakenly, we must believe — opposed by the higher officials of the Catholic Church. The mystic attainment to God, the ascetic self-discipline, the consecration of all action to holy service, were combined with the sincerest group effort of the era to restore integrity and respect to the Church of which they were a part; yet they were condemned as a group, individually persecuted, and finally expelled from their monastery. It is a mark of the temper of the time that the buildings of these religious ones, who had saints among them, were burned and the bones of their dead exhumed and defiled.

Nevertheless, out of France of the seventeenth century it is not Pascal or Mère Angélique or the saintly Bishop Fénelon who best proves the ability of the individual human soul, despite discordant, even chaotic events, to walk serene in the presence of God. Rather it is their obscure contemporary, the holy-minded lay monk Brother Lawrence, who places his feet on the "way" and turns neither to right nor to left because of the controversies and breaches of his day.

Pascal's is incomparably the more noted name. Blaise Pascal is celebrated as scientist, inventor, writer. In his early years he was accepted among the great thinkers of France, and his "defection" to religion evoked a storm. After three centuries he is read, quoted, commended, and condemned. Brother Lawrence was, in all senses, a humble servant during his lifetime. He was author of a very few conversations, maxims, and letters — so few that together they hardly make up a pamphlet. To-day one may speak of him to librarians and professors, even possibly to a churchman, and strike no spark of recognition. Yet in a curious way his conversations have survived, have been frequently reprinted, and have been internationally circulated in just the way of the *Tao Teh Ching* or Boehme's *The Way of Christ*. Like Lao-Tse, Lawrence was single-minded, selfless, unworldly; like Jacob Boehme he was sweet of character, saintly, and wholly devoted to God. The "book" of his sayings, happily entitled *The Practice of the Presence of God*, reveals at its best Christian simplicity and mystic warmth.

As historians view it, Blaise Pascal was much more truly a product of the age. He advanced the study of mathematics, particularly in the field of conic sections and the differential calculus, invented the basic calculating machine at the age of nineteen, demonstrated the practical uses of the barometer, founded the science of the theory of probability (not for its modern uses in calculating insurance premiums and the like, but to help a professional gambler), and, one among many practical business schemes, established a public omnibus system for Paris. This was the man, well born, recognized as a genius in the fields of scholarship, research, and business enterprise, admired and fêted, who renounced worldly activities and spent his later years in contemplation, in writing religio-philosophical essays, and in charitable works. He underwent conversion at the age of thirty-one, on a night late in 1654, and thereafter wore sewn in his coat the scrawled record of the experience. He went to the refuge at Port Royal in 1655.

Except for his renunciation and retreat, Pascal's history fails to parallel at any point that of Brother Lawrence, who was humbly born, whose activities during the 1640's and '50's are completely lost to record as pertaining to one known only as a soldier, then a man-servant; who, converted as a youth, spent years and years searching for his path of devotion, entering the Paris monastery of the Carmelites probably in 1666.

If upon the far from happy Pascal and upon all those who found asylum at Port Royal there was the impress of the strife of the times, if their self-imposed silence was often broken and their teaching often deranged through controversy and intervention, there was this other one, at the Carmelite Monastery in their own Paris, who was enabled to carry on as a blessed solitary, attaining to God's presence, habitually "schooling the soul only to find joy in that Companionship."

In early life Brother Lawrence had gone to the wars against the Protestants, and had been lamed; and he had known the mystic's usual period of search, doubt, and minor defeat between the day of his first illumination and his finding of peace. But practically all that we know of his life and his writings is from that period after he entered the monastery, when, as he put it, "I abode lovingly united to God's will — and that was my whole business."

No other revelation of the mystic's oneness of mind, of his single, humble, and intimate devotion, of his living in the felt presence of God, is so simple, so touching. One feels, in reading, the utter sincerity, candour, and generosity of Brother Lawrence. His soul is alight with the sense of the divine in all things; if he is asked to serve in mean and small ways, he acts as happily as in large matters, because to him it is all God's work; his consciousness of Divine presence is no less when he is employed in the kitchen than when he is before the altar. In his character one feels a native sweetness, an unconscious sunniness. It is a quality not uncommon among the mystics and seers, but hardly universal; for Augustine, as we know, could be dark-minded and thunderous, and Blake frequently let himself be irritated or tortured into testiness and protest. Brother Lawrence was rather of that gentle, all-loving group of mystics that is most beautifully exemplified in Jesus, in the Buddha Gautama, and in Lao-Tse. He is akin, by the same token, to Saint Francis and to the gentle Fra Angelico.

His sweetness is not on the sentimental side; for the man had dignity and reserve. He constantly, moreover, translated inspiration and benevolence into deed. He praises consistently the life of adoration and consecration that holds the soul in communion with God; but the greater space is given to the idea that adoration and consecration can be expressed in, and implicit in, work.

He speaks often of "the simplicity and purity of the heart," and he would have devotion come from these, rather than from mental decision. The "way" is to be found "by heart and by love rather than by thought." God flashes the light of faith and the sunshine of His presence into the heart of the humble, and "If you would go forward in the spiritual life, you will do better to leave aside the laboured conclusions and the subtle reasonings of the unguided intellect." In this he is, of course, the perfect intuitive.

Though unlettered, perhaps educated not at all beyond reading and writing, Brother Lawrence achieved spiritual education. When a M. Beaufort, a Grand Vicar, had been directed by Cardinal de Noailles to put into writing some of the spoken ideas of Brother Lawrence, he betrayed his own surprise that one so lowly born and fixed in menial work should exhibit so much sound wisdom and exceptional powers of expression.

"What he spoke," M. Beaufort records, "was very simple, but to the point and filled with sense. Beyond a somewhat rough exterior, one encountered singular sagacity, a range of mind beyond that of the usual humble lay brother, and a penetration far surpassing my expectation. A man of affairs, capable of giving wise and safe counsel. . . ."

M. Beaufort got down a good deal of the matter of the *Conversations* in Brother Lawrence's own terse, economical sentences; and there are extant sixteen letters, all but three written to a *religieuse* of the Carmelite order, exhibiting in general the same directness, brevity, and pithiness. From this sort of writing, not intended for publication, he turned at times to efforts to "commit his thoughts to paper." Usually he tore up the compositions when he saw how inferior they were to the inspiration he had had from God, "lacking God's greatness and goodness"; but the manuscript of a small sheaf of *Maxims* was found among his letters after his death.

With men as with God he exhibited a rare balance of humility and confidence, of self-giving and independence. On the one hand he insisted upon total renunciation and surrender to God's will as prerequisites to entering the Presence. "We must distrust our own strength utterly, and commit ourselves to His safe-keeping." But he walked with a high head, maintaining a dignity in submission. To God he said in effect: "I have put myself in your keeping, it is Your business I am about, and so everything will be all right." He refused to enter into incessant prayer on his knees, or to carry asceticism over into mortification; for he had schooled his soul until his every intention and every action, "his common business," was addressed to God. M. Beaufort, writing of his character, sums up his virtues in these words:

> This good Brother kept steadfastly in the Way of Faith, which never changes. He was constant in studying the duties of that station in which God had put him, striving only to excel in discharging those duties. . . . Spiritual contemplation and prayer render him humble, gentle and patient, but also strong as iron to resist temptation, so that not the desire for pleasure nor fear of suffering has hold upon him. The joy of contemplation transcends all other pleasures, for thus he dwells with God, in love. The vision he has seen, in the unchanging light of faith, pales the attractions offered by the world. . . . He longs for nought else because he has his heart's desire, so far as one in this life can. There is for him no fear, since no thing on earth can injure him, no thing turn his heart from the love of God. He need solicit no boon of peace, for his soul lives in tranquillity, conscious of a world designed for good. The perturbance of anger he knows not. . . .

Indeed, Brother Lawrence made clear to Beaufort that the only occurrence that could bring sorrow to him would be loss of the sense of God's presence; but, he added, he apprehended no danger in that direction, being aware of God's complete goodness.

"Brother Lawrence" was the name in religion of Nicolas Herman, a native of Lorraine. Nothing is known of his early life except that he was born in the year 1611 and that he came of a family in humble circumstances. As a youth he fought in the wars waged in the name of the Holy Roman Emperor against the Protestant sovereigns of the North. It is supposed that he served in the army of Wallenstein in Germany. He was severely wounded and after his recovery he walked always with a pronounced limp.

About the time of his army service, when he was eighteen years of age, he experienced his first revelation from God. The disclosure was no more than comes to millions of men each year: the sight, in midwinter, of a dormant, leafless tree. As he gazed upon the trunk and branches, in which all life was asleep, he experienced a vision of the tree as it would be in summer, garbed in countless thousands of leaves, with flowers, then fruit; and therein he felt a sense of God's power and bountifulness that never left him. Reflecting upon the leafless tree and God's way with it, he was then and there, he said, "converted." He felt that he had been specially favoured in the revelation, and he thenceforward struggled to loosen the ties of the world upon him.

A great many years later Brother Lawrence told M. Beaufort that he had then been kindled with such a love for God that he was not sure it had been increased through four decades of living since. The leafless tree, he said, "first flashed in upon my soul the *fact* of God." From the hour of conceiving that "notion and esteem" of God's power, wisdom, and goodness, "he had no other care but to reject scrupulously every other thought, in order that he might perform each act for the love of God."

In the years following his conversion he worked as a manservant. For a time he was a footman in the establishment in Paris of one M. Fieubert, described as "the treasurer." It is not unreasonable to believe that Nicholas Herman felt a certain fitness in dedicating himself to a servant's work. He said of himself, as regards his employment as footman, that "he was a great awkward fellow who broke everything." While Beaufort confirms this to the extent of speaking of "a rather rough exterior," he speaks of his keen perception and his goodness of heart. "Despite his goodness," he adds, "Brother Lawrence was intensely human. His manner was open and frank so that one immediately had confidence in him."

How long he was in domestic service, how well he discharged his tasks as servitor, whether he succeeded in co-ordinating his primary business of serving God with his duty to M. Fieubert: all this is unreported. The first datable event of his mature life is his entry into the Carmelite Monastery in 1666.* In that year he was fifty-five years old.

As there is the open question whether his life had been normally blameless or sinful before the incident of the leafless tree, so also there is only the faintest light upon his way of living in the years between his conversion and his decision to join the Carmelite order. In late life he often spoke of his "sins" in that early period; but it is not unusual for saints to magnify the transgressions of their unregenerate days. The very purity and holiness of their existence after illumination and dedication makes earlier lapses — be they only pleasure taken in pleasant food or trim clothing or innocent personal love — seem evil and monstrous. The age was one of violence and of easy morals on the one hand, but of strict, almost fanatic rectitude on the other. Brother Lawrence, so far as anyone knows, may have truly sinned, or he may have known only those commoner pleasures of the senses in the pursuit of which the average man spends his life.

Mentally and spiritually he experienced a long period of doubt and tribulation. There were four years of trial when, despite his dedication of his life to God, despite his effort to do every act as if it were in His service, he seemed to fail miserably, even succumbing to worldly temptation. Though he had "resolved to make the love of God the end of all his actions," he had trouble in schooling his mind to reject desires and vacillation. He was plagued, moreover, by fear for his soul's salvation.

> I was for a long time certain in my mind that I would be damned, so certain that all the people in the universe could not have persuaded me from it. But I found it possible to

---

* Even this date may be in error. Most editors of Brother Lawrence's book have accepted it, doubtless because M. Beaufort mentions August 3, 1666, as the day of his first meeting with the author of the *Conversations*. But in a letter written by Brother Lawrence in 1689 he states categorically that he has "lived in religion" — that is, within the monastic order — "for more than forty years." This would suggest that he became a lay brother between 1645 and 1649. The matter is relatively unimportant, since it is his spiritual life that interests the world.

reason in this way: "I have entered the spiritual life purely for the love of God, attempting to act only in accordance with His will; whatever shall become of me, whether I may be lost or saved, I will continue always in the path of God's love and will. At least there will be this to my credit, that until death I had put my every effort into loving and serving Him." The torture of mind persisted for four years, and my suffering was acute, but at last I saw that it all came about through lack of faith. Seeing that, I was freed and entered into a life of continual joy.

Even so it took him additional years to perfect himself in a discipline that would habitually bring his mind about to God in any uncertainty or crisis. "Having given myself wholly to God, I renounced for love of Him everything that was not He. I began to live as if there were no one save God and me in the world. . . . As often as I could I placed myself as a worshipper before Him, fixing my mind upon His holy presence, recalling it when I found it wandering from Him. This proved to be an exercise frequently painful, yet I persisted through all difficulties. . . ."

Again he said that he had been very sensible of his own faults, but that he had refused to be too discouraged about them. He confessed them freely to God, "but did not plead with Him to forgive them." After confessing, "he went back in peace to his accustomed love and adoration." He came to the conclusion that "It is idle thoughts that spoil all — the mischief begins there." In summary of the struggle of that period and the coming of a second illumination, Brother Lawrence much later wrote to one of his superiors in the brotherhood:

For the first ten years my suffering continued. The feeling that my devotion was not so intense as I wished it to be, the recollection of my past sinfulness, and the great difference between my worthiness and the bounty God poured upon me: all this caused me suffering. Often I fell, and presently rose again. . . . When I had accustomed myself to the thought that I should end my days in this struggle — though it did not diminish my trust or my faith — I was changed suddenly. My soul, escaping tiresome discussions, attained a profound inward peace, as if it had come to its own home and place of rest. Since that day I walk before God simply, humbly, in faith, and lovingly, nor do I do anything that may be apart from His design.

He came early to the conclusion that mortification of the flesh was not a necessary part of the struggle to reach God. One's love of holiness would lead to a certain degree of asceticism; but "all the possible kinds of mortification cannot abate one sin." As for the wickedness one saw all about, he was not at all surprised or alarmed by it. "When he was told of the sins of the wicked in this world, he found nothing to wonder at; on the contrary he marvelled that there were not more transgressions, considering all the corruptions into which desire can lead a man. . . . And since God permitted evils, for reasons which must be useful in His design and providence, and could remedy the mischief done by such evil, he would pray for the sinners; then, putting the matter aside, resume his peaceful service. . . ."

At some time during this period, we are told, Nicolas Herman decided to take himself out of the world of men to become a solitary, after the pattern of the hermits of the East. But he failed to find peace in a life of complete withdrawal. Or perhaps he could not reconcile physical idleness (and the begging that accompanies it) with the Christian injunctions to work and serve.

He told M. Beaufort that when he entered the order of the Barefooted Carmelite Friars, whether in 1666 or earlier, "he had desired to be received into the monastery, believing that he would be disciplined for his awkwardness and his faults, sacrificing his worldly life and its pleasures"; but he found that he need not have troubled his mind in that matter, for he experienced nothing but satisfaction in the monastic life. He did, however, relax and draw away from the routine practised by the brothers. Before long he had substituted his own way of devotion — the Practice of the Presence of God, which forms the substance of the published *Conversations* — for that of the other friars. There are misunderstandings over this, perhaps jealousy and complaints, and one of the most cogent and beautiful of Brother Lawrence's letters is a justification to a Superior of his conduct and his manner of adoration:

> As a novice, in the beginning, I spent those hours appointed for personal prayer in an effort to turn all my thoughts toward God. I then laboured to convince myself of the divine

existence, though less by means of reason and the deductions of the intellect than by the appeal of faith to the heart. Thus I came shortly to the sense of God's nearness, and to the knowledge that I wanted only to abide in His presence.

Prayers in the ordinary sense ceased to have meaning for him. Finally:

"I have quitted all forms of devotion and all set prayers except those to which my position as a friar obliges me. Now my only business is to remain in the holy presence of God . . . or better, in an habitual, silent and hidden conversation of my soul with God, a thing of joy and inward rapture not to be exposed before others. . . ."

In spite of his independence and self-reliance, once he had settled into monastic existence he continued to rely upon the purging and tonic effect of confession. "I have no need," he said, "of a director to advise me, for I am schooled to love and follow God in all things. But I much need a confessor to absolve me."

His superiors in the monastery assigned him to the kitchen for his daily periods of labour. He was irked at first, but, calling upon his faith, he philosophically acquiesced. Before long he was able to lift himself into the Presence among his stoves and pans as readily as out of doors in nature or in the silence of the oratory. Of this matter he said:

With me, my time of labour is no longer different from the time of prayer. Amid the clatter and confusion of my kitchen, when numerous people are calling various orders, I hold to God, and with as great tranquillity as though I were on my knees at the blessed sacrament. . . . In His service I turn the cake that is on the pan before me. When that service is done I kneel down in submission before Him, for it is through His grace that I have work to do. Then I rise happier than a king. For me it is enough that I but pick up a straw from the ground for the love of Him.

Brother Lawrence once wrote down an account of his way of approach to his menial work, recording the sort of prayer he improvised as he laboured: "At the beginning of my work I would speak to God with a child's faith: 'O God, Thou art with me and it is Thy will that these outward tasks are given me to do; therefore I ask Thee, assist me, and through it all let me continue in Thy presence. Be with me in this my endeavour, accept the labour of my hands, fill my heart as always.' . . . Having completed the task, I would ask how I had performed my duty. If well, I gave thanks to Him. If badly, I asked His forgiveness."

For fifteen years he had laboured in the monastery kitchen, when M. Beaufort talked with him, and although he had at first undertaken the work with aversion (as he admitted) he had found it all easy. He added that he was pleased to continue in the post; though he would as easily quit it for another if the occasion arose, since he knew where to turn for unfailing assistance.

Although he had thought of himself as unfitted for business, he had been sent into Auvergne to purchase the brothers' supply of wine, and had come off splendidly. During a second trip into Burgundy he encountered difficulties due to his lameness, the many casks on the boat acting as obstructions over which he could only roll. But again the business transaction went off to everyone's satisfaction, for which the grateful brother gave credit to his ever-present Guide. He said that upon occasions of this sort he would speak to God, saying: "It is Your business I am about." Then, without worry or uneasiness, he closed the business, always to the brothers' advantage.

Of Brother Lawrence's friendships with men or women there is little record left to us. Of the sixteen extant letters the greater part seem to have been written, in reverent affection, to a Mother Superior of the Carmelite order.* From these same letters one infers a familiar companionship with books; for in the opening lines of a letter written in 1685 he speaks of receiving two books from a Sister, and of sending to the Reverend Mother "one of those books treating of the Presence of God — a subject containing the whole of the spiritual life." It is tempting to speculate upon the identity of this work, so near in its content to his own personal

---

* Brother Lawrence would find many fellow-spirits among the holy women of his own order. The Reformed Carmelite establishments constituted one of the glories of Catholicism in France at this troubled time. The inspired Mme Acarie had stamped the movement with both the holiness and the mystic sanctity of Santa Teresa. It was Mme Acarie's daughter, Mother Marguerite, who said that "the spiritual life is constituted in a very few words and a very great inclination to God."

philosophy and "way" that he felt impelled to recommend it to a fellow-pilgrim on the mystic road. The least dangerous hazard would be that he transmitted to his friend a copy of Santa Teresa's *The Castle of the Soul* or one of the treatises upon Divine Love by Saint John of the Cross.

Brother Lawrence's dependence upon the Bible as the foundation and centre of all reading is what one would expect of a Christian student in his time. Beaufort records that "in his reading Brother Lawrence esteemed the Holy Gospel far above all other works, because he found his faith nourished incomparably in the simple and pure words of Jesus Christ." Certainly he would know Saint Augustine and Thomas Aquinas and his own spiritual ancestor, Thomas à Kempis. The profound treatises of Ruysbroeck would be open to him, and the books of Saint Bonaventura; but the *Treatise on the Love of God* by Saint Francis de Sales would be nearer to him in both time and spirit — though possibly suspect to Rome because the Quietists made much of it.

Brother Lawrence, however, was as contemptuous of books as of anything in the world — they seemed so mean and inadequate when he meditated upon the splendour of God's direct speaking to his soul. "I have not found my manner of life in books," he avers. Only the Creator, he noted, can be the teacher of Truth in its fullness and grandeur. Labour as man will intellectually, he can only produce a theory of life or religion; but in a single flash God illumines with knowledge and understanding the heart of the humble. Neither art nor science can help very much.

All that I have heard from other men, all that I have learned from reading, all that my mind could reason out, as touching on God, cannot content me, seems low, indifferent and heavy as compared to the unspeakable riches He spreads forth. Faith alone reveals Him, reveals to me what He is. Faith illumines Him, instantly. Oh, the schools! . . . We toil and exercise our intellects, in reason and science, forgetting that we achieve only a reflection, a copy, when we might turn our eyes to the Incomparable Original.

Brother Lawrence's personal and original way of finding God aroused misunderstanding among the brothers, who were content with a set devotional routine. Evidently they reported what seemed to them his inactivity in prayer, his self-reliance and "delusion." He was "questioned and obliged to open himself." His answers, as reported by M. Beaufort, seem to have satisfied fully the Superior who interrogated him. He explained how he had trained himself to live continuously in God's presence and how he accomplished his work of scullion or cook without losing communion with Him. And, adds Beaufort, "as Brother Lawrence found so much advantage in walking in the presence of God, he earnestly recommended this way of life to other men. No argument, however, was as effective as the example of his own devotion, for his countenance reflected a winning inward sweetness and calm."

He took philosophically such disappointments as came to him. "One day," writes Beaufort, "I told him right out that a project of great consequence to him, which was close to his heart, and for which he had long laboured, would not be carried out, because the Superiors had decided against it. He replied simply, 'We cannot but believe that they have reasons for rejecting it. Our duty is to assent and say no more about it.'"

One can see Brother Lawrence, with his curious balance of humility and independence, of deference and dignity, before the Superior or the Bishop, answering questions about his faith, obviously and unmistakably a man of rare saintliness and piety, yet equally clearly a maker of his own rules of devotion, a silent accuser of much that the Church exacted from its members. It is to the credit of his superiors and of the Carmelite Order that the inquisitors sufficiently recognized his sincerity and his holiness to pass over the charges and leave him in peace.*

The letter of justification addressed by Brother Lawrence to "My Reverend Father" constitutes one of the boldest and most reasonable defences of "companionship with God" written by the humble friar. He reviews his career, tells how he came to distrust

* At this time Mme Guyon was under punishment for her mystic beliefs, and copies of her books were being burned throughout France. She was to die in an enforced retirement after serving terms in the Bastille and other prisons. Her defender, Archbishop Fénelon, was within the decade to be silenced and disgraced. The Spanish seer Molinos, who influenced both Mme Guyon and Fénelon as he was later to inspire the Quakers and numerous Quietist pilgrims to America, was already a prisoner of the Inquisition, destined to die tragically in a Roman dungeon. The charges of the Church against Mme Guyon and Fénelon were exactly those that could be brought against Brother Lawrence: advocacy of a way of knowing God's will not sanctioned by the Church; too great reliance upon the soul's individual communion with the Holy Spirit; consequent neglect of the routines and forms provided by the Church.

the more usual "methods" of attaining spirituality, and how he substituted his own way of worship.

During the first year, during the times of devotions, I gave my thoughts to death, judgement, heaven and hell, and my own sins. The rest of the day, even in my hours of labour, I gave myself over to the consciousness of God, schooling myself to feel His presence as with me or in me. This continued for some years, until the time of prayer also came to be a time of His presence, a matter of joy and elation to me. . . . Since that time I walk before God in all simplicity, in utter trust, humbly and lovingly, and I attempt to do nothing and to think nothing that might be outside His design for me. . . . I feel assured beyond any question that my soul has been with God these thirty years.

The letter is remarkable for its undercurrent of self-reliance and certainty; there is expressed an implicit confidence that the Father Superior will fully understand. He pleads for no forgiveness; instead he notes that "with a sensible regret" he has confessed his sins to God, has asked forgiveness there, and has surrendered himself to the Divine will; and that "The King, merciful and full of beneficence, far from punishing me, has held me in love, summoned me to His table, afforded me the key to His riches. . . ."

Rarely outspoken in criticism, Brother Lawrence nevertheless by indirection suggested that churches and churchmen would profit by substituting for set devotional forms — "trivial devotions," he called them — the simple practice of the presence of God. The mystic way, he said, should be the very spirit of the Church, for it alone is sufficient to perfect the human soul. "Many fail in Christian progress because they stick fast in penances and set exercises." Even prayers may obscure God rather than bring the prayer close to Him. "Even in the time of set devotion when our voice is lifted in prayer, we should school ourselves to pause, if only a moment, to adore God in the centre of our being, to be conscious of His presence, to keep a hidden tryst. . . . I am certain that it is a common fault, even among men of religion, to overlook this pausing in their affairs to adore God in the depths of their souls, to enjoy renewal through the peace of knowing Him."

Later in his life the reputation of Brother Lawrence for saintliness and sagacity so increased, despite his low station, that men of note outside the monastery began to seek him out. One of these was M. de Chalons, who had been Cardinal de Noailles. It was at his direction that M. Beaufort, his Grand Vicar, held conversations with the friar, attempting to set down a report verbatim of his thoughts.

When the *Conversations* were first published in 1692, a year after the death of Brother Lawrence, M. Beaufort showed his surprise that there had grown up a public interest in the saintly friar. His Preface begins: "During the past year death has taken many members of the Order of Barefoot Carmelites, brothers leaving rare memories of lives spent in virtue; but Providence, I can see, desires that men's eyes should be drawn chiefly, among them, to Brother Lawrence."

Fénelon, Archbishop of Cambrai — who was, as Vaughan says, "dignified and gentle, graceful as a courtier, and spotless as a saint, the most pure, the most persuasive, the most accomplished of religious guides" — Fénelon was among the pilgrims who came to the Carmelite monastery in Paris to talk with Brother Lawrence. He found the friar dangerously ill, for this was very near the end of his life.

Only one question asked by the celebrated divine has been recorded. "If God permitted a choice, would he desire to live longer in order to increase in holiness, or to be received at once into Heaven?" The reply came instantly: That choice lay with God, he said. "For his part, he but waited in peace until God should show him His will." On his deathbed, Saint Francis de Sales had answered a similar question with memorable words: "If it is His will, I will it too"; and one cannot but believe that Fénelon knew of the instance. Nor is it improbable that Friar Lawrence was conversant with Saint Francis' life too. The Savoyard Saint, the holy Bishop of Cambrai, and the lay monk of the Barefoot Carmelites: they were as much of a single spirit as any group of mystics in history. As Brother Lawrence was the simplest man of the three, it is he who has put the thought of the trust in God in the simplest words and the most direct statement: "I am in God's hands, He will do as He wishes with me. . . . If I can no longer serve Him here, He will take me elsewhere to serve."

Outside the monastery walls, France was still the scene of disorders and minor civil wars. The cause of the Huguenots had declined until it had become hopeless. The extirpation of the Protestant bands was being accomplished with ferocity and cruelty. The Catholic reaction had served to purge the Church of its worst evils, and seldom had so many admirable men and women of blameless lives, combining great scholarship with saintliness, served Catholicism as in seventeenth-century France. The extremists had nevertheless gained control of the machinery of the Church, and after the revocation of the Edict of Nantes they joined with a State avid to stamp out heresy. Even a brother immured in a monastery could not escape the impact of the disorders.

A soldier wounded in the wars was the occasion of a letter written by Brother Lawrence to a friend in 1688. In it he applies his philosophy to the life at arms. Expressing admiration for the young man, but excusing him for having in him "something of the world and an excess of youthfulness," he hopes that suffering will serve to deepen his character. "It should impel him to place his trust in the One who accompanies him everywhere. Let his mind turn to Him constantly, especially when danger is greatest. To lift up the heart a little is enough. A remembrance of God, a moment of spiritual worship, upon a march, when a sword is drawn, is a prayer acceptable to God. This reliance, far from lessening a soldier's courage, will fortify it even in the extremities of danger. Let him be with God the most he can."

After he was seventy-eight years old, in the final two years of his life, Brother Lawrence suffered from physical ailments, and he was in correspondence with one of the Mothers, sixteen years his junior, who likewise suffered. In his letters he gently rebukes her for not finding comfort in God, for not giving thanks for whatever circumstances He may place her in; though there is a note of kindly concern over her pains. "Since in His mercy He grants us yet a little interval, let us turn to Him in earnest. . . . With an open heart renounce all that is not His. . . . You will tell me that I am always saying this one thing. Truly yes; for it is the best way I know."

Again he writes: "Lift up your heart to Him, the least little thought of Him will be acceptable. You need not cry very loud. He is nearer to us than we know." And: "They are happy who suffer with Him. . . . Worldly men find sickness a thing of pain, grief and distress, not a favour from God. Those who can think of it as His doing, a part of His mercy, and a means for our salvation, they find in it sweetness and consolation. . . . Often God is nearer to us in sickness than in health. Rely, then, upon no other physician."

As the last months pass by, his mind becomes even clearer as regards faith, and he feels himself more completely in the Presence. "In a little while I must go to Him. What comfort I find in faith! By so much is my sight cleared that I can say, no more do I believe, but I *see*." He adds that "to suffer something for His sake" is a foretaste of Paradise; while the most delicious pleasures would be a Hell if he could relish them out of God's presence. As a whole, life still found him jubilant. "I do not know how God will use me. But I am continuously happy. All the world knows distress and pain; but I, undeserving, am filled with joy so great I can hardly contain it."

On February sixth he wrote his last letter, to "My good Mother," repeating his expressions of thanks for "the bitter with the sweet, if it be from His hand," echoing his central thought: "He is present within us; seek Him not elsewhere." On the second day following he took to his bed for the last time. The final Sacraments of the Church were given him. To a Brother who was watching at the bedside, who asked him what was in his mind, he answered: "I am doing that which I shall be doing through eternity, thanking God, praising God, adoring God, offering him the love that fills my heart."

On February 12, 1691, painlessly and in peace, Brother Lawrence slipped away from his body, to enter into a new phase of a long-established companionship.

Brother Lawrence's meagre writings, together with his reported "conversations," Beaufort entitled, perhaps over-fully but with admirable fitness to content, *The Practice of the Presence of God the Best Rule for a Holy Life*. No other arranged title could summarize so well the philosophy or belief of Brother Lawrence.

What he had accomplished that is rare if not unique was to simplify a philosophy of life until it is contained in hardly more than a single injunction; and to his genius as spiritual philosopher he had added the gift of almost miraculously apt and simple speech.

There is no one quotation that can be lifted out of the text and offered as the key passage. Rather he repeated his central injunction tirelessly, in the conversations, in the letters, in the *Maxims.* Often he leads into his subject with some such simple introduction as this:

> Men invent means and methods of coming at God's love, they learn rules and set up devices to remind them of that love, and it seems like a world of trouble to bring oneself into the consciousness of God's presence. Yet it might be so simple. Is it not quicker and easier just to do our common business wholly for the love of Him? Thus we put His consecration upon all we lay our hands to, at the same time establishing communion of our hearts with His, summoning the sense of His abiding presence. There is need of neither art nor science. We go, as we are, to Him, unpretending, single hearted.

The Maxims, perhaps, contain the most concise exposition of the central thought:

> In the spiritual life, that devotion which is the most characteristic and the most fundamental is the practice of the presence of God. It is the schooling of the soul to find its joy in Divine Companionship: the holding of humble and affectionate converse with Him, ceaselessly. . . . We should so rule our actions that they be little acts of tribute to God — but let them not be studied, only natural, welling up from the simplicity and purity of our hearts. . . . It would seem almost beyond belief if one could foresee the nature of the converse the soul holds with God at these times. He seems to delight so in this communion that, upon the soul utterly committed to Him, He bestows joys beyond number. As if He would not have it turn again to earthly things, He provides for the spirit abundantly. Thus it gains a Divine nourishment, an unbounded felicity, of a sort beyond human thought or conception; and this with no more effort on its part than simple assent.

Occasionally Brother Lawrence admits the difficulties of coming unhindered to a consciousness of the Divine presence; and once, in the *Maxims,* he lists (quite as if he had been studying the Oriental mystics) three ascending stages of passive and conscious union. He concludes: "The third, or *actual* union of the soul with God is *the perfect union.* . . . In this actual union the soul is intensely alive. Its operations are quicker than fire; it is more resplendent than the unclouded sun. . . . It is a state of the soul — if only words will serve me! — simple but profound, filling us with exaltation yet with serenity, with a divine love that is both ardent and humble. The soul is lifted to a summit where it cannot but adore Him, embracing Him with a tenderness that is inexpressible."

In some of the *Maxims* especially (and these are the only writings direct from Brother Lawrence's hand except the presumably extempore letters) there are passages descriptive of mystic union in the higher and purer sense, as approaching ecstatic abandonment of self in God's Being. But throughout the writings there is reiteration of the importance of that other phase of his "way," the methodical schooling of one's self "to establish a continual consciousness of God's presence by constantly conversing with Him."

It is in one of his letters to the Mother Superior that he describes most fully the joys he has had from this continuous practice. Speaking of himself in the third person, explaining the experiences as those of "a member of our society," he adds: "If sometimes in the press of outward affairs he seems to lose a little of the sense of Divine presence, or absents himself, God presently makes felt in his soul a summons, and he answers and converses. . . . Then he feels that the love of God, satisfied with a few words, reposes again in his soul, at the core and depth of his being. The experience so assures him that God is always at the centre of his soul that doubt of Him is inconceivable. You may judge what content and tranquil joy are his, when this treasure is continual."

Brother Lawrence leaves no doubt that there were for him also occasional sudden illuminations, experiences of rapture and ecstasy. His conversion at eighteen had come about through a vision so clear, so startling, so vivid that his life and his desires were instantly changed. One remembers, too, his account of his years of doubt and mental disquiet, and his "sudden illumination" and emergence into a realm of profound peace. Of his later transports he speaks quite freely; though he tries to guard against the literal minds and the uninitiated who would misunderstand or misconstrue in worldly terms or mock. "You must know," he writes in the

Maxims, "that the benevolent and caressing light of God's countenance kindles insensibly within the soul, which ardently embraces it, a Divine and consuming flame of love, so rapturous that one puts curbs upon the outward expression of it." He speaks also of "joys and raptures of the spirit, not only inwardly but outwardly felt, so that one is at pains to moderate them and keep their appearance from others."

He tried, sometimes in direct description, sometimes by metaphor, to transmit the *feeling* of mystic union, to express that which is so nearly inexpressible. "In measure as our faith, through this spiritual practice, opens our understanding of the hidden mysteries of God, we recognize in Him a beauty beyond compare, surpassing boundlessly all that is known on earth, and all that is conceivable of the holiest men and angels. Already we relish, we taste, this beauty, this bliss. . . . Our desire is set aflame in the consuming fire of His love, which burns to ashes all that pertains not to Him. No longer can the soul be content away from Him, for this union creates within the heart a consecrated passion, a holy desire, an ardent fire. . . ." Then more calmly he adds: "Thus the soul comes to a knowledge of Him, abundant, profound; it attains to an unclouded vision."

Once at least Brother Lawrence reverses the meaning of the terms "real" and "visionary" in a way common among the seers of the Orient, and often baffling to the "practical" thinkers of the West. "The world that is with us," he says, "has lost reality. Those things that my outward eye reports flow by as fantasies and dreams. That which I discern with the eye of the soul alone exists and is the object of my desire."

One of the images developed to suggest the infinite sweetness of the mystic experience is that of being taken to the Bosom of God. Almost as if he were thinking of God as Mother as well as Father, Brother Lawrence writes: "He converses and delights Himself with me continually, in a thousand and a thousand ways, and treats me as if I were His favourite one. . . . From Him I experience more of sweetness and delight than is felt by a babe at its mother's breast. In default of words, I would choose to speak of this state as attainment to the Bosom of God, for its inexpressible sweetness."

In the end the reader may ask, "What is the message Brother Lawrence has left?" Nowhere does he pause to say, "This is my message." He lived his own philosophy, and he did not think of himself as a leader of opinion or as a man with a mission. His one known interlocutor, Beaufort, said that "All his life he took pains not to come into the stare of men."

When Beaufort was sent by Cardinal de Noailles to elicit and record Brother Lawrence's thoughts, the monk showed some suspicion. Beaufort reports that Brother Lawrence warned him that in such an enterprise complete surrender and dedication to God were necessary. "One must watch attentively, he told me, for human passions which may taint spiritual projects as well as others; that God alone could inform one of the purity or unworthiness of one's design. If my desire was sincerely to serve God, I might come to him for the conversations as often as I wished; if not, I should visit him no more."

Perhaps the main outline of the way followed by the saintly friar, and commended to us, can be put down fairly thus:

Surrender of all to God; love of Him; living continuously in consciousness of His presence; occasional ascent to the blissful experience of soul-union with Him. Brother Lawrence pauses to make other points: the need for renunciation, for rigid self-discipline (but without mortification), for charity, for humility; and the superiority of the way of the heart over the way of the intellect — but these are secondary. Central, fundamental, outstanding in each group of writings or reported sayings is the importance of the habit of quickening the soul into the sense of the Divine presence. Brother Lawrence is certain that common men can school themselves in this devotion, if only they care enough as against their care for the pleasures of the world. "Everyone," he says, "is capable of such affectionate converse with God."

As near to an epitome of his writings — and therefore as near to a "message" — as any sequence in the texts left to us is one that may be pieced together from a letter written to a Mother Superior in 1685 and from Conversation IV (with only a little rearrangement, and much abridgment) as follows:

> Were I a preacher I would above all else preach the practice of the presence of God. Were I a teacher I would direct all the world to that spiritual practice, so fundamental do I consider it, and so simple to attain.
>
> There is not in the whole world a manner of life more delightful and rewarding. . . . For the right practice of it, one

must empty the heart of all else, to permit God sole possession; and as He must possess it wholly, so He must be free to dispose of everything as He pleases, and to employ the heart as He wills, through our utter surrender. . . .

The main thing is that we make one unreserved renunciation of everything which we are sensible does not lead to God. Then we need only recognize Him intimately present with us; address our intention to Him over and over; entreat His assistance in knowing His will in all things doubtful, and in knowing how best to discharge those duties which plainly He requires of us — offering every act to Him before we undertake it, and rendering thanks for His aid when we have done.

The most effective way of going to God is that of doing one's common business without any purpose of pleasing men but purely for love of Him.

One deludes oneself in believing that the times of prayer should be considered different from other times. Action has its responsibility to God as prayer has its.

We ought, then, once for all place our unreserved trust in God, completely surrendering ourselves to Him, assured that He will not fail us.

The steps in what may be called the personal path of the pilgrim are described, at one point in the *Maxims,* more categorically:

The first is *a great purity of life,* a guarding oneself watchfully lest one do, say or think a thing displeasing to God, and, in failure, an immediate and sincere repentance thereof, and humility in entreating forgiveness.

The second is *a positive faithfulness in the practice of His presence,* a keeping of the soul's eyes upon God, calmly, trustfully, humbly, with a love that leaves no room for care or doubt.

The third is *a looking to God when taking up any common task,* a prayer to Him at the beginning, a reliance during discharge of the task, and thanks when it is completed. . . .

The fourth is *an offering up of words of love,* in silence and hiddenly: as, "My Lord, I am wholly Thine," and "O God, make my heart even as Thine," or such other words of loving trust as may rise out of occasion. Be heedful that the mind wander not back to the world; let it be steadfast to God.

If this way to the practice of the presence of God is not without difficulties at first, yet faithfully followed it leads to the most marvellous effects upon the soul, drawing down God's grace abundantly; insensibly the soul becomes illumined and contains the constant vision of God loving and loved. This is the holiest, most real and most inspiring of all manner of devotion.

France in the seventeenth century was committing itself more assiduously than any other nation to the faith that man can advance without a faith. Midway between the sceptic Montaigne and the brilliantly atheistic Voltaire there stands, in the range of French letters and philosophy, the different and lonely figure of Pascal, mystically converted and trying vainly to stem the tide of irreligion and scepticism.

Beside him, almost unnoticed in his own time, there is this other constructive mystic, too humble to challenge the attention of historians or philosophers, yet author of a booklet strangely circulated in countless editions and treasured through more than two centuries by pilgrims seeking the way back to faith and divine companionship. Saintly but unsainted, uneducated but a natural teacher of men, Brother Lawrence seems destined to influence increasing numbers of spiritual seekers, as the Age of Enlightenment — which may better be termed the Age of Exclusively Intellectual Enlightenment — is ended in the wars bred by sceptic individualism and enlightened thinking.

Brother Lawrence had one idea that he restated again and again — an idea that might prove to be the key to regeneration of millions of individual men. Just before he died he once more put that "single saying" in memorably simple words: "If in this life we would know the serene peace of Paradise, we must school ourselves in familiar, humble and loving converse with God."

X. A MYSTIC IN THE AGE OF ENLIGHTENED SCEPTICISM: WILLIAM BLAKE

OF ALL the latter-day saints, William Blake was the one least limited by mortal nature. He believed that the soul is, during its time-conditioned life on earth, a wanderer from the realm of pure spirit, from an Eden that exists eternally in a Golden Age. Throughout life he kept contact with the Golden Age, with Eternal Childhood, through visions. Death, he said, is no more than the soul's passage from one room to another.

"Just before he died," reported one who was there, "his countenance became fair, his eyes brightened, and he burst into singing of the things he saw in Heaven." Thus William Blake brought down to a dingy room in crowded London, for the thousandth time, some of the light of Paradise. It was apparent not only to his faithful wife, who accepted his visions as reality, but to a neighbour woman who had come in to help Mrs. Blake. Observing how the cramped, dark room had lighted up, she said simply, "I have been at the death of a saint."

London had not been aware of this saint among her children. For six years he and his wife Catherine had lived in two dim rooms off the Strand. The one in which he died had served as kitchen, bedroom, and workshop. From it he was carried to an unmarked grave. Beyond a handful of personal friends not a dozen people in England counted him among the immortals. His poems had been forgotten. His drawings and paintings still carried the critics' labels, "incomprehensible" and "rude." Few knew the sweetness of character of the man and his integrity. Fewer still realized the connection between his lovable character and the visions he saw; between the man and the pictures he painted and the poems he wrote, as by dictation from Paradise.

A saint William Blake was, though a saint with a difference, a saint curiously enamoured of the Devil; a loving, forgiving saint in living, but flawed with some very human frailties. Londoners, in so far as they knew of this obscure artist, noted the frailties and heeded the critics who spoke of "madness." The churchmen had no knowledge of him or his visions; his only "connection" was with an obscure Swedenborgian group. Even his friends distrusted his admiration for the Devil, missing the point that his Satan is still very much a Prince of the Angels, the original Archangel, demonstrating a laudable imagination and freedom and courage, as against the dull routine and timidity associated with orthodoxy.

"The man of conventional faith," said Blake, the too-slavish "reasoning man," has forfeited imagination and daring. Having lost Satanic imagination, he dog-trots a dull round of sense-existence. The law, the Church, the school, help to fix him in unimaginative conformity. There are even artists who press art down into imitation and simulation. It is necessary to overthrow Reason as god, to restore Heaven and Hell in one undivided Eden, to recover thus Infinity.

Let the world of rationalization and of the senses, he pleaded, be consumed in the fires of imagination. Free the eternal soul; let it taste again Infinity. In a key line he writes that "If the doors of perception were cleansed, everything would appear to man as it is, infinite."

As poet and designer William Blake spent fifty years trying to cleanse those doors, to open the gateways of his fellow-men's perceptions to the glories of the infinite. By right, he believed, every man is clairvoyant, partaking of Imagination, divine by intuition. To perceive more and more of Heaven in everything is the most important task in the world. The artist's business is to transcend earth-things and reveal the glories beyond.

His lapses from loving-kindness were due to high-temperedness and exhausted patience. When he and his beloved Catherine had not enough to eat or when copper plates or gravers or colours were lacking on his work table, he was led into petulance and even, on rare occasions, into complaint. In a journal he wrote down bits of doggerel embodying these complaints and lampooning those who had crossed him. The squibs in verse, not intended for publication, were somehow saved (though many major poetical works and also paintings have been lost or destroyed); and unsympathetic biographers have magnified their importance.

Against the few evidences of petulance and anger, it is possible to pose the truth that the man was honest, loyal, unselfish, and generous. He was temperate in habit and punctilious in money matters. Although he considered law, especially moral law, unimportant, he was faithful to and utterly considerate of one woman all his life. (Catherine's only known complaint, made after thirty-four years of companionship, was that her husband was so much away in Paradise.) However resentful he might have felt toward those who criticized or attacked him or stole his ideas, he eventually forgave them and felt pity for their meanness. Forgiveness, he said, is the very heart of Christian living.

Beyond the tamer virtues of the man are the unexplainable attributes — his burning imagination, his exalted spirit. From childhood he was a visionary in the truest sense. When he regarded common things he saw through to God's hand within, to essences and eternal forms and dæmons. When he looked beyond things he saw that other world that encloses this — saw Eden, or God, or Eternity.

Blake had a seer's awareness together with an artist's passion and genius for revelation. He recorded his images and visions with dramatic power and profound feeling, in both words and graphic design. He wrote, madly they will tell you, revealing mysteries, majesties, sublimities, and sometimes tendernesses beyond the capacities of other men. With his pen and brush and graver he traced designs in which a second beauty is given up, in which forms are created that not only illustrate the theme but have an æsthetic vitality of their own, disclosing the healing rhythms and profound order beyond nature.

As artist he practised second sight and brought down Imagination and Divinity to man. As poet he summed up the mystic's aspiration:

> *To see a World in a Grain of Sand*
> *And a Heaven in a Wild Flower,*
> *Hold Infinity in the palm of your hand*
> *And Eternity in an hour.*

Saints were out of fashion at the time of Blake's appearance upon the earth — perhaps never more so in the history of mankind. The expansion of civilization during the seventeenth and eighteenth centuries had been physical and commercial. The economic and political march of events arrived at a crisis as Blake came to manhood, in the American and French Revolutions. Materialism had swept over the Western world in a mighty engulfing wave. Europe had entered the final phase of civilization tested by physical, not spiritual, gain. Already the black waters of industrialism were over Britain. From the spread of the factory system Blake gained a new metaphor, speaking of England's "dark Satanic mills," extending the figure to cover all that is blighting and gloomy and constricting.

The contemners of official religion had won their fight in most of the countries of Europe. The churches were in general disestablished. The ruling power had gone over to kings and parliaments. The institution of religion was fighting for survival.

The Church of England had made an expedient compromise and had escaped some of the bitterness and disorder incidental to the Reformation. The mould of Catholicism had been retained, under English control, at first royal, then parliamentarian. But in Blake's time the high English ecclesiastics, through complacency and political expediency, had depressed the Church to the lowest point touched in its history. Nowhere had class and privilege brought more sinister inequalities. The lower clergy were hardly less poor than the wretched workers whom they were powerless to help. Services were notoriously neglected or perfunctory. The outstanding religious mystic of the era was in every sense outside the Church.

William Blake was hardly less outside the recognized cultural development of his time. Not only a stranger to the universities but wholly uneducated, he distrusted the entire intellectual establishment, especially as it was paraded in the works of the eighteenth-century "Classic" poets, the artificial and chit-chat essayists, and the materialistic philosophers. He revolted from the Augustan standards, from all that was intellectual, scholarly, and refined, vaulting into spontaneity and lyric passion a quarter-century before the revolution that is known as Romantic. But, along with saints, poets who sang from the heart were out of fashion. Nor was Blake the graphic artist less obscured and neglected, in the furore over the showy and popular painting of the Reynolds-Gainsborough school.

The times, in short, were unspiritual, realistic, with power in the hands of the shrewd, the cunning, and the rewards accruing to the conformist and the "practical" artist.

Even in an era so unpromising, there are born mystics and seers, other-worldly and self-effacing. In France Brother Lawrence, humblest of the major mystics, had died just before the end of the seventeenth century. There had appeared no other whose light shines quite so clearly. But almost contemporary with Blake there is Louis Claude de Saint-Martin, born in 1743, a learned, sincere student of the spiritual life, a writer of mystical treatises and preacher in several countries. When he was middle-aged he was introduced to the works of Jacob Boehme, and he became translator and apostle of that "incomparable" one.

Stripped of his properties during the Revolutionary disorders because he was an aristocrat, he was thereafter a wanderer, and he signed certain of his books "by the Unknown Philosopher." Although he had been involved in the tide of pseudo-scientific occultism then sweeping over Europe, he attained to illumination, preached effectively the importance of living in consciousness of God, and wrote suggestively of a world of men united in a spiritual theocracy.

In Germany there were innumerable devotees of occultism and numerous societies of sincere quietists, pietists, and other followers of the inner light, but there were no outstanding seers and prophets. Whole congregations of God-seeking German people were escaping to England and America.

From Sweden came the one international figure, the one seer who, in eighteenth-century Europe, had visions, claimed divine enlightenment, and challenged world attention: Emanuel Swedenborg. His books are rather revelations of a new Christianity than mystical treatises. Indeed they are so much in the nature of realistic reports, replete with physical detail, so lacking alike in divine imagination and mystic illumination, that the seers in the line from Plotinus and Boehme, though grateful to the Swedish visionary for, so to speak, shaking up Christendom, parted from him upon mature test of his "system."

Swedenborg's theosophy was conceived on the plane of intellect and fancy, falling short of that warmth and surrender proceeding from ecstatic divine union. Much of his doctrine was calculated to evoke a purer Christianity in living than was common among either Church members or dissenters; especially his insistency upon Christ as crucial, his urging to regeneration, and his certainty of an influx from God into each man's soul. William Blake, who as a youth may have seen Swedenborg as an old man in the streets of London, was fired by the brilliance of the seer's picturing, but he wrote critically later, when he had found missing the elements of creative imagination and mystical warmth.

England of the eighteenth century had known two native mystics whose names live on in the annals of spiritual progress; though both curiously compromised, obscuring those ends of participation and experience that seem primary to most initiates. The one, William Law, who lived until 1761, became in middle life an apostle of Jacob Boehme. Although he spent years celebrating the Illuminate of Goerlitz, and thus influenced his friends and his readers towards the most human and the most restrained type of mysticism, he lacked, in both his life and his spiritual writings, the note of joyous self-surrender.

The other, John Wesley, also brought up firmly in the Church of England, was struck forcibly in the early years of his ministry by the faith of the Moravians. It was during the prosecution of his mission to America, in 1735, that he first remarked their personal holiness, their Christ-centred consciousness, and their resultant tranquil-mindedness. But it was only after his return to London that he encountered a Moravian minister who was able to lead him, in 1738, to illumination. He noted the event afterward as his conversion, his entry into "real" Christianity. So avid was he for fullest "living in Christ," for divine light, that he, a minister of the Church of England, entered the Moravian Church. He made a pilgrimage to Herrnhut, in Saxony, where the Moravian Brethren were combining elements of their earlier primitive Christian faith with Lutheran doctrines as modified by Count von Zinzendorf, who came fresh from devotion to Spener and Boehme.

Wesley drank deep of the fountain of quietist spirituality. But his burning zeal to evangelize, his restless-mindedness, and doubtless the ties to his old companions of the Methodist circle at Oxford recalled him from the mystic path. The rest of his history is familiar: his loyalty to the Church of England, its disapproval and passive discipline, the extraordinary success of his and Whitefield's open-air services, and eventually the birth of a sect, the Methodist, destined to become far more numerous than the Anglican confession. Blake could hardly have escaped a certain influence of the Wesleyan "dissenters."

Although professional philosophers had proved themselves dry and intellectual and calculating, concerned hardly at all with the highest experiences possible to the human being, discounting the testimony of the soul, certain ones among them had recently opened a vista into regions where a mystic philosophy might seem valid. A generation before Blake, Bishop Berkeley had spoken out against materialism and the reality of matter, finding import instead in the realm of mind and imagination. Before Berkeley there had been Benedictus Spinoza, the Jewish philosopher of Holland, who had glorified intuition as the highest mode of knowledge. He had also arrived at a sort of divine pantheism (as against pantheism with the emphasis on nature) and a doctrine of the immanence of God in all things, which were part way along the road to mysticism. But Spinoza remains a justifier of the mystics and not one of them, though as persecuted and harried as any.

William Blake is described by a friend, in 1826, as advocating "a strange compound of Christianity, Spinozism, and Platonism." The Christianity is there in a primitive purity. Platonism is implicitly there (though Blake associated Plato with Greek or classic ideas and art and criticized him as would any bemused romantic). The Spinozism is, however, only apparent and fortuitous. Blake, like Spinoza, was a rebel against orthodoxy, a profoundly religious man, and a misunderstood major prophet. But Spinoza was an intellectual, opening the way to the validity of mystical experience so far as argument can. William Blake *was* the mystic, imagining, visioning, walking with God. That both men met abuse, neglect, and dishonour in their lifetimes was a sign of the disability of prophets and seers, whether intellectual or intuitive, from 1650 to 1850.

Blake, as mystic, is both artist and message-bearer. His poems and his designs are as direct, as crystal clear, as immediately joyous as any known to man. They bind profundity to simplicity, they escape all need of gloss or explication. He is the most genuine and most illuminating mystic in the British line, and not to be matched in any country in the Western world during his century.

On November 28, 1757, a son was born to the hosier, James Blake, and his wife Catherine, in a house in Broad Street, Golden Square, London. The child was named William. There had been two sons born of the marriage before William, only one surviving, and there were to be two sons and a daughter afterward. He was thus one of a considerable family, in respectable but plain circumstances, living in rooms over the hosiery shop. The city streets were his playground; but greater London was a cluster of towns and villages, and at no more cost than a few minutes' walk the child could come to those parks and fields that are pictured so clearly and beautifully in the many lines descriptive of "England's green and pleasant Land."

William Blake as a babe was christened — "one in a batch of

six"—orthodoxly; a circumstance unexplained, since his father was a dissenter, an attendant at Moravian services, and a convert to Swedenborg's ideas. There is evidence that William Blake seldom again entered any Anglican Church, after being carried to St. James's in Piccadilly for his baptism. The Moravians, on the other hand, might have fathered many of his ideas, about the unfathomableness of God, the accessibility and humanity of Christ, the secondary nature of law, and the meaning of the Last Judgement; all this beyond the basic resting upon enlightenment and "divine operation." The Moravian hymns, moreover — no other sect worships so largely in song — probably influenced the early poetic writing of Blake.

Swedenborg more directly fired the imagination of the visionary child. The books of the seer certainly would be about the house of the hosier Blake. The Lord appearing as a Sun, the golden palaces of Heaven, and the arched caverns of Hell, as described in the treatise *Concerning Heaven and Its Wonders, and Concerning Hell; From Things Heard and Seen*, would be exciting and electric to a visionary boy who himself at the age of four had seen God's face at the window.

As he matured, learning to value creative imagination above all else, he was destined to detect too much of physical reporting in Swedenborg's records and too little of supersensuous understanding. But to a lad of eight or ten these "visions," approved by his parents, these ramblings in heavens and hells, amid angels and spirits, with talk of the Golden Age and the New Jerusalem, and of "correspondences" between nature and Heaven, and of the implantation of God in man — all this served to fire William Blake, and to provide symbols and names that were with him for sixty years after.

When he came to passages identifying the year 1757, his own birth-year, as marking the end of the first Christian era upon earth and the advent of a second Church and Kingdom, he could not but visualize himself as a knight of the faith if not a chosen prophet and builder of the New Jerusalem. He was already poet and artist. Already he saw heaven and earth as created, and to be redeemed, by Poetic Imagination, and he visioned the earthly Christendom as a City of Art.

The child seer was fortunate in his parents. The father, who believed implicitly the flesh-and-blood Swedenborg's reports of conversations with the angels, was inclined to doubt at first the authenticity of his own child's visions of Heavenly Beings. But the mother intervened for William when, at eight, he returned home radiant at seeing a tree simply full of bright-winged angels at Peckham Rye by Dulwich Hill. Thereafter James Blake held his peace. Better still, the elder Blake determined to shield so clairvoyant and sensitive a child from the rigours and the mind-closing effects of common schooling. The boy learned reading and writing, along with religion, at home. He never received any other systematic education. He was free to read, to imagine, to wander in solitude, loving nature, detecting God's hand in tree and flower, in rock and field. The one binding, inspiring source of his ideas was the Bible. Beside Swedenborg's books there were the more imaginative ones of Jacob Boehme; but perhaps William's favourite among prophets was Ezekiel.

Solitary as he was by nature, and introspective, William Blake yet had normal companionship. One of his three brothers, Robert, was especially dear to him.

When it became clear that William would be happy only in a vocation within the arts, he was entered as a student at Pars' Drawing School in the Strand, where he underwent the usual course of copying outlines and shading from casts of antique sculptures. His father supplemented this schooling by purchasing plaster models of hand and head and foot and the usual little casts of imitations of "The Gladiator" and the "Venus de Medici" so that drawing could go on at home. He also indulged a passion the boy had formed for prints, supplying small sums to be spent at print-shops or at auctions.

A contemporary tells how Langford the auctioneer came to admire and favour the boy; getting his bid, he would "knock down a cheap lot with friendly precipitation." The twelve-year-old thus trudged home often carrying the prize of an original Dürer, or engravings after Michelangelo (his highest idol) or Raphael. So early, his preference began to tend away from all that fashionable London counted significant. It was Dürer whose clean line most influenced his own engraving method. It was Michelangelo who ever came first to his mind when he wanted to name a creative genius in contrast to the stylish illustrators of the Reynolds school or to the baroque followers of Rubens.

The youth apparently looked to making a living as a painter, and in 1771, when he was thirteen, the question arose of the change from a student's estate to apprenticeship. "A painter of eminence was proposed" (in the words of Tatham, Blake's first biographer) "and necessary applications were made; but from the huge premium required, he requested, with his characteristic generosity, that his father would not on any account spend so much money on him, as he thought it would be an injustice to his brothers and sister. He therefore himself proposed engraving as being less expensive, and sufficiently eligible."

Here again a hitch occurred, because the youth took exception to the face of his proposed master when he and his father were interviewed. The engraver, the famous W. W. Ryland, was at the very top of the profession; he was Engraver to the King. The clear-seeing William looked deeper. "Father," he said once they were outside, "I do not like the man's face; it looks as if he will live to be hanged." James Blake let his son make the decision. They never went back to complete the arrangement. Ryland, caught in crime, was hanged twelve years later.

At a cost of fifty pounds William was apprenticed for a seven-year term to James Basire, a friendly, considerate engraver with a shop in Great Queen Street. Basire was no genius, nor was he specially fitted to guide the hand of a divinely endowed artist; but he was, fortunately, a bit old-fashioned, holding to the severe line-engraving of his predecessors as against the modish softening and especially the stippling processes of Ryland, Bartolozzi, and others. In William Blake he found an ideal helper, clean and accurate in drawing and soon accomplished in use of the clean-burrowing burin.

In those days the processes of photography and photo-engraving were unknown, and whatever reproductions were made of famous (or other) works of art were printed from hand-engraved copper plates. In the second half of the eighteenth century the vogue for large reproductions had grown, and engravings might measure two, even three feet in dimension. The amount of hand labour that went into cutting the lines on the copper was enormous. The master engraver, his assistants, and his apprentices might all be called upon to put forward the work on a single plate over a period of months. What part William Blake played in engraving Basire's prints in the years 1771–3 cannot be known.

His second assignment, to work that occupied him from 1773 (when he was sixteen) to 1778, must be accounted a capital influence upon his tastes and development. Basire, having orders for engravings of antique monuments — and desiring to get William

WHEN THE MORNING STARS SANG TOGETHER. WATER-COLOR PAINTING BY WILLIAM BLAKE, FROM THE *JOB* SERIES. PIERPONT MORGAN LIBRARY, NEW YORK.

out of the shop, where two new and "cunning" apprentices were playing upon him — sent him to Westminster Abbey to sketch the historic tombs there, and subsequently to churches elsewhere in London and in the environs. For years the imaginative youth spent his daylight hours among Gothic tombs and other mediæval relics. What dreams, what visions, then passed before his inner eye, what sharpening of his imaging faculties came about in those days of solitude, contemplation, and devoted designing, one can only infer from the reading of the mystic and prophetic books of later years. The impressionable boy who had chosen Michelangelo and Dürer as exemplars now as a youth recognized the Gothic art of England as similarly profound, spiritual, and exciting. Thereafter he was never to mistake the expiring neo-classicism or the prettified baroque of contemporary Britain for imaginative art. For all time he was turned away from the Greek current; his themes will be not of Attica and the Isles, of Parnassus and Olympia, but of Jerusalem and the Christian Heaven, of Atlantis and Albion and America; especially of a timeless realm of the spirit, of the unspoiled Eden of the Golden Age, of Eternity and Paradise.

William Blake in those years was saturated in a spiritual atmosphere and confirmed as a solitary, independent creator. The conditions of his work, the solitude, the hushed religious activities about him, the silent association with monument after monument, brought alive his clairvoyant faculties. The visions he had known in childhood were continued. Christ and the Twelve Apostles appeared to him in a vision in the Abbey. From the subjects of his drawings he absorbed much of the symbolism and "colour" that went into his epic works later, and he established himself in a sort of design (basic to his paintings as well as his engravings) that is best described as monumentally large and majestic.

During the apprentice years he spent at least some of the winter months making engravings from the antiquarian drawings. Many of these, utilized as illustrations in books about the historic monuments of England published during the following decade, have been traced as the apprentice's work, though signed, of course, by Basire. The youth at the same time was sketching on every possible occasion; and at least one independent engraving, after a drawing (now lost) of Michelangelo's, survives with a "W. Blake" signature and the date 1773.

In a second field the boy was proving himself a prodigy. He was writing poetry with a clear sweet beauty hardly surpassed in the range of English literature. The sheaf of poems composed from his twelfth to his twentieth birthday contains some of the most felicitous lyric pieces in the language, and certainly it marked the emergence of the most spontaneous and original genius since Elizabethan times. There are those who count "To the Muses" the turning point from the poetry that had represented England for a century past to the lyricism and spontaneity that will usher in Shelley and Keats and Burns. In those stanzas to the Muses, beginning with the so simple lines:

> *Whether on Ida's shady brow,*
> *Or in the chambers of the East,*
> *The chambers of the sun, that now*
> *From ancient melody have ceased . . .*

and ending with the equally simple:

> *The languid strings do scarcely move!*
> *The sound is forced, the notes are few!*

he wrote the death-song of a period. In those lines, says Arthur Symons, "the Eighteenth Century dies to music."

A more characteristic loveliness lights up a "Song" said to have been composed by Blake at the age of fourteen. A certain sweetness of character, a childlike directness, and a genius for pictorial imagery are implicit in this ballad-like song, and its theme of a strangely lost liberty is not unconnected with the thought behind the prophetic books of twenty years later. It is the lyric beginning

> *How sweet I roamed from field to field*
> *And tasted all the summer's pride . . .*

If the youth's days were filled with designing and visioning, with reading and writing, he yet had time for an interest in the political topics of the day. Independent in all matters, a rebel in many, he sided with the American Colonists in their struggle for freedom, and against his Government and King. America was "withering" under the "devastating British rule" — though by the time he got to the writing of an epic poem entitled *America*, in

1793, his simple and direct ideas on the subject had become involved in a vast system of cosmic projection and universal contention. America is glorified because America is Revolt. Albion is castigated because Albion has permitted Urizen, the serpent Reason, to drive out the arts and inspiration and to put in chains the spiritual man. A host of Blake's symbolic figures, cosmic, theological, mythical, ride into the poem, in gorgeous imagery but to the obscuration of the simple and vehement sympathy of the poet for the Colonists in 1776.

It was in 1778 that William Blake came to his twenty-first birthday. He was still unknown as a poet. As an artist he was only graduating from his apprenticeship. He decided upon further studies and entered classes at the Royal Academy's Antique School. Already an accomplished draughtsman, he did his routine renderings well. Nevertheless he disagreed with his teachers and indiscreetly upheld the claims of Michelangelo against professorial praise of the fashionable courtly painters. Sir Joshua Reynolds suggested that he design with "less extravagance and more simplicity" — a cut that went deep.

Altogether his art schooling left him with a profound distrust of routine classes, professors, and the Royal Academy. To draw from the posed model, he said, can only lead to the smell of death. From then on he dispensed with models, whether antique statues or arranged natural figures. He said that "All forms are perfect in the Poet's mind, but these are not abstracted nor compounded from nature, but are from Imagination." Water-colour paintings began to come from his hand in profusion in the years 1778–81, fixing the mode in which his major works were to appear.

At this time Blake was still living with his father in the Golden Square district, which was then fashionable enough and was home to many a celebrity of the art world. Among near neighbours were Angelica Kauffman, Francesco Bartolozzi, Henri Fuseli ("foreigners" formed a sizable element in the top ranks of English artists still), and — from 1781 — John Flaxman. Blake, now twenty-three, might well consider himself a successful beginning artist, since he showed a water-colour at the Royal Academy Exhibition of 1780 and was receiving from publishers commissions to engrave illustrations, from designs by Thomas Stothard and others, in sufficient volume to constitute a "living." For some years, apparently, he wrote practically no poetry, a loss to the world not to be estimated. One engraving after his own design, dated 1780, is typically and powerfully Blakean: a radiant figure of an angel-man, lighting up the earth, symbolizing perhaps Morning, or the Day of Glory. It might have been conceived as a frontispiece for Boehme's *Aurora*.

Love had had its place in Blake's early poems, but the sentiment seems to have been reflective or imaginative, not born of experience. At twenty-three, handsome, athletic, and electrically alive, he began to be attracted; and at least one fair girl, harmlessly playful, kept company with him. But he, serious-minded, demanding not only fidelity but an exclusive loyalty, frightened her away. He was then and there, he insisted, "cured of jealousy" — but left heart-broken. While still suffering he met the daughter of a market gardener at Battersea and, telling her of his misfortune and disappointment, found her so charmingly sympathetic that he straightway transferred his devotion. Nor could he have hoped to find so perfect a mate had he spent years wearing out his heart-sickness. Catherine Boucher brought him — beyond that loveliness of outer being that means so much in an artist's wife — an understanding mind, utter loyalty, and all that is implied in the word helpmate. Catherine was illiterate (for female education was then hardly existent, except for the wealthy few), and a year later when they were married she signed the parish register with a cross.

It was William who asked for the year between troth and marriage, that he might save enough to set up housekeeping. Visionary and impulsive as he was, he still would not rashly expose Catherine to the hazards of an obscure poet-artist's life. He spent the interval consolidating his position as a commercial engraver.

On a Sunday in August 1782, at Saint Mary's Church in Battersea, the two were married: the genius Blake, twenty-four years old, fiery but tender, rapt but solicitous, and Catherine, twenty, outwardly lovely, inwardly pliant, and to be shaped by her husband into "my shadow of delight," as he phrased it a quarter-century later.

They set up their own establishment in rooms in the Leicester Square district of London. He kept at his engraving, producing mostly illustrations for books from other artists' designs. In leisure he went about the education of Catherine, methodically and with full regard to his own belief in the imaginative and artistic as against the rational faculties. She, intuitive and eager, learned to be as her husband would have her. As she acquired the rudimentary tools, reading and writing, so also she learned to draw and to colour and even to engrave, thus entering into his work-life as a partner after her household duties were done.

Catherine had her own sort of second sight, and during the nearly half a century of living with the seer she never once questioned the reality of his visions, and she granted absolutely the necessity to follow divine dictation. She entered with him into prayer and came at times to share his visions; at other times she was content, though summoned perhaps from sleep at night, to sit silent beside him while for hours he worked as poet or designer to record the glories of his second seeing.

Though he needed no model, yet out of his love for her, because her mortal being represented symbolically those elements of spiritual beauty which he visioned in the unseen world, he portrayed Catherine in many of his most moving paintings and prints, as Eve, as the stately wife of Job, as the Attendant Spirit in "Comus," as angel or queen or Madonna. She also appears as Enitharmon, who is to the poet Inspiration, Pity, Feminine Imagination, and sometimes Desire.

Their circle of friends was, beyond the two large families, that of the young artists, especially the illustrators and engravers. Through Flaxman, also recently married and a neighbour, Blake was introduced into one of those literary *salons* that so flourished at the century's end. At the highly decorated home of the Reverend and Mrs. Henry Mathews a score of secondary literary lights were accustomed to gather to discuss the arts and politics and to scintillate to the best of their ability. Into this atmosphere of combined pretence and genuine wit came Blake, the utterly unknown poet — though a promising designer, and a forceful, sometimes dogmatic talker. It did not take the Mathewses long to discover that they had snared a young lion, and that he could be fascinating and terrifying by turns. Encouraged to read some of his poems, he not only read but sang the words to tunes made up at the moment. The hearers, so one of them reported, listened "with profound silence," and he was allowed by "most" to possess "original and extraordinary merit." "His tunes," continues the same reporter, "were sometimes most singularly beautiful, and were noted down by musical professors."

So far were the members of the circle impressed that Flaxman (or perhaps Mrs. Mathews) was able to persuade Henry Mathews to bear half the cost of publishing Blake's poems, Flaxman contributing or securing the other half. The contents of *Poetical Sketches; by W. B.* were those pieces written from the author's twelfth to his twentieth year (there having been now some years of silence, while the author turned designer and engraver). The volume was small — only seventy-four pages — and ill-printed; and it was discredited from within by a preface from the Reverend sponsor's pen explaining that the poems are "the production of untutored youth" and expressing the hope that their "poetic originality" will carry them, despite "irregularities and defects."

The sponsors generously gave the edition to Blake to do with as he wished. But he had turned diffident and made no effort to circulate the copies or to put them into the hands of reviewers. Whether he foresaw that the poems would receive, in that time, no more than the sort of lame praise or patronizing apology written into the preface, or genuinely hated the bungling job of editing and printing, he set the edition aside and went about his engraving business. It is possible that he too recognized certain literary defects, and certainly about this time he began to write poetry again, slowly, producing those pieces which would appear in 1789 as *Songs of Innocence,* and establishing a higher standard of excellence.

Blake, or perhaps the Blakes, could not long frequent a *salon* where the atmosphere and talk were so different from that of their own simple way of life. Or perhaps it was that the habitués tired of a certain "unbending deportment" on the young poet-seer's part ("what his adherents are pleased to call his manly firmness of opinion," adds the gossipy reporter of the soirées, one John Thomas Smith). One can see the unyielding revolutionary, the outspoken critic of the Church, the scornful contemner of Reason, in the polite circle of conforming artists, of reasonable talents, in a clergyman's house, among pseudo-classic ornaments and knickknacks: the honest straight-cutting William Blake, with the wife who had no education and none of the artificial graces of mind that belong to the successful dilettante — the wife he idolized — and one needs none other than the simplest facts of temperament and aims to know that the visits could not last.*

---

* There was one regular visitor who must have recognized for what it was the second sight, the divine awareness, of young William Blake. A fellow-

WILLIAM BLAKE

In the summer of 1783 the engraver Ryland, whose end Blake had foreseen, was put to death on the gallows. Blake's mind and imagination worked over the scene; and the place, Tyburn, and its symbolic "tree" became a permanent part of the imagery of desolation and cruelty in the later epic poems. During the following summer Blake's father died. The elder son, James, took over the hosiery business in the family home; and now William and Catherine came to live next door, where William, with the engraver James Parker as partner, set up a print-selling shop on the ground floor. William's favourite brother, Robert, came to live with him and Catherine. Besides designing and painting, engraving (from other men's designs), and print-selling, William now undertook to teach Robert, an apt pupil, the arts of drawing and engraving. In both 1784 and 1785 Blake exhibited water-colours at the Royal Academy Exhibitions, in the former year two treatments of a less than popular theme, the abominations of war; in the latter, four less controversial designs, three of them Biblical.

William Blake had definitely put himself into trade, and the hours for writing poetry or for painting were few. This was to him a sort of self-betrayal, a treason to his spiritual self. He therefore experienced periods of intense suffering. A climax came when the beloved younger brother, Robert, who for two and one-half years had lived with him and Catherine, died. Through two weeks before the end William kept watch at the bedside day and night, tending the sick one, knowing the near presence of Death, sunk in visions. When Robert breathed his last, William saw his brother's spirit come out of the body, rise "clapping its hands for joy," and disappear. William then fell into a sleep that lasted three days.

Ridding himself of partner and shop, Blake took Catherine to new lodgings in Poland Street. While he could not wholly escape the established routine, he somehow shifted his obligations— disregarding his brother James's "bread and cheese advice" — so that the commercial engraving consumed less time, permitting a return to poetry. He was reading extensively, not only his favourite poets, Shakespeare, Ossian, Chatterton, but the philosophers (among them the hated apostles of rationality, Bacon and Locke) and spirit, Thomas Taylor, was frequently there: he who had translated the *Enneads* of Plotinus and other classics of mysticism. It was Emerson who told Wordsworth that every library in America held Taylor's translations and that he found it "incredible" that no Englishman knew of the man. "A man of imagination" and "a feeder of poets," he called him.

scientists — and still Swedenborg and Boehme. He read several books on æsthetics, writing his comments on the page margins.

These early marginalia on art have not survived, as did the notes on Sir Joshua Reynolds's *Discourses on Painting* of a later period. But the latter-day comments afford an inkling of what Blake was thinking about art in England under the R.A. and "this President of Fools." He felt keenly his own inability to find time for original work, and he felt that the artists that he most cared for were, like himself, unjustly "depressed." He lays the "oppression" to Sir Joshua "and his gang." He earns for himself the reputation of being a dissenter and an eccentric, even a madman.

It is a story as old as art and patronage. William Blake, having resolved to make a living for himself and Catherine, having thus cut himself off from poetry for a considerable term of years, had now equally cut himself off from a career of creative painting by dissenting from current standards. He had not saved himself from the injury most tragic for the artist, periods of unproductiveness.

The changes in the year 1787 brought back some margin for creative effort, at least for poetry, but the following few years intensified the seriousness, even the melancholy, of his view of the outward world. With Catherine he found a healing companionship. Among the brightest entries in the record of the times are those of rambles together into the countryside, sometimes a walk of thirty miles in a single day. There were, too, the visions "away in Paradise"; and there were good friendships on earth. In a circle that met at the home of the publisher Joseph Johnson, the poet became intimate with some of the leading radicals and controversialists of London: William Godwin, Mary Wollstonecraft, then writing *A Vindication of the Rights of Woman*, and Thomas Paine, just publishing *The Rights of Man*. It was Blake who, by his urging, saved Paine from arrest, aiding him to escape to France.

The part Paine had taken in the American Revolution, his intimacy with Washington, Franklin, and others of the erstwhile rebels, his daring defiance of Pitt and His Majesty's Government, and now his open advocacy of the revolutionary elements in France were more exciting to Blake's mind than anything he had found in his social and political reading. The inception of his epic poems, *America*, *The French Revolution*, and *Europe*, probably dates from their talks together; and, more important, Blake's imagination was fed, toward completion of that symbolic structure

THEN A SPIRIT PASSED BEFORE MY FACE, THE HAIR OF MY FLESH STOOD UP. ENGRAVING BY WILLIAM BLAKE, FROM THE *JOB* SERIES. ROSENWALD COLLECTION, NATIONAL GALLERY OF ART, WASHINGTON. (PHILADELPHIA MUSEUM OF ART PHOTO).

SAINT PAUL PREACHING AT ATHENS. WATER-COLOR PAINTING BY WILLIAM BLAKE. MUSEUM OF ART, RHODE ISLAND SCHOOL OF DESIGN, PROVIDENCE.

which would underlie the action and thought of all the epic poems.

He contradicted Paine on many matters of religion and spiritual philosophy, but the man was a valued fellow-spirit in the realm of revolution. The circle of which he was a part became the "Revolution Society." Blake even wore the red cap of Liberty on the streets — a circumstance fortunately not uncovered by the prosecution when, many years later, he was in danger of hanging upon charges of seditious speech.

The year 1789 had seen the appearance of the *Songs of Innocence,* a small collection, but containing some of the most felicitous lyrics in the language. The freshness, the spontaneity, the simplicity of the early *Sketches* are again beautifully manifested. The book opens with the well-nigh perfect proem:

> *Piping down the valleys wild,*
> *Piping songs of pleasant glee,*
> *On a cloud I saw a child,*
> *And he laughing said to me:*
>
> *"Pipe a song about a Lamb!"*
> *So I piped with merry cheer* . . .

Nor is the quality less pellucid and tender and light-hearted in "A Dream," "The Lamb," "The Little Girl Lost," "A Cradle Song," and "Nurse's Song." It is Blake most himself, with a child's insight and a child's joy, a seer speaking with the simplicity that passes understanding. That the Christ appears in gentlest reference, that two or three of the poems may be read (after long acquaintance) as allegories of the soul, may be put down to the poet's growing resolve to turn all his creative work to the one purpose of revealing a spiritual life beyond the mundane one.

When he adds, in 1794, a second sheaf entitled *Songs of Experience,* the revelatory aim is made plain in the opening lines of the introduction. The singing quality is not impaired. Nevertheless there is a great deal less of joyous lyricism, less of innocent laughter, in the *Songs of Experience.* Against a refrain of childish abandon is set an answering refrain of dread and grey despair, of the hidden worm in the rose, of trembling fear and iron chains. With the mention of God comes the image of the binding Church, of constrictive religion, of a priestcraft. Well-nigh unbearable is the new version of "A Little Boy Lost," in which a child with intuition of God's presence is caught up by the Priests, and —

> *The weeping child could not be heard,*
> *The weeping parents wept in vain;*
> *They stripped him of his little shirt,*
> *And bound him in an iron chain;*
>
> *And burn'd him in a holy place,*
> *Where many had been burned before. . . .*

Several of the poems are dark versions of subjects treated lightly in the *Songs of Innocence*. In "Holy Thursday" there had been the unforgettable picture of the child-singers "walking two and two, in red and blue and green," into St. Paul's. But the new version fairly rushes into indictment of cruel Albion. The opening lines, economic and stinging, are:

> *Is this a holy thing to see*
> *In a rich and fruitful land, —*
> *Babes reduced to misery,*
> *Fed with cold and usurous hand?*

There is a change of mood also away from tenderness to a fearful wonder — but no pessimism — in the poem that corresponds, in the later collection, to "The Lamb" of the *Songs of Innocence*. It is "The Tiger," the most quoted of Blake's works.

But it is another poem, "The Garden of Love," which above all indicates the change in Blake's thought, seeming to mark full stop after the carefree lyricism and sheer felicity of the first and second books. He goes to the Garden of Love and finds a chapel "built in the midst," and graves about,

> *And priests in black gowns were walking their rounds,*
> *And binding with briars my joys, and desires.*

In other poems he slashes at the Government and the Church that seem to him to abet the commoner evils, war, commerce, harlotry. In "London" he gets back to the ultimate cause, law, misused reason: "the mind-forged manacles." Nevertheless he visions deliverance of man from those manacles, a glorious return to liberty, Imagination, Eden. Henceforward his writings will increasingly serve that vision. Now, in 1789, while the innocent, lyric phase is slowly closing, the purposeful, prophetic phase is opening.

Tiriel, unpublished during his lifetime, is first of the epic poems. It fixes much of the symbolism woven later into the several treatments of the struggle between Imagination and Reason, between the inspired poet-seer and the shapers of the sluggish materialist world, between Love and Law. *Tiriel*, however, is neither clear nor sustainedly poetic. It is the poet feeling his way into a new métier. Out of a cancelled afterpiece he carried over to his next work, *The Book of Thel*, two key lines to go into a telling introductory stanza:

> *Does the eagle know what is in the pit?*
> *Or wilt thou go ask the Mole?*
> *Can Wisdom be put in a silver rod?*
> *Or Love in a golden bowl?*

William Blake was one of the most reverent and spiritual men of his time, and his growth as artist is not to be distinguished from his religious development. His cleavage from the established Anglican Church, as from the Catholic, was now complete. A certain amount of symbolism and imagery in the poems of the period seems to hark back to Swedenborg's writings, though mixed with original conceptions and bits suggested by Ossian. There is influence, too, out of the Hindu Books of Wisdom, which had just appeared in Wilkins's translation. He painstakingly annotated the text of two books, one newly published, by Swedenborg; but the study of them substantially ended his loyalty to the Swedish seer. He uncovered evidences of legalism and literalism, and he thought he had discovered an adherence to the doctrine of predestination as binding and as damnable, he felt, as Calvin's.

Already Blake had published (in a small way) his own first prose summaries of religious thought: brief tables of "principles," under the titles *There is No Natural Religion* and *All Religions Are One*. Together the works constitute a warning against conceiving life as limited by man's sense-perceptions; a denial of Reason (or Ratio) as in any way final or primary; and an affirmation of faith in Man as Poetic Genius and as Godlike source of all religions. There are aphorisms that Blake never improved upon:

The bounded is loathed by the possessor.

He who sees the Infinite in all things, sees God. He who sees Ratio only, sees himself only.

Therefore God becomes as we are, that we may be as He is.

Two years later, in 1790, he published *The Marriage of Heaven and Hell*, the essay in verse, rhythmic prose, and epigram which Swinburne was to characterize as "the greatest of all Blake's books and about the greatest produced in the Eighteenth Century in the line of high poetry and speculation." There is very little aid now from the singing poet of innocent childhood. The lamb has given way to the tiger.

The Marriage of Heaven and Hell includes in its ill-related parts, especially in the "Memorable Fancies" and in the "Proverbs of Hell," so much that is essentially Blakean that it may be put down as his first substantial prophetic work. It is here that the key line of his working philosophy occurs: "If the doors of perception were cleansed, every thing would appear to man as it is, infinite." Blake's basic mystical doctrine is illumined also in a question put in couplet form:

How do you know but every Bird that cuts the airy way,
  Is an immense world of delight, clos'd by your senses five?

The epigrams and summaries repeat favourite thoughts of the author:

Jesus was all virtue and acted from impulse, not from rules.

All deities reside in the human breast.

The man who never alters his opinion is like standing water, and breeds reptiles of the mind.

The eagle never lost so much as when he submitted to learn of the crow.

The tygers of wrath are wiser than the horses of instruction.

It is in this book that Blake declares himself a disciple of Satan. The trail of thought is devious, and the purport obscure unless the reader remembers that Heaven and Hell were one Paradise before Adam's fall. In general the affirmation is that contraries are necessary; with the advent of a new Heaven, "the Eternal Hell revives"; evil arises out of energy, but energy, Satan's medium, is necessary to combat the sluggish, restrained life and the passive, slavish religion introduced by the "good"; and, as the author phrases it in an epigram written over one of the illustrations:

> *Death and Hell*
> *Teem with life.*

William Blake *is* the Devil now, consciously, purposefully, perversely; just as in other times he will be Los, the Sun, Imagination, Revolution. He sees himself using the Devil's means to prove to mankind that the body is in no way distinct from the soul, that the spiritual overlies all. "This I shall do by printing in the infernal method, by corrosives." He adds: "I was in a printing house in Hell, and saw the method. . . ."

As a matter of fact Blake was already printing his own books "by corrosives," in a manner not known before, and his rooms in Poland Street must have smelled at times very like the Printing House of Hell. Back in 1783 he had been disgusted at the uncraftsmanlike printing and casual publishing of the *Poetical Sketches*. From then on he had cast about for a way to stamp his books, physically as well as in the writing, with his own personality. No "regular" publisher would touch his compositions anyway, not even the lovely and immortal *Songs of Innocence*, and certainly not mad conceits such as *The Marriage of Heaven and Hell*. He must multiply copies in his own way.

Committing the matter to the spirit, he experienced a vision in which his brother Robert revealed to him a method of engraving a copper plate in reverse of the usual intaglio method, the impressions to be taken off the lines left standing (after the corrosive bath) in relief. The "print" would constitute all the lettering together with the basic lines of an illustration or illumination; all colours beyond the first would be painted in by hand.

The morning after receiving this revelation Blake sent Catherine out with all their money to purchase the small materials necessary for the first production of "the author and printer, W. Blake."

From that day he made a part of his living by writing, engraving, printing, colouring, and selling his own compositions in this highly personal method (though he sometimes varied the process, from relief to etching or engraving in intaglio). He made usually a detailed coloured sketch of each page, and he taught Catherine to take impressions and to build up the prints in colour. Blake ground and mixed his own inks and colours, and Catherine bound the sheets together; so that no process in the production of the final book was in other hands than his own, except the making of the paper.

At first the pages were very small, for copper plates were costly. And in general Blake's literary compositions were small in bulk, because to print and colour great numbers of pages would involve an impossible amount of labour. For a like reason Blake as painter is known almost wholly by pictures of modest size, in what would be for others "minor" works: because he never got to the point of affording costly colours on costly canvas.

At just this time Blake is coming to the fullness of composition, the weighted order, that will characterize the illustrations of the prophetic books as well as the best of the independent paintings. Though the picture field is small, the picture is solid, spacious, "of a certain magnitude." The water-colours of later years, measured in inches rather than feet, lack nothing of the monumentality of design and grandeur of statement found in larger masterpieces.

"A Song of Liberty" appears at the end of *The Marriage of Heaven and Hell*. It is like an exultant cry over the birth of Orc, or Revolution. This "son of fire" is, no doubt, the poet himself. Henceforward the way for him is clear. He will be the affirmer of Liberty, the destroyer of the monster Urizen.

By 1793, at the age of thirty-five, he is deep in his mission of revealing the truth through the prophetic poems. Two of them appear (that is, the plates are engraved, and perhaps the first five or ten copies are offered) during that year. One is *Visions of the Daughters of Albion*, an occasionally beautiful if not always clear glorification of the holiness of love. It gives forth flashes of the old felicity, coupled with deeper meaning:

Arise, you little glancing wings and sing your infant joy!
Arise, and drink your bliss! For every thing that lives is holy!

The other is *America*, the narrative poem about the oppression of the American Colonies. It ends with the flight of Revolt to Europe — a reminder of the French Revolution. During this very year Louis XVI and Marie Antoinette have been guillotined in Paris. Revolt has freed America, settled in Europe.

When, however, in the following year Blake publishes a long poem entitled *Europe: A Prophecy*, it contains no word of contemporary history, but tells only how Orc, Revolt, gets to France. It is notable especially for its indications of Blake's thinking on liberty of action, on an England chained to Reason and Law, on Bacon as representative of rational philosophy, on civilization built around fears and "Thou shalt not." Increasingly the figures of Blake's mature mythology appear: Urizen, Los, Enitharmon, and the others.

A book of engravings issued in 1793 has been lost, no copy surviving. But the designs accompanying the epics have a largeness, a depth of purpose (sometimes going far beyond the text), and an independent formal beauty not often associated with the word "illustration." The frontispiece of *Europe: A Prophecy* is the frequently reproduced picture of the Ancient of Days laying out the boundaries of the universe with a compass. Blake had experienced, at the top of the stairs as he came into the house, this vision of the Creator.

William and Catherine Blake, in 1793, moved their scant goods across the Thames to Lambeth. They took a good house of three stories, not detached but with a small garden of its own, with a view at the back to Lambeth Palace and the Thames — by far the most sizable of all their dwellings. The poet-artist was never more certain of the aims of the good fight before him, never surer that the cause and the target were materialism and lack of vision.

In the years 1793–4 the Blakes approached prosperity. They hired a servant (Blake would wince at the word), and thus Catherine both had time to enter more into the work of printing and colouring, and found leisure for activities impossible at any other time in their lives. They went together on long walks into the country. And William got about among more kinds of people, for beside work on his own books and engraving, he was teaching. Some of his pupils came from homes of wealth, and Blake sometimes found himself invited after lessons for dinner or an evening gathering. The testimonials to his "entertaining and pleasant" ways at this time afford evidence that his native spirit was in no way depressed, however far his convictions had carried him as regards England's social decadence and religious depression.

Prosperity did not long tarry. Through a channel not identified, Blake was offered the position of drawing teacher to the children of the royal family. He saw only servitude ahead in such a post, and he declined. Quixotically he dismissed all his pupils, believing that to continue any teaching while refusing to tutor the royal children would be interpreted as an affront to the King. As to the servant, Mrs. Blake had found her negligent if not unclean and had sent her away. Never again were Blake and his wife to have "help."

The shorter poems he was now writing were put down in a sort of daybook — later known as the Rossetti Manuscript — which also came to contain doggerel jottings and the first sketches for illustrations or paintings. For a quarter-century it served as a catch-all for stray compositions. Splendid and immortal poems took shape therein, to be followed by journalistic notes and lampoons. It was in 1794 that Blake added the plates of *Songs of Experience,* mostly from the daybook, to the *Songs of Innocence* to make up a single printed volume of fifty-four leaves.

In the same year he put out a slight book of designs, *For Children: The Gates of Paradise,* containing seventeen plates. They are curiously assorted, illustrating vaguely the author's growing, and shifting, philosophy. Some of the plates, which are hardly more than emblems, point up the familiar Blakean objections to Law, Commandment, Doubt. One shows "the Father and the Sons" closed naked in a cramped dungeon. The engraved legend reads: "Does thy God, O Priest, take such vengeance as this?" The most engaging of the plates is a simple little design entitled "I want! I want!" It shows a man starting up a ladder that reaches to the moon.

Charming in their simplicity, the engravings of *The Gates of Paradise* nevertheless underline the seriousness of Blake's thinking at this time, if not a recurring depression of mind. Some biographers have ventured the thought — bolstered with unconvincing "evidence" from the poems — that there was a period of strain between the poet-husband and the wife. Psychoanalysts have inferred that of course Blake must have found himself unhappy, bound to a woman not far from illiteracy; that of course he longed to, and probably did, indulge in extra-marital affairs. But nowhere does a personal rift find mention. Every contemporary observer confirms the impression of an idyllic companionship and a perfect mutual trust.

But Blake broke out again and again in laments over the state of social and religious civilization in England, and indulged in scornful denunciation of rulers, priests, and stupid conforming fools. He hates the British genius for compromise, implies that England, in escaping Revolution, has sold her soul to commerce.

> *Britannia's Isle*
> *Round which the Fiends of Commerce smile . . .*

is the scene of every degrading inhumanity. In "Auguries of Innocence" he is terribly specific:

> *The whore and gambler, by the State*
> *Licenc'd, build that Nation's fate.*
> *The harlot's cry from street to street*
> *Shall weave Old England's winding sheet.*
> *The winner's shout, the loser's curse,*
> *Dance before dead England's hearse.*

Yet through it all is a light of faith. Blake sees — for the visions are with him still, unfailing, more glorious — he sees that there is a source from which man can recover all that he has sacrificed in his blind devotion to law, to rationalism, to his own Satanic mills. Like every true mystic he is constructive: uncovering evil, he affirms the good; showing the need of withdrawal, he counsels action; destroying one world, he poses another more glorious. He is the man of action, affirmation, faith.

William Blake in his writing had passed through three phases: first, a singing of the innocent beauty of the world, a poet's revelation of the joyful and the spiritual in simplest things, with a poet's subtle intimations of a "voice of Heaven" through all; second, a crying out at the inhumanities of the world, especially in Albion, under a twisted rendering of Christianity, a phase in which the darkness is only occasionally illumined by the truth or faith that these evils are good in reverse, order perverted, that a cleansing of the vision will restore Eden; and third, a serious balancing of criticism of the current order with revelation, a balance of realistic attack and inspired prophecy, a purposeful limning of the sad world where "five windows light the cavern'd Man," but only to the end that the reader may discern, beyond Man self-closed in sensual existence, a Heavenly glory, a mystic life.

Cloudily the next mythological poem, *The Book of Urizen*, tells of the fall of the world out of the boundless, eternal, blissful universe — and all because of the monster Urizen, Reason, moulder of laws by virtue of cold intellect. In a sequel, *The Book of Ahania*, Urizen again controls the world, and, "shrunk away from Eternals," he writes "his book of iron." The fourteen stanzas of Ahania's lament are among the most musical, among the richest in imagery, to be found in Blake's pages. It is a flash of the "pure poetry" of the years of the *Songs of Innocence*, unweighted by prophetic purpose.

In the *Book of Los*, a comparatively short epic poem of the year 1795, Los, the Eternal Prophet, the One beyond Jehovah, at once Imagination and the Source — and yet Poet, Artist, the individual prophet Blake — appears, is encased in adamant rock, falls "ages on ages," rises again, confronts Urizen, but is tricked by the monster of Rationalism. In a companion piece, *The Song of Los*, Blake identifies Newton and Locke, the philosophers of science and rationalism, as Urizen's advocates in Albion; in the following verse he names Rousseau and Voltaire; and then "the deceased gods of Asia." In a poem undated, but presumably of this period, he more specifically throws out his defiance to the sceptics and Deists:

> *Mock on, Mock on, Voltaire, Rousseau:*
> *Mock on, Mock on: 'tis all in vain!*
> *You throw the sand against the wind,*
> *And the wind blows it back again.*
>
> *And every grain becomes a Gem*
> *Reflected in the beams divine. . . .*

And how were William and Catherine Blake living while he wrote these epic pieces, which practically no one in his time would care to read as poetry or prophecy either, while the two of them laboriously produced the books "in illuminated printing"? Certainly not by the sales of books, for copies brought incredibly low prices. Blake was feeling again the chains of iron. He had got back to doing commercial engraving as a means of keeping a roof over their heads and food in the cupboard. Catherine was all sympathy, faith, and loyalty when William poured out to her his visions and schemes. That did not prevent her placing before the poet and artist, when he sat down for his dinner, an empty plate, as a sign that there was neither food nor money in the house. Then less poetry, more commercial engraving: the old, trying business of graving copper plates from other men's uninspired designs.

About this time he finds, mercifully, a patron who appreciates his water-colour paintings, and from 1795 on he does increasing numbers of important designs in the medium. Left to his own preferences in subject matter, he chooses Biblical figures and incidents. A blessed patron is Thomas Butts, who recognizes genius and lets the artist choose theme and treatment.

A publisher, too, in 1795, comes to Blake with a commission to design more than five hundred illustrations to the currently popular *Night Thoughts* by Edward Young. An opportunity! But when publisher and artist sit down together it comes clear that this will again be somewhat in the nature of a work of love. Blake sets his price. The publisher halves it, halves that again, and then cuts once more. Blake cannot afford to refuse even so: he accepts and produces 537 designs in water-colour at an average price — incredible! — of ninepence.

A factor had been that Blake would engrave the illustrations from his own drawings, and thus be presented to a wide audience. But the first "part" of the *Night Thoughts,* of four projected, failed to please the subscribers, who loved the poem because it was commonplace and disliked the disturbingly original and uncommon designs provided for it. And Blake was partly to blame in that he, not finding inspiration in Young's text, added imaginative material, partly out of his own personally created mythology. In any case, the following three parts were cancelled, the most of the projected engravings were not made and not paid for, and there was no introduction of Blake's talents to a wide public.

In effect he had spent the better part of a year producing drawings that can have netted him hardly more than a shilling a day. There were no epics or books of his own designs composed that year, and only one, *Vala,* during the nine years thereafter. He had stepped so deep into the current of commercial work again, and so disastrously, that nothing could save his mortal fortunes but further traffic with the publishers.

In the years 1795–1800 he engraved illustrations, from designs by various artists, for poetical works, for a history of England and a history of Rome, for a book of travel, and for essays in medicine and æsthetics. He even engraved business cards. Nevertheless he and Catherine were close to penury. In a letter written in the summer of 1799 he exclaims: "As to myself . . . I live by miracle." And: "As to engraving . . . I am laid in a corner as if I did not exist . . . but I laugh at Fortune and go on. . . . I think I foresee better things than I have ever seen."

The better things, for some years further, turn out to be not material but spiritual. Yet one actual happening lightens the prospect. Thomas Butts promises to accept up to fifty water-colour paintings at a guinea apiece, and the artist may choose his own subjects. Was ever so perfect a patron? When commissions for engraving fail to come in, Blake turns happily to creation of those incomparable paintings that at once illuminate and illustrate Bible incidents and Bible thought. Occasionally he produces something out of his own mythology, or a commentary such as the "Newton," showing the scientist symbolically writing in darkness.

It was Thomas Butts who embroidered upon an incident occurring in the garden at Lambeth, until he had a story that went the rounds and perhaps had to do with the myth of Blake's "madness." Calling one day at the house, Captain Butts failed to find William and Catherine at home, but going to the garden he came upon them in a little summer house, unencumbered by any clothing at all, reciting to each other the rôles of Adam and Eve from *Paradise Lost*. And, added Butts, he was invited in — which is, after all, the only incredible detail. Later, sensational writers built up the tale shamelessly.

One cannot live indefinitely on guinea-apiece paintings, and it is a different sort of patron, a fussy, serious, conceited little man, one William Hayley, who determines the next major move in the Blakes' game of life. Hayley, after a few trial commissions, invites Blake to move to Felpham in order to be on the ground, so to speak, to engrave the plates for a life of Cowper, for which he is writing the text. The commission seems an attractive one. Blake goes to Felpham, a village on the Sussex coast, to make final arrangements, and he rents a cottage within sight of the sea. He is delighted in every way, with the place and with the new plan of life. In the interval before he takes Catherine and their goods — chiefly his proof-press, his engraving plates and portfolios of

SATAN ROUSING THE REBEL ANGELS. WATER-COLOR PAINTING BY WILLIAM BLAKE. VICTORIA AND ALBERT MUSEUM, LONDON. (CROWN COPYRIGHT).

THE GREAT RED DRAGON AND THE WOMAN CLOTHED WITH THE SUN. WATER-COLOR PAINTING BY WILLIAM BLAKE. ROSENWALD COLLECTION, NATIONAL GALLERY OF ART, WASHINGTON. (PHILADELPHIA MUSEUM OF ART PHOTO).

prints — to the new home, he is enthusiastic in writing of the prospect to his friends. He tells Hayley, just before their departure from Lambeth: "My fingers emit sparks of fire with expectation of my future labours." And of Catherine's anticipation of Felpham: "My wife is like a flame of many colours of precious jewels whenever she hears it named."

At first it proves to be indeed "Sweet Felpham . . . Heaven is there." There is a ladder of Angels from Heaven, and a splendid staircase in the reverse direction. William's beloved brother Robert is close by again, to be reached in vision. To Flaxman, William writes of the cottage: "No other formed House can ever please me so well; nor shall I ever be persuaded, I believe, that it can be improved either in Beauty or Use. . . . Heaven opens here on all sides her golden Gates; . . . and now begins a New Life."

The New Life began in the autumn of 1800. The following spring: "Sussex is certainly a happy place, and Felpham in particular is the sweetest spot on Earth, at least it is so to me and my good Wife." But in the winter the cottage proves to be damp and unhealthful; Catherine especially succumbs to ague and rheumatism. Worse, William Blake is drawn by his patron into a routine of filling orders, with seldom a chance to write a line of verse or to paint an independent picture. Hayley, who at first "acts like a prince," decides to set Blake's life right by teaching him practical ways of earning money, and by ruling out imagination, visions, and mysticism. He secures for the artist commissions to paint miniatures, portraits of the gentry. Blake himself is surprised to find that he can work excellently "from Nature." There are engravings to be done for Hayley, some for the biography of Cowper, others for the patron's ballads and books of poems. There is a series of tempera paintings of nineteen heads of eminent poets (including Hayley's deceased son) for the decoration of Hayley's library. There is even a period of teaching drawing to the children of Lady Bathurst.

In January, 1802, he writes to Butts indicating clearly the impossibility of the situation. "I find on all hands great objections to my doing anything but the meer drudgery of business, and intimations that if I do not confine myself to this, I shall not live." Hayley, himself a poet, though a superficial one, distrusts Blake's glorification of Imagination, and he hates Blake's poetry. Hayley, orthodox passive Christian, dislikes the Bible, which is to Blake the incomparable treasury of imaginative literature. Hayley wants to be a Greek, and at the same time he likes best the contemporary German poets, especially Klopstock; and Blake is anything but Greek and German. Hayley is a born compromiser, Blake is positive, headstrong, a fighter to the end. When Lady Hesketh, Cowper's cousin, objects strenuously to a design for the biography, Hayley, backed by Blake, takes a strong line and insists upon inclusion of the plate; but then he gives in and forces the artist to "modify" the design. The patron, moreover, has been training Blake as amanuensis in preparing the Cowper text, and in the evenings they proof-read Cowper's translation of *The Iliad* and compare the text with the original Greek. Blake learns Greek for the purpose — excellent education and discipline in other circumstances, for one deficient in the languages and prejudiced against the Greeks since youth. But the whole business interferes with vision and consumes the time that might otherwise be available for his own writing.

For a long time Blake hides his resentment. He confides to his friends something of his bafflement; and in his private daybook he jots down doggerel lampooning his patron. He was the more disturbed because the removal to Felpham had opened again the gates of vision. Never else had his letters been so full of angels met, of "fourfold sight," of divine meanings detected in grains of sand and whispering leaves, and in the morning light. Sometimes he reaffirms his faith in the Spirit, and in its infallible rightness as guide. Again he speculates on the temptations put in the way of the mystic traveller. "I am," he writes to Butts in 1802, "under the direction of Messengers from Heaven, daily and nightly; but the nature of such things is not, as some suppose, without trouble or care."

At no other period in his life is the struggle so shattering. Never else does he act out so explicitly in his own person the drama that is at the heart of his epic poems, the contest between Reason and Spirit. A year later he writes more hopefully to Butts, affirming that "I have conquer'd, and shall go on conquering. Nothing can withstand the fury of my Course among the Stars of God. . . ."

Catherine was his unfailing companion and aid. She kept his house and she spent long hours at the printing press, while Blake painted miniatures, engraved illustrations for the biography and plates for Hayley's ballads, helped Hayley collect material for the new books, and learned Greek (and something of Latin and Hebrew too). In his renewed resolution he produced occasional water-colours and began the writing of his monumental poem *Jerusalem*.

But Hayley, sensing resentment and rebellion, redoubled his efforts to make a sensible man of his protégé. He sincerely believed that Blake should consider himself fortunate in his present well-paid circumstances. The patron even tried to win over Catherine, whom he praised to others as a perfect wife and a delightful being — and a good printer besides. But her loyalty proved to be on the other side.

In the spring of 1803 the friction between patron and artist-amanuensis is open. The stage is set for a final quarrel and break. But suddenly an event occurs that, threatening tragedy, brings out every good characteristic in the patron. It proves to Blake an over-all loyalty and goodness of heart on Hayley's part, and brings him around to gratitude and sincere appreciation.

Blake is arrested on charges of "assault and seditious words" in August, 1803. Returning to his cottage, he has found a strange man in his garden and, without pausing to ascertain whether the fellow has a reason for being there or not — he has, being hired as sub-gardener — Blake has ordered him off the place. Meeting with an impertinent refusal, Blake forcefully ejects him. The man wanting to force a fight and being abusive and profane, Blake steps into the road, parries the blows, swings the fellow around, and forcibly marches him by the elbows to a near-by inn. There they are separated, with nothing further than threats of vengeance.

Four days later the artist is haled before a court at Chichester. His "victim" proves to be a soldier of the Royal Dragoons quartered in Felpham. Determined to get even with the unimpressive little man who has shamed him publicly, he has cooked up with a companion the charge that Blake in his anger made seditious utterances. Blake had shouted, he testified, "Damn the King, his country and all his subjects." Despite the agreement of all witnesses that they had heard nothing of the sort, Blake was bound over to appear for examination in October, at which time, when he pleaded not guilty, the date of the trial was set for January 1804.

The situation was serious enough. A verdict of guilty would mean execution. If the prosecution lawyers searched the records they might find that the accused had once gone about the streets proclaiming his republicanism by wearing the red cap of Liberty. He had supported the Revolution in France and had helped Thomas Paine to escape from England. He had outspokenly defended the American Colonists against His Majesty's Government. In his epic poems he had repeatedly scourged princes and governors and the law. He had even depicted his Sovereign (George III was in 1804 again insane and under restraint) as sickening and trembling before the terrible and glorious spectacle of America's liberation. He had used the name Albion as symbol of the whole discreditable, nay Satanic, civilization cut off from God. There was reason to believe, moreover, that the judges were prejudiced against him.

In his favour was the fact that no accuser or lawyer would be likely to read his epic poems, much less understand them. And Hayley, the celebrity of the neighbourhood, was on his side. Hayley proved, indeed, a sterling friend. He put up bail money, and he secured the services of an eminent lawyer for the defence. Catherine was, as Blake wrote to Butts, "terrified"; and indeed she went into a grave illness that was not completely cured until after the trial.

In the meantime Blake, softened by the spontaneous show of loyalty on Hayley's part, sought to terminate the patron-protégé association without further friction. He even took upon himself the responsibility for the differences that had arisen. To Butts he wrote: "Perhaps the simplicity of myself is the origin of all offences committed against me." He and Catherine moved from the cottage by the sea back to London in September. They took two rooms in a house on South Molton Street. These rooms were to be their home and their workshop through eighteen years.

In January he went to Chichester to "get rid of this infernal business of the soldier." He faced his accusers before a bench of seven justices. In spite of a hostile summing-up by the Duke of Richmond, a verdict of not guilty was rendered. Blake was free from a shadow that had been over him a half-year.

He returned to London to find that "My poor wife has been near the gate of death"; but once he is restored to her unharmed, she begins "to resume her health and strength." They seem at the moment to be entering (once more!) upon a new life. He has commissions for engravings, he is writing poems again, Butts will take pictures. At this time Blake is in his forty-seventh year.

A great deal of Blake's expanding faith and of his exuberance finds expression in one of his longest poems, *Vala*, which he had started to write during the years at Lambeth and continued at Felpham. Now he takes it up again in a fire of enthusiasm. He tries to make it a summary of his mythology and philosophy, though as always he tells the cosmic story partly in terms of his own experience, in terms of William Blake and Catherine, of Hayley and the cottage at Felpham, of the trial justices and Chichester. The symbolism is confused, though Urizen and Orc, and Los, Enitharmon, and the others reappear. Uneven and confused though it be, the poem is one of the richest in the English language. There are scores of pages of gorgeous description and imagery. At the head of the manuscript Blake placed a quotation in Greek, which is in effect a restatement of his resolve to fight the powers of darkness and reopen the way to Eden. It is from Paul's Letter to the Ephesians, and reads: "Ours is a conflict not with flesh and blood, but with dominion and despotisms, and the rulers who have depressed this world into darkness, with the spirit of evil in heavenly places."

Blake's enthusiasm, gratitude, and faith shine out like stars in the letters he wrote to Hayley during 1804. He was doing an extraordinary amount of errand-running for his patron still, in connection, more or less, with the engraving of two plates for Hayley's *Life of Romney*. He is content again with engraving as a basic occupation. His words about the craft are among the truest ever spoken in regard to it. "I curse and bless Engraving alternately, because it takes so much time and is so untractable, tho' capable of such beauty and perfection." And: "Engraving is Eternal work" — "Eternal" meaning of the Golden time before the Fall, glorious, true. "O Glory! and O Delight!" he breaks out in a letter of October, 1804. Despite the long hours of labour with the coppers, despite the renewed errand-running, he has turned another milestone, has looked back over twenty years which seem now to have been marred by doubt, perturbation, and lapses from faith, has found new conviction and firmness. "For now! O Glory! and O Delight! I have entirely reduced that spectrous fiend to his station . . . and my feet and my wife's feet are free from fetters. . . . I thank God that I courageously pursued my course through darkness."

This renewal of vision occurred on the day after a visit to an art exhibition where he saw works of masters never before open to him. "Suddenly . . . I was again enlightened with the light I enjoyed in my youth" — a light which, he explains, "has for exactly twenty years been closed from me as by a door and by window-shutters." The door and the shutters do not, this time, signify for him the bonds of iron of commerce, but rather a failure of his own.

He was grateful for many other things in that year after his escape from the shadow of the gallows: for Catherine's return to health, for the friendship of Flaxman, for the remittances from Hayley on account of the engraving, for the promise of "work in abundance." But the year is hardly out when the view of himself as inspired and happy in the joint rôle of engraver and creative artist blurs. By the autumn of 1805 the old division is tragically evident. Abundance of work has meant many commissions, but the labour has become tedious, the business intercourse irritating, sometimes intolerable. Believing absolutely in his own art, and positive by nature, Blake is utterly unfitted to serve officious authors and tasteless publishers. His last attempt to be reasonable and practical and conciliating is almost at an end.

Late in 1805 he seems to be saved by a generous commission to design illustrations for an edition of Blair's *The Grave*. Presently, having delivered drawings that please, he is told by the publisher, one Cromek, that a commission to engrave the illustrations will follow. Blake's friends are delighted. Cromek feels that he has "discovered" Blake — who is still, one must remember, an obscure artist despite Hayley's patronage, and forgotten as a poet. Cromek, though shrewd and scheming, sincerely wishes to help; it is a time when, as he remarks, the artist-poet and Catherine are "reduced so low as to be obliged to live on half a guinea a week."

But Cromek has only limited funds, and, finding some opposition to Blake, wanting also to append the name of the most fashionable of engravers to the title-page of the book, he cancels Blake's commission to engrave the plates and employs Louis Schiavonetti to render the designs on copper. Thus Blake finds himself displaced by one of the men he most despises among artists, a prettifying, conforming purveyor of sentiment. Beyond the disaster of losing the promised payment, he suffers the degradation of seeing his designs presented to the public in weakened and sweetened form. Schiavonetti, master of the wiggly line and of the soft effects of stippling, made Blake's figures so pretty that the public loved them, at the expense of both spirit and plastic vitality.

When Blake protested, Cromek wrote vigorously in his own defence, using plain words. "What public reputation you have, the reputation of eccentricity excepted, I have acquired for you. . . . I was determined to bring you food as well as reputation, though from your late conduct, I have some reason to embrace your wild opinion, that to manage genius, and to cause it to produce good things, it is absolutely necessary to starve it." Cromek had, indeed, some points on his side in the ages-long battle between uncompromising genius and business for profit. But with all other questions swept away by time, it is clear that art was, in the episode, degraded. And with Blake art was synonymous with religion, with Eternity.

Cromek, if not wholly guilty of tricking Blake in the matter of Blair's *The Grave*, proved himself truly a rascal in another transaction. Seeing at Blake's home a sketch for a painting of the Canterbury Pilgrims, he conceived the idea that a proper picture on that subject might be a great popular success. Failing to get the design from Blake, he went to Thomas Stothard and suggested a similar composition. Stothard's painting, for which he paid sixty guineas, was then publicly exhibited and, aided by adroit publicity, became a sensational success when shown through the country. It brought in imposing profits. This time Blake was simply and unanswerably the victim of dishonesty, but he could do nothing about it.

From then on to that day when a new conversion taught him to forgive his enemies and to be content with whatever lot came to him, his life was a series of small fortunes and greater misfortunes, with lapses into lampooning those who had victimized him, and lapses into hack work. In 1808 he exhibited two water-colours at the Royal Academy after nine years' absence, his last (and fifth) showing there. His works went unnoticed, being hung in the Drawings and Miniatures room.

In that year Leigh Hunt published in his weekly journal a derogatory and malignant criticism of Blake's art, especially as seen in the Blair set of illustrations. Unaccountably he found the designs indecent (even in Schiavonetti's softened versions); and he poked fun at Blake's "attempts to represent immateriality." This unfair criticism — which was, for Hunt, mere space-filling and "debunking" at the expense of an obscure illustrator — did much to spread the opinion that Blake was insane.

Commissions for paintings came at intervals, and Blake put an immense amount of labour and vision into his most elaborate and intricate picture, a "Last Judgement," fitting it out also with a written commentary. For Sir Thomas Lawrence, now fabulously successful, Blake did by request a replica of an earlier picture, "The Wise and the Foolish Virgins." But at this time the Blakes were falling away from many of their friends and former associates. Poverty had something to do with it, also a certain testiness not far short of bitterness that took hold upon the artist's mind under disappointments. As if to keep alive an old grievance, Cromek announced an engraving by Schiavonetti from Stothard's *Canterbury Pilgrims*, to follow up the success of the cabinet painting.

Taking up the *Discourses on Painting* of Joshua Reynolds (who had died in 1792) and finding his most cherished beliefs about art there negated, Blake wrote the marginalia that afford one of the clearest views of his own æsthetic. Many of Sir Joshua's passages provoke merely an impatient exclamation: "Nonsense!" "A lie!" "Villainy!" "Idiot!" Occasionally there is a "True!" or "Excellent!" Oftener there is considered or caustic refutation. Most valuable is the occasional declaration of Blake's own principles. "All forms are perfect in the Poet's Mind, but these are not abstracted nor compounded from Nature, but are from Imagination." And "God forbid that Truth should be confined to Mathematical Demonstration!" Commenting on the matter treated by Sir Joshua under the rubric "Invention; — Acquired by being conversant with the inventions of others. — The true method of imitating, . . ." Blake writes: "When a man talks of acquiring Invention and of learning how to produce Original Conception, he must be expected to be called a fool by men of understanding."

The miscellaneous daybook received, in those days of renewed bafflement and depression, many a doggerel bit about Cromek and Stothard and Reynolds, even about Flaxman (who writes coldly to Hayley: "At present I have no intercourse with Mr. Blake"). It all leads up to the only answer Blake can with dignity make: an exhibition of his own. He will show his paintings and express his views on art in a descriptive catalogue.

The exhibition is, of course, a failure. It is poorly attended and it entails a financial loss. It is held in rooms at the house of

Blake's brother James, the hosier. Only sixteen paintings are shown. They include five pictures since lost. Among the others are "The Canterbury Pilgrims" (not one of the artist's most inspired works), "The Spiritual Form of Pitt Guiding Behemoth," and "Jacob's Ladder." The showing is representative. But London simply does not want what Blake has to offer.

The *Descriptive Catalogue*, however, serves to fix Blake's thoughts about graphic art toward a time when he will be recognized as a genius; and particularly it serves to express his faith in a spiritual or divine origin of creative works of art. With the so-called *Public Address*, written about the time of the exhibition but left unpublished, it constitutes a personal æsthetic of extraordinary cogency and persuasion. The artist is especially impelled to defend those works he has translated from vision.

"A Spirit and a Vision are not, as the modern philosophy supposes, a cloudy vapour, or a nothing: they are organized and minutely articulated beyond all that the mortal and perishing nature can produce. He who does not imagine in stronger and better lineaments, and in stronger and better light than his perishing and mortal eye can see, does not imagine at all. The painter of this work asserts that all his imaginations appear to him infinitely more perfect and more minutely organized than anything seen by his mortal eye." He returns to the attack upon realism: "No man of sense can think that an imitation of the objects of nature is the art of painting, or that such imitation, which any one may easily perform, is worthy of notice, much less that such an art should be the glory and pride of a Nation." He reaffirms his admiration for Michelangelo, Raphael, and Dürer as surpassing masters.

The only wide publicity evoked by the exhibition and its *Catalogue* appeared in the weekly *Examiner*. Robert Hunt, brother of Leigh, resumed the abuse of Blake — "an unfortunate lunatic whose personal inoffensiveness secures him from confinement." More specifically he reports the exhibition: "The poor man fancies himself a great master, and has painted a few wretched pictures. . . . These he calls an exhibition, of which he has published a catalogue, or rather a farrago of nonsense, unintelligibleness and egregious vanity, the wild diffusions of a distempered brain." Thus the critical brains of London, 1809, in reference to a creative figure whom modern critics list among the clearest-seeing, most inspired artists of the nineteenth century. Blake's only answer is postponed until the issuance of his next epic poem, *Jerusalem*, when the Hunts will appear vaguely as a three-headed monster, on the side of Urizen against the Man of Imagination. But even the Hunts will presently be forgiven.

Among the visitors to the exhibition was one who became a friend and patron sixteen years later, Henry Crabb Robinson. Through him a copy of the *Descriptive Catalogue* passed into the hands of Charles Lamb, who saw Blake's paintings, and a decade and a half later remembered them as "marvellous strange pictures, visions of his brain, which he asserts that he has seen. They have great merit." Lamb found it harder to characterize Blake's poems, but, when queried by a friend in 1824, he answered that he had heard "The Tyger" recited. It was "glorious," he added, "but alas! I have not the book, for the man is flown, whither I know not — to Hades or a Mad House. I look on him as one of the most extraordinary persons of the age." William and Catherine were then living a few blocks away in two cramped rooms, lost to sight except to a small circle of devoted friends and disciples.

And indeed the years 1809–20 made up a period of lessening production and increasing obscurity. Blake prepared additional copies of the prophetic books, sometimes colouring the plates. He had a certain amount of engraving to do, including hack work for the Wedgwood Potteries, of soup tureens, butter boats, and the like. He continued for a time to paint water-colours for Butts and others. But the event of the later years is the issuance of two further epic poems.

In 1808 or 1809 the first copies of *Milton* have been produced. The text, started back in 1797, was still incomplete in 1808 — nor were more than two "books," of twelve originally projected under the title, ever published.

Milton is a personal as well as a "prophetic" poem. It goes over the ground of Blake's trials at Felpham, but it also treats in grand style of the hindrances to, and the promise of, man's return to the Golden Age. The poet Milton is glorified, yet is shown to have been misled into a repressed or law-bound sort of Christianity (which is sometimes called Puritanism). In the poem he is led through redemption, arrives at a new purity through self-annihilation, receives into himself "Jesus the Saviour, wonderful." He is then the perfect Man of Imagination confounding "the Spectre, the Reasoning Power in Man."

The poem is one of the grandest in conception, with gorgeous descriptions of the Elements, of Time and Space and the Cosmic Vortex, of the Eternal Void and the External Spheres, of Los and the Zoas and the Immortal Starry-Ones, of Eden and of the City of Art. In it Blake is once more the man of burning faith and militant affirmation. His prefatory poem is one of his most haunting compositions. Here occur the unforgettable lines:

> Bring me my bow of burning gold!
> Bring me my arrows of desire!
> Bring me my spear! O clouds, unfold!
> Bring me my chariot of fire.
>
> I will not cease from mental fight,
> Nor shall my sword sleep in my hand,
> Till we have built Jerusalem
> In England's green and pleasant land.

The stanzas again and again ring with calls to service and words of re-dedication. There is one other fresh current of thought, and with it a moderating, warming humanness: Jesus is shown as the Inspired Man, the Saviour. There is a revelatory vision at the end, of Jesus entering into Albion's bosom, while the Zoas raise their trumpets and sound the news to the four winds.

A set of the *Milton* plates was printed in 1815 or soon after (the paper is watermarked 1815). Even so late, eighteen years after the first writing, the poet has been making erasures and revisions. He is now largely engaged in hack work for Wedgwood and others; in producing a series of paintings in illustration of *L'Allegro* and *Il Penseroso;* and (with Catherine) in printing an occasional set of plates of one or another of the older epic books. But he has yet one prophetic poem to give to the world, *Jerusalem*.

For twenty years, at intervals, he has worked upon this epic. He believes it to be his crowning production. It attempts the bringing together of his cosmic conceptions, his philosophic principles, and his call to Man. Not clear in its main outlines except to those who have been introduced earlier to his interpretations of world philosophy and Christianity, and to the figures of his mythology, it is yet a magnificent and flaming composition. With unusual explicitness he announces his theme:

> . . . *Of the passage through*
> *Eternal Death! and of the awakening to Eternal Life.*

Again it is the story of Man misled, of Albion asleep in Death, and of the ways to awakening. We must, Blake warns, distinguish between Eternal Man and Man in his present state, rational, law-bound, doubting. The message is that time-conditioned creation, the sleep of Death, will end, Eternal Life will be restored; the rationalizing power, which brings in its train materialism, will succumb before Imagination; the gulf between Heaven and Hell will be closed, and physical, generative life and the natural world will disappear in the Universes of Delight, in "the Communion of Saints and Angels"; there is hope in finding the Christ in Man's self: everything else will be swept away when Albion, the Universal Man, takes Jesus to himself — thus Eden, Jerusalem, the Life of Immortality, will be attained. It is Albion aroused, possessed, in vision, who speaks the lines:

Awake, Awake, Jerusalem! . . .
Awake and overspread all nations as in ancient time;
For lo! the night of Death is past and the Eternal Day
Appears upon our hills. Awake, Jerusalem, and come away!

There are in *Jerusalem* a hundred references to Blake's own circumstances and struggles. There is that telling line where the Sons of Eden praise Los, "Because he kept the Divine Vision in time of trouble." There is, too, the repeated stressing of the thought, expressed in the foreword, that "the spirit of Jesus is continual forgiveness of Sin" — a thought that is reshaping Blake into a mould of gentleness and fellowship.

His mysticism, ripened, clarified, finds direct expression:

. . . In your own bosom you bear your Heaven
And Earth and all you behold; though it appears Without it
  is Within,
In your Imagination, of which this World of Mortality is but
  a shadow.

As always in his "illuminated" books — and he never, after appearance of his first book of poems, intended that any of his writings should appear without the illustrations — the text of *Jerusalem* gains by continual reference to, or consciousness of, the accompanying designs. If Blake was still capable, in his enforced obscurity, of rising to perhaps the greatest poetic magnificence of his career, he also was at a new summit in his mastery of the art of design. The illustrations, appearing on every text page, are dramatic, powerful, and moving beyond any earlier series. The finest of the plates are both profound and ecstatic. It is common men's misfortune that only six copies of the book are known. Such were Blake's circumstances that he coloured only one copy (though fragments of a second coloured copy, said to have been owned by Ruskin and to have been cut up by him for his systematic scrapbooks, exist).

The text of *Jerusalem* was Blake's last considerable literary work. There are no more epic poems; and there is only one poetic work. The slight *Ghost of Abel,* engraved on two pages, appears thereafter, in 1822. There is also a short illustrated prose piece on a single sheet, the *Laocoön,* which is hardly more than a collection of random notes on art. It is of interest for some of the aphorisms restating the artist's beliefs, and as indicating a growing identity, in his mind, of art and religion. "Israel deliver'd from Egypt, is Art deliver'd from Nature and Imitation. . . . A Poet, a Painter, a Musician, an Architect: the Man or Woman who is not one of these is not a Christian. . . . In Eternity all is Vision. . . . The Old and New Testaments are the great code of Art. . . ."

Unpublished but inscribed in the daybook was a poem entitled "The Everlasting Gospel," which Blake wrote probably just before 1820. Its argument — and it is more polemical than poetic — fits in with the poet's personal change of thought at the time. It is, that forgiveness of sins is the heart of the revelation of Jesus to mankind. There is nothing in the *moral* aspect of Christianity, Blake avers, that the Greeks and Romans did not bring forward before Jesus. Over-concentration upon the moral code has made most men unbelievers in regard to all that is implied in the forgiveness of sins, which can only come with the taking on of the Christ. Moral righteousness, supported by law, results in the justice of revenge, the accusation of sin, and devotion to "the Roman virtues, warlike fame"; it blinds its adherents to all the mystic and spiritual blessings of living with the indwelling Christ.

Blake went on to put forward those ideas that have sometimes led profane philosophers to mark him as a forerunner of Nietzsche and the doctrine of the superman. He asks that the reader throw off the conception of Jesus as humble and law-abiding. Jesus broke man-made laws when it would serve his mission to do so. He was proud and triumphant — to men. When man unites his soul with Jesus' spirit, he will not be humble in the sense stressed by the churches; having God within one, knowing the Eternal, makes for a "triumphant pride."

Two of Blake's lines in this connection have been widely attacked as blasphemous, because the attackers held in mind man in his usual degraded estate, not Man-in-Christ or Christ-in-Man:

> *Thou art a Man, God is no more,*
> *Thy own humanity learn to adore.*

Taken in its context the passage is reverent and pregnant with meaning. It is God who speaks:

> *If thou humblest thyself, thou humblest Me;*
> *Thou also dwell'st in Eternity.*
> *Thou art a man, God is no more,*
> *Thy own humanity learn to adore,*
> *For that is my Spirit of Life.*

Never perhaps has humanity been more eloquently glorified — but humanity purified, dedicated, absorbed in God. Nothing could be farther from the sensual, wilful Superman of Nietzsche.

Forgiveness of sins! It is the most difficult obstacle to get over, for the man who turns from nominal Christianity to attempt living as Jesus lived. One who is positive, even extreme in opinion, who has been injured, who has been one of the clearest-seeing, most divinely gifted artists of the age, yet treated with indifference, abuse, or patronizing friendliness — how could such a one embrace that ultimate Christian requirement, forgiveness of one's enemies? Yet Blake, reading through his Bible for the hundredth time, sees the figure of Jesus emerge in new meaning, new glory. This is the crowning vision. Where a thousand earlier visions had fed the poet's art and shaped his thought, this one, of the triumphant, understanding, Divine Christ, changes his own life. It is a personal conversion, as well as a revelation to be blazoned forth in word and design. Fully, unreservedly, he takes to himself the truths of which he is writing, which inspire his painting.

What is it that "converts" him? It is, first of all, the realization of the spiritual greatness of Jesus. William Blake had spoken of the Saviour and had glorified His sacrifice much as the churchmen had. Suddenly through his new reading of the story he is afire with excitement over the *life* of Jesus. It is His way of living, not His way of death, that will regain Paradise for man. The grandeur of His sacrificial death is merely the inevitable dénouement of an existence on earth wholly in the consciousness of God. He is the man of Imagination breaking away from all precedents, at once Rebel and Prophet. He lays down instructions for living so different and so wonderful that men still cannot comprehend that they are meant for ordinary people, that they will cure ordinary evils. "Forgive your enemies."

William Blake is not an ordinary person. He has since childhood consorted with angels; he has spoken with God. He sees now, nevertheless, that in reading the message of the Christ he has held reservations, has clung to personality, has failed to rise above resentments. But at last he will cast in all. He dedicates himself, in the opening stanzas of *Jerusalem:*

> *O Saviour, pour upon me thy Spirit of meekness and love!*
> *Annihilate the selfhood in me: be Thou all my life!*
> *Guide Thou my hand. . . .*

The poet's hand, he confesses, has trembled upon the rock of ages. But now his infirmities and his problems — yes, his enmities and his resentments — will fall away incidentally to his "self-annihilation," in order that he may be one with God. How small are his own troubles, his own affairs, in the light of Jesus' words, in the illumination of the vision of man "returning wearied," and then "awaking into His Bosom, in the Life of Immortality"! How petty to hold to personal resentments, disappointments, ambitions, when one has known that light! What *completeness* of life is in this Jesus, humble toward God but terrible in the presence of hypocritical mortals, loving and forgiving to the sinning woman but a scourge to the men who have turned the temple to the uses of Mammon, needing no law because transcending the reasons for and the provisions of law, reconciling human and divine, transcending death as well as earthly life. William Blake took Jesus to himself — and forgave his enemies.

In his writings — and the final version of *Jerusalem* is of the period of conversion — he can thunder still against the Law of Moses and the "Ancient Heavens . . . writ with curses from pole to pole," and against the mistaken Jehovah of the law-led multitude; but the greater emphasis is on Jesus rolling away Moses' commandments and those wrathful Heavens, on Jesus offering the mystic union with God in place of the moral holiness of conventional churchmen.

Having cast out resentments, Blake faced the world with new love. Though poverty-stricken still, he ended the long period of retirement. He went about with dignity despite what must have appeared to many a shabbiness of dress. In 1819 and 1820 he was seen much at exhibitions in London in the company of friends, although he made no further effort to show his own works at the galleries.

A glimpse of him in the latter years is afforded in the diary of Lady Charlotte Bury. Knowing nothing of him as poet, she describes him, as encountered at Lady Caroline Lamb's, as an eccentric artist. "He looks careworn and subdued; but his countenance radiated as he spoke of his favourite pursuit. . . . Every word he uttered spoke the perfect simplicity of his mind, and his total ignorance of worldly wisdom." Lady Charlotte has sat by the brilliant Thomas Lawrence at dinner, and she indulges in a comparison of the two painters, not at all to the credit of England's most popular artist of the day. "Sir Thomas Lawrence looked at me several times whilst I was talking with Mr. Blake, and I saw his lips curl with a sneer, as if he despised me for conversing with so insignificant a person."

Nevertheless Lawrence, though everything Blake was not, fashionable, successful, superficially facile, an R.A. and a Knight, had bought a painting by Blake, which he kept on his studio table. Lawrence, moreover, helped in 1820 to save a series of woodcuts by Blake from the sort of softening, not to say mutilation, suffered by the designs for Blair's *The Grave* fifteen years earlier. A Dr. Thornton had commissioned Blake to illustrate a school edition of the *Pastorals* of Virgil. The artist for the first time forsook copper engraving in favour of wood, and miraculously he created designs as beautiful as anything being produced in the medium. The little pictures compress almost an incredible amount of meaning and of woodcut-loveliness in tiny compass, being especially noticeable for the masterly play of light in each print. But Dr. Thornton, with an eye educated to the pale, conventional thing, judged the set of prints amateurish and strange. He was all for having the designs re-engraved by a "regular" artist. Chancing to show Blake's proofs to a group of artists, John Linnell and Sir Thomas Lawrence among them, he was dissuaded from discarding the set. Nevertheless the publishers lined up the designs four to a page, and finding that the dimensions did not come right, they sawed off a sizable piece of each engraved block — a bit of desecration for which the picture-lover can find no words acid enough. Dr. Thornton, moreover, apologized for the illustrations in a prefatory word: "They display less of art than genius, and are admired by some eminent painters."

However deeply Blake may have been hurt by the incident, he reserved his criticism until he could attack the blindness and the fashion-serving and the bowing to false gods that lay behind the personal action. He even engraved a copper-plate illustration for Dr. Thornton four years later. It may be that the low estimate he held of Virgil's ideas made him unconcerned about the book. Ever since he had encountered the Roman poet's famous line, "Let others study art: Rome has somewhat better to do, namely war and dominion," he had kept Virgil's name on the list of Caesar-worshippers and arch-materialists.

For a lifetime the story of Job had been familiar to William Blake. The symbolism of the character and the superb poetry of the story had been a part of his spiritual and poetic background. As once he had "taken on" the prophet Ezekiel, he later felt himself identified with Job, the man of worldly misfortune redeemed by faith. If anyone could *feel* the character of Job, certainly the aged William Blake could. And so, when in 1820 or 1821 Thomas Butts agreed to take a series of paintings or coloured drawings based on the Bible story, the artist entered upon one of the happiest tasks of his career.

Nobly he fulfilled the commission. With love and vision and mature artistry he set about designing a series of twenty-one pictures. The designs turned out to be — as Butts doubtless was glad to have them — far more than a set of illustrations for a loved and familiar story. For Blake interpreted *Job* as an allegory illustrating his own knowledge of God, the cosmos, and Man. Here is the Mundane Shell in which Reason has constricted humankind. Here is Job, Man, actually in the image of God. Here is the Heaven of Blake's vision, with the angels who had visited him so often. Here are the Blakean symbols of Art (a Gothic structure), of Imagination (the Sun, Los), of Materialism or Reason (the serpent).

Above all, here is acted out the story of the loss of the state of Innocence, of Eden, through Rationalism and moral righteousness; the degradation and affliction of Man; and the redemption through cleaving to, and right understanding of, God.

The majesty, the power, and the formal beauty of the *Job* designs render them among the greatest illustrative works in the range of world art. They are opulent in all the elements of design except colour. They carry a wealth of both direct and symbolic meaning and are abundantly packed with figures. But most notable is the symphonic effect of the rhythmic and melodic designing. The elements are used to create "movements" that are at once mathematical and musical. Those who speak of the secret of modern art as lying in plastic rhythms or form-orchestration discover in the *Job* designs an extraordinary revelation of four-dimensional composition.

William Blake is now in his mid-sixties. He is himself a Job-like patriarch, an Israelite of God, at once an Isaiah and a John of Revelations. There has gathered about him a little group of understanding artists, younger men who believe implicitly in his genius, his Divine authority, his speaking for God. They find him gentle, tolerant, and wise beyond any contemporary artist or poet or philosopher. John Linnell, who has been a disciple since 1818, is leader of the circle. It is he who, in 1823, commissions the artist to make a duplicate set in full size of the *Job* drawings, at a cost of one hundred pounds, to be paid at the rate of one pound and fivepence each week, with a further provision for a set of engravings in reduced size.

Among those who joined with Linnell in honouring Blake with their loyalty and friendship were Samuel Palmer, George Richmond, Frederick Tatham, Henry Walter, and Edward Calvert — artists all, or art students. Awakened, each in his own way, to new vision by the revelations of Blake's genius, they dreamed of establishing an island of poetic romanticism in the current of British art, a current flowing ever more swiftly in the channels of conventional, not to say mechanical, naturalism. No one of them was endowed with Blake's gift of imagination and mystic insight, and ultimately they failed to offer an arresting challenge to the story-book realism of the time, to Wilkie and Mulready, Landseer and Frith. Inspired as they were by Blake's words and his example, and utterly loyal, they yet, because their eyes did not open naturally upon the inner world, settled upon the lesser

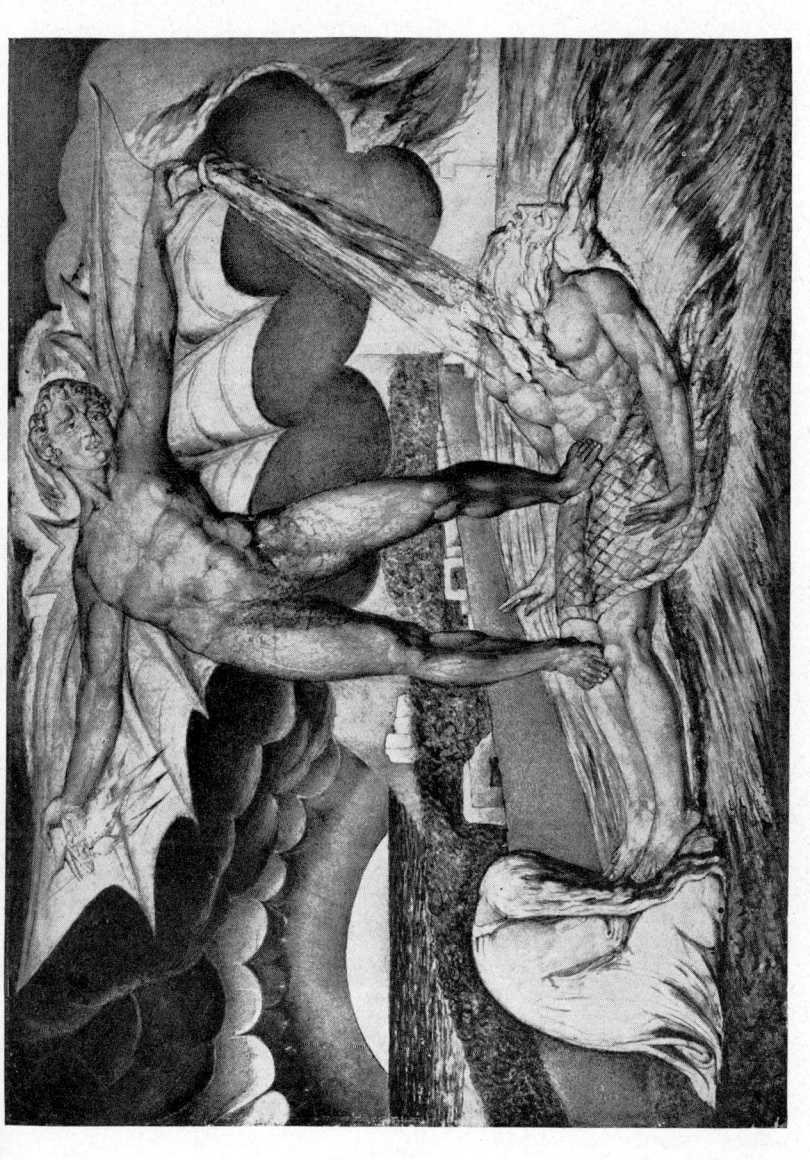

SATAN SMITING JOB WITH BOILS. WATER-COLOR PAINTING BY WILLIAM BLAKE, FROM THE *JOB* SERIES. NATIONAL GALLERY, MILLBANK, LONDON.

THEN WENT SATAN FORTH FROM THE PRESENCE OF THE LORD. ENGRAVING BY WILLIAM BLAKE, FROM THE *JOB* SERIES. PRINT ROOM, NEW YORK PUBLIC LIBRARY.

of the seer's works for emulation. They translated the other-worldliness of Blake into its most easily apprehended form: the soul at repose spelling pastoralism, the Golden Age an Arcadian romanticism.

Samuel Palmer gained the most of strength and of insight into Blake's way of utilizing formal elements for rhythmic effect. Edward Calvert produced some excellent and exquisite prints, directly in line from the Virgilian pastoral series that had so distressed Dr. Thornton. The one really Blakean picture that survived from the "school" is "The Creation of Light," painted by George Richmond when he was seventeen years old: a typical prophetic subject treated with surprising maturity of conception, rich means, and a considerable reach after mystic overtones. But Blake died within two years. The boy Richmond then went to Paris to study, exchanged the prophetic for the scientific eye, and, after a runaway marriage, decided that the artist's first business is to make a living by art. He became a foremost portraitist and never got back to revelation.

John Linnell, though the leader of "The Ancients," as the disciples began to call themselves, and an almost fanatic admirer of Blake's work, was the least touched in his professional life by the example of the master. He found in his companionship a further impetus toward a solitary and loving study of nature and toward a vital religion; but the impress of a literal education was too strong to permit play to his own imagination. He continued to be a competent engraver and a painter of veracious landscapes. Nevertheless it was he who led in homage to the master, and it was he who contrived that Blake, in the final five years of his life, should receive enough orders to keep him and Catherine from actual starvation.

Blake had ever been a child at heart and an instinctive friend of children. Child, youth, or man, each soul evoked from him the same simple understanding response. The Ancients, ranging in age from the thirty-three years of Linnell (in 1825) to the sixteen of Richmond, soon learned that they could talk with William Blake as with any other fellow-student, and their love for him and their looking to his wisdom became the dominating fact of their lives.

The Blakes had moved in 1821, as a matter of economy, to two rooms in a house on Fountain Court, an inlet from the Strand. There, in quarters not unrespectable but certainly dark and cramped and unsuited to more than modest housekeeping, they carried on their activities in designing, engraving, and printing as well. The back room, which had a window looking narrowly out between two building walls to the Thames, affording a vista much valued by Blake, held a bed for sleeping, an open fireplace for both warmth and cooking, and a work table for engraving.

While inevitably this became a place of meeting for the disciples, the more frequent gatherings took them to Calvert's house on Brixton Road, Hampstead, or to Linnell's farm-home at North End, where Blake became a regularly expected visitor. Palmer deserted London and retired to a picturesque retreat at Shoreham, whither the other Ancients went at intervals to talk and sketch in "the Valley of Vision." Once the patriarchal Blake, only a year before his death, went down with the Calverts in the carrier's van, behind eight horses and bells, to be one of the meeting of Ancients there, to dream, talk, and plan with them.

The simple and friendly relationship of the youths to the older man is indicated in a record left by George Richmond. Suffering from depression about his work, he called at the home of the Blakes, to find them having tea. He explained his trouble, saying: "For a fortnight I have been deserted by the powers of invention." William Blake turned to Catherine for answer. "It is just so with us, is it not," he said, "when for weeks together the visions forsake us? What do we do then, Kate?" She answered: "We kneel down and pray, Mr. Blake."

The greater number of glimpses of Blake the man in the final years are of his regular Sunday appearances at the home of the Linnells at Hampstead. He loved to take part in the interminable conversations about art and to meet the older painters who came there, Constable among them; he loved to sit in the garden or to muse from some vantage point facing the countryside; he loved to look on at the family life of his hosts and their children. He was especially partial to Mrs. Linnell's singing; and occasionally he recited or sang songs of his own, to tunes of his own. He worked with little Hannah Linnell on her drawings. The mood of his life at this time is clear in a saying of his to a little girl who was introduced to him at a friend's home. Putting his hand on her head, he said: "May God make this world as beautiful to you as it has been to me."

Blake's health had been excellent through more than sixty years, but now it began to decline. Sometimes he was confined to his bed; but there he worked at his drawings. To an artist who complained of ill-health he said simply, "I work on, ill or well." About 1822 he touched closest to starvation. He sold the engravings he had collected in a lifetime of study. Linnell, aided by Lawrence and others, prevailed upon the Royal Academy to send Blake twenty-five pounds, a generous gesture, considering his outspoken condemnation of fashionable artists and art-depressing schools. It was the only money ever received by the Blakes (so far as is known) for which the artist did not return value in engraving work or prints or paintings.

By 1823 Linnell had evolved that plan by which he was able to supplement Blake's other earnings by instalment payments for drawings and engravings to be produced as time permitted. It was a generous and tactful way of guaranteeing that the wolf would not actually enter the door of the Fountain Court rooms. It enabled the artist to work further on the *Job* designs during the years 1823–26, first upon a full-size duplicate set of twenty-one coloured drawings, then on a series in pencil in reduced size, as guide to the engravings, on a third set in colour, and finally upon the engraved plates.

The book of engravings appeared in 1826. The translation of the values of the coloured designs to the values of copper-plate engraving had been accomplished with superb artistry. The formal, spiritual, and emotional values of the originals were retained. Special values possible to execution with the burin were added — a brilliant clarity, a dramatic simplicity, and a heightened play of black-and-white. Blake's genius as an engraver had matured thus late in life, his masterpiece appearing in his sixty-eighth year. It is a production placed by many with the engraving masterpieces of all time.

To the end Blake's preference in art remained in religious and visionary fields. In 1825 or 1826 he painted in water-colours a series of twenty-eight designs illustrating Bunyan's *Pilgrim's Progress*. He started then also to produce an ambitious set of paintings dealing with the materials of Dante's *Divine Comedy*. In order to be more in the spirit of the original, he resumed study of the Italian language.

His reading, like his work, lay largely in spiritual fields. His Bible was much with him; indeed he was still planning new Biblical pictures. He projected also a specially interpreted *Bible for*

Visionaries, wherein the *spirit* of the texts would be graphically brought out. Boehme was again in his mind. And he returned to praise of Swedenborg: "He was a divine teacher. He has done much good." He was stirred, too, by the books of the prophetic Scotch preacher, Edward Irving, then minister of the Caledonian Church in London. The French mystics, Fénelon and Mme Guyon, attracted him.

Happy in his reading, in his affectionate companionship with Catherine, in his friendships, in his work, he passed the final two years in an atmosphere of exceptional peace and well-being. Illnesses intruded, were a nuisance, but he did not take them too seriously. If one of them should take him off, it would be the happy occasion of his soul returning to that land of morning gladness which he had so often visited in vision. Once he spoke candidly of the poor lodgings in which he and Catherine lived and worked: "I live in a hole here." Immediately he added: "But God has a beautiful mansion for me elsewhere."

Crabb Robinson, who had been attracted to Blake's only exhibition sixteen years earlier, met the artist at a dinner party in 1825. In the following two years or less before Blake's death he put down in his diary accounts of their many conversations. The one a mystic and poet, the other a legal-minded barrister and realist, they yet respected each other's views; and Crabb Robinson through the diary preserved one of the most vivid first-hand views of the seer. The reports cover many of the truths and principles basic to Blake's life. As to vision: "I have had it from earliest infancy. All men partake of it, but it is lost by not being cultivated." And: "No education should be attempted except that of cultivation of the imagination and the fine arts." Of the chasm between Inspiration and Nature: "One power alone makes a poet: Imagination, the Divine Vision. Natural objects always did and now do weaken, deaden and obliterate Imagination in me." "When I am commanded by the Spirits, then I write. . . . Everything is the work of God."

The diary goes on to report Blake as averring that he has often conversed with Voltaire. Asked in what language, he replied: "To my sensation it was English. It was like the touch of a musical key. He touched it probably in French, but to my ear it became English." And: "I have written more than Voltaire or Rousseau — six or seven epic poems as long as Homer, and twenty tragedies as long as 'Macbeth.'"

Blake's closest friend among the older artists, Henry Fuseli, had died in the spring of 1825. Late in 1826 Flaxman passed away. Blake, informed by Crabb Robinson of the sculptor's going, said smilingly: "I thought I should have gone first. I cannot consider death as anything but a removing from one room to another."

He had been seriously ill during the summer. Nevertheless he pushed on with the Dante designs. He was destined to complete only seven of the more than one hundred projected engravings, but he left a large number of the unfinished water-colour drawings. In general they are original, imaginative, and among the most felicitous of his works; but they fail to have the monumentality and "sense of glory" of the *Job* and the *Jerusalem* series — an indication less, perhaps, of lessening insight and a failing hand than of a theme not within his own brooding and visioning. In the *Job* series and in the Biblical subjects generally he had lived the subject-matter and revealed himself; as also in the plates for *Milton* and *The Song of Los*. Dante, whom he concluded before the end to be an "atheist — a mere politician busied about this world," stirred him less profoundly.

It was perhaps in his last year that he made five sketches for illustrations of the apocryphal *Book of Enoch*. They are so spirited and so indicative of second meanings that the series, had the artist not died that year, might have ranked with the major prophetic works. He was busy at intervals finishing or repainting some of the earlier pictures, including an "Ugolino" and the since lost monumental fresco "The Last Judgement" — which he spoiled, as he thought, in the working-over. Desultorily he was writing too.

In a letter to John Cumberland dated April 12, 1827 Blake writes: "I have been very near the gates of death, and have returned very weak and an old man, feeble and tottering, but not in Spirit and life, not in the real man, the Imagination, which liveth for ever. In that I am stronger and stronger, as this foolish body decays." He includes in the letter, apologetically, a list of the prices at which he can deliver copies of his illuminated books — to print the *Jerusalem* "will cost my time the amount of twenty guineas" for the 100 plates. He adds that "The little card I will do as soon as possible," referring to a visiting or message card which turned out to be his last engraving: a little panel bearing the name "Mr. Cumberland" surrounded by floating figures. Thus in the last weeks he was taken from the Dante and Enoch paintings to produce a commissioned commercial item. With his signature he put down his age, 70, and the date, 1827.

At the beginning of that year the Linnells, genuinely worried over the inadequacy of the Blakes' dark rooms on Fountain Court, conceived the idea of removing the elderly couple to their own London house in Cirencester Place (then vacant because they were staying at their farm in Hampstead). They would make no charge for rental. Blake seemed at first tempted. But after he had "entreated Divine help" he refused. Trying conditions of living were no new thing to him and Catherine. Financial dependence upon others would be a surrender.

Toward the end of June he made his last visit to the Linnells at Hampstead, and returned home exhausted. After that he was much in bed. He could work with his designs there, but writing was difficult. "Kate," he one day said, "I am a changing man. I always arose and wrote my thought, whether it rained or snowed or shone, and you sat beside me; this can no longer be." And again: "I have no grief but in leaving you, Kate. . . . Why should I fear death? Nor do I fear it. I have endeavoured to live as Christ commanded, and have sought to worship God truly in my own home, when I was not seen by men."

Propped up in bed, he was working over a print of the Ancient of Days laying out with Golden compasses the circle of the Earth, when he was overtaken by one of the recurrent seizures. When he was again able to sit up, on Sunday, August 12, his habitual mood of patience had turned to one of exhilaration and gladness. He called for the print of the Ancient of Days and went on with the colouring of it. Saying "There, I have done all I can. It is the best I have ever finished" — and he *had* put a special glory of colour in it — he thrust it aside. Seeing Catherine as in a sudden revealing light, he said: "Kate, you have ever been an angel to me. I will draw you." Putting down the sketch of her, he began to sing ecstatically "Hallelujahs and songs of joy and triumph." He was interrupted by one of the little group of friends at the bedside who asked where he would prefer to be buried. He specified Bunhill Fields, where his people were, and he asked for the Anglican service. He also gave directions to Catherine about the disposition of his manuscripts and prints, suggesting Frederick Tatham as one to act with her in all matters.

Then to Catherine he said: "My beloved, I am going to that country which I have all my life wished to see. I am happy, hoping

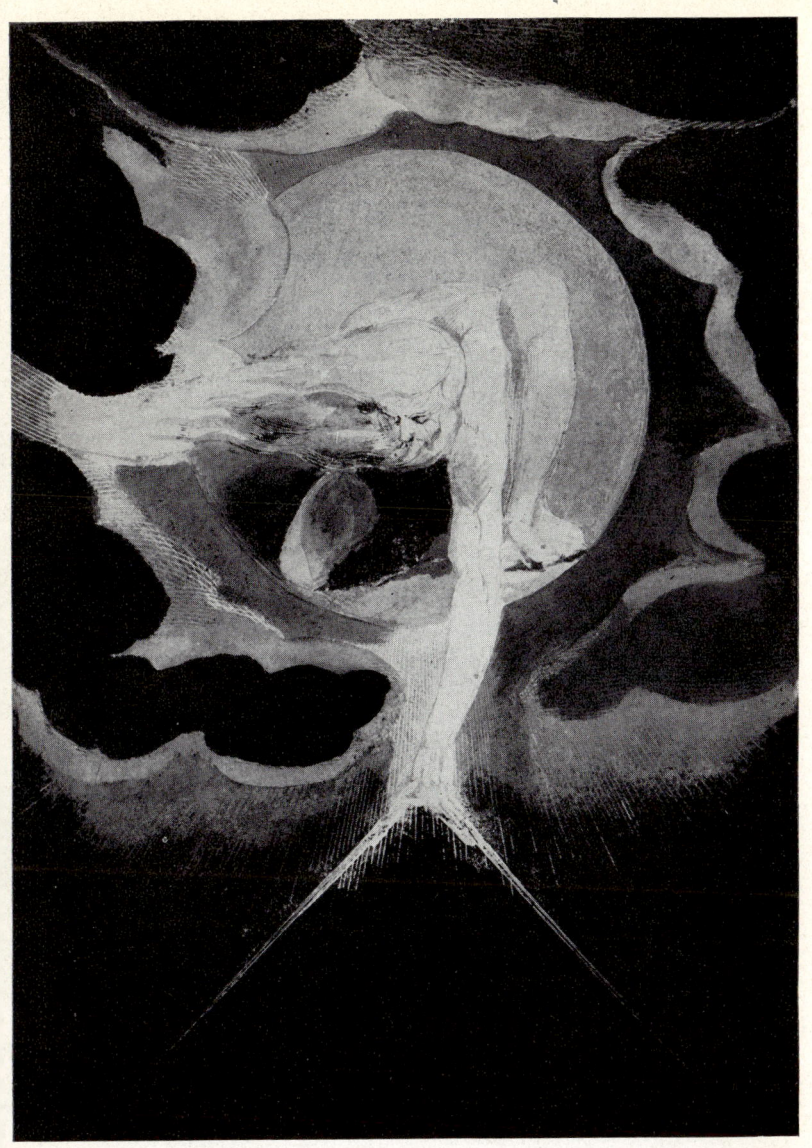

THE ANCIENT OF DAYS LAYING OUT THE CIRCLE OF THE EARTH WITH GOLDEN COMPASSES. COLORED PRINT BY WILLIAM BLAKE. ROSENWALD COLLECTION, NATIONAL GALLERY OF ART, WASHINGTON.

BLAKE DETHRONING URIZEN. COLORED PRINT BY WILLIAM BLAKE, FROM *MILTON*. ROSENWALD COLLECTION, NATIONAL GALLERY OF ART, WASHINGTON. (PHILADELPHIA MUSEUM OF ART PHOTO).

for salvation through Jesus Christ. But we shall not be parted. I shall always be about you, to take care of you." He took up again his joyful singing — songs described by Catherine as truly sublime in music and in verse. He paused to say to her of the songs, as he had said so often of his pictures and his poems: "My beloved, they are not mine. No, they are not mine."

Catherine, Frederick Tatham, George Richmond, and a neighbour woman were beside him in the late afternoon as the end approached. In Richmond's words, "His countenance became fair, his eyes brightened, and he burst out singing of the things he saw in Heaven." It was six o'clock when his soul passed outward, to regain Eden and the Eternal Golden Morning. The mortal body became still, even to the artist hands that had so seldom rested and the poet lips that had given utterance to so many immortal songs. The one among the attendants who is known only as "a neighbour woman" spoke the fairest epitaph: "A Saint has passed."

The funeral cost twenty-five shillings, and the grave was unmarked. Catherine, believing implicitly in her husband's continued presence, went on tranquilly, even smilingly, into a lonelier life. She accepted a place made for her by the Linnells at first, then went to act as voluntary housekeeper for the Tathams. She inventoried the stock of copper plates and prints and paintings left unsold, printed new impressions from some of the plates, and set about selling enough of the pictures to cover her modest expenses. Her friends found purchasers for some of the larger works. When the Princess Sophia asked that she accept a gift of one hundred pounds, Catherine returned the money, saying that, however thankful, she did not need it, that it would doubtless do more good elsewhere. In all matters she made her decisions only after "consulting Mr. Blake." Four years after his going, when she was on her death-bed, instead of singing joyful songs she kept calling to William to say that she was coming, that it wouldn't be long now.

An unfortunate postscript to the life and death of William Blake tells of the heritage of pictures, poems, and books he left to mankind. Catherine bequeathed to Frederick Tatham everything not sold. Tatham probably profited more by the sale of Blake's prints and books than by creations of his own during the following forty years. If his "service" to Blake had ended there, all might be considered well. But Frederick Tatham, being converted to the stricter tenets of the "Angels" of the Irvingite Church, took it upon himself to censor Blake's writings. He burned a reputedly large number of unpublished manuscripts. There is no trace of those "twelve tragedies as long as 'Macbeth' "; and even allowing for hyperbole, it is likely that we have lost some of the "six or seven epic poems as long as Homer." How much else, by way of religious speculation and other prose comment, may have been then destroyed, no one can venture to say. Crabb Robinson made mention of manuscripts "in immense quantity." It is true, too, that certain surviving prints have been mutilated (perhaps by others than Tatham) at those points where Blake pictured mortal love to suggest the bliss of heavenly attachment.

Other hazards, fires, attic rats and mice, and carelessness, have accounted for many of the larger paintings, and for some books of which only the titles survive. It is likely that the works of no other major poet or artist of modern times have been so neglected, mutilated, and, in great part, destroyed.

"All choice things," wrote the poet Novalis, "have a reference to mysticism." Poetry by its very nature, compounded of the indescribable elements of music, fastidious choice of words and images, and spiritual or emotional revelation, is, in its higher ranges, mystical. In its simplest lyrical form the mystic element is spontaneous, unemphatic, hidden to the perceptions of the uninitiated — as in Blake's "Piping down the Valleys Wild"; while in purposive mystic verse the other-worldly theme may be declared, the message made the central concern.

As a poet, William Blake at first sang lightly and felicitously, then wrote seriously and emotionally, and finally flashed and thundered in epic and tragic strain. His works illumine more brightly than those of any other poet the range of mystic or divine poetry.

From "Piping down the Valleys Wild" he goes on to the thoughtful but still "childlike" "The Lamb," identifying a lamb, a little child, the poet, and the Lamb of God in one Unity. A further stage is marked in the imaginative, allegorical, but still simple "Land of Dreams," in which the opening line, "Awake, awake, my little boy!" cloaks so many undeclared meanings, opens so many vistas into unseen lands. In the unpublished *Auguries of Innocence* — "To see a world in a grain of sand" — is perhaps the first direct statement of the poet's purpose to adopt consciously the mystic's attitude in his poetic writing. Thereafter the lines frankly charged with spiritual import are commoner:

> *I am in God's presence night and day,*
> *And He never turns His face away. . . .*

Finally, about the year 1788, the urge to speak the message direct becomes overwhelming and Blake turns to composition of the books variously called epic, prophetic, and unintelligible. When he incorporates a lyric passage he loses nothing of the sweet singing quality, the unique felicitous charm, that spells Blake for those readers who have not progressed beyond *Songs of Innocence* and *Songs of Experience*. But the characteristic poetry of the mature Blake is epic composition on grand themes, vast in conception, philosophic and prophetic in intention, packed with titanic, not to say cosmic figures. It is at once tender and terrible, musical and shattering, idyllic and profound. Sometimes there is an almost unbelievable juxtaposition of gorgeous measures and careless, awkward versifying.

Blake cannot indeed be wholly exculpated from accusations that his expression is uneven and that his epic poetry is occasionally unintelligible. Every critic in his own time turned back upon the prophetic books. It is to be remembered, nevertheless, that even the early lyrics that are a delight to all readers to-day found only an exceptional champion in the poet's lifetime or during fifty years after. Nor were editions of the epics made available to searchers until near the end of the nineteenth century. Little wonder then that hardly more than a grudging praise has been accorded to any one of the prophetic or mystical books by influential critics, up to the 1940's. "Confused," "unintelligible," "eccentric" are judgements heard not only in college halls but in books about English literature and about Blake.

Nevertheless, despite obvious faults, the long prophetic poems are likely to make their way into treasuries of the classics. Their faults are those especially apparent and specially irritating to the "authorities" of eighteenth- and nineteenth-century literature, to the polished neo-classic intelligences of Blake's own time, and to the soft-speakers of the Victorian era. Their virtues seem to some readers to be of the flaming sort that burns away imperfections. Surely the grandeurs of *Milton* and *Vala* and *Jerusalem* are not to be foregone because the passages are not all of an equal poetic excellence; or again because one must know something of Blake's total philosophy and mythology to extract all the meaning.

William Blake was a seer and a visionary in an age of worship of science. He was a Man of Imagination in a generation of reasoners. He was a rebel Christian, a follower of Jesus, in an era of nominal, rationalized Christianity. His whole poetic pæan was a hymn to God in praise of His Golden Age and a repudiation of the rationalism that seemed to him to have enslaved the men of earth to lawgivers, empire-makers, and the keepers of a law-bound church.

When William Blake as poet set about proving his contentions that the eternal and holy quality can be found in every thing, that the sense-detected material world is less real than the surrounding spiritual universe, and that the greatest happiness is to be found in communion with God — Whom he variously termed Imagination and Eternal Spirit, and the One beyond Jehovah — he built barriers of "unintelligibility" between his poems and those who should have been his readers.

The half-secret thing that binds all his prophetic works together, that illuminates each one, is the mystic's conception of the universe as Eden, of a timeless Golden Age in which man is restored to God, to unlimited Imagination, the animal self annihilated, the vision cleansed, the soul one with Jesus. It is an interpretation of Christianity as true and as beautiful as any known to us.

Nor is there anything of religiosity or puritanism in his poems. Far from denying the senses, Blake pleaded for richer use of them, though for enjoyment not with them so much as *through* them. They are often the channels to vision, to detection of the divine — "the chief inlet of the soul," he called them. His own contact with, as it might be, angels, or the Spirits of Milton and Shakspere, or with God was sometimes spontaneous and sometimes evoked by the sights and sounds and smells of nature. When he had gone to the seashore to live he wrote: "Heaven opens here on all sides her golden gates." He spoke too of the pleasures of sex as a gateway to vision, a holy gateway opening upon the clearest Eternal seeing of which the soul is capable. He is tolerant of sense enjoyment as he is tolerant of reason when utilized for its own necessary purposes. But as he thundered at reason usurping the place of intuition, imagination, and vision, he thundered at imprisonment to the senses.

If the light-heartedness seems to go out of the verse in the final years, and the pregnant sense-images give way to abstract ideas, there is no weakening of the translucent singing quality of those invoking lines with which Blake delighted to introduce the heavier prophetic works. The singing leads to profound revelation. The *Milton* starts with the superb hymn containing the lines "Bring me my bow of burning gold." The last epic, *Jerusalem*, is introduced with stanzas more personal and graver, but direct and simple:

> Again he speaks in thunder and in fire! . . .

The thunder and the fire in *Jerusalem* are sublime, majestic, at times terrifying. There are unforgettable titanic figures and stupendous cosmic vistas. It is in this poem, too, that William Blake most exactly describes his intention as a poet:

> . . . I rest not from my task!
> To open the Eternal Worlds, to open the immortal eyes
> Of Man inwards into the Worlds of thought, into Eternity
> Ever expanding in the Bosom of God, the human Imagination.

As he was a mystic among poets, so William Blake was a seer in the truest sense among graphic artists. He pleaded for second seeing over and over again, and he utilized notably those formal devices that render art a medium of revelation rather than imitation. Of the eye which sees only "that faint shadow called natural life," he wrote:

> This life's dim window of the Soul
> Distorts the Heavens from pole to pole,
> And leads you to believe a lie
> When you see with, not thro' the eye.

Guarding against the deduction that he is advocating fable or allegory, which may not rise above natural or "vegetative" statement, thus remaining "an inferior kind," he avers that "Vision or Imagination is a representation of what eternally exists, really and unchangeably. . . . This world of Imagination is Infinite and Eternal, whereas the world of generation, or vegetation, is finite and temporal. There exist in that Eternal world the permanent realities of every thing which we see reflected in this vegetable glass of nature. . . ." The artist's business is to grasp the permanent or Eternal reality; for himself, he experienced, he said, "fourfold vision."

Of the artist who works in single vision, by "nature's law," Blake said scornfully — and the passage is a favourite quotation of to-day's Moderns: "A man sets himself down with colours and with all the articles of painting; he puts a model before him and he copies that so neat as to make it a deception: now let any man of sense asks himself one question: Is this art? Can it be worthy of admiration . . . ? No man of sense ever supposes that copying from nature is the art of painting; . . . everybody may do it and the fool will often do it best."

Some of the overtones of Blake's paintings are of the sort that never will become apparent to the man of single vision, to the literal, unmusical man. They are formal, rhythmic, contrapuntal, of an element to be experienced but not identified. In the enrichment of design through the rhythmic devices Blake proves himself a master. He instinctively uses the abstract geometry, the organization of backward-forward movement within picture space, which is the central formal aim of a whole school of Moderns; which was an aim also of Tintoretto, Michelangelo, El Greco, and certain others of the old masters.

Blake seldom, however, played for abstract effect alone. His plastic structure in-forms the picture, is not its sole reason for being. The subject values, the meanings, are underlined, not overshadowed, by his design method. His mysticism lies not only in his way of utilizing the indescribable properties of four-dimensional design to afford an experience of rhythm or movement or melody, but also in his use of character and places and objects. As it is necessary to know something of his cosmography and mythology to gain all the pleasure and understanding possible out of the prophetic poems, so one gains immensely by such knowledge in contemplating the illustrations of *Jerusalem;* or the print (for *Milton*) of "Blake Dethroning Urizen"; or "When the Morning Stars Sang Together" — a glorious picture on all accounts, but the richer in spiritual significance when one realizes (it may be only subconsciously) that Job, his wife, and his comforters are encased in "the mundane shell," and that the feeling of the angels "shouting for joy" in Eden above is a feeling that runs through all Blake's descriptions of Eternity, through his descriptions of the bliss known to visionaries, to men such as the reborn Job.

The radiant splendours and symphonic grandeurs of the Biblical pictures were but one side — the prophetic — of Blake's designing. He could be simple, melodic, and felicitous upon occasion; and the mystic overtones, the emanations, were then in no way left out. Some of the "illuminations" for the *Songs of Innocence* and *Experience* are of that harmonic, beguiling sort. But most felicitous and most charged with meaning are the best of the miniature designs cut on wood for Dr. Thornton's Virgil: miracles of pastoral feeling, miraculously lighted and serenely realized. "They are," wrote the youthful Samuel Palmer, " 'visions' of little dells and nooks and corners of Paradise: models of the exquisitest pitch of intense poetry. . . . There is in all, such a mystic and dreamy glimmer as penetrates and kindles the inmost soul, and gives complete and unreserved delight, unlike the gaudy daylight of this world." And yet Dr. Thornton, looking with only single vision, had described the Virgil engravings which he would have destroyed, as coarse and amateurish. Perhaps one must be already something of a mystic, must already have cleansed the vision, to savour the spiritual values in the works of an artist such as William Blake, or to know what he meant when he said that "Art is a means of conversing with Paradise."

In poetry William Blake held to Imagination, which he also called God. In graphic art he held to intuition, clairvoyance, and revelation. So too in living he held to mystic perception, vision, and "converse with God" as the highest good of existence. The quality of his personal mysticism was deep, penetrating, and intense.

Despite lapses into mortal despair and irritation, he was one of the happiest men of his time. He habitually found beauty in — or through — nature; he consorted with the spirits of the great of all times and with the angels; and he was summoned periodically into God's presence. Life was never single to him. For everything material there was a spiritual "correspondence." A walking excursion into the country was a trip to Heaven, "displaying the Eternal Vision, the Divine Similitude." At his work table a moment's contemplation opened the way into the mansions of Paradise.

His beloved Catherine stated that William believed "that the inner world is all-important; that each man has a world within greater than the external." She believed implicitly in him and accepted without question his visions and his reports of meeting spirits or angels, or it might be Milton or Plato or Jesus. She sat by him gladly for hours when he rose at night to take down Divine dictation. He looked at her, as at all else, with second sight, so that she was to him Pity, Forgiveness, Desire, "Lovely delight of Men, Enitharmon."

Blake's works tell a single, meaningful story, forming a narrative framework for his mysticism. It is a story at once vast and precise. It proceeds by flashes and bursts; and the precise details at one place are sometimes at variance with those revealed at another, where a more meaningful conception has taken possession of the poet. Nevertheless he does keep a direction fairly clear, by dropping in guide lines or brief summaries in praise of the "life in divine vision." These range from the unforgettable abstract statement:

> *To see a World in a Grain of Sand*
> *And a Heaven in a Wild Flower,*
> *Hold Infinity in the palm of your hand,*
> *And Eternity in an hour —*

to the triumphant cry in his last prophetic poem, after his climactic turning to Jesus:

> *He is become One with me!*

No "system," Christian or classic or Oriental, was big enough to contain the poet's conceptions of the cosmogony, of the geography of Heaven and Earth, and of the fall and rise of Man. He took as basis the Christian story (for the Bible was in every sense the first book in his life), but he borrowed from sources as far apart as the ancient Vedic gods, the Atlantean legends, and the visions of Boehme. He invented, if not gods, the emanations of gods, and he imaged a Heaven of dimensions almost beyond human faculty to grasp. He enlarged, he reinterpreted, he embroidered; then in a flash he soared away from all he had adapted or created.

The gist of the story is this. The beginning is in neither a Creation nor a Chaos. "Eternity exists . . . independent of Creation." There is, independent of any act or beginning, the timeless Paradise, the unlimited Golden Age. There is an unnamable God, Eternal Spirit, embracing the Oneness of all that is. He is Imagination and Poetic Genius. To be in his estate is to be in Paradise, Eden, Jerusalem.

There arise four elemental beings, the Zoas, and one of them, Urizen, Reason, desiring to rule, stirs up a struggle for supremacy. Mastering the others, he writes his books of Law. Aspiring even to be God, Urizen (who thus becomes a false Jehovah) creates the limited or temporal world. Typifying Reason or Rationalism, he tries to take the throne of Spirit, a second Zoa, named Urthona. He makes himself ruler of the created, time-conditioned universe.

Man is thus separated from God and placed in the mortal or vegetative world, "a world of generation and death." The earth, with all having to do with it, is now material, illusory, and divided. It is a shadow, a poor copy of the Eternal, Imaginative, Spiritual Reality. For Man the fall is a personal one because he descends from Eternal Life to "the land of death eternal."

The single-sighted man, without Imagination, remains in a state of living death. But Poetic Man discovers, beyond each material aspect of life, a corresponding spiritual "existence," the Divine Reality. In fact, Imagination is the man, once he opens the gateway of vision inward.

The prophetic books treat mainly of Urizen's adventures in gaining supremacy over the other Zoas and of the attempts of Los, the Sun of Imagination, to bring fallen Man to vision, judgement, and redemption. Urizen may be called directly "Reason" or he may take on something of Satan. Blake once represented Reason's submission and the triumph of Imagination in a little drawing that shows a girl and two small children riding happily on the back of a serpent. The girl controls the monster by reins: Imagination or vision controlling Reason.

But before this happy dénouement — never quite accomplished in any of the surviving prophetic books — there are vast struggles among the Zoas, who confusingly live, die, live again, beget Emanations, even beget each other, and, though sometimes trying to aid Man, only succeed in keeping him in slavery to the law-obsessed Urizen. To Los and Enitharmon is born Orc, Revolt, and he seems on the way to stirring sluggish Man to overthrow all the institutions by which Reason has corrupted and ruled men. But Orc appears very little toward the end. Rather it is Jesus, taking an increasingly central place in the cast of characters as Blake matures, who brings hope, even certainty, of redemption, of restoration of the Golden Age, of reconstitution of the One.

Man plays a rather pitiable rôle through most of the story. For lack of Imagination he has taken to seeing everything "in reason," trusting his five physical senses. From innocence he has fallen into experience, and from there into arguing good and evil. The next step is laws — and now government, religion, philosophy, and education are simply floundering in a swamp of moralizing, law-making, prohibition, and punishment. The network or crust of laws and curses about Man is the "mundane shell" shown in certain of the prints, caverning Man, and described in the poems as a "frozen net."

In all consideration of Man the distinction must be made between man fallen into this degraded estate, infected by time, and Man before the Fall (or after regeneration), the Human-Divine dweller in Paradise. Man since Adam, enslaved, bound up in self, law-ridden, is merely the spectre, the mortal shadow, of the Divine Man identical with God, inseparable from Jesus, Man as Imagination and Poetry.

Albion, who had symbolized England in the early poems, became in the later poems man in his degraded state. Originally, it seems, Albion was identical with Jerusalem, one with Eternity. Once he is "the King of Men," and again "Albion, our Ancestor, patriarch of the Atlantic Continent." But later he is representative man — that is, fallen man — a symbol of the human race under Reason's cold rule. The struggle, then, is to awaken Albion by means of vision so that he will see life about him for what it is, a cold, ugly routine of materialism; so that he will rise again and claim Jerusalem.

At the triumphant close of the final epic, *Jerusalem*, it is Jesus before whom Albion stands "in the clouds of Heaven, fourfold among the visions of God in Eternity." And it is only by contemplating the Divine Mercy of Jesus and exercising His Divine Vision that Albion is enabled to cast off selfhood, pass through the "furnaces of affliction," and awaken to Eternal Day. Jesus, for William Blake, is God and the inmost in Man, is Faith, is Art, is the means to salvation, and, in the end, the Sea in which the soul is immersed.

In many passages of *Vala* and *Jerusalem* the poet restates the thoughts of the Sermon on the Mount or of the charge to the Disciples. Once he writes:

> *Go, therefore, cast out devils in Christ's name,*
> *Heal thou the sick of spiritual disease,*
> *Pity the evil, for thou art not sent*
> *To smite with terror and with punishment.*

The Blakean story thus ends with the Christian-mystic thought that Jesus has shown the "way." Though for nearly two thousand years poets and prophets have failed to stem the flood of materialism, now new poet-seers arise, revolution stirs, a call goes out to awaken, to rebuild Jerusalem, to seek Eden and "the Mystic Union of the Emanation in the Lord."

And what is the personal application of the vast fable? What is the individual's path? Is there a single illuminated "way" indicated through the immensities of Blake's magnificent, confused drama?

One may begin, as the poet began his writing, among simple everyday things, finding in flowers, in a grain of sand, in a tear, the spiritual impress, the reality of the Divine. Potentially each man is All — "in every bosom a universe expands" — and the beginning of the "way" lies in himself, in an inner eye too long disused, in a capacity for vision and self-surrender and soul-unfoldment.

We cannot all, obviously, begin with that "fourfold sight" which rendered angels visible to William Blake:

> *With angels planted in hawthorn bowers*
> *And God himself in the passing hours, . . .*
> *With a thousand angels upon the wind —*

but we can have faith from his example that, once the doors of perception *are* cleansed, every common thing will appear "as it is, Infinite." And, Blake says, "He who sees the Infinite in all things, sees God."

One warning Blake uttered repeatedly. Reject nothing, for all is holy. Instead of trying to set off good from evil — the moralists, especially the law-makers and the churches, are practically absorbed in the business — cultivate Vision; and arriving thus at a vantage point whence the world is viewed in the light of the Spiritual, you will find that everything in mortal existence falls into place. In that revealing light evil will be seen as the absence or negation of good. A great deal of so-called sin will prove only illusion, having seemed evil because of mortal lack of understanding. "Error is created. Truth is Eternal," he wrote. Forgiveness, in Jesus' sense, Blake adds, will do wonders here.

Perceiving the divine in everything, exalting all because God embraces all — "Everything on Earth ... in its essence is God" — might lead to no more than a pantheistic understanding, an enlightened nature-worship, if one fails to heed the poet's further revelation. To him it is not that each object is important because existing in the Body of God, so much as the truth that God, existing in all that is, is all-important. The one half of the struggle upward is the cultivation of multifold vision, the training of the faculties of spiritual seeing, of clairvoyance. There then remains the more purifying, the more holy, half of the "way," the process that ends with the restoration of Oneness with Divinity.

Religion was to Blake the highest activity of man. Vision led to no other consciousness so joyous as that of the Christ in the heart. In early life he spoke of the supreme attainment as return to Imagination. He wrote that "Imagination is the Divine Body in every man." But then, as he found that his own life had not been cleared of the material element, even of some very unspiritual resentments, though he attained to Poetry and Vision and fourfold seeing, he turned increasingly to the Saviour. He conceived the word "Saviour" not as connoting atonement in the churches' sense; for sins did not seem to him important and called for little consideration, being illusory, having no standing in the spiritual world. Rather Jesus was the guide and companion of the "way," the One easily "taken on" because Human, the expression of God in man.

There is no plainer, more artless invitation to follow Blake as mystic than that inserted at the opening of the final book of *Jerusalem*. There he placed the lines:

> *I give you the end of a golden string,*
> *Only wind it into a ball,*
> *It will lead you in at Heaven's gate*
> *Built in Jerusalem's wall.*

The string end is the understanding of living in God as the one worthy aim of human life. Take hold of that understanding and cling to it — though the string disappear for considerable periods while Blake marshals his gods and spectres and emanations, and

THE ANGEL OF THE REVELATION. WATER-COLOR DRAWING BY WILLIAM BLAKE. METROPOLITAN MUSEUM OF ART.

WILLIAM BLAKE

men, through vast cycles of adventure — hold to that understanding and the string will reappear at intervals in the reading, to mark the individual's way to Heaven's Gate. The reappearances might almost be numbered — in this fourth book of *Jerusalem* — indicating steps not unlike the stages of spiritual progress as prescribed by some Hindu "Guru."

Step One is the awakening to vision.

Step Two is the passing through affliction, or it may be only the recognition that life as lived, in the net of rationalism and materialism, without Divine illumination, is affliction.

Step Three is the recognition that civilization and unillumined religion are infected like all else on the mortal plane. At this stage, with this recognition, Forgiveness enters the heart — and one has begun to take on the attributes of Jesus.

With Step Four the pilgrim arrives at realization of the Divine in man, is awakened to universal love, and sees the vision of the brotherhood of men as implicit in the fellowship of Christ.

The progress from this stage to the next is inevitable, and perhaps imperceptible. Man learns that brotherhood cannot exist except by the "mysterious offering of self for another." The self must be given away, annihilated. The soul then finds its own Christhood.

In the story of Albion — "the representative man" — Albion finally throws himself into the furnaces of affliction. Thus the last obstruction to clear-seeing is swept away. He passes through Heaven's Gate, arrives at Oneness with all that had been divided from him, in Eternity.

And so, says Blake, may you and I, at the end of the golden string — so may we be transported, by the "way" of awakened Imagination, recognition of worldly life as a living death, annihilation of selfhood, and regeneration: so may we be transported into that Eternal Imagination, in which our soul is at one with Jesus, in which we know God.

That is the consummation, the mystic's advent of the Golden Age. The prophecy has been fulfilled: "God becomes as we are, that we may be as He is." The pilgrim has travelled the way and has found Him; and He is within.

William Blake was, as certain philosophers have pointed out, a forerunner of Nietzsche and of the cult of exalted individualism. Aphorisms of his, wrested from their context and set up without regard to the total structure of his beliefs, seem to glorify the expression of exuberant personality, to exalt certain commonly condemned instincts, to praise the will to act decisively — and seem to condemn Christian humility. But the only "superman" pictured ultimately in Blake's works is the man strong enough, inspired enough, to break the hold of mortal things, annihilate selfishness, and rise to mystic union with God.

All the negation and pessimism to be uncovered in the prophetic books has to do with man in his fallen state, rational, corrupt, selfish, and with institutions infected with mortality, degraded by the misuse of reason. The poet's excoriations of humility are held in limits: he scorns the "humble toward man" but goes on to extol the "humble toward God." He derides the art and the religion of fallen man: the shallow, "copying" art fashionable in his time and the compromised Church with its lame dependence upon moral law; but creative art and God-illumined religion are inseparable from the Eden to which his Imaginative Man is to be restored.

He glorifies Art as Paradise. "The City of Art" is another name for Jerusalem. God is Eternal Poetic Genius. Religion is the highest state to which the individual may aspire. (All this in contrast to Nietzsche's thesis that art and religion are *in toto* illusory, or else a sort of invented fog in which man hides from reality.)

Nietzsche and Blake alike scorn slave psychology and the cautious, "reasonable" spirit; but in Blake's philosophy this spirit and the evils it has bred — law, militarism, false religious doctrine, false art, imperialism, realistic education — will be resolved into nothingness. Nietzsche attacks Jesus as symbol of humility, slavishness, and a moralism designed to protect the weak, as nullifying joy and impeding the will to power. Blake attacks the too frequent conception of Jesus as exclusively a refuge for the weak and the meek, a comforter of the miserable, and a means of "magic" salvation. But in all spiritual literature there is no more reverent and exalted picture of Jesus as the mystic redeemer of man than his.

In short the Nietzscheans pose as protagonist on the modern stage of life a ruler of earth by the power of intellect and will, an individual who is a superman only physically and intellectually. They stop short of any belief in or comprehension of a spiritual region of being. Blake, on the other hand, though he can be said to go along with them brilliantly in his preliminary destructive phase, rises to prophecy in the purest realms of religion, of spiritual faith. He foreshadowed the figures of the nineteenth-century era of negation and revolt. But he transcended the philosophies of his own time and of all those decades following when philosophers (including Nietzsche) had lost the sense of God.

Considering the drift of men during the twentieth century to the rediscovery of the truth that balanced living has its spiritual side, a side predominant in determining the happiness of existence — even scientists admitting a spiritual necessity, independent of rational activity — considering this later drift, one may feel certain that Nietzsche is the lesser, Blake incomparably the greater modern seer. William Blake must himself have seemed, to many an exasperated and embarrassed contemporary, the assertive Schopenhauer-Nietzsche superman. But he added the only qualifications that can make the presence of the superman tolerable: spiritual control of rational activity, mystic understanding, an all-embracing love.

One may believe that he is the more modern in that he carried on the ages-old mystical tradition, reaffirming in the era of intensified materialism the Christian truths that the Kingdom of God is within you; that a rebirth, the birth of the spirit, opens the way of vision, of a "new life"; and that the mystic knowing of God, in each created thing and in an unbounded communion, is the highest good open to man.

Almost it might be said that he spent his life repeating one truth: that Paradise, with all that the word implies of Heavenly bliss and consciousness of God's presence, can be brought down to the individual, or, if you will, that he can be lifted up, even in mortal life, to that realm of Divine illumination and experience. Blake's unique importance in the history of prophecy and mysticism is that he expressed with more beauty than any other, in poetry and in painting, this message of the Spirit, in terms essentially Christian yet universal.

He is the more convincing in that in his own life he set up the example of a visionary never compromising or withdrawing; holding to Vision and affirming the importance of mystic communion even in the stream of common affairs. And when most buffeted and all but destroyed (as mortals' standards go) he rose to a final triumph of faith in a climactic conversion, arrived at peace in life, and attained frequent communion with God.

Afterword

In mysticism, I believe, lies the essence of the religious life. Without the mystical element, religion is external and strengthless. Most of the mystics I have portrayed in this book have been men of religion in a special sense, founders of sects or saints dedicated to holy service. They have been men of older times. If I were adding further studies, however, to a collection already beyond its planned length, I should be tempted to include the biography of a modern lay mystic, one who has had to meet the challenge of contemporary scientists.

The story of mysticism does not end with the last of the seers interpreted in the preceding chapters. It seems true that in the Western world there have not been, in a hundred years, distinctive and prophetic mystics of the stature of Jacob Boehme and Brother Lawrence and William Blake. There have been, nevertheless, poets expressing the oneness of the individual soul with all deity and all life, and there have been minor spiritual prophets who have claimed considerable followings in both Europe and America. As for the truce with science I may quote a passage from a writer who was not one of the great figures in mysticism, who yet got to the heart of it in simple words while exploring subjects that are closer to biology and psychology.

Edward Carpenter wrote, late in the nineteenth century: "Of all the hard facts of science . . . I know of none more solid and fundamental than the fact that if you inhibit thought (and persevere) you come at length to a region of consciousness below or behind thought and different from ordinary thought in its nature and character — a consciousness of quasi-universal quality, and a realization of an altogether vaster self than that to which we are accustomed. And since the ordinary consciousness, with which we are concerned in ordinary life, is before all things founded on the little, local self, and is in fact *self*-consciousness in the little, local sense, it follows that to pass out of that is to die to the ordinary self and the ordinary world. It is to die in the ordinary sense, but in another sense it is to wake up and find that the I, one's real, most intimate self, pervades the universe and all other beings — that the mountains and the sea and the stars are a part of one's body and that one's soul is in touch with the souls of all creatures. Yes, far closer than before. It is to be assured of an indestructible immortal life and of a joy immense and inexpressible — 'to . . . sit with all the Gods in Paradise.'"

The eminent scientist who wrote those words, suggesting the vaster "self" of the mystic as a fresh field of scientific research, could write also an eloquent description of the actual attainment of spiritual union: "The Man at last lets Thought go; he glides below it into the quiet feeling, the quiet sense of his own identity with the self of other things — of the universe. . . . He leans back in silence on that inner being, and bars off for a time every thought, every movement of the mind, every impulse to action, or whatever in the faintest degree may stand between him and That; and so there comes to him a sense of absolute repose, a consciousness of immense and universal power, such as completely transforms the world for him. All life is changed. . . . For the ceaseless endeavour to realize this identity with the great Self, there is no substitute. No teaching, no theorizing, no philosophizing, no rules of conduct or life will take the place of actual experience. This is the Divine yoga or union, from which really all life, all Creation, proceeds."

Edward Carpenter was a poet-scientist. If one were writing his story as a type-mystic, one would be constrained to sketch his background in the tradition of English poetry. In the literature of no other nation does mystic poetry bulk so large or assay so rich. One might go back as far as Spenser for a beginning, and along the way spend fascinated hours with Henry Vaughan and with Richard Crashaw. Thereafter there was no other to rival the intensity of William Blake's feeling or the prophetic grandeur of his poetry. But Coleridge struck the mystic note, and with Wordsworth a sort of nature-mysticism arrived at full flower. The "Ode on the Intimations of Immortality" justly became a classic of mystic verse. After Wordsworth came Browning, whose spiritual speculation was on the intellectual side; but as a foil to it there appeared, during his lifetime, a classic of the mysticism that unfolds thoughtlessly within a pagan communion with nature: the autobiography, in poetic prose, of Richard Jefferies, called "The Story of My Heart."

In America the communities that grew out of the Quietist, Quaker, Moravian, Shaker, and other congregations seeking asylum failed to find voice in the nation's literature, or to produce any widely heard mystic prophet. Rather, it was the group in New England named the Transcendentalists that is best known as affording a mystical bent to philosophy and writing. Emerson was the genius of the movement, a true philosopher and illuminator of the way. His gathering up of the wisdom of the East as well as the West, of ancient knowledge as well as modern, is perhaps too little appreciated by his fellow Americans. Where he was indebted to the Vedas and to the Buddha, to Plotinus and to Boehme, his companion Thoreau was uniquely native and self-sufficient in his mysticism. He was a child of seclusion and solitude, a liver of the interior life of nature, with a Franciscan understanding of the animals other than man.

But of all American poets Walt Whitman was the one who most heartily and eloquently gave his life to glorifying universality and "unseen existences." He was on the pagan side; indeed he seems to have accepted God and Christ only out of a great impartiality, a love of all that ever was, is, or will be. But he detected the soul, its limitlessness, and the light in which it shone:

> *Light rare, untellable, lighting the very light,*
> *Beyond all signs, descriptions, languages.*

A proper treatment of Whitman's poetry in relation to the tradition of mysticism has not yet appeared. When his poems in mystic vein are drawn clear of the other pieces, and from what is plain "barbaric yawp," it may be that he will seem the principal figure after Blake in the line of mystic singers. Whitman, Wordsworth, Browning, Jefferies, Emerson — any one of these might afford materials for a chapter in the account of mysticism since Blake.

But in the world-view the poets — excepting Lao-Tse — have left monuments less splendid than those bequeathed by the seers who are better called philosophers, or practical mystic guides. Of those who lived in the later nineteenth century the one who perhaps surpassed all others, for holiness, and for the typically modern attempt to fuse all mystic techniques, Christian and Eastern, into one way of communion with God, was the Hindu who took the name Ramakrishna. In America the message of Ramakrishna was put forward by Vivekananda, whose books upon the Vedantic philosophy have formed a bridge for many readers between the thought of the West and the thought of the Hindus.*

---

* I am impelled to add that, of all the deficiencies or omissions, as I have felt them, in the pages of this book, the greatest is at the point where an exposition of Hindu mysticism might have appeared. The reasons lie espe-

AFTERWORD

Although the twentieth century seems not to have produced a mystic philosopher of the insight and influence of those treated in my main chapters, there never has been a time when so many societies, foundations, and presses have been devoted to the propagation of spiritual ideas, and particularly to the clarifying of one universal way to union with the Divine. There are minor prophets all about us, and there is a rising tide of interest and of vocation toward the inward life. If new major prophets come not immediately, we may well be patient, for we are dealing with slow-moving forces, indeed with a thing that is certain and eternal. We can be assured that they will arrive among men again; for mysticism is the very core of living, ever-lasting and ever-recurrent.

The realm that is opened by the mystics, as we have now sensed from their lives and their writings, is a land of unimaginable majesty and radiance. Is it to be still something of a secret realm? What of the common man of our present-day materialistic civilization? Is he to be excluded? Let us be candid. The horizon that stands behind the eyes, the vista that lures the inward vision, the realm so fair that initiates returning from it count all that is admirable on earth a mere shadow of it — all this is still for most men territory lost at birth, and during life unexplored.

Vaguely it is a familiar land, remembered as the native country of the soul. Children have memory of it, as if they had but recently come away. At rare intervals the adult may be confronted with the actuality of it, perhaps when transported in love, or in the hours when the tangible world recedes before the advance of death. In the one case he puts the vision down as a gain of early rapturous love, not to be recaptured. In the other he has turned too late from the darkness of practical living to the gates of vision. Upon rare occasions the man may, as an effect of symphonic music, or poetry, or a play at the theatre, be delivered from the world and washed to that shore. Equally rarely, and unaccount-

---

cially in the fact that the classics of Vedantism are anonymous, and thus ill fitted to enter into my plan to present the history of mysticism through a series of biographies; and in a certain duplication which would have occurred in connection with the chapter on Buddhism (itself an outgrowth of Hinduism). It should be noted that in the West many prominent proponents of the mystic life have been, in recent decades, members of the Theosophic movement, which has drawn especially upon the wisdom of India.

ably, one may slip over to it from sleep, and return reluctantly, conscious of its blessed peace and its abiding radiance.

Every man has two selves. Those vistas and voyages and intimations are glimpses and quests into the realm and the life of a second, a commonly submerged, self.

Ordinarily the upper self takes charge during the early stages of the passage on earth that we call life, and directs the voyage until its end, or near its end. The man is content to be one person, one self, in spite of the vague consciousness that another sleeps within him. He sets his course by observation, by studying the routes taken by other ordinary men. He arrives at the island called security. There the necessities of physical living and the pleasures of the senses, even intellectual recreations, are his, seemingly forever. The perils of the voyage of life seem past. The one self has succeeded. The man has no need of the other person he might have been.

But the island of security turns out to be illusion — never more so than in the war-sundered twentieth century. It is seen that voyagers who utilize only the upper, superficial self, on the material, the creaturely side of being, carry their own storms and destruction to whatever isle or haven. The course they have travelled brings them at last to a prison of the mind and senses, and to the pillories of war, disease, and enslavement. It is then that the traveller oftenest rediscovers how fair might have been the other path, how superior the realm of the spiritual self, which he has left aside, with all of faith and imagination and spiritual initiative. Too late he has looked inward, has faced that other horizon.

Yet there is the example of men who have forsaken or compromised the way of common, practical life to enter the realm of the spiritual self. Their testimony is recorded in books open to all eyes, books commonly called "holy" and "sacred," so excellent is their message, or "mystical," so different is the glory and truth therein from the easily understood pleasures spread in the records and novels of this world. Those explorers have experienced the highest happiness open to human beings. They have walked with God. They have lost themselves in Divine Presence. In that mergence they have known a timeless bliss and the inexpressible comfort of peace.

Returned to their accustomed life, they have perceived more spontaneously the beauty of the world and have affirmed more readily the nobility of mortal life. They have come back gladdened, vitalized, inspired. For the mystic wanderer counts his journeying, not as an escape from living, but as an interval of illumination and renewal. To meet the problems of common life he has brought back an incorruptible certitude and a steadfast bravery. In no other way can man come fully to the inner fearlessness, the fortification, that renders him invulnerable to the shocks and stabs of earthly existence.

Not war or human infamy or personal disaster can shake the returned pilgrim's faith in the orderly processes and the spiritual importance of the universe. These soul-wanderers, finders of peace and harmony and order, are, indeed, our only true philosophers. They have gained a perspective upon the constructive processes of the universe, the origin and significance of living, and the impermanence of human evils and ills. To a degraded world they speak of a main direction, a continuing purpose, an incorruptible good. They alone have seen life whole.

Latter-day pragmatists and sceptics, letting pride of intellect rise up between them and open-mindedness, mistrusting the hiddenness of the mystic realm, have attacked the explorers of the inner world, declaring them to be groping conjurers and dealers in mystery. They have assailed mysticism as a nebulous thing, compounded of confusion and darkness. But invariably the great mystics have come back from their meditation and their transports speaking of the clarity, the illumination, and the lucent understanding experienced in the world of the other self. As it is the world of the Spirit, they have spoken oftenest of a return to the illumination that is God.

There, indeed, is the central "mystery" of their activities, the consummation almost too sacred and too secret for words: they have experienced the presence of God. That experience, that surrender and loss of self in Divinity, if it be not the *summum bonum* of religion, as some of us believe, is yet a prime factor in every inspirational faith, in every joyous communion from Taoism, Buddhism, and the Greek Mystery Faiths to essential Christianity and Moslemism; and the partakers of that hallowed communion are to be identified as the truest religious leaders in history, although frequently they have been denied, if not persecuted, by the established churches from which they sprang.

Their teaching rises above the intricacies of dogma and the divisions of sects. Theirs is less a plea for an exclusive religious life than an invitation to practise life whole; that is, as an activity of both selves. To-day we all exist in a divided if not anarchic world society of men. To follow the example of the mystics would mean healing and orderliness, fraternalism and freedom and peace. Wide-spread obedience to them would open the road to the only binding union, of love, self-discipline, and communal giving.

These, then, have been the mystics — the explorers of the second world, the seers, the saints — among matter-of-fact human beings. It had seemed to me that a history of them would be at once a biography of God on earth and a record of the highest in human happiness. It would be a reminder, too, that in whatever depths of selfish warring, common depravity, or moral confusion mankind may have sunk, there have been always spiritual guides, adventurers in holiness and calm, proving by example the wisdom of divine union, and its accessibility.

A Descriptive Reading List, with Acknowledgments

THIS BOOK is an introductory and elementary study, rather than a treatise addressed to scholars and initiates. Therefore I shall attempt, in the lists that follow, to point the way to profitable *general* reading, avoiding the deeply philosophical and esoteric works. Keeping in mind the needs of the common reader, I will describe those books that seem at once inclusive, authoritative, and readable.

GENERAL. There is one volume that is a treasury of excerpts from and brief biographies of leading mystics: *Hours with the Mystics*, by Robert Alfred Vaughan (London & New York, 9th ed., no date, originally published in 1856). It is readable, even chatty, but it is written unsympathetically, and it tends to be openly hostile to the Catholic seers. Outside the Oriental field, where it is both begrudging and misinformed, it has the virtues of inclusiveness and suggestiveness. A brief review, more speculative than historical or biographical, is *Mysticism throughout the Ages*, by Edward Gall (London, n.d.). It is a good background book, though over-brief in its presentation of Christian mysticism. *Lamps of Western Mysticism*, by Arthur Edward Waite (New York, 1923), includes, between grouped speculative essays, a review of fifteen centuries of Western mysticism.

A fairly good introductory book on the theoretical side is *The Theory and Practice of Mysticism*, by Charles Morris Addison (New York, 1918). But most convincing and richest in illustrative matter, though confined to a personal view of Christian mysticism, is *Mysticism*, by Evelyn Underhill (London, 12th ed., revised, 1930). In no sense a survey, yet presenting a series of cogent and unconventional "slants" upon mystical religion, is *Mysticism of East and West: Studies in Mystical and Moral Philosophy*, by William Loftus Hare (New York, 1923). The student entering this field soon learns that certain authors can be especially trusted to yield rich return for time given to their books. Among them, beside Evelyn Underhill, I would place Rufus M. Jones, who writes thoughtfully and urbanely, out of a lifetime of devoted study; though it is only as a series that his books can be described as a survey of any extensive era of mystic development.

I. LAO-TSE AND TAOISM. The only book of considerable weight now generally available is *The Way and Its Power: A Study of the Tao Te Ching and Its Place in Chinese Thought*, by Arthur Waley (London, 1942). It is valuable in many ways, but more so to the specialist in sinology than to the beginning reader; and the included "philological" translation seems somewhat less true to the spiritual values than several other versions. Perhaps the most readable is *The Tao Te Ching*, translated by Ch'u Ta-Kao (London, 1937). It is reprinted complete in *The Bible of the World*, edited by Robert O. Ballou (New York, 1939). Other good versions are: that of Lin Yutang, included in his valuable anthology, *The Wisdom of China and India* (New York, 1942); that of Wai-Tao and Dwight Goddard, published with supporting essays under the title *Lao-Tzu's Tao and Wu-Wei* (Thetford, Vermont, 1939); and that of Lionel Giles, published as *The Sayings of Lao Tzu* (London, 1909, in the Wisdom of the East series). *The Canon of Reason and Virtue*, by Paul Carus (Chicago & London, 1927), includes considerable introductory matter and suggestive commentary, as well as the Chinese text, but the translation loses in the effort to transpose parts of the original into rhymed English verse. At the moment of completing this list there appears a new version, *The Way of Life according to Laotzu*, by Witter Bynner (New York, 1944). Introduced by an excellent brief essay, the translation is among the most satisfying.

A book indispensable for the scholarly approach is *The Texts of Taoism*, by James Legge (London, 1927, in the Sacred Books of the East series, vols. 39 & 40). Included are the writings of Chuang-Tse as well as those of Lao-Tse, in reputedly literal translation, with scholarly introductions. A more readable selection from Chuang-Tse's writings can be found in *Musings of a Chinese Mystic*, with an introduction by Lionel Giles (London, 1927, in the Wisdom of the East series). In the same pocket-size library is the only easily available selection from the writings of Lieh-Tse, published as *Taoist Teachings*, translated with introduction and notes by Lionel Giles (London, 1939).

One of the most prized introductory books, *The Story of Oriental Philosophy*, by L. Adams Beck (New York, 1928), includes chapters on Lao-Tse and Chuang-Tse; and the interpretations are the more illuminating because the author was a thorough mystic.

READING LIST

For historical background readably presented, see *A Short History of Chinese Civilization*, by Tsui Chi (New York, 1943). One can recommend highly *The Vision of Asia: An Interpretation of Chinese Art and Culture*, by L. Cranmer-Byng (New York, 1933). As regards Chinese art in relation to mysticism the books of Laurence Binyon and Ananda Coomaraswamy are most useful.

[I owe thanks to all the authors whose books are mentioned above. To James Legge I am especially indebted, since I used his nearly literal translation, by courteous permission of the Oxford University Press, as basis for my own "versions" of the poems of Lao-Tse herein presented — though I worked with frequent reference to ten other translations. The excerpts from Chuang-Tse also are "after" Legge. One excerpt, from Lieh-Tse, is based on a translation by Giles. I concede that the deeper merits of my "versions" should be credited to Legge and the others, while I assume responsibility for the actual wording of every line.]

II. THE BUDDHA. The most readable introduction is *The Gospel of Buddha: Compiled from Ancient Records*, by Paul Carus (Chicago & London, 1915), wherein the standard tales of the life and preaching of the Buddha are pieced together into a running story. A similar useful compendium, including a great deal more material, is *Buddhism in Translations: Passages Selected from the Buddhist Sacred Books*, translated by Henry Clarke Warren (Cambridge, Massachusetts, 1915, in the Harvard Oriental Series). An extraordinary amount of valuable translated material, from Chinese and Japanese as well as Pali and Sanskrit sources, appears in *A Buddhist Bible*, edited and published by Dwight Goddard (Thetford, Vermont, enlarged ed., 1938). One of the best introductory books, combining biography and interpretation, is *Buddha and the Gospel of Buddhism*, by Ananda Coomaraswamy (London, 1928).

Among the many biographical treatments are *The Life of Buddha*, by A. Ferdinand Herold (New York, 1927), in story form; the fully fictionized *The Splendour of Asia*, by L. Adams Beck (New York, 1937); and *The Life of Buddha as Legend and History*, by Edward J. Thomas (New York, 1927). The famous poetic treatment, *The Light of Asia*, by Sir Edwin Arnold, is available in innumerable editions.

Beyond all these books are many scholarly translations and interpretations. The advanced reader should consult especially the texts of T. W. Rhys Davids, Samuel Beal, and C. A. F. Rhys

Davids. There are shorter but authoritative expositions of various aspects of Chinese, Japanese, and Indian Buddhism in the Wisdom of the East series. An excellent brief history of India, with due attention to its religions, is *Pageant of India*, by F. Yeats-Brown (Philadelphia, 1943). The mysticism of the Hindu religion, as well as that of Buddhism, is treated in *Hindu Mysticism*, by S. N. Dasgupta (Chicago & London, 1927).

[My chief indebtedness here is to the late Dr. Carus. I have exceptionally leaned upon *The Gospel of Buddha*. Certain of my paragraphs are hardly more than paraphrases from his pages — which in turn were taken from a score of Buddhist classics. The Open Court Publishing Company has courteously permitted this reliance upon his text. At times I have gone back to his sources, in the writings of Samuel Beal, T. W. Rhys Davids, and others. I owe a considerable debt also to *The Bible of Buddhism;* and to Dr. Ananda Coomaraswamy for permission to quote two or three brief passages from *Buddha and the Gospel of Buddhism*. A slighter acknowledgment is owing to each of the authors mentioned in the two paragraphs above.]

III. GREECE. Widely accepted as the standard translation of Plato is *The Dialogues of Plato, Translated with Analyses and Introduction* by B. Jowett (London, 5 vols., 3rd revised ed., 1924). There is a more convenient edition: *The Dialogues of Plato*, translated by B. Jowett (New York, 2 vols., 1937); from this is taken *The Works of Plato*, selected and edited by Irwin Edman (New York, n.d., in The Modern Library), a readable condensation. The Greek text appears with the translation in *Plato, with an English Translation,* by H. N. Fowler (London & New York, 10 vols., 1913–26, in the Loeb Classical Library). For commentary see especially *Plato, The Man and His Work,* by A. E. Taylor (New York, 1936); and *The Myths of Plato,* by J. A. Stewart (London, 1905), which has translations as well as commentaries. *Greek Religious Thought from Homer to the Age of Alexander,* by F. M. Cornford (London & New York, 1923), is exceptionally inclined to take account of the mystical element. Satisfactory biographies of Socrates are *Socrates,* by A. E. Taylor (New York, 1933), and *Socrates: The Man and His Mission,* by R. Nicol Cross (London, 1914).

There is no satisfactory book about Pythagoras in print; but many libraries have copies of a multigraphed compilation entitled *Pythagoras Source Book and Library,* by Kenneth Sylvan Guthrie (Alpine, New Jersey, 1919–20). It includes translations of all the known ancient biographies, the fragmentary writings attributed to Pythagoras, and writings of his followers. Most standard histories of Greek philosophy include chapters upon Pythagoreanism. Among books on the Greek mystery religions, an exceptionally meaty one is *From Orpheus to Paul: A History of Orphism*, by Vittorio D. Macchioro (New York, 1930).

[I owe a debt here to the translators of Plato, especially to Benjamin Jowett. The excerpts are mostly from *The Dialogues of Plato*, translated by B. Jowett (Clarendon Press, Oxford); though I must add that in several cases I have made my own paraphrases, after study of other translations. The excerpts from Iamblichus and Photius are based on Guthrie's translations; or, more rarely, on those of Cornford.]

IV. PLOTINUS. There is an excellent introductory work, condensing the *Enneads* for general reading, in *The Essence of Plotinus*, by Grace H. Turnbull (New York, 1934). The book includes also a condensation of Porphyry's biography of Plotinus and extracts from Plato and other writers contributing to Neo-Platonism. Its text is largely from the complete translation by Stephen MacKenna. The more advanced student should go to MacKenna's imposing work direct, for it is the outstanding translation: *Plotinus: Treatises Comprising the Enneads*, translated from the Greek by Stephen MacKenna (London, 5 vols., 1917–30). A second translation, excellent in parts but careless in others, is *Plotinus: Complete Works*, by Kenneth Sylvan Guthrie (London, 1918). Standard works about Plotinus and Neo-Platonism are *The Philosophy of Plotinus*, by W. R. Inge (London, 2 vols., 3rd ed., 1929); *The Neo-Platonists: A Study in the History of Hellenism*, by Thomas Whittaker (Cambridge, 1928); and *Select Passages Illustrating Neo-Platonism*, by E. R. Dodds (London, 1923).

[By courteous permission of the Oxford University Press I have sometimes quoted from, sometimes paraphrased, parts of the *Enneads* as they appear in Miss Turnbull's *The Essence of Plotinus*. My debt to the book, and to Stephen MacKenna's work beyond, is heavy. Perhaps one-fourth of my paraphrases are based, however, upon Guthrie's text. My two excerpts from Philo are based on texts appearing in *The Message of Philo Judæus of Alexandria*, by Kenneth Sylvan Guthrie (London and North Yonkers, 1909). My debt to Inge, Dodds, and Whittaker is general rather than particular, but none the less real.]

V. CHRISTIAN MYSTICISM. An excellent simple treatment is *The*

Mystics of the Church, by Evelyn Underhill (New York, n.d.). Each chapter is followed by a reading list. The same author's *The Mystic Way: A Psychological Study in Christian Origins* (London & New York, 1913) is a larger and more speculative work, dealing especially with primitive Christian mysticism. *Christian Mysticism*, by William Ralph Inge (London, 6th ed., 1925), is a briefer review, also excellent. *Among the Mystics*, by William Fairweather (Edinburgh, 1936), treats briefly a great many Christian mystics from the Apostolic Fathers to the nineteenth-century British poets, with short excerpts. A readable account of some of the "movements" within Christianity, including ones essentially mystical, such as the Montanist, the Franciscan, and the Port-Royalist, is to be found in *Group Movements throughout the Ages*, by Robert H. Murray (New York & London, n.d.). Very good, too, is the group of studies of Augustine, Francis, Brother Lawrence, and others entitled *Strangers and Pilgrims*, by Willard L. Sperry (Boston, 1939).

There are innumerable biographies of Paul, and there is even a considerable literature on Paul's mysticism, including *Paul the Mystic*, by James W. Campbell (New York, 1908). Every reader should have *The Confessions of Saint Augustine;* an excellent translation is that of Edward Pusey, available in many editions. For other of Augustine's writings see *The Works of Aurelius Augustine, Bishop of Hippo*, translated by Marcus Dods (Edinburgh, 14 vols., 1871–74). A suggestive and useful comparison is set up, within the Catholic view, in *Western Mysticism: The Teaching of Saints Augustine, Gregory and Bernard on Contemplation and the Contemplative Life*, by Cuthbert Butler (New York, 1924). The book includes generous passages from the writings of those Saints. Of the several biographies of Saint Bernard, perhaps the most sympathetic to his mysticism is *The Life and Times of St. Bernard*, by l'Abbé Ratisbonne (New York, 1863).

[I have quoted several passages from Dom Cuthbert Butler's *Western Mysticism*, by kind permission of E. P. Dutton & Company; and I have paraphrased other passages after comparison with other translations. The excerpt from the treatises of the False Dionysius is based on a translation in *Mysticism: Its True Nature and Value*, by A. B. Sharpe (London, 1910). The passages from Saint Augustine are in general from, or based upon, the Pusey translation.]

VI. MEDIÆVAL. There are many biographies of Saint Francis,

but not all do justice to his mysticism. There is an inexpensive volume in Everyman's Library that includes the interesting "official" life by Bonaventura and two classics of Franciscanism: *The Little Flowers, and the Life of St. Francis, with the Mirror of Perfection* (London & New York, 1912). Especially on Franciscan mysticism there is *The Mysticism of St. Francis of Assisi,* by D. H. S. Nicholson (London, 1923). Broader in scope and more popular in style is *Mystics and Heretics in Italy,* by Émile Gebhart (New York, n.d.). There are several very good biographies of Saint Catherine, but outstanding for scholarliness, sympathy, and literary value is *Saint Catherine of Siena: A Study in the Religion, Literature and History of the 14th Century in Italy,* by Edmund G. Gardner (London & New York, 1907). For the story of the English mystics of the same period the reader may turn confidently to *Studies of the English Mystics,* by William Ralph Inge (London, 1907).

Meister Eckhart: A Modern Translation, by Raymond Bernard Blakney (New York & London, 1941), is the outstanding book in its field. It includes an excellent translation of about one-half of Eckhart's writings, and a brief introduction. *Mysticism East and West,* by Rudolf Otto (New York, 1932), provides, through a comparison of Eckhart's doctrines with those of the Hindu mystic Sankara, a profound scholar's interpretation of the two philosophies. A good running account of the activities and beliefs of Eckhart, Tauler, Suso, Ruysbroeck, and the Friends of God can be found in *Friends of God: Practical Mystics of the 14th Century,* by Anna Groh Seesholtz (New York, 1934). Broader in its range and lighted with the wisdom of a lifetime devoted to mystic study is *The Flowering of Mysticism: The Friends of God in the 14th Century,* by Rufus M. Jones (New York, 1940). About the life and the doctrines of Ruysbroeck the fullest treatment in English is *Ruysbroeck the Admirable,* by A. Wautier d'Aygalliers (London & New York, 1925). There is a translation of Maurice Maeterlinck's essay *Ruysbroeck and the Mystics* (London, 1908), now out of print, but worth seeking out at the libraries. Good translations of *The Imitation of Christ* are widely available; and there is an excellent edition in English of the *Theologia Germanica,* translated by Susanna Winkworth (London, 1937, in the Golden Treasury Series).

[I owe a debt of gratitude to Professor Blakney and to his publishers, Harper & Brothers, for permission to reprint passages from *Meister Eckhart: A Modern Translation* and to paraphrase other passages. Some minor excerpts are taken from the book by Anna Groh Seesholtz, by courtesy of the Columbia University Press; and a few lines from Professor Jones's *The Flowering of Mysticism*, by courtesy of the Macmillan Company, and from Professor Otto's *Mysticism East and West*, by courtesy of the same publishers. Part of the indebtedness here goes back to an earlier version by C. deB. Evans. The very brief excerpts from English mystics are from *Studies of English Mystics*, by Dean Inge, and from Miss Underhill's *Mystics of the Church*. To the named works of Nicholson and Gebhart, and to the publishers of the Everyman's Library volume of Franciscan biography, I acknowledge a slighter but sincerely felt indebtedness.]

VII. FRA ANGELICO. There are few biographies of Fra Angelico in English, and unfortunately there is none that treats especially his mysticism. Admirable for other reasons, as accounts of his uneventful life and as criticism of his art — and generously illustrated — are *Fra Angelico*, by Wilhelm Hausenstein (London, 1928), and *Fra Angelico*, by Langston Douglas (London, 1902). All biographical studies lean heavily upon a chapter in Vasari's *Lives of the Italian Architects, Painters and Sculptors*, published in 1551 and available in many modern editions.

VIII. BOEHME. As a readable introduction to the mysticism of the Reformation period and of Protestantism there is *Spiritual Reformers in the 16th and 17th Centuries*, by Rufus M. Jones (London, 1928). Few books cover a period so adequately. The separate biographies and interpretations of Boehme are mostly out of print, but the larger libraries may have some of these works: *Jacob Boehme: His Life and Teaching: or Studies in Theosophy*, by Hans Lassen Martensen (London, 1885), the fullest speculative treatise; *Personal Christianity, a Science: The Doctrines of Jacob Boehme*, by Franz Hartmann (New York, 1919), containing a biography, introduction, and a great many brief passages from Boehme's books; and *The Mystic Will, Based on a Study of the Philosophy of Jacob Boehme*, by Howard H. Brinton (New York, 1930), a sound and useful study, midway between the introductory books and those designed for advanced students of religious philosophy.

The only book by Boehme easily obtainable in English is *The Signature of All Things*, by Jacob Boehme (London & New York, 1940, in Everyman's Library). This is hardly a representative work, but included in the volume is the more satisfying dialogue, *Concerning the Supersensual Life*. Fechner's otherwise rare biography of Boehme appears as a preface to *De Electione Gratiae, and Quaestiones Theosophicae*, by Jacob Boehme, translated by John Rolleston Earle (London, 1930), in a series that includes Earle's translations of *The Six Theosophic Points* and other treatises. For notes on other books by Boehme the reader can best consult Brinton's *The Mystic Will*.

[I have become indebted to all the books named above. To the Franz Hartmann volume I owe a special debt: a number of my quotations of Boehme are taken therefrom, by courteous permission of the Macoy Publishing Company; though the bulk of my excerpts are from those translations published in earlier centuries, especially the Law and Sparrow editions, and from Boehme's letters. Some lesser passages are from the books of Brinton and Jones; one considerable excerpt follows fairly closely the translation by Earle, and bits are quoted from the biography by Fechner. I am grateful to Professor Jones for the sort of stimulation and influence that cannot be measured; and in fairness I must note an indeterminate debt to Professor Brinton, and to his publishers, the Macmillan Company, and to a fugitive pamphlet about Boehme by the late Alexander Whyte.]

IX. BROTHER LAWRENCE. Of the many editions of the small writings of Brother Lawrence the only one available in recent years has been *Brother Lawrence: The Practice of the Presence of God the Best Rule for a Holy Life* (New York, 1895). This contains a brief preface, the *Conversations*, and fifteen letters. There is an edition (Philadelphia, n.d.) containing an added letter and a translation of the original preface of 1692. Its text is reprinted in *The Book of Christian Classics*, edited by Michael Williams (New York, 1933). Out of print, but to be found in libraries, is *The Spiritual Maxims of Brother Lawrence, together with The Character and Gathered Thoughts* (London, n.d., in the Heart and Life Booklets series).

[By courtesy of the Fleming H. Revell Company I have drawn freely upon their edition, the one noted above as in print, for quotations from the *Conversations* and the letters. By courtesy of H. R. Allenson Ltd., London, I have similarly drawn upon the *Maxims*. I have paraphrased freely after comparing as many texts as I could assemble; but this does not lessen my gratitude to these publishers.]

X. BLAKE. There is a truly monumental edition of Blake's writings, published by the Nonesuch Press, but it is both costly and rare. A one-volume complete edition, also rare, reproducing the Nonesuch Press text, appeared as *Poetry and Prose of William Blake*, edited by Geoffrey Keynes (New York & London, 1927). Next best is *The Poems and Prophecies of William Blake*, edited by Max Plowman (London & New York, n.d., in Everyman's Library), nearly complete. Good, too, is *Poems of William Blake*, edited by William Butler Yeats (New York, n.d., in the Modern Library). It includes an excellent introduction, the early poems, and a very few selections from the prophetic works.

The standard biographies are generally out of print, but not unusual in old-book stores. Especially compact and sound is *The Life of William Blake*, by Mona Wilson (London, 1932). This is a shorter version of the *Life* that appeared in sumptuous form as supplement to the Nonesuch Press *Writings* in 1927. Less systematic, even discursive and gossipy, but a treasury of materials, is *The Life of William Blake*, by Thomas Wright (Olney, Bucks, 2 vols., 1929). It includes 135 illustrations. An admirable treatment, interpretative as well as biographical, is *The Real Blake: A Portrait Biography*, by Edwin J. Ellis (New York, 1907). Briefer, breezy, and readable is *William Blake in This World*, by Harold Bruce (New York, 1925). A biography that especially stresses Blake's spiritual growth is *William Blake: the Man*, by Charles Gardner (London & New York, 1919). Farther back are the source books, from Smith (1828) and Tatham to the great work of Gilchrist (1863), and on to Swinburne, Langridge, and Symons.

On Blake's mysticism the chief work is *William Blake: His Philosophy and Symbols*, by S. Foster Damon (Boston & New York, 1924). The only "in print" interpretation of Blake's philosophy, well worth reading but not along the mystical line, is *William Blake's Circle of Destiny*, by Milton O. Percival (New York, 1938).

[My debt here is primarily to Random House, New York, and the Nonesuch Press, London, for courteous permission to reprint the excerpts from Blake's writings, and to Geoffrey Keynes, who edited their edition. I owe gratitude also to Thomas Wright, from whose biography I mined materials not readily found elsewhere; but also to Mona Wilson, Edwin J. Ellis, Charles Gardner, and Harold Bruce, who variously contributed to my knowledge and interpretation of Blake's life. I have, indeed, consulted and drawn upon all the books named in the three paragraphs above. Without

READING LIST

adding a special reading list in connection with my Afterword, I may note here that the two quotations from the writings of Edward Carpenter are from *The Art of Creation* (London, 1907); and from *The Drama of Love and Death* (New York & London, 1912), by courtesy of the publisher, Mitchell Kennerley.]

Index

Abelard, 167, 170
Academy of Plato, 89, 108–9, 115
Acarie, Mme, 296
Adams, Hannah, 206
Addison, Charles Morris, 386
Adornment of the Spiritual Marriage, The, by Ruysbroeck, 209, 210
Æsthetics, 34–6, 96–7, 139–41, 215–17, 233–7, 346, 347, 367–9, 376
Age of Reason, Greek, 86–9, 98–9
Alara Kalama, 54
Albertus Magnus, 167, 177, 188, 192
al-Ghazali, 191
All Religions Are One by William Blake, 329
America by William Blake, 320–1, 333
Ammonius Saccas, 124–5, 158, 160
Ananda, 64, 65, 71–2
Anaximander, 93
Ancestor worship, 7–8
Angela of Foligno, 183, 220
Angel Brothers, the, 239, 281
Angelico, Fra, 121, 213–37, 289, 393
Angélique, Mère, 286
Anselm, Saint, 164
Anthony, Saint, 157
Antonino, Fra, 219, 221, 225, 227, 228, 230
Apollonius of Tyana, 122–4, 140
Aquinas, Saint Thomas, 164, 167, 177, 188, 192, 202, 297
Arabian philosophy, 191–2
Arianism, 163
Aristotle, 109, 119, 124, 139, 167, 192
Arnold, Sir Edwin, 388
Artists and mysticism, 34–6, 97, 139–41, 215–17, 224, 231–7, 347, 368–9
Aryan peoples, 43–4
Ascent of Mount Carmel, The, by Saint John of the Cross, 246
Asceticism, 54–5, 67, 78, 94, 129, 198, 200, 294

Asita, 48
Asoka, 45, 74–5
Asvaghosa, 76
Atman, the, 46, 54, 60, 78, 79
Augustine, Saint, 89, 127–8, 132, 135, 159, 160–3, 169, 171, 173, 183, 191, 211, 289, 297, 391
Aurora, The, by Jacob Boehme, 243, 248–52, 253, 274, 322
Autobiography of Suso, 207–8
Averroes, 191
Avicenna, 191

Bacon, Francis, 285, 325, 333
Bacon, Roger, 177
Ballou, Robert O., 387
Bartolozzi, Francesco, 318, 321
Bax, Clifford, 258
Beal, Samuel, 39, 388–9
Beck, L. Adams, 381, 388
Beghards, 187, 204–5
Beguines, 204–5, 208
Behmenists, 239, 282
Benedetto, Fra, 218, 221, 227, 230
Berkeley, Bishop, 314
Bernard, Saint, 143, 152, 164, 168–75, 191, 192, 198, 270, 391
Binyon, Laurence, 388
Birgitta, Saint, 184
Blake, William, vii, 84–5, 121, 144, 197, 289, 309–77, 379, 395
Blakney, Raymond Bernard, 197, 392–3
Boccaccio, 213
Boehme, Jacob, 112, 121, 144, 170, 238–83, 287, 313, 314, 317, 360, 370, 380, 393–4
Boethius, 89, 166
Bonaventura, Saint, 181–2, 183, 185, 297
Book of Ahania by William Blake, 336
Book of Divine Comfort by Eckhart, 189
Book of Divine Consolations by Angela of Foligno, 220

INDEX

Book of Heavenly Wisdom by Suso, 207–8
Book of Los by William Blake, 336
Book of Tao, 9, 10–29, 31, 32, 36–7
Book of the Kingdom of God's Lovers by Ruysbroeck, 208
Book of the Master, 204, 211
Book of the Nine Rocks, 211
Book of the Sparkling Stone by Ruysbroeck, 209
Book of Thel by William Blake, 329
Book of Urizen by William Blake, 336
Brinton, Howard H., 393–4
Brothers of the Common Life, 210
Brothers of the Free Spirit, 205–7
Brothers of the New Spirit, 205
Browning, 379
Bruce, Harold, 395
Brunelleschi, 213, 215, 218, 222
Buddha, the, vii, 8, 38–85, 144, 289, 388–9
Buddhism, 8, 29, 38–85, 110, 144, 380, 388–9
Buddhist Brotherhood, 60–73, 77–8, 81
Bury, Lady Charlotte, 354
Butler, Dom Cuthbert, 197, 391
Bynner, Witter, 387

Cabbalism, 122, 247, 279
Caesar-worship, 145, 159
Callippus, 109
Calvert, Edward, 356–7, 358
Calvinism, 260–1
Cambridge Platonists, 89, *and see* Neo-Platonism
Campbell, James W., 391
Carpenter, Edward, 378–9, 396
Carus, Paul, v, 9, 11, 39, 387, 388–9
Cassianus, 159
Castle of the Soul, The, by Santa Teresa, 246, 297
Catherine, Saint, 143, 184–5, 199, 213, 218, 219, 231, 392
Ch'an Buddhism, 29
Chinese art, 34–6, 233–4, 236
Christian mysticism, *see* Way, the Christian

Christianity, 40, 118–19, 122, 127–8, 132, 134, *and see* Way, the Christian
Ch'u Ta-Kao, 9, 387
Chuang-Tse, 4, 8, 18, 27, 30–4, 387–8
City of God by Saint Augustine, 128, 135, 160, 162
City of God, Christian, 84–5, 160
City of Peace, Buddhist, 84–5
Clara, Santa, 183, 220
Clement of Alexandria, 158
Cloud of Unknowing, The, 186
Coleridge, 379
Colombini, Giovanni, 185, 213
Concerning Heaven and Its Wonders, and Concerning Hell by Swedenborg, 316
Concerning Mystical Theology by the False Dionysius, 164, 186
Confession, 69, 295
Confessions of Saint Augustine, 128, 160–3, 391
Confucianism, 28–9
Confucius, 2–5, 12, 24, 27, 28–9, 31
Constable, 358
Constantine, 159
Contemplation, 83–4, 137, 165–6, 170, 181
Conversations of Brother Lawrence, 289, 292, 300, 302–8, 394
Coomaraswamy, Ananda, 39, 388–9
Cornford, F. M., 389, 390
Counsel of Love, A, by Johannes Dominici, 219
Cranmer-Byng, L., 388
Crashaw, Richard, 379
Cross, R. Nicol, 389
Cynics, 109

Damis, 123
Damon, S. Foster, 395
Dante, 183, 213, 359, 361
Dark Ages, the, 166
Dark Night of the Soul, The, by Saint John of the Cross, 246
Dasgupta, S. N., 389
Davids, Rhys, 39, 388–9
d'Aygalliers, A. Wautier, 392

INDEX

della Quercia, Jacopo, 214
della Robbia, Luca, 228
Descriptive Catalogue, Blake's, 347, 348
Devadatta, 64, 66
De Vita Contemplativa, by Philo, 120
Dhyanas, the, 84
Dialogues of Cassianus, 159
Dionysian Mysteries, 90–2
Dionysius, the False, 163–6, 167, 183, 186, 191, 391
Divine Comedy by Dante, 183, 359, 361
Dodds, E. R., 390
Dods, Marcus, 391
Dominic, Saint, 218
Dominici, Johannes, 218–19, 224, 227
Donatello, 215, 218, 228
Douglas, Langston, 393
Duccio, 213, 215, 236
Dürer, 317

Earle, John Rolleston, 394
Eckhart, Meister, 144, 170, 175, 177, 187–203, 204, 207, 208, 209, 239, 245, 265, 392–3
Edman, Irwin, 389
Education, 20, 70, 96, 108
Eightfold Path of Virtue, 59, 68–9, 82
Eleusinian Mysteries, 88, 90
Ellis, Edwin J., 395
Emerson, 88, 283, 325, 380
Enneads of Plotinus, 89, 125, 127–42, 160, 192, 390
Erigena, 89, 164, 166, 167, 169, 192
Essenes, 120, 146, 154
Eternal Life, The, by Jacob Boehme, 261–2, 265
Eucleides, 107
Europe by William Blake, 326, 333
Eustochius, 127
Evans, C. de B., 393

Fairweather, William, 391
Fechner, Hermann Adolph, 394
Felicitas, 157–8
Fénelon, Bishop, 287, 298, 300, 360

Flaxman, John, 321, 323–4, 339, 344, 346, 361
For Children: The Gates of Paradise by William Blake, 334
Forty Questions of the Soul, The, by Jacob Boehme, 257
Four Degrees of Burning Love, The, by Richard of Saint Victor, 171
Fowler, H. N., 389
Fox, George, 240, 281–2
Francis de Sales, Saint, 297, 300
Francis of Assisi, Saint, 175, 177–83, 185, 190, 201, 202, 209, 219, 220, 289, 391–2
Franck, Sebastian, 245
Frankenberg, Abraham von, 266, 283–4
Fraticelli, the, 205
French Revolution, The, by William Blake, 326
Frerots, the, 205
Friend of God from the Oberland, 204, 211
Friends of God, 183, 187, 189, 203, 204–7, 208, 239, 245, 392
From Things Seen and Heard by Swedenborg, 316
Fuseli, Henry, 321, 361

Gall, Edward, 386
Gandhi, 46
Gardner, Charles, 395
Gardner, Edmund G., 392, 393
Gates of Paradise, The, by William Blake, 334
Gautama, 48, *and see* Buddha
Gebhart, Émile, 392
Gertrude the Great, Saint, 184
Gesuati, Society of the, 185, 213
Ghiberti, 215, 218
Gichtel, Johann Georg, 280
Giles, Lionel, v, 387, 388
Giorgione, 236
Giotto, 183, 213, 215, 220, 236
Giovanni of Fiesole, *see* Angelico, Fra
Gnosticism, 122, 132, 150, 158, 163, 207, 278–9
God, conceptions of, 7, 41, 45, 77,

86–7, 90, 96, 100, 109, 130–4, 143, 146, 165, 196, 273–4
Goddard, Dwight, 9, 39, 387, 388
Godwin, William, 326
Goethe, 281
Golden Age, the Chinese, 1, 2, 5–7, 10
Government, the art of, 22–4, 30, 62
Gozzoli, Benozzo, 230
Grace, 16, 260–1
Greco, El, 236, 368
Greek philosophy, 86–9, 92, 94, 119, *and see* Pythagoras, Socrates, Plato, *etc.*
Green Isle Community, 210–11
Gregory the Great, 127, 166–7, 169, 173, 198, 391
Groenendael community, 208–10
Groot, Gerhard, 210
Guthrie, Kenneth Sylvan, 389, 390
Guyon, Mme, 298, 360

Hare, William Loftus, 386
Hartmann, Franz, 393–4
Hausenstein, Wilhelm, 393
Hayley, William, 338–44
Hedonists, 109, 119
Hegel, 191, 261, 281
Herman, Nicolas, 291, *and see* Lawrence, Brother
Hermitic mysticism, 157
Herold, A. Ferdinand, 388
Hierocles, 124
Hildegard, Saint, 184
Hinayana Buddhism, 75–6
Hinduism, 40, 41, 43, 45, 54, 73–5, 79, 380–1, 389
Homilies of Saint Macarius the Great, 157
Hotham, Durand, 282, 283
Hugo of Saint Victor, 164, 171
Humility, 25–6, 29, 376
Hunt, Leigh, 345–6
Hunt, Robert, 347
Hylton, Walter, 186

Iamblichus, 92, 96, 116, 164, 390
Ideas, Plato's doctrine of, 109, 112, 113–15, 116, 119, 133, 140, 279

Ignatius of Loyola, Saint, 246
Imitation of Christ, The, 210, 392
Imitation of the Poverty of Jesus Christ, 204
Incarnation of the Son of Man, The, by Jacob Boehme, 258
Inge, W. R., 390, 391, 392, 393
Inpouring Light of God, The, by Saint Mechthild, 184
Intuition, vii, 20, 195–6, 310
Irving, Edward, 360, 364

Jacopone da Todi, 182–3
Jefferies, Richard, 379
Jerome, 127, 159
Jerusalem by William Blake, 341, 348, 349–51, 352–3, 361, 365, 367, 368, 372, 374–5
Jesus, vii, 6, 19, 42, 144, 145–50, *and see* Christianity *and* Way, the Christian
Jewish mysticism, 120, 122, 146
Job, Blake's illustrations for, 355–6, 359, 361
Johannes Scotus Erigena, *see* Erigena
John, Saint, 122, 149, 150–3, 164, 173, 174, 191
John of Saint Paul, Cardinal, 179
John of the Cross, Saint, viii, 171, 246, 297
John the Scot, *see* Erigena
Jones, Rufus, v, 386, 392–3, 394
Jowett, B., 91, 132, 389–90
Judaism, 119–20, 122, 124, 145–6, 150, 154, 163, 164
Julian of Norwich, 185, 186

Karma, 46, 54, 79
Keynes, Geoffrey, 395
Kondanna, 60
Kuhlmann, Quirinus, 280

Lamb, Charles, 348
Lao-Tse, vii, 1–37, 42, 70, 97, 166, 202, 287, 289, 380, 387–8
Law, William, 314
Lawrence, Brother, 284–307, 312, 394
Lawrence, Thomas, 346, 354–5, 359

iv

INDEX

Legge, James, v, 9, 387–8
Lieh-Tse, 30–1, 387–8
Lin Yutang, 9, 387
Linnell, John, 355, 356–7, 358, 359, 362, 363
Lippi, Filipino, 228
Little Garden of Devotion by Frate Ricardo, 219
Locke, 325
Lorenzetti, the, 215
Luther, Martin, 211

Macarius the Great, Saint, 157
Macchioro, Vittorio D., 390
MacKenna, Stephen, v, 132, 390
Maeterlinck, Maurice, 392
Mahayana Buddhism, 75–6
Manichæism, 163
Marguerite, Mother, 296
Marriage of Heaven and Hell, The, by William Blake, 330–1, 332
Martensen, Hans Lassen, 393
Martini, Simone, 213, 236
Martyrs, Christian, 157–8
Masaccio, 223, 228, 230
Mathematics and mysticism, 94, 116, 235
Maxims of Brother Lawrence, 290, 303–8, 394
Maximus the Confessor, 167
Mechthild, Saint, 184
Medici, Cosimo de', 222, 224–7
Meditation, Buddhist, 83–4
Merswin, Rulman, 210–11
Michelangelo, 213, 317, 319, 368
Michelozzo, 213, 215, 222, 225, 226, 227
Milton, 283, 348–9
Milton by William Blake, 348, 365, 367
Mohammedanism, 40, 172, 192
Molinos, 298
Monaco, Lorenzo, 213, 220
Montaigne, 308
Montanists, 157, 391
Moravian Church, 280, 283, 314, 316, 379
More, Henry, 282
Murray, Robert H., 391

v

Music and mysticism, 94, 96–7
Mysterium Magnum by Jacob Boehme, 261
Mystery religions, Greek, 87–92, 94, 138, 145, 152, 154, 158, 390

Nature mysticism, 180–1, 209, 258–9, 271–2, 365, 379, 380
Neo-Platonism, 89, 105, 113, 115, 116, 118, 120, 122, 124, 127–42, 158, 159, 160–3, 166, 183, 191, 192, 245, 279, 282, 315, 390
New Devotion, the, 210
Nicholas V, Pope, *see* Parentucelli, Tomaso
Nicholas of Basel, 211
Nicholson, D. H. S., 392, 393
Nietzsche, 351, 352, 375–7
Nirvana, 38–42, 57, 62, 70, 77–8, 80, 82–4, 144
Non-resistance, 17–18, 24, 26, 67, 147, 158
Novalis, 281, 364
Numenius, 124

On the Consolations of Philosophy by Boethius, 166
On the Election of Grace by Jacob Boehme, 260–1
Origen, 158, 171
Orphic Mysteries, 88, 90–2, 93, 102, 110
Ossian, 329
Otto, Rudolf, 392–3

Pacifism, 21–4, 67, 74, 246
Paine, Thomas, 326–7
Palmer, Samuel, 356–7, 358, 369
Pantheism, 272, 315
Paracelsus, 244, 246–7, 252
Paradise, 5–7, 38–42, 82–4, 111
Parentucelli, Tomaso, 224, 225, 227, 228–31
Parker, Edward Harper, 11
Pascal, Blaise, 286–8, 308
Paul, Saint, 84–5, 143, 149–50, 153–8, 160, 164, 169, 171, 173, 174, 343, 391
Penn, William, 240, 282

INDEX

Percival, Milton O., 395
Perpetua, 157–8
Petrarch, 213
Pettignano, Pier, 182, 183
Philadelphians, 239, 282
Philo, 88, 119–22, 124, 150, 151, 279, 390
Philosophy, origin of word, 94
Philostratus, 123, 139–40
Photius, 98, 390
Pietists, 282–3, 313
Plato, vii, 87, 88–9, 91, 98, 99, 103, 106–17, 118, 119, 120, 122, 124, 127, 128, 139, 141, 160, 167, 279, 315, 389–90
Platonic love, 115–16
Platonists, the, 282, *and see* Neo-Platonism
Plotinus, 88–9, 105, 116, 118, 121, 122, 123, 124–42, 158–9, 160, 161–2, 164, 167, 192, 196, 380, 390
Plowman, Max, 395
Poetical Sketches by William Blake, 324, 331
Porphyry, 124, 125–7, 133, 135, 390
Port Royal community, 286–7, 288, 391
Poverty, 180, 201
Practice of the Presence of God, The, by Brother Lawrence, 287–308, 394
Prayer, 100, 138, 198, 299
Predestination, 260–1, 329
Proclus, 164
Protagoras, 87
Pusey, Edward, 391
Pythagoras, 87–8, 92–8, 101–2, 123, 124, 389–90
Pythagorean brotherhoods, 88, 93–8, 107–8, 119, 123

Quakers, 239–40, 281–3, 379
Quietists, 297, 298, 313, 314, 379

Raimondo, Fra, 218
Ramakrishna, 46, 380
Ratisbonne, l'Abbé, 391

Revelation of Divine Love by Julian of Norwich, 186
Reynolds, Joshua, 321, 326, 346
Ricardo, Frate, 219
Richard of Saint Victor, 164, 171
Richmond, George, 356–7, 358, 363
Ripafratta, Fra Lorenzo, 219
Robinson, Henry Crabb, 348, 360–1, 364
Rogatianus, 126
Rolle, Richard, 185–6
Rosetti Manuscript of William Blake, 334
Rousseau, 336
Ruysbroeck, 171, 208–10, 297, 392

Saint-Martin, Louis Claude de, 312–13
Saint Victor Monastery, 171
Sakyamuni, 48, *and see* Buddha
San Marco Monastery, Florence, 225–8
Sankara, 46, 392
Sanskrit language, 43
Savonarola, 225
Scale of Perfection, The, by Walter Hylton, 186
Schelling, 261, 281
Schiavonetti, Louis, 344–5, 346
Schlegel, Friedrich, 281
Scholastics, 167, 170
Schopenhauer, 261, 281, 377
Schweinitz, Sigismund von, 266
Schwenckfeld, Caspar, 245
Seekers, the, 282
Seesholtz, Anna Groh, 392–3
Sermons on the Song of Songs by Saint Bernard, 170
Seven Beguines, The, by Ruysbroeck, 209
Sextus Empiricus, 96
Sharpe, A. B., 391
Signature of All Things, The, by Jacob Boehme, 258–9
Signorelli, Luca, 229
Smith, John Thomas, 324
Society of Friends, *see* Quakers
Socrates, 87, 88, 98–106, 107, 110, 113, 114, 389

vi

INDEX

Songs of Experience by William Blake, 327–8, 334, 365, 369
Songs of Innocence by William Blake, 324, 327–8, 331, 334, 365, 369
Sophia, 207, 253, 277–9, 284
Sophists, 98, 107
Spark in the Soul, The, 211
Spener, Philip Jacob, 280, 314
Spenser, 379
Sperry, Willard L., 391
Spinoza, Benedictus, 315
Spiritual Tabernacle, The, by Ruysbroeck, 209
Spirituals, Franciscan, 182, 190
Starnina, Gherardo, 220
Stewart, J. A., 389
Stoics, 109, 119
Story of My Heart by William Jefferies, 379
Story of the Mustard Seed, 76
Stothard, Thomas, 321, 345, 346
Sufi mysticism, 171–2, 192, 277
Suger, 168
Suso, Heinrich, 187, 199, 207–8, 209, 392
Swedenborg, Emanuel, 313, 316, 329, 360
Swinburne, 330
Sze-Ma-Ch'ien, 9

Talks of Instruction by Eckhart, 187, 189
Tao Teh Ching, 11–29, 31, 32, 36–7, 287, 387–8
Taoism, 3, 4, 11–37, 97, 134, 166, 387–8
Tathagata, the, 48, *and see* Buddha
Tatham, Frederick, 318, 356, 362–4
Tauler, Johannes, 187, 188, 192, 203–4, 206, 208, 209, 210, 211, 239, 265, 392
Taylor, A. E., 389
Taylor, Thomas, 325
Teresa, Santa, viii, 171, 246, 296, 297
Tertiaries, Franciscan, 183, 190, 204, 205
Tertullian, 158

Teutonic Philosopher, the, 257, *and see* Boehme, Jacob
Thales of Miletus, 93
Theologia Germanica, 163, 211, 239, 245, 265, 392
Theosophical Questions by Jacob Boehme, 266
Theosophic movement, 381
Theosophick Philosophy Unfolded by Jacob Boehme, 283
Therapeutæ, 120
There Is No Natural Religion by William Blake, 329
Thomas, Edward J., 388
Thomas à Kempis, 210, 297
Thoreau, 380
Three Principles, The, by Jacob Boehme, 254–5, 277, 279
Threefold Life of Man, The, by Jacob Boehme, 255–6, 275
Tieck, Johann Ludwig, 281
Tintoretto, 236, 368
Tiriel by William Blake, 329
Titian, 236
Transcendentalists, the, 283, 379–80
Transmigration, 79, 94
Treatise on the Love of God by Francis de Sales, 297
Tsui Chi, 9, 388
Turnbull, Grace H., 132, 390

Uccello, Paolo, 228
Underhill, Evelyn, vi, 386, 391, 393

Vala by William Blake, 337, 343, 365
van Beyerland, Abraham Willemsoon, 281
Vasari, 217, 228, 231–3, 234, 393
Vaughan, Henry, 379
Vaughan, Robert Alfred, v, 300, 386
Vedantism, 41, 45–6, 74, 79, 370, 380, 381
Victorine school of mystics, 171, 183, 192, 198
Victorinus, 159, 160
Virgil, 355
Visions of the Daughters of Albion by William Blake, 332

Vivekananda, 380
Voltaire, 308, 336, 360

Wai-Tao, 387
Waite, Arthur Edward, 386
Waldensians, 205
Waley, Arthur, v, 9, 11, 387
Walter, Henry, 356
Walther, Balthazar, 253, 256–7, 259, 263
Warren, Henry Clarke, 39, 388
Way, the Buddhist, 41, 42, 59–85
Way, the Christian, 143–4, 146–75, 177–211, 216–17, 231–7, 269–84, 289–308, 373–5
Way, the Taoist, 3, 4, 9, 11–29, 31–4, 35, 36–8
Way to Christ, The, by Jacob Boehme, 259, 261, 287
Weigel, Valentine, 245
Wesley, John, 314

White Brothers, the, 205
Whitman, Walt, 380
Whittaker, Thomas, 390
Whyte, Alexander, 394
Williams, Michael, 394
Wilson, Mona, 395
Winkworth, Susanna, 392
Wollstonecraft, Mary, 326
Wordsworth, 379
Wright, Thomas, 395

Yeats, William Butler, 395
Yeats-Brown, F., 389
Yin-Hi, 10
Yoga, 82

Zealots, Franciscan, 182, 201
Zen Buddhism, 29
Zenophon, 99, 106
Zinzendorf, Count von, 280, 314

A NOTE ON THE TYPE USED IN THIS BOOK

The text of this book is set in Caledonia, a Linotype face designed by W. A. Dwiggins. Caledonia belongs to the family of printing types called "modern face" by printers — a term used to mark the change in style of type-letters that occurred about 1800. Caledonia borders on the general design of Scotch Modern, but is more freely drawn than that letter.

Mr. Dwiggins planned the typographic scheme and designed the binding. The book was composed, printed, and bound by The Plimpton Press, Norwood, Massachusetts.

THIS BOOK HAS BEEN PRODUCED
IN FULL COMPLIANCE
WITH ALL GOVERNMENT REGULATIONS
FOR THE CONSERVATION OF PAPER, METAL,
AND OTHER ESSENTIAL MATERIALS